SAGE was founded in 1965 by Sara Miller McCune to support the dissemination of usable knowledge by publishing innovative and high-quality research and teaching content. Today, we publish over 900 journals, including those of more than 400 learned societies, more than 800 new books per year, and a growing range of library products including archives, data, case studies, reports, and video. SAGE remains majority-owned by our founder, and after Sara's lifetime will become owned by a charitable trust that secures our continued independence.

Los Angeles | London | New Delhi | Singapore | Washington DC | Melbourne

CLAIMING INDIA

CLAIMING INDIA

*French Scholars and the Preoccupation
with India in the Nineteenth Century*

JYOTI MOHAN

Los Angeles | London | New Delhi
Singapore | Washington DC | Melbourne

First published in 2018 by

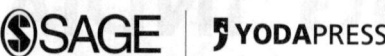

SAGE Publications India Pvt Ltd
B1/I-1 Mohan Cooperative Industrial Area
Mathura Road, New Delhi 110 044, India
www.sagepub.in

YODA Press
268 AC Vasant Kunj
New Delhi 110070
www.yodapress.co.in

SAGE Publications Inc
2455 Teller Road
Thousand Oaks, California 91320, USA

SAGE Publications Ltd
1 Oliver's Yard, 55 City Road
London EC1Y 1SP, United Kingdom

SAGE Publications Asia-Pacific Pte Ltd
3 Church Street
#10-04 Samsung Hub
Singapore 049483

Published by Vivek Mehra for SAGE Publications India Pvt Ltd, typeset in 11/13 pt Trebuchet MS by Zaza Eunice, Hosur, Tamil Nadu, and printed at Chaman Enterprises, New Delhi.

Library of Congress Cataloging-in-Publication Data

Names: Mohan, Jyoti, author.
Title: Claiming India: French scholars and the preoccupation with India during the nineteenth century/Jyoti Mohan.
Description: New Delhi: SAGE Publications India, 2018. | Includes bibliographical references and index.
Identifiers: LCCN 2017046534| ISBN 9789352804658 (print (hb): alk. paper) | ISBN 9789352804672 (e pub 2.0) | ISBN 9789352804665 (e book)
Subjects: LCSH: India--Civilization--Historiography. | India--Civilization--Study and teaching--France--History--19th century. | France--Colonies--India--History--19th century. | Postcolonialism--India--History--19th century.
Classification: LCC DS435 .M64 2018 | DDC 954.03/1--dc23 LC record available at https://lccn.loc.gov/2017046534

ISBN: 978-93-528-0465-8 (HB)

SAGE Yoda Team: Arpita Das, Amrita Dutta and Guneet Kaur

For my mother whose perseverance saw me through...

Thank you for choosing a SAGE product!
If you have any comment, observation or feedback,
I would like to personally hear from you.

Please write to me at **contactceo@sagepub.in**

Vivek Mehra, Managing Director and CEO, SAGE India.

Bulk Sales

SAGE India offers special discounts
for purchase of books in bulk.
We also make available special imprints
and excerpts from our books on demand.

For orders and enquiries, write to us at

Marketing Department
SAGE Publications India Pvt Ltd
B1/I-1, Mohan Cooperative Industrial Area
Mathura Road, Post Bag 7
New Delhi 110044, India

E-mail us at **marketing@sagepub.in**

Get to know more about SAGE

Be invited to SAGE events, get on our mailing list.
Write today to **marketing@sagepub.in**

This book is also available as an e-book.

Contents

List of Tables

List of Figures

List of Images

Acknowledgements

This enormous and time-consuming project has seen more milestones of my life than I would sometimes like to remember. On the other hand, with the hindsight that historians are notorious for, I cannot imagine that this book would have taken the form it has today, without these milestones. For my husband who has painstakingly supported me in my often bewildering mood swings for fifteen years. My children, Nandika and Arjun, taught me that there are other important and fulfilling roles in life. My brother Anand was always my most exacting critic and without his interest in my dissertation (from which this project grew), I can truly say it would never have been completed.

My friend and co-conspirator since our days of graduate school, Marcy Wilson, has been around for my marriage, the birth of my two children and has constantly reminded me that it was worth finishing even when the kids enticingly beckoned for me to shelve the project indefinitely. Several people provided much intellectual sustenance—Professor Richard Price, Professor Paul Landau, Professor Jeffrey Herf, Professor Mrinalini Sinha, Professor Brett Berliner, and Professor Gyanendra Pandey. The companionship of several participants at the University of Liverpool's project on France-Britain-India shaped this project in important ways. In particular, the feedback of Ian Magedera and Kate Marsh was indispensible.

My first baby, Swami, taught me about unconditional love and comfort. His warm tail-wagging presence and unstintingly generous face washes put smiles on my face and laughter in my heart when the dark side of graduate school threatened to break me down. To all graduate students out there, doubting themselves, and their ability to push to the finish line, you can do it. Don't ever think you are any less intelligent than when you started out. Seek out those who build your confidence and provide you with intellectual and emotional nourishment. Avoid people who try to break you, and there will be many.

My biggest debt of gratitude is to my mother. She put her own life on hold to become chief babysitter and housekeeper, leaving me free to do research. More importantly, her emotional support and desire to see me finish kept me from quitting during my most depressing and lonely periods. Thank you amma.

Introduction: The Last King of France Found...in India?

If France ever returns to a monarchy, the King of France would arrive in state from the Indian city of Bhopal. Balthazar Napoleon de Bourbon is the closest living link to the French royal family of Bourbons. Born in Bhopal and Indian in every way except for his name and lineage, he represents the complex link between India and France. Descended from cousins of Louis XVI and Marie Antoinette, the ancestors of this down-to-earth, middle-class Indian, who may lay claim to the *fleur de lis,* arrived in India in swashbuckling style, in a story involving kidnapping, piracy and shipwrecks in the middle of the sixteenth century. France's story in India thus goes back more than 400 years!

Beginning with humble trading origins, the French desire to colonize India reached its height in the eighteenth century, when the global Anglo-French rivalry over world domination led to the Seven Years' War. France's defeat in the war meant the downfall of her hopes for an Indian Empire, and the start of the Company Raj. Determined to hold on to at least the vestige of glory in India, the French retained five small posts or Comptoirs here: Chandernagore, Pondichéry, Karaikal, Mahe and Yanaon. Surrounded by the burgeoning British Indian Empire these Comptoirs languished as sleepy outposts in the French colonial empire for the better part of 150 years, content to watch the world go by, and occasionally aiding the colonial effort in South East Asia.[1]

---

[1] The comptoirs served as ports of call on the way to and from South East Asia. During the late nineteenth and twentieth centuries

From 1817 to 1947 the Comptoirs continued in a state of tranquility. With the independence of British India[2] the movement for independence in French India gained momentum until finally France gave up her colonial claims on India in 1954. French colonial writers describe this period from 1817 to 1954 as one where the French India posts developed educational, economic, political, and judicial structures in peace and harmony with their colonial masters.[3]

France's colonial career in India in fact, extended beyond the British Empire in India. While British India acquired its independence in 1947, the French Comptoirs were declared independent of France only in 1954 and in fact, the actual union with India occurred after a brief military siege of Pondichéry in 1963. Ironically 'French India', as the Comptoirs and loges were collectively called, outlasted the Raj, and ensured that the French were the longest lasting colonial power in India, from the first French Governor General of Pondichéry, François Martin in 1699 to 1963: a career of 264 years in comparison to the British colonial administration of 190 years.[4]

This book examines the process by which images and histories of India[5] were created in France. France

---

Pondichéry also supplied labour, administrators, and traders to the area. Emmanuel Divien, *The Development of Tamil Society in Pondicherry, 1706–1898*. PhD Thesis, University of Madras, 1975.

[2] I use the term 'India' for the late nineteenth century and beyond since the British had now defined the geographical limits of 'India'.

[3] For example, Louis Rousselet, *L'Inde des rajahs: Voyage dans l'Inde centrale et dans les présidences de Bombay et du Bengale* (Paris: Hachette, 1875) and Pierre Loti, *L'Inde (sans les Anglais)* (Paris: Calman-Levy, 1903).

[4] From Clive's military success in 1757 to the independence of India in 1947.

[5] It is important to distinguish between the geographical entity of India and the people. I refer to India as the people who inhabit the South Asian region, comprising roughly the modern nations of India and Pakistan.

continued to be a colonial power in India even though it was no longer the dominant *colonizing* power. As a result of this situation, France was in a unique position in India as a subordinate colonial nation—a subaltern. This book refers to France as a 'subaltern' in India with reference to this historical situation where France continued to occupy colonies in India as a secondary, or subaltern power. The approach is taken from Kate Marsh who notes that, 'French language writing on India cannot be examined and appreciated fully without engaging methodologically with France's politically subordinate status in India, thus proposing, instead of the traditional binary relationship between colonizer and colonized, a triangular model composed of India (the colonized), the "subaltern colonizer" (France), and the dominant colonizer(Britain).'[6]

I do not seek to define what India 'really' was (an impossible task!);[7] rather, I aim to study the *process* of creating India in the French imagination. An important argument for this project is that the colonial imagination, which constructed unreal, 'phantasmatic'[8] images of colonies did so in order to further specific national

---

[6] Kate Marsh, *Fictions of 1947: Representations of Indian Decolonization in French-language Texts* (New York: Peter Lang, 2007): 13.

[7] As Sunil Khilnani points out in *The Idea of India*, the need to define India in finite terms was a product of the colonial denigration of the land and people. This led to multiple definitions of India, each bounded by specific geographical, ideological, philosophical, and cultural agendas, each necessarily lacking in a holistic view of India. Sunil Khilnani, *The Idea of India* (Delhi: Penguin, 1997).

[8] I take this term from Panivong Norindr, *Phantasmatic Indo-China: French Colonial Ideology in Architecture, Film and Literature* (Durham and London: Duke University Press, 1996). Norindr uses various moments in French literary representations and colonial representations of 'l'Indochine' to argue that these constituted an unreal, imagined romance, far removed from reality, and that the very notion of 'Indochine' itself was a 'phantasmic' creation in French colonial imagination.

colonial aims. This imagination was embedded in an artificial archive of knowledge, expressed in part, through
academic monographs and museum exhibits. As Thomas
Richards notes, the notion of 'empire' and the unity that
the term suggests was conferred by creating an imaginary
world—through documentation and paperwork, through
literature and exhibitions, through intellectual peregri-
nations—which served to convince both the métropole
and the rest of the world about their territorial overlord-
ship over what was really a 'paper empire',[9] an empire
in thought, an epistemological empire. The project really
involved a 'colonization of knowledge' where one nation
could convince itself, the 'colonized' nation, and the
global onlookers that it ruled over a land by virtue of
copious claims to do so—all of which were expressed in
print. The nineteenth-century empire was thus an empire
of knowledge where colonial nations evoked their empires
and their rule over them by pointing to their monopoly of
knowledge about that empire. I use this term to denote the
intellectual archive which comprised 'India' in French academia, particularly the works of French experts on Indian
culture, popularly called 'Indologists', during the nineteenth century. Beginning with Antoine de Chézy, Eugene
Burnouf, Julien Vinson, Sylvain Lévi, Auguste Barth, and
Emile Sénart, I move to Gustave le Bon and Paul Topinard
who defined India as a racial entity, thus incorporating the
French imagination about India into the prevailing anthropological debates of the mid-nineteenth century.

Finally, there is what Nicholas Bancel and Pascal
Blanchard call 'colonial memory'. From colonial imagination and the creation of an archive came colonial memory.
Despite the death of the colonial era, the modern world is
still left with many vestiges of the colonial past. Some of
these are real—architecture, language, and government.
But far more deep-rooted and therefore more influential in

---

[9] Thomas Richards, *The Imperial Archive: Knowledge and the
Fantasy of Empire* (New York and London: Verso, 1993): 4.

the way people imagine one another is colonial memory. For Nicholas Bancel and Pascal Blanchard, 'colonial memory' is a construct, created by the players in a nation's colonial history, as much as by the literature, films, music, plastic arts, it is essentially the 'official memory' of colonization. According to them, 'memory, as an intercession between the realities of the present and the recessive logic of the narrative that orders a direction to these, is a process, a permanent reconstruction, and (also) leaves immediate, indelible tracks, (which are) incorporated in the social imagination.'[10] This book treats the popular uses to which the academic images of India were put as part of 'colonial memory'. Whether academic monographs inspired school textbooks, or artistic masterpieces, they can be interpreted as the introduction of the erudite into the popular imagination and memory. In attempting to bridge the gap between the intellectual archive and popular memory, I look at history textbooks of French and francophone school children in the late nineteenth and early twentieth centuries, to assess the impact of intellectual creations of 'India' on the 'colonial memory' of school children.

Whether or not these images embodied the 'true India' is not as important in this study as the rationale behind the conception of a specific India. The lens through which different European powers like Britain, France, Portugal, Germany, and Denmark viewed India was as varied as the images of India which were created. So, for example, British images of India were those of an unruly country in need of British guidance;[11] while Germany

---

[10] 'La mémoire, comme intercession entre les réalités du présent et la logique recessive du récit qui ordonne un sens à celles-ci, est un processus, une reconstruction permanente, et elle laisse aussi des traces, immédiates, indélibles, incorporées dans l'imaginaire social.' Nicholas Bancel and Pascal Blanchard, 'Mémoire coloniale: resistances à l'émergence d'un débat', *Culture post-coloniale 1961–2006*. Edited by Pascal Blanchard and Nicholas Bancel (Paris: Éditions Autrement, 2005): 24.

[11] See for example, James Mill's monumental *History of British India* (London: Baldwin, Craddock and Joy, 1817).

created a romantic image of a country which had given birth to language and civilization,[12] and, by contrast, Portugal focused on her little island of Catholic converts in a sea of Hindu idolaters.[13] The very diversity of such images exposes the fallacy that histories were unbiased accounts. Moreover, different perspectives illuminate different aspects of realities as well. Colonial histories often tell us more about the concerns of the colonizing power than an accurate account of the colony. I examine the different 'Indias' produced by French academics and study some of the appropriations of these 'Indias'. These differences are important in studying not only the trajectory and impact of colonial policy and implementation in France, England, Portugal and Denmark (the remaining colonial powers in India in the nineteenth century), but also provide an insight into present-day conceptions in France of what constitutes India and how different communities in India perceive themselves. The erstwhile French India posts, for example define their 'Indianness' in ways that can be traced directly to the specifically French project of constructing a cultural image of India. Religious tension between Hindus and Muslims, as a conspicuous example, is lacking in these areas, although caste distinctions are prominent in the way Pondichériens identify themselves.[14]

---

[12] See Friedrich Max Müller, *India: What Can it Teach Us? A Course of Lectures Delivered before the University of Cambridge* (Cambridge: Longmans Green, 1883), Lecture I.

[13] See *The Goa Inquisition, Being a Quarter-centenary Commemoration Study of the Inquisition in India*, edited by A. K. Priolkar (Bombay: Bombay University, 1961).

[14] Jacques Weber, 'Acculturation et assimilation dans les Établissements français de l'Inde. La caste et les valeurs de l'Occident', *Comptes rendus trimestriels des séances de l'Académie des Sciences d'Outre-Mer*, tome XXXVIII2–1978: 187–215 and 219–24. This is not to say that the French India posts have never seen any communal conflict. However, the records of the *Chaudrie*, or local Tribunal courts would indicate that skirmishes between castes were more the rule. Religious conflicts, when they did occur, were often due to outside influence,

Contrast this to the neighbouring state of Tamil Nadu, which was part of British India and where not only caste, but also communal tensions run high.[15] As Narayani Gupta points out, there were also differences in political experience; the *Comptoirs* came to representative government through developments in France while British India had to mount a campaign for the same rights.[16]

THE 'ORIENTAL RENAISSANCE' AND THE PLACE OF INDIA

Focus on India was not unusual in nineteenth-century Europe. The Neo-classical Renaissance of the Long Century was supplemented by an intense interest in the Orient as an exotic entity. Raymond Schwab dedicated a considerable part of his life to documenting this 'Oriental Renaissance' in nineteenth-century Europe.[17] Following Schwab, William Halbfass,[18] Roger Pol-Droit[19] and Alex Aronson made similar

---

and as such, the French administrators were not particularly concerned with the possibility of religious tensions between Hindus and Muslims. Narayani Gupta also notes that caste distinctions were emphasized in the Comptoirs while religion was the basis of distinction in British India. Narayani Gupta, 'The Citizens of French India: The Issue of Cultural Identity in Pondicherry in the XIX century', *Les relations historiques et culturelles entre la France et l'Inde XVII–XX siècles*. 2 volumes (Sainte-Clotilde: Le Chaudron, 1987): 164–65.

[15] This aspect of Anglo-French colonial difference in India has been tentatively approached by Niels Brimnes, *Constructing the Colonial Encounter. Right and Left Hand Castes in Early Colonial South India* (Richmond, Surrey: Curzon Press, 1999), and Emmanuel Divien, *The Development of Tamil Society in Pondicherry, 1706–1898* (PhD Thesis, University of Madras, 1975).

[16] Narayani Gupta, 'The Citizens of French India: The Issue of Cultural Identity in Pondicherry in the XIX century'.

[17] Raymond Schwab, *The Oriental Renaissance* (New York: Columbia University Press, 1984).

[18] Wilhelm Halbfass, *India and Europe* (Albany, N.Y.: State University of New York Press, 1988).

[19] Roger Pol-Droit, *L'Oubli de l'Inde* (Paris: Presses Universitaires de France, 1989).

attempts to document the enormous influence of India and the East in the development of nineteenth-century European philosophy.[20] These scholars adopted the term 'Oriental Renaissance', after the work of Edgar Quinet[21] for this philosophical movement to the East. Camille Jullian, writing about the work of Orientalists Silvestre de Sacy and Abel Rémusat noted that, 'Their articles in the *Journal des Savants*, everywhere reprinted, suggested to the learned world that the Orient was at that time absorbing all the scholarly energy of France.'[22]

In part, the focus on the Orient came about as a result of colonial ambitions in the East and the desire of European colonizers to 'know' their Eastern subjects in order to better exploit and govern them.[23] Many scholars who have studied the *Comptoirs* stress that the economic attractiveness of the India trade continued far beyond the downfall of colonial hopes. Louis Dermigny and Sudipta Das for example, stressed the continued commercial attractiveness of India to French merchants after the French East India Company's monopoly was revoked in 1769 in the aftermath of the Seven Years War.[24] Paul Butel who has studied the private archives of individuals to explore

---

[20] Alex Aronson, *Europe Looks at India* (Bombay: Hind Kitabs, 1946).

[21] Schwab, *The Oriental Renaissance*: 11.

[22] Camille Jullian, *Extraits des historiens français du XIX siècle* (Paris: Hatchette, 1906). Cited in Schwab, *The Oriental Renaissance*: 99.

[23] See for example, Lewis Pyenson, *Civilizing Mission: Exact Sciences and French Overseas Expansion, 1830–1940* (Baltimore: Johns Hopkins Press, 1993) and Michael A. Osbourne, *Nature, the Exotic, and the Science of French Colonialism* (Indianapolis: Indiana University Press, 1994).

[24] Louis Dermigny, *La Chine et l'Occident. Le Commerce à Canton au XXVIII siècle* (Paris, 1964). Quoted in Paul Butel, 'French Traders and India at the End of the Eighteenth Century', in *Merchants, Companies and Trade. Europe and Asia in the early Modern Era*, edited by Sushil Chaudhury and Michel Morineau (Cambridge England: CUP, 1999): 298.

the trade between India and French ports like Bordeaux and Marseilles, notes the petition of a merchant, Louis Monneron (whose company was based in Pondichéry till 1787) to the National Assembly and later again to Napoleon stressing the importance of maintaining the trade route via the Suez.[25] As Butel points out there was a tendency among both ports and Parisian financial circles of returning to the commercial routes of the Indian Ocean which had created so many fortunes in the eighteenth century.

But the images of India which were popular with French academics derived only partly from colonial and economic interests. During the nineteenth century, French academics used India to demonstrate a plethora of theories. Earlier scholars of Indology took their cue from Schwab whose impressive documentation of the Western preoccupation and development of Oriental studies is simultaneously a tribute to the pure pursuit of knowledge. His 'Oriental Renaissance' was a veritable encyclopaedia of developments in Oriental knowledge and studies in the West but it made no connection with larger intellectual or political currents which impacted the extent and trajectory of Oriental studies. As a corrective to this otherwise impeccable scholarship, this book explores some of the religious, philosophical, and anthropological discourses that French Indologists created for India, just as Kamakshi Murti, who has studied the effects of German Indology in the discourses of racism which developed during the twentieth century.[26] Murti argues that German Indologists claimed a spiritual, if not territorial connection with India by virtue of the 'Aryan' parallels in the past of the two countries. In the French case, where India could easily

---

Sudipta Das, *Myths and Realities of French Imperialism in India* (New York: Peter Lang, 1992).

[25] Ibid.

[26] Kamakshi P. Murti, *India: The Seductive and Seduced 'Other' of German Orientalism* (Westport, CT: Greenwood Publishing Group, 2001).

have been a French rather than a British colony, the need to 'claim' a mastery of India was linked directly to national pride. At the beginning and the end of the nineteenth century, India figured prominently in colonialist rivalry with England. While this rivalry was articulated largely by the colonialist press and by individuals, often the academic discourse on India was appropriated to serve these ends. In a telling statement of French disappointment in losing her Indian Empire, Naudet claimed that although France had lost her temporal claims to India, she was still the intellectual master of India through the work of the Indic scholars of the nineteenth century.[27] According to Schwab,

> ...it was England's great disgrace to be too self-seeking in India to avoid violent reactions, after fits and starts of adaptation...The conquerors felt obligated to defend their conquest, which meant exalting their own race and religion...reinforcing the English prejudice of Western superiority and minimizing, for the parent state, the phenomenon of the Oriental Renaissance.[28]

Despite the fact of French defeat in India, perhaps *because* of her marginal political position, Schwab highlights the development of 'a scientific passion which no ulterior political motive could alter.'[29]

French studies on India were thus shaped and legitimized by the *loss* of India. Binita Mehta argues that France's unique relationship with India stemmed from this territorial loss and that France's shortlived hopes of colonizing India and the loss of India created a powerful hold over

---

[27] M. Naudet, 'Notice historique sur MM. Burnouf, Père et fils', in *Mémoires de l'Académie des inscriptions et belles-lettres* 20 (Paris, 1854): 310.

[28] Schwab, *The Oriental Renaissance*: 43.

[29] Ibid.: 45.

French dramatists.[30] According to her, nineteenth-century French views of India were influenced to some extent by the loss of France's Indian colonies after nearly a century of fighting the British. The French wished to recapture their past glory in India, and they accomplished this through literature.[31] In her study of journalistic representations of India in the twentieth century, Kate Marsh also notes that since France never actually colonized India, but had to be content with ruling over five tiny Comptoirs in place of the dreams of an Indian empire, French writing on India must be interpreted in the context not just of romanticism, but of a yearning for 'what may have been'—the unreal nostalgia for what had been and a romantic projection of what may have been.[32]

Mehta focuses on plays and Marsh on the polemic of journalists. This book examines academic views and works on India. Among French academics there was no such overt yearning, or rhetoric of empire. Despite French marginalization in India, Paris was indisputably the centre of Indic studies well into the nineteenth century. In fact, the first Chair of Indology at the Collège de France was created in 1815, and the pre-eminent *Journal Asiatique* in 1822, well after the French dream of Empire in India was laid to rest. Indology continued to survive and flourish in Paris. Part of this fascination with India was due to the revival of Classical studies, but French scholars, having taken up Indological studies from an interest in human history could not escape the public view that having irrevocably lost India to the British the French could at least claim a superior understanding of India. This understanding led to clearly different images of India from the colonizing British

---

[30] Binita Mehta, *Widows, Pariahs and Bayadères. India as Spectacle* (Lewisburg: Bucknell University Press, and London: Associated University Presses, 2002): 14.

[31] Ibid.: 156.

[32] Marsh, *Fictions of 1947*: 19.

works which stressed the backwardness of India and her need for British tutelage, or even the occasional American evangelical work emphasizing the oppression of Indian religion.

'ORIENTALISM' AND INDIA

Edward Said published an influential book, titled 'Orientalism' in which he argued that the colonizing West had constructed an exotic, essentialist 'Other' which embodied the civilizing mission, by defining the East as degenerate, effeminate, despotic and superstitious, among other epithets.[33] Overnight no scholar examining colonial history could ignore Said. Among the scholars who vigorously agreed with Said was Rana Kabbani,[34] who was influenced by his theoretical writings about the construction of the Orient in the colonial imagination as an exotic and diametrically opposite land to the civilized West.

Many scholars have studied the creation of India in the popular sphere. Binita Mehta, for example, cites the 'invention' of India in the West as a constant theme in Western writing on India from ancient times.[35] Jackie Assayag,[36] Srilata Ravi,[37] Christian Petr,[38] Jean Biès,[39] Catherine Weinberger-Thomas,[40] and Richard Andersen[41]

---

[33] Edward W. Said, *Orientalism* (New York: Pantheon Books, 1978).

[34] Rana Kabbani, *Europe's Myths of the Orient* (Indianapolis: Indiana University Press, 1986).

[35] Binita Mehta, *Widows, Pariahs and Bayadères*: 27.

[36] Jackie Assayag, *L'Inde fabuleuse: le charme discret de l'exotisme français : XVII–XXe siècles* (Paris: Kimé, 1999).

[37] Srilata Ravi, *L'Inde romancée: l'Inde dans le genre romanesque français depuis 1947* (New York: P. Lang, 1997).

[38] Christian Petr, *L'Inde des romans* (Paris: Ed Kailash, 1995).

[39] Jean Biès, *Littérature française et pensée hindoue des origines à 1950* (Paris: C. Klincksieck, 1974).

[40] *L'Inde et l'imaginaire*. Edited by Catherine Weinberger-Thomas. (Paris: Purusartha, 1988).

[41] Richard Anderson, *India in Romantic and Parnassian French Poetry* (New Haven: Yale University Press, 1950).

also focused on the hold which India had upon the popular French imagination. Based on studies of French plays, poems, novels, travelogues and operas these scholars posited the creation of an India which was dominated by clichés of bayadères, oriental tyrants, widows, and brave European adventurers. The plethora of scholarly literature produced in the wake of Said's *Orientalism* paid due homage to the influence of India in the creation of Western, specifically French Orientalism.[42] The exoticism of nineteenth-century literature was echoed in art. As Amina Okada notes, the lithographs, etchings and watercolours in travelogues, and journals like *Le Tour du Monde* and *Le Monde Pittorresque* reinforced the notion of 'India' as a land of princes, spirituality, demons and barbaric customs (like thuggee and sati), bayadères and beauties, of beautiful landscapes and a vestige of France's colonial dreams.[43] Another theoretical framework which proved valuable to this study is the Foucauldian discussion of 'power-knowledge' by ruling classes of people to create and disseminate powerful images of their subjects, which eventually, came to be internalized by these very subjects.[44] Importantly, Foucault's model allowed for a degree of agency and choice to be exercised by subject populations. An important area where natives had considerable agency was in the relaying of information about their cultures and pasts to their colonial masters. Bernard

---

[42] For example Lisa Lowe, *Critical Terrains. French and British Orientalisms* (Ithaca: Cornell University Press, 1991), Dorothy Figuiera, *Translating the Orient: The Reception of Sakuntala in Nineteenth-century Europe* (Albany: State University of New York Press, 1991), and Jenny Sharpe, *Allegories of Empire. The Figure of Woman in the Colonial Text* (Minneapolis: University of Minnesota Press, 1993).

[43] Amina Okada and Enrico Isacco, *L'Inde au XIXe siècle: voyage aux sources de l'imaginaire.* (Marseille: AGEP, 1991).

[44] Michel Foucault, *Discipline and Punish: The Birth of the Prison* (New York: Vintage, 1995). In this edition, the term 'power-knowledge' is replaced by 'governmentality'.

Cohn argued that co-operation and resistance by Indians in their relations with European colonialists produced a distinct interpretation and understanding of the Indian past.[45] Cohn's work was unique in arguing for a *relationship* between Indians and European colonizers, in contrast to earlier works which had presented Indians as entirely passive in the creation of 'India'. Even if Indians were in an inferior position, they were the primary informants who contributed to the discourse of Indology.[46] While this book focuses on French writings about India, an enormous corpus of literature which necessitated the exclusion of Indians as direct agents in the dialogue of history, it is crucial to remember that Indians often participated in the production and dissemination of these images, and in focusing on French academia I do not mean to negate or minimize the contribution of Indians.

The application of Said and Foucault to South Asia has led to groundbreaking works like Carol Appadurai Breckendridge and Peter Van der Veer's edited volume, *Orientalism and the Postcolonial Predicament: perspectives on South Asia.*[47] Their work demonstrated that Said's open-ended model of Orientalism could be applied to specific linguistic and literary developments in colonial South Asia. The work of the Subaltern Studies collective which studied the perspective of groups and individuals outside of the hegemonic power structure, was also crucial to re-conceptualizing the power discourse in the description of South Asian colonial history, particularly Ranajit Guha's *Dominance without Hegemony: History and Power in*

---

[45] Bernard Cohn, *Colonialism and its Forms of Knowledge* (Princeton: Princeton University Press, 1996).

[46] Bernard Cohn, 'The Command of Language and the Language of Command', in ibid.

[47] *Orientalism and the Postcolonial Predicament: Perspectives on South Asia.* Edited by Carol Appadurai Breckendridge and Peter Van der Veer (Philadelphia: University of Pennsylvania Press, 1993).

Colonial India[48] and Gyanendra Pandey's *The Construction of Communalism in Colonial North India*.[49] These works have been immensely helpful in conceptualizing the argument of this book.

According to Amartya Sen, India has been represented in three ways in Western writings: exoticist, magisterial and curatorial.[50] Ronald Inden has similarly categorized Western writings on India as possessing 'descriptive' and 'commentative' aspects which claim to represent the thought and acts of the Indian to the reader,[51] 'explanatory' or 'interpretive' aspects which intervene between the reader and the Indian to explain the apparently distorted thought of the Oriental to the rational Western reader,[52] and 'hegemonic' accounts which present the Indian civilization in the authoritative voice of the colonizer.[53] Echoing Schwab and Naudet's sentiments about British writings being tainted by the necessity of rule, Sen and Inden present 'hegemonic' accounts as possessing the least accuracy of all Indological accounts.

An excellent narrative and analytical work is Inden's *Imagining India*, which examines the use of various metaphors about India in Western writing, such as India as a female, Indian thought as a dream, Hinduism as a jungle or a sponge and caste society as a centrifuge.[54] He notes that his study is about the agency of individuals, specifically

---

[48] Ranajit Guha, *Dominance without Hegemony: History and Power in Colonial India* (Harvard, Mass: Harvard University Press, 1998).

[49] Gyanendra Pandey, *The Construction of Communalism in Colonial North India* (Delhi: OUP, 2006).

[50] Amartya Sen, 'Indian Traditions and the Western Imagination', *Daedalus*, Vol. 126, No. 2, *Human Diversity* (Spring, 1997): 1–26.

[51] Ronald Inden, *Imagining India* (Oxford: UK; Cambridge, Mass., USA: Basil Blackwell, 1990): 38. He provides the example of Louis Renou.

[52] Ibid.: 42. Inden criticizes this as being too reductionist in explaining the Indian within one single rubric or logic.

[53] Ibid.: 43.

[54] Ibid.: 1.

the capacity of people to order the world around them. In respect to imperial formations centred on India, Inden posits the existence of two periods: the Anglo-French period where Orientalist discourse and notions of India in the West were dominated by the Anglo-French schools of thought, and the imperial formation of the US and USSR in the contemporary period. According to Inden, such a framework is made possible by the fact that earlier, Spanish-Portuguese thought formations of the sixteenth to eighteenth centuries were dominated by Christian theology, while the Anglo-French (in which he includes the German and American Orientalist schools) centred primarily on the Hegelian-Marxist notion of a natural science or philosophy.[55] However, in analysing the entire Western discourse on India prior to the twentieth century in terms of the Hegelian model, Inden simplifies the complex process of identity formation and colonial and political aims which co-opted India as a metaphor or example of the 'other'. Moreover, in assigning all Europeans the simple position of power over India, Inden also negates the important distinctions which came to represent different descriptions of India—British, French, German, and Portuguese.

The Foucauldian model is adopted as an approach in this book to argue for the influence of French images of India. Since France was part of the ruling colonial West, the academic study of India in France had far greater impact in the West (on German and American Indology, for example) than any academic studies by Indians themselves.[56] Foucault's model also allows for a multiplicity of images. For instance, popular stories like Voltaire's *Zadig et la destinée* (1747), *Lettres d'un Turc sur les Fakirs et sur son ami Bababec* (1750), *Histoire d'un bon brahmin* (1761), and

---

[55] Ibid.: 32.

[56] For example, the prominence of Indian reformer and intellectual Raja Ram Mohun Roy among European intellectuals was due to his mastery over English and his popularity with European Indologists.

Bernadin de Saint-Pierre's *La Chaumière indienne* (1790) were full of the standard clichés of India as a land of serpent charmers, fakirs, exotic women, a land of danger and sensuality. While these images continued to dominate the theatrical and literary representations of India in nineteenth-century France, the new generation of academics strove to break away from their romantic predecessors and establish themselves as scientists who followed a rigorous academic process of investigation and presentation and did not allow their opinions to cloud their research. The Indologists of the nineteenth century tried to capture the essence of India in a progression of dominant 'isms'. Thus India as a land of Brahminism gave way to India as the land of Buddhism, which was subsumed by India as the land of the Aryans and then to a hybrid 'Hindu' entity.

Another singular aspect of this work is its scope. While not exhaustive, I have tried to provide at least snapshots of pre-modern images of India in France before focusing on the long nineteenth century. For instance, a fourteenth-century work, the *Mirabilia Descripta* by a Friar Jordanus is contrasted with the compendium of proselytizing Jesuit missionaries in sixteenth- and seventeenth-century India, the *Lettres édifiantes et curieuses*[57] to demonstrate not only the enduring European interest in India, but also that images of India had historically been the result of particular intellectual and political agendas, whether conversion or conquest. The description of works by missionaries also provides a good foil for the later works by academics, who prided themselves on their 'rational, non-biased judgment'.

In terms of academics, this book rather ambitiously stretches from the Enlightenment to the early twentieth century. From the works of the French *philosophes*,

---

[57] *Lettres Édifiantes et Curieuses, Ecrites de Missions Etrangères, par quelques Missionaires de la Compagnie de Jésus* (Paris: Nicolas Le Clerc, 1702 to 1776), 34 volumes.

particularly Voltaire and Montesquieu and their impressions of India, to the writings of Indologists in the early twentieth century, the *longue durée* lens allows me to follow certain particular characteristics of French descriptions of India, such as their anti-Islamic stance and the notion that regardless of the state of contemporary India the Indians had once possessed a great civilization, while simultaneously looking at the subtle shifts within these characteristics, and specific stimuli to create such images of India. Another undertaking of this work is to compare the kinds of writing that described India across different academic fields like Indology, Sociology, Anthropology, Linguistics and Philology, and History and analyse whether the writings corresponded to field-specific models or whether they revealed consistent themes based on arguably external influences, such as France's colonial policy.

Admittedly, the material researched for this work was scholarly and primarily meant for an intellectual, even academic readership. Beyond a typical historian's fascination with obscure works, why should anyone care what kinds of images the French produced about India? Did it even matter? Here, I make my biggest gamble. I want to convince you about the importance of all these images. They did matter. They set the path for ordinary thousands, millions of Europeans, who knew nothing about India except what they were told in newspapers, entertainment and schools. Particularly, in schools. Most Europeans, and in fact children of the Francophone world, encountered India first, as a distant country in their school textbooks. This is where they first learned of its existence and its history. This is where they formed their first opinion of India. Beyond France, histories of India in French school textbooks were taught all over the French colonial world, as well as in French-speaking countries like Belgium. The impact of these works reached far beyond the geographical confines of France. And these textbooks were hybrid accounts of all the various images of India that had been created in abstruse works on Indology, Sociology and the like. My argument is that, regardless of who you are, and where you are from, you will recognize the images I describe in this book as defining 'India' in some way for you. An 'India' which was created in France.

Chapter 1

India: A Land of Wonders or of Monstrosities? The Writings of Missionaries

IMAGE 1.1: Postcard from French India, 1910; French missionary and local statue

IMAGE 1.2: Postcard from French India, 1910; gopuram

Image 1.1 above is a postcard from French India dated to 1910. It shows a French missionary standing next to a statue of a local God sculpted in the traditional, 'Dravidian' style[1]

---

[1] The term 'Dravidian' itself was popularized by Europeans seeking to differentiate Northern from Southern India. In its various interpretations, and certainly in art and architecture, the word usually referred to

and described as the 'face of the devil', while Image 1.2 is the picture of the gopuram, or tower topping a local temple. The contrast between the obviously negative left image and the neutral right image was typical of French missionary sentiments about Indic religion as far back as the fourteenth century.

Initially the focus on Indian religion was the work of missionaries who accompanied explorers to the East looking for heathens to convert to Christianity. This aspect of proselytization was also prominent in sixteenth- and seventeenth-century writings of travellers and traders. The later works were intended to be both a catalogue of curiosities and strange customs, and helpful advice for subsequent travellers and traders to interact successfully with Indians. Religion continued to pique the interest of Enlightenment *philosophes* who searched for spiritual and philosophical traditions which were distinct from the Classical tradition of the Christian Church. India and China in fact provided the intellectual impetus for the Enlightenment attack on the Church. Since the origin of scholarship in Enlightenment Europe that studied the 'Orient' was spurred by the works of missionaries writing about the East, it becomes crucial to examine the image of India described in these works.[2]

I focus on two works: the fourteenth-century *Mirabilia Descripta* of the Dominican missionary Jourdain du Séverac and the later letters of Jesuit missionaries which were compiled into the *Lettres édifiantes et curieuses*. I decided to use the *Mirabilia,* because it is the first extensive account of India written by a Frenchman. The *Lettres édifiantes*

---

an inferior form marked by outrageous features on statues, a garish and aesthetically repulsive efflorescence of colour and tasteless overcrowding of friezes and panels.

[2] According to Županov, accounts of the Jesuits provided much of the philosophes' information about India. Ines G. Županov, *Disputed Mission: Jesuit Experiments and Brahmanical Knowledge in Seventeenth Century India* (Delhi: Oxford University Press, 1999): 44.

represent the latest attempt of men of the cloth, to describe India, before the full-scale advent of Imperialism. These two works are by no means definitive works on India. However, they were extensively quoted by others writing about India and therefore offer one image of India that was cited by French writers.

An overview of pre-nineteenth century French writings reveals that there were specific professions or occupations that presented India. Broadly, one can speak of 'missionary views',[3] and 'secular views'.[4] A substantial body of research already exists on the works of secular travellers.[5] The work of missionaries is only now being examined. This chapter focusses on missionary writings for three reasons. First, it

---

[3] I use the term 'missionary views' to broadly indicate the views of men whose primary aim in writing about India was for the purpose of spreading Christianity.

[4] I use the term 'secular views' to represent the views of men who travelled to India as merchants, mercenaries and even tourists as opposed to missionaries who were sent to India in pursuit of their evangelical duties. While many of these men were deeply religious and expressed their opinion of Indian religion, their fundamental purpose in travelling to India was not to effect conversion, so they have been grouped into 'secular views'.

[5] Most of the current research on India in the sixteenth to eighteenth centuries has used the works of travellers and observers like Jean Baptiste Tavernier and Le Gentil, physicians like François Bernier and Charles Dellon, engineers like Legoux De Flaix, architects like Claude Martin, and most of all mercenaries like Allard, Ventura, Réne Madec, Law de Lauriston, Dubois de Jancigny, Gentil, Claude Martin and Benoit De Boigne. For travellers see Edward Farley Oaten, *European Travellers in India during the Fifteenth, Sixteenth and Seventeenth centuries. 1909.* (New York: AMS Press, 1971 reprint); and *Distant Lands and Diverse Cultures: the French Experience in Asia 1600–1700*, edited by Glenn J. Ames and Ronald Love (Westport Ct and London: Praeger, 2003). For the work of mercenaries see Jean Marie Lafont, *Indika. Essays in Indo-French relations 1630–1976* (New Delhi: Manohar, 2000) as well as *La présence française dans le royaume sikh du Penjab: 1822–1849* (Paris: École française d'Extrême-Orient, 1992).

fills a gap in the scholarship on pre-colonial modern India.[6] Second, the work of missionaries becomes especially important for this intellectual history, because the aim of French missionaries in India by the late seventeenth century was to record information as amateur scientists as much as it was to effect conversions to Christianity. The mission writings are representative of the earliest *educated* Western descriptions of India. These early representations were considered so valuable that nineteenth-century works on India relied greatly on missionary accounts of the previous centuries. Citing Pierre Filliozat, William Halbfass in his essay on India and Europe noted that,

> The birth of Indology as a real science is the result of a collaboration between Indian traditional scholars and French missionaries. The first work that can be recognized as an achievement is a grammar of Sanskrit written in Latin, in about 1733. It is probably the work of J.F Pons, a Jesuit, who resided in India, especially at Chandranagore, Karaikal and Pondicherry, in the first decades of the eighteenth century.[7]

Third, this chapter explores the possibility that French views of Indian religion dominated French writing about India from the early modern to the modern period. Interest

---

[6] The scholarship on 'secular' writers like Tavernier, Bernier, Charles Dellon and Le Gentil is fairly extensive. Apart from numerous translations of their accounts and monographs dedicated to these individuals, it is very common for their works to be used as sources for the modern period in Indian history. For instance, Binita Mehta, *Widows, Pariahs and Bayadères. India as Spectacle* (Lewisburg: Bucknell University Press, and London: Associated University Presses, 2002); and Kate Teltscher, *India Inscribed: European and British Writing on India, 1600–1800* (Delhi: OUP, 1995) are among the more recent works which examine the impact of these writers on the image of India in France.

[7] Wilhelm Halbfass, *India and Europe. An Essay in Understanding* (Albany, N.Y.: State University of New York Press, 1988): 44. Cited from P. S. Filliozat, 'The French Institute of Indology in Pondicherry,' *Weiner Zeitschrift für die Kunde Südasiens* 28 (1983): 133. I have discussed this issue on pages 74–76.

in India during the Middle Ages was sporadic at best and limited to missionaries who sent back reports of the strange lands and the heathens whom they had attempted to convert. Some scientific interest in the Indian systems of medicine and astronomy did present itself during medieval contact with the Arabs, who had adopted many of the astronomical and medicinal practices of India. As the famous twentieth-century Indologist Jean Filliozat points out, however, the possibility of appreciating India for itself was remote in the hyper-religious environment of medieval France.[8] It was only with the Renaissance and later on with the Enlightenment that Europe would truly be ready to accept the possibility that there were other cultures as developed as their own.[9]

Among the rare missionaries in India was the French Dominican missionary Jourdain de Séverac, who visited India as far back as the fourteenth century. His account and observations about India and the people of India are contained in a couple of long letters,[10] as well as the *Mirabilia*,[11] and formed the beginning of a valuable corpus

---

[8] Jean Filliozat, 'La naissance et l'essor de L'Indianisme', *Bulletin de la Société des études indo-chinoises de Saigon,* Vol. 29, issue 4, (1954): 268.

[9] Ibid.

[10] The two letters of Jordanus to missionaries wishing to work in the East are in the BNF, dated to October 1321 and January 1324. They total about 29 pages. Friar Jordanus, *Mirabilia Descripta. The Wonders of the East.* Trans. Col. Sir Henry Yule. Hakluyt Society Publication no. 31, first series, (1863): preface, iv–vi. The Mirabilia was previously published in *Receuil des Voyages et de Mémoires publié par la Société de Géographie,* vol. 4 as *Description des merveilles d'une partie de l'Asie: imprimé d'après un manuscrit du XIVe siècle par le P. Jordan ou Jourdain Catalani,* ed. Eugène Coquebert de Montbret. The Mirabilia was also partially reproduced in Henri Cordier, *Mirabilia Descripta-Les Merveilles de l'Asie, par le Père Jourdain Catalani de Séverac* (Paris: P. Geuthner, 1925).

[11] Published as Friar Jordanus. *Mirabilia Descripta. The Wonders of the East.* Trans. Col. Sir Henry Yule. Hakluyt Society Publication

of information available to missionaries who made the long, arduous, and often dangerous journey to India in subsequent centuries. Jordanus is a particularly important source because he was among the first Western missionaries in India.[12] He wrote his *Mirabilia* while at the Papal court in 1329, and soon after was appointed the first Latin Bishop of Columbum in South India. These incidents combine to make him an influential source.[13] I examine the work of Jordanus in contrast to the later writings of the Jesuits. By the seventeenth century the new geographical and scientific discoveries and incipient long distance trade between Europe and the East led to an increased vigour in seeking information about new lands.[14] As R. K. Kochhar points out, traders only explored the coastline of India. Geographical exploration was left to the Jesuits, who had the training, the time, and the opportunity to criss-cross the country. They had also the necessary discipline to make careful observations, to record them faithfully, and to

---

no. 31, first series, 1863. Also published as *Receuil des Voyages et de Mémoires publié par la Société de Géographie*, Vol. 4.

[12] John of Montecorvino was possibly the first to visit India on his way to China in 1291–92. See James Ryan, 'European travellers before Columbus: The fourteenth century's discovery of India', *Catholic Historical Review*, Vol. 79 Issue 4 (October 1993). http://search.ebscohost.com/login.aspx?direct=true&db=aph&AN=9409090099&site=ehost-live. Accessed on December 31, 2007.

[13] As pointed out in Ibid.

[14] In the preceding years there had been several Jesuit missions which had attempted to effect conversions in North India. A notable work was that of Father Pierre Du Jarric, who came to the Mughal court during the late sixteenth century. Jarric studied the writing of all previous Jesuit missions in India and compiled a *Histoire des choses plus mémorables advenes tant en Indes orientales...*which essentially detailed the Jesuit missions thus far in India. His work was translated and published in English in 1926 as *Akbar and the Jesuits: An Account of the Jesuit Missions to the Court of Akbar* (Oxon: Routledge Curzon, 2005 reprint). A valuable account of Jesuit Missions, Du Jarric did not concern himself too much with a description of the country and people; hence I have left it out of this study.

transmit them regularly.[15] In 1687 Louis XIV sent a mission of 14 Jesuits to Siam. Designated 'Mathematicians of the King' they were to collect whatever information they could about the country and its culture in order to understand the peoples of India, Siam, China, and Japan.[16] Expelled from Siam in 1688, only three Jesuits made it to the coast of India alive, including Pères Bouchet and Richaud. The observations of these missionaries along with others who were travelling in India at the time were recorded in the collection *Lettres édifiantes et curieuses*.[17] By the

---

[15] R. K. Kochhar, 'Secondary Tools of Empire: Jesuit Men of Science in India', in *Discoveries, Missionary Expansion and Asian Cultures*, edited by Teotonio R de. Souza (New Delhi: Concept Publishing Company, 1994): 175.

[16] Ibid.

[17] The *Lettres* which deal with India are records by Pères Tachard, Papin, Bouchet, Pons, Calmette and Mauduit and Coeurdoux. They contain detailed descriptions of the people and customs, which allow a better analysis of their image and representation of India for this study. The *Lettres* seem to have gone through several versions and translations. According to Ines G. Županov in her *Disputed Mission*, a total of 34 volumes were published between 1703–76, edited by LeGobien (Vols 1–7), the China expert du Halde (9–26), 27,28,31,33,34 by Patouillet and possibly René Maréchal or J. B. Geoffrey for vols 29, 30, 32. In addition a number of translated, abridged, and altered versions were published well into the nineteenth century: 12–13. In this study I refer to the earliest English translation of the *Lettres*, which was published even before the French originals were compiled. This edition was compiled by John Lockman under the title of *'Travels of the Jesuits, into various parts of the world: particularly China and the East-Indies. Intermix'd with an account of the manners, government, civil and religious ceremonies, natural history, and curiosities, of the several nations visited by those fathers. Translated from the celebrated Lettres édifiantes & curieuses. To which is now prefixed, an account of the Spanish settlements in America, with a general index to the whole work* (London: T. Piety, 1762, 2nd Ed). The first edition was published in two volumes in 1743, London, by John Noon. The French originals were published periodically by the Paris Jesuit Mission in 34 volumes dating from 1702 to 1776 as *Lettres Édifiantes et Curieuses, Écrites de Missions Etrangères, par quelques Missionnaires de la Compagnie de Jésus* (Paris: Nicolas Le

time the Jesuits of the *Lettres édifiantes* began sending
back their impressions of India their views were certainly
not as favourable as Jordanus'. However, in examining
both Jordanus' work as well as the *Lettres édifiantes et
curieuses* one can see the beginning of a 'French' image
of Indian religion.[18] Moreover, the *Lettres* are important
simply because, as Kate Teltscher points out, between the
years 1700 and 1750 Europe viewed India primarily through
the medium of the letters of the French Jesuits.[19] In terms
of geography these two works both focus on the southern
part of India thus providing a long-term picture of continu-

Clerc). For a description of the various versions of the *Lettres,* see David
Clines, 'In Search of the Indian Job', *Vestus Testamentum,* Vol. 33. 4
(October 1983): 399–404.

[18] There is an emerging corpus of scholarly work which examines
the work of the Jesuits in relation to science, astronomy and their interaction with the native people. Although these aspects are not central to
this work, they are valuable additions to the history of South Asia. See
for example, S. M. Razaullah Ansari, 'Introduction of Modern Western
Astronomy in India during 18–19 Centuries', *History of Indian Astronomy,*
edited by S. N. Sen and K. S. Shukla, (New Delhi: INSA, 1985): 363–402;
Jacques Pouchepadass, 'L'Inde au miroir de l´histoire et des sciences
du temps présent', *Passeurs d´Orient. Encounters between India and
France,* edited by F.Gros (Paris: Ministry of Foreign Affairs, 1991):
52–57; Dhruv Raina, *Nationalism, Institutional Science and the Politics
of Knowledge: Ancient Indian Astronomy and Mathematics in the
Landscape of French Enlightenment Historiography,* (Institutionen för
vetenskapsteori, Göteborgs Universitet, 1999) Rapport Nr. 201; Dhruv
Raina, 'Jean-Baptiste Biot on the History of Indian Astronomy (1830–
1860): The Nation in the Post-Enlightenment Historiography of Science',
Indian Journal of History of Science 35.4 (2000): 319–46; Dhruv Raina,
'Betwixt Jesuit and Enlightenment Historiography: The Context of
Jean-Sylvain Bailly's History of Indian Astronomy', *Revue d'Histoire de
Mathématiques* 9 (2003): 101–53; Virendra Nath Sharma, 'The Impact
of Eighteenth Century Jesuit Astronomers on the Astronomy of India and
China', *Indian Journal of History of Science* 17.2 (1982): 345–52; Ines
G. Županov, *Disputed Mission;* Ines G. Županov, *Missionary Tropics: The
Catholic Frontier in India (16th–17th Centuries)* (Ann Arbor: University
of Michigan Press, 2005).

[19] Teltscher, *India Inscribed*: 5.

ity and change in the representation of peninsular India until the eighteenth century. I use Jordanus as an early work and the Jesuit *Lettres* as the latest representation of India by French missionaries, thus comparing and contrasting the 'missionary view' of India from the thirteenth to the eighteenth century. There are a number of common elements in the work of Jordanus and the Jesuits, including a consistent anti-Muslim stance, coupled with an intense interest in the origins of Indian religion, and a more tolerant view of Indian religion as opposed to Islam.[20] In contrast Jordanus was more forgiving of the peculiarities of the Indians while the Jesuits had harsher criticisms, even though Europe knew more about the East by the eighteenth century.

THE MUSLIM ENEMY

The first common feature of 'missionary views' from the fourteenth to the eighteenth century was their anti-Muslim view. In the context of the Crusades and the long standing antipathy between Christianity and Islam as the two major proselytizing religions of the world, this is not a surprising element of Jordanus' writing.[21] Travelling to India in order to convert the heathen peoples of the East, Jordanus came into direct conflict with Muslims. In fact, as James Ryan points out, most Christian martyrs in this period suffered at the hands of the Muslims, since they 'courted confron-

---

[20] I use the term 'Indian religion' because this is the term used both by Jordanus and the Jesuits, in preference to 'Hindu religion'. Presumably they used the term in recognition of the fact that there were many sects and groups within Hinduism to the extent that the only common features of Hinduism were likely to be geographically determined (i.e., people followed the same customs within a particular region) rather than united by religion.

[21] Rana Kabbani also argues that the anti-Muslim view of Europe was a post-crusade development. Rana Kabbani, *Europe's Myths of the Orient* (London: Macmillan, 1986): 4.

tation...knowing full well they had offended Islamic sensibilities'.[22] As a result of their activities, four missionaries were put to death in India, an event which Jordanus, who was travelling at the time, missed. He returned in time to bury the martyrs ruing his narrow escape from their fate. 'Woe to that most evil hour, the hateful hour, in which for the salvation of others I so unhappily separated myself from my holy companions, ignorant, alas for me! of their future crowns.'[23] His account of the Muslims was therefore extremely harsh. At various points in his text Jordanus contrasts the Muslims with other people unfavourably. The following quote contains his impression of the Persian Muslims whom he contrasts with the Hindus:

> This Persia is inhabited by Saracens and Saracenised Tartars, and by schismatic Christians of divers sects, such as Nestorians, Jacobites, Greeks, Georgians, Armenian, and by a few Jews[24]... the people of this realm live all too

---

[22] James D. Ryan, 'Missionary Saints of the High Middle Ages: Martyrdom, Popular Veneration, and Canonization', *The Catholic Historical Review* 90.1 (2004): 7. Ryan notes that Islam, like Christianity, being a proselytizing religion, came into conflict with the European missionaries, especially the Franciscans and Dominicans who regularly challenged the Muslims with their open denunciations of Allah and the Prophet.

[23] Arthur C. Moule, 'Brother Jordan of Séverac', *Journal of the Royal Asiatic Society of Great Britain and Ireland* (1928): 373. Cited in Friar Jordanus. *Mirabilia Descripta*: 17.

[24] Ibid. In several passages Jordanus dismisses sects of Christianity which he found as heretics. The people of Ethiopia, for instance, 'are all Christians but heretics' (p. 46). In India, Jordanus speaks of, 'a scattered people, one here, another there, who call themselves Christians, but are not so, nor have they baptism, nor do they know anything else about the faith...'(p. 23). Furthermore, 'Of the Caspian Hills I say that there they sacrifice sheep upon a cross, and they call themselves Christians, though they are not so, and know nothing of the faith' (p. 51). In terms of the history of the period, Jordanus displays a fairly typical view of 'heretics' since the Catholic Church was actively engaged in defining the limits of Catholicism and heresy during this period. See Malcolm

uncleanly, for they sit upon the ground, and eke [*sic*] eat upon the same, putting mess and meats in a trencher for three, four, or five persons together. They eat not on a table-cloth, but on a round sheet of leather, or on a low table of wood or brass, with three legs. And so six, seven, or eight persons eat out of one dish, and that with their hands and fingers; big and little, male and female, all eat after this fashion. And after they have eaten, or even whilst in the middle of their eating, they lick their fingers with tongue and lips, and wipe them on their sleeves, and afterwards if any grease still remains upon their hands, they wipe them on their shoes. And thus do the folk all over those countries, including Western and Eastern Tartary, except the Hindus, who eat decently enough, though they too eat with their hands....[25]

Jordanus' use of descriptions like 'unclean' and 'decent' indicate his belief that the Persians and the Tartars, who were mostly Muslim, were unhygienic and uncivilized while exonerating the Hindus from the charge. His criticism stemmed from the growing science of hygiene in Europe which was motivated, in part, by the plagues which had struck Europe as a result of bad hygiene. However, at the time that Jordanus was writing, most of Europe was still in a state of 'the great unwashed' and although they did use rudimentary cutlery to eat, most often these were not washed after meals either![26] In effect, there was little sanitary difference between the use of cutlery for eating

---

Lambert, *Medieval Heresy: Popular Movements from the Gregorian Reform to the Reformation* (Maldren, MA: Blackwell Publishers, 2002).

[25] Ibid.: 9–10.

[26] Norbert Elias, *The Civilising Process*, (Oxford, 1978–82), Vol. 1: 99–113. Also Roy Wood, *The Sociology of the Meal* (Edinburgh, 1995). The custom of washing one's hands before and after meals seems to have come into existence in the homes of the rich only by the late fifteenth century. See Paul Lacroix, *Manners, Custom and Dress During the Middle Ages and During the Renaissance Period*. Project Gutenberg E-Book.

in Europe, and the use of hands for eating in the East. In India where the tradition of eating with one's hands still exists, the unsanitary aspect was removed by the otherwise extreme cleanliness practised, particularly through the insistence on frequent washings. In fact the notion that Muslims were unclean was a common myth which had grown out of the antagonism of the Crusades.[27] The fact that Jordanus singled out the Muslims cannot be dismissed. His description of Arabia, for instance, is unequivocally critical. 'The natives of this Arabia are all black, very crafty and lean, with voices like that of a little boy. They dwell in caverns and holes on the ground: they eat fish, herbs and roots, and nothing else.'[28] Or even stronger, 'This Turkey, which is called Asia Minor, is inhabited by the Turks, and by a few schismatic Greeks and Armenians. Which Turks be most rascally Saracens, and capital archers withal, and the most warlike and perfidious of all mankind.'[29] Lamenting the lack of missionaries in the East to effect conversions, he lashed out at the 'preachers of the perfidious and accursed Saracens.... For their preachers run about, just as we do, here, there, and everywhere over the whole Orient, in order to turn all to their own miscreance. These be they who accuse us, who smite us, who cause us to be cast into durance, and who stone us....'[30] The adjectives which stand out strongly in these quotes are 'craft and lean', 'rascally

---

[27] The common description in medieval and early modern times of the 'filthy Saracen' grew into a conviction which continues to be popular in the West, that of Muslim uncleanliness. See *Western Views of Islam in Medieval and Early Modern Europe: Perception of Other*. Edited by David R. Blanks and Michael Frassetto (New York: St. Martin's Press, 1999).

[28] Friar Jordanus. *Mirabilia Descripta.*: 45.

[29] Ibid.: 58.

[30] Ibid.: 56. Also see James D. Ryan, 'Missionary Saints of the High Middle Ages: Martyrdom, Popular Veneration, and Canonization', *The Catholic Historical Review* 90.1 (2004): 1–28 for details of the suffering of Jordanus at the hands of the Muslims.

Saracens', 'perfidious', 'warlike' and 'accursed'. They are all used in connection with Islam rather than an indictment of the inhabitants of Turkey. For instance, Jordanus heaps abuses only on the Saracen Turks, while noting that there were some Greeks and Armenians living in Turkey, emphasizing his concern that the preachers of the Saracen (Islamic) religion attempt to convert people to their own 'miscreance', presumably Islam. In fact, the thirteenth century was the era when Christians and Muslims were competing to covert Africans and Asians.

The anti-Islamic sentiment was a strong characteristic of missionary writings even in the seventeenth century. By the time of the Jesuit missions the need to openly avow one's allegiance to Christ was no longer considered a glorious way to achieve martyrdom. Rather the Jesuits stressed the fact that they were working to effect conversions and foolhardy denunciations of Allah and the Prophet Mohammed would not achieve much towards this goal.[31] Nevertheless, these missionaries considered Islam to be far worse than any other Indian religion. For instance, Father Bouchet,[32] writing in the first decade of the eighteenth century about his travels and efforts at conversion in the southern kingdom of Carnata in India wrote,

---

[31] Father Martin to Father de Villette, Balasore Bengal. John Lockman, *Travels of the Jesuits, into various parts of the world: particularly China and the East-Indies. Intermix'd with an account of the manners, government, civil and religious ceremonies, natural history, and curiosities, of the several nations visited by those fathers. Translated from the celebrated Lettres édifiantes & curieuses. To which is now prefixed, an account of the Spanish settlements in America, with a general index to the whole work.* Vol. 1 (London: T. Piety, 1762, 2nd edn): 2.

[32] Bouchet arrived in India in about 1688 and was appointed to establish a new mission at Madura in 1702. He was then appointed Superior of the Mission in Carnata. Father Tachard, Superior of the Jesuit Missions in India, to Count De Crecy. Pondichéry, February 1703. Ibid.: 481. For information about Bouchet, see Francis Clooney, *Fr. Bouchet's India: An 18th Century Jesuits' Encounter with Hinduism*, (Chennai: Satyam Nilyam Publications, 2005).

> The Preachers of the Gospel are frequently imprisoned, and otherwise abused, in their Mission; which is owing to the Avidity of the *Mohammedans*, who are but too apt, of themselves, to persecute `em, from the natural Aversion they bear to the *Christian* Name...The *Indians* [under the Muslims] are quite miserable, and reap very little Benefit from their Labours.[33]

Bouchet does not similarly criticize non-Muslim Indian rulers of exploiting their subjects, making the emphasis on the cruelty and oppression of 'Mohammedans' the central theme. Further evidence of the animosity of Muslims to Christian missionaries is found in the letter of Father De La Lane to Father Morgues in 1709 that

> The Country is very populous, and abounds with a vast Number of Towns and Villages; but 'twould be much fuller of Inhabitants, if the *Moors* or *Mohammedans*, subject to the *Great Mogul*, who subdued it, did not impoverish their People by their perpetual Exactions.... The Oppression in which the *Heathens* live under the Government abovementioned, would be no obstacle to propagating our Religion, were not the *Moors*, at the same Time, the implacable Enemies of the *Christian* Name.[34]

Once again, there is no mention of the numerous Hindu feudatories of the 'Great Mogul' in exploiting the people even though historians have pointed to the general equality in the economic conditions between Hindu and Muslim feudatories of the Mughals during the seventeenth and eighteenth centuries.[35]

---

[33] Father Bouchet to Bishop Huet, formerly Bishop of Avranches. Ibid., Vol. 2: 374.

[34] Father De La Lane to Father Morgues, Pondichéry, Jan. 1709. Ibid.: 373.

[35] There has long been a debate between economic historians of India regarding the state of decline [notably Irfan Habib, *The Agrarian System of Mughal India 1556–1707* (Delhi: OUP, 1999)] or of economic

Father Mauduit, the missionary in charge of the mission at Pondichéry who had established the mission there some years before had already described the Muslims as having 'infested all the Country....The Face of the Country is beautiful, and seeming very populous; but it was more so before the *Moors* had usurped it.'[36] Mauduit's primary mission was to explore Carnata and the opportunities for conversion there. In his extensive travels through the area he describes his encounter with a friendly Muslim Doctor as 'a Person of Learning and Capacity...a worthy Man...yet this Doctor was a *Mohammedan*, that is, a Person still more remote from the Kingdom of Heaven than the Heathens themselves.'[37] If any clearer example of Mauduit's animosity to Islam can be found, it is in his conclusion.

> The Advantage I have gained by these Journies is, I now know the several Places wherein Missionaries may be sent. The Season seems to be come, for us to labour with Success at the Conversion of the Idolaters of those Countries, which have so long been overspread with Darkness. All imaginable Dispatch should be used, lest the *Mohammedans*, who get Possession of all these Countries by insensible Degrees, should force the Inhabitants of them to embrace their abominable Religion.[38]

Jordanus had expressed a similar anguish about the power that the Muslims held in India. In his primary task of conversion Jordanus acknowledged that the Hindus were

---

growth [notably Shireen Moosvi, *People, Taxation, and Trade in Mughal India* (New Delhi: Oxford University Press, 2008)] during the Mughal period of Indian history. The state of the economy and of the oppression of the people stemmed from the demands of the cities and of the land-owning class (zamindars) regardless of their religion. Moosvi emphasizes the religious compositeness in the ruling class under Mughal rule.

[36] Father Mauduit to Father le Gobien, Carnata. January 1702. Ibid., Vol. 1: 430.

[37] Ibid.: 432.

[38] Ibid.: 440.

idolaters. Yet he wrote of Hindu idolatry favourably as compared to Muslim rule. Describing the conquest of central
India by the Khilji Sultanate of northern India, Jordanus
wrote,

> In this India the greater part of the people worship idols,
> although a great share of the sovereignty is in the hands
> of the Turkish Saracens, who came forth from Multan
> and conquered and usurped dominion to themselves not
> long since, and destroyed an infinity of idol temples, and
> likewise many churches, of which they made mosques
> to Mahomet, taking possession of their endowments and
> property. 'Tis grief to hear, and woe to see!'[39]

As Maduit and Jordanus stressed, Muslims were accused
of destroying the beauty of India and looting the wealth
of the country. But their greater crime was the aggressive
spread of Islam in their dominions. While both Idolatry and
Islam were heathen religions, the latter in its direct challenge to Christianity was considered by them to be the
greater evil.

The conclusion of Mauduit's letter and even of
Jordanus' anti-Islamic rhetoric seems to indicate that
the primary proselytizing purpose of the missionaries in
the East was to counter the spread of Islam by effecting
conversions to Christianity. In this aspect the missionaries
were united.

THE ORIGIN OF THE INDIAN RELIGION

Jordanus and the Jesuits were also unanimous in proclaiming the antiquity of Indian religion, and the essential unity
of a religious power despite the worship of several idols.
According to Jordanus, 'They make idols after the likeness
of almost all living things of the idolaters; and they have
besides their god according to his likeness. It is true that

---

[39] Friar Jordanus. *Mirabilia Descripta.*: 23.

over all gods they place One God, the Almighty Creator of all those....'[40] The supposition that Indians recognized a single Godhead among the thousands of Hindu gods and goddesses and the understanding that these were all different manifestations of a single divinity continued to exist among Frenchmen who studied Hinduism. Filliozat points to Blaise Pascal, a seventeenth-century intellectual, who noted that, the very existence of 'false religions' proved that there was a greater truth and a greater power.[41] Pascal shrewdly pointed out that the fuss was not about 'false' religions as much as it was about the surprise that so-called savages could have a religion, thus putting not only theories about what constituted civilization to the test, but also questioning the greater power of Christianity, since 'savages' obviously knew about the Great Deluge and other mythic events.[42] By the time the Jesuits were writing their letters, the origin of Indian religion was a matter of great interest. Many of the Jesuits who travelled to India were also intellectuals and men of science. Several of them were members of the *Académie des Sciences*[43] and the tone of

---

[40] Ibid.: 24.

[41] Blaise Pascal, French mathematician, philosopher and spiritual writer, was born in 1623 at Clermont-Ferrard and died in 1662 in Paris. His best-known work is a collection of essays titled '*Les Pensées*' which although unfinished, is essentially an apology for the Christian Religion 'which the increasing number of libertines rendered so necessary at that time'. See Blaise Pascal, *Pensées*, no. 817. Trans. W. F. Trotter (1660). Cited in Jean Filliozat, 'La naissance et l'essor de L'Indianisme', *Bulletin de la Société des études indo-chinoises de Saigon*, Vol. 29, issue 4, (1954): 268.

[42] Blaise Pascal, *Pensées*. Also, Jean Filliozat, 'La naissance et l'essor de L'Indianisme", *Bulletin de la Société des études indo-chinoises de Saigon*, Vol. 29, issue 4, (1954): 268.

[43] According to Georges Naidenoff, among the Jesuits who were also members of the Académie des Sciences were Fontenay, Tachard, Gerbillon, Lecomte, Bouver, and Visdelov. See Georges Naidenoff, 'Endeavours of the Missionaries', in *The French in India: from Diamond*

the *Lettres* they sent back grew increasingly more scientific as the eighteenth century progressed. The *Lettres* reflect this trend towards recording information about a country and its people not only for the purpose of conversion but also to further knowledge.[44] For instance, Father Bouchet provided extensive comparisons between Hinduism and Judaism in a long letter.[45] 'In this present Letter I shall set before you, and I compare some Conjectures, which, I believe, will be thought important. The Design of them is to prove, that the *Indians* borrowed their Religion from the Books of *Moses* and the Prophets.'[46] Bouchet then

---

Traders to Sanskrit Scholars, edited by Rose Vincent (Bombay: Popular Prakashan, 1990). Also see the decline of Jesuit membership in the Académie during the eighteenth-century in James E. McClellan III, 'The Académie Royale des Sciences, 1699–1793: A Statistical Portrait', *Isis*, Vol. 72, No. 4 (December, 1981): 555.

[44] As Županov points out, the Jesuits used the epistolary form of writing. The goals of the order as stipulated by Ignatius Loyola were two-fold. The first was service and the glory of god, the second the service of the Jesuit order to enable the realization of these goals. The founder had prescribed subjects for Jesuit writing, especially for those stationed outside Europe. There were to be four components of Jesuit-written composition and correspondence cast in a specified narrative form. The first were accounts of kings and nobles, and these were to be recorded as dramatic, theatrical vignettes. The second was to deal with the life, habits, and customs of the common people, and these virtually took the form of ethnographic descriptions. Naturally there were disputes within the order and it was prescribed that these disputes be couched in dialogical or polemical terms. And finally, their own individual ambitions were sublimated in the rhetoric of sainthood and utopianism. See Županov, *Disputed Mission*: 7.

[45] Wilhelm Halbfass also notes Bouchet's comparison of Indian beliefs with Hebrew beliefs. See *India and Europe*: 44.

[46] Father Bouchet to Bishop Huet, formerly Bishop of Avranches. John Lockman, *Travels of the Jesuits, into various parts of the world: particularly China and the East-Indies. Intermix'd with an account of the manners, government, civil and religious ceremonies, natural history, and curiosities, of the several nations visited by those fathers. Translated from the celebrated Lettres édifiantes & curieuses. To which is now prefixed, an account of the Spanish settlements in*

proceeded to compare and analyse incidents and figures in Hindu religion and mythology to Noah, Abraham, Moses, and incidents in the Old Testament.[47]

> Among these Customs, which the *Indians* must neces-sarily have borrowed from the *Jews,* and still practice in this Country, I include their frequent Bathings, their Purifications, their extreme Aversion to dead Bodies, the bare touching of which, they imagine to be Pollution. Add to these, the different Order and distinction of Castes; and the inviolable Law, by which all Persons are commanded not to marry out of their own Caste or Tribe.[48]

He concludes his letter:

> I will here end the long Letter which I have taken the Liberty to address to your Lordship. I therein have given you an Account of such Particulars as were told to me by the *Indian* Nations, who, in all Probability, were antiently [sic for 'anciently'] *Christians,* but fell back, many Ages since, into the Errors of Idolatry...You may perceive, that, at the same Time we win over these abandon'd Nations to *Christ,* we endeavour to be of some Service to the *Literati* in *Europe,* by our Discoveries in Countries with which they are not enough acquainted.[49]

These comparisons between Hinduism and the Old Test-ament clearly set out the reason why Europeans tended

---

America, with a general index to the whole work. Vol. 2 (London: T. Piety, 1762, 2nd edn): 241. For a good discussion of this topic, see David Clines, 'In Search of the Indian Job', *Vestus Testamentum*, Vol. 33, Issue 4 (October 1983): 398–418. Also see, Francis X. Clooney, *Fr. Bouchet's India: An 18th Century Jesuits' Encounter with Hinduism*, (Chennai: Satyam Nilyam Publications, 2005).

[47] Father Bouchet to Bishop Huet, formerly Bishop of Avranches. John Lockman, *Travels of the Jesuits*, Vol. 2: 241–63.

[48] Ibid.: 264.

[49] Ibid.: 277.

to look upon Hinduism more favourably. According to Brett Berliner, the 'Christianization of Hinduism' where individual elements of Hindu mythology were compared to Christian mythology may have accounted for the longstanding admiration that many Frenchmen held for India.[50] After all as Father De La Lane put it, 'I shall now give you a Sketch of the Religion of these *Indians*. They doubtless are truly Idolaters, since they worship strange Gods. Nevertheless, it appears plainly to me, from some of their Books, that they had antiently [sic for "anciently"] a pretty distinct knowledge of the true God.'[51] The comparisons between Christianity and Hinduism as possessing the same fundamental beginnings began in the time of Jordanus and continued in the work of the Theosophists down to the colonial period.[52] In their anti-Muslim stance and their opinion that Hinduism held a long-lost belief in the True God, missionaries were united through the centuries. Apart from rhetorical denunciation of the 'false prophet' Muhammad and the 'false God' Allah, none of the missionaries writing about India actually described what they found so objectionable about Islam or Muslims. In sweeping statements they presented Muslim rulers as harsh tyrants—cruel despots who laid the land to waste and oppressed their non-Muslim subjects. In reality, historians of modern India have demonstrated that individual rulers had their own policies—some were tyrants, others benevolent.[53] Religion had little to do

---

[50] Brett Berliner, Department of History and Geography, Morgan State University. Personal communication, December 2006.

[51] Father De La Lane to Father Morgues, Pondichéry, January 1709. John Lockman, *Travels of the Jesuits* Vol. 2: 377.

[52] Louis Jacolliot was a prolific writer, colonial official and fervent believer that Christianity was derived from Hinduism. His works on the subject include *La bible dans l'Inde* (1869) and *Christna et le Christ* (1874). Jacolliot's ideas were extensively quoted by the famous Theosophist Madame Blavatsky in *Isis Unveiled* (1877).

[53] See *The Cambridge Economic History of India: c.1200–c.1750* (Cambridge: CUP, 1982). Edited by Tapan Raychaudhuri, Irfan Habib, Dharma Kumar, Meghnad Desai.

with these regimes—there were Hindu and Muslim tyrants, just as there were enlightened rulers of both religions. The fact that missionaries chose to single out Muslim rulers for criticism highlights the antipathy they had for Islam, which, according to religious historian Tomoko Masuzawa stemmed from a longstanding anti-Semitic feeling in Europe.[54]

THE EFFECTS OF 'CIVILIZATION'

There were many differences between the views of Jordanus and the later Jesuits. Although they both held that Hinduism had once been a 'true belief', Jordanus held a more favourable view of Indians than the Jesuits. His account of the Hindus was relatively gentle and descriptions of the caste system and customs like Sati were described without the condemnation of later Jesuit writers.

Take for example, Jordanus' description of sati:

> In this India, on the death of a noble, or of any people of substance, their bodies are burned; and eke [sic] their wives follow them alive to the fire, and, for the sake of worldly glory, and for the love of their husbands, and for eternal life, burn along with them, with as much joy as if they were going to be wedded; and those who do this have the higher repute for virtue and perfection among the rest. Wonderful! I have sometimes seen, for one dead man was burnt, five living women take their place on the fire with him, and be with their dead [sic].[55]

Jordanus did not experience the revulsion that later Jesuits described. Instead he described the ceremony as resulting in 'worldly glory', 'eternal life', 'joy', 'virtue' and 'perfection', a 'wonderful' ritual in its performance and the attitude of the performers. In contrast to later

---

[54] Tomoko Masuzawa, *The Invention of World Religions* (Chicago: University of Chicago Press, 2005): Chapter 6.

[55] Friar Jordanus. *Mirabilia Descripta*: 20–21.

Jesuit observers of sati, Jordanus' description stressed the voluntary aspect of sati where widows *chose* to burn with their dead husbands. His admiration for the *satis*— the women who burnt themselves—stands out against the descriptions of the later Jesuits. There was not a single word of remonstration or criticism in Jordanus' account of sati. Almost 400 years of history and the beginning of colonialism changed this view. A French Jesuit missionary in India wrote about sati in 1701:

> 'Twas with Tears I beheld the Sad Remains of a diabolical Ceremony which the *Moors* have endeavoured to abolish, since their being Masters of the greatest part of this Country. Not many Days before, a Woman, either out of the Love she bore her deceased husband, or from a Desire of spreading her Name, had thrown herself on the funeral Pile, whilst her Husband was burning on it, and in this manner had been consum'd to Ashes. There were still seen the Necklaces, Bracelets, and other Ornaments of that unhappy Victim of Satan, hanging on the Boughs of the Trees, which stood round the Place where this Sad Ceremony was performed....[56]

The above quote stands out in its condemnation of the custom of sati as a 'diabolical' and 'sad' ceremony which had consumed a 'victim of Satan'. It also presents a stark contrast to Jordanus' description of sati as being a ceremony which added to the glory of women who performed it, a ceremony which was 'wonderful' and not 'diabolical' in its difference from Europe. While Mauduit described the same motives for Sati—love or a desire for glory—as well as the voluntary nature of the act, he described the performer as 'that unhappy victim of Satan'. Considering that Jordanus was as fervent in proselytizing as the Jesuits of the eighteenth century, the change in European views

---

[56] Father Mauduit. Written from Carnata, 1701. From John Lockman, *Travels of the Jesuits* Vol. 1: 425.

of strange and exotic customs from being 'boundless marvels'[57] to being 'monstrosities'[58] came with the addition of a colonizing motive to the religious zeal.[59] All of Jordanus' descriptions of the nature and culture of the people of India were written from his own experiences or from the explanations of locals. He included aspects of India based on its variance with Europe as a catalogue of the strange and fantastic. While in Turkey and Islamic India he played the outraged missionary, and in southern India he played the tourist, taking simple delight in witnessing exotic rituals. He employed a narrative style at all times, justifying customs like sati in terms of the natives' belief that it brought greater glory to the woman performing it. His proselytizing and resulting criticism was directed entirely towards Islam. By the time the *Lettres* were being written, the European economic interest in India was well-advanced, and trading depots, factories and a flourishing trade in cotton, tobacco, tea, spices and other luxury goods had begun a period when European traders scrambled to secure their footing in India by establishing their own colonies. The *Lettres* of the Jesuits were translated into English solely because they provided valuable information—geographical, social, political and religious—which helped English merchants in their dealing with the Indians in the south of India. For their part, the Jesuit missionaries could not have been unaware or even uninfluenced by the emerging theory that European, Christian culture was a superior civilization which owed other, lesser civilizations the opportunity to develop through the *mission civilisatrice*. What is interesting to note in this transition is that the voice of the native has been removed. While Jordanus

---

[57] Friar Jordanus. *Mirabilia Descripta.*: 12.

[58] Father Bouchet to Bishop Huet, formerly Bishop of Avranches. John Lockman, *Travels of the Jesuits* Vol. 2.

[59] Gayatri Chakravarty Spivak, 'Can the Subaltern Speak?' in *Marxism and the Interpretation of Culture*, edited by Cary Nelson and Lawrence Grossberg (Chicago: University of Illinois Press, 1988).

described the customs and religion *as explained to him* by the natives, the Jesuits presented their own understanding of these customs. Even where explanations were sought, the Jesuits dismissed them as irrational and further evidence of the backwardness of native customs. While the latter's understanding of native customs could very likely be coloured by Enlightenment discourses about individual rights, their refusal to accept anything other than a European moral compass was a new development of the colonial era.

These impulses were missing in Jordanus, who wrote,

> In this lesser India are many things worthy to be noted with wonder.... Here be many and boundless marvels; and in this First India beginneth, as it were, another world; for the men and women be all black, and they have for covering nothing but a strip of cotton tied around the loins, and the end flung over the naked back....[60]

The part of Jordanus' work which describes 'lesser India' includes parts of South India, including the Malabar, which were later to become the working grounds of the Jesuits.

About the personal qualities of the Hindus, Jordanus added to his observation about their cleanliness to attribute to them the qualities of being 'true in speech and eminent in justice, maintaining carefully the privileges of every man according to his degree as they have come down from old times'.[61] Jordanus further demonstrated his sympathetic view of Hinduism in analysing their abstinence from beef. Traditionally cited as a common superstition of Hindus, Jordanus notes that the Indians, 'never kill an ox, but rather honor him like a father; and some, perhaps even the majority, worship him.... This is because oxen do all

---

[60] Friar Jordanus. *Mirabilia Descripta*: 12.
[61] Ibid.: 22.

their services, and moreover furnish them with milk and butter, and all sorts of good things.'[62]

Jordanus even compared the Hindus' idol worship with the veneration of idols of the Virgin Mary in Europe. According to him, in South India, the Hindus often asked their Gods for boons, particularly to be cured from an illness. Upon their boon being granted, they adored their Gods and carried around their idols much in the manner of processions bearing the Virgin Mary in Europe.

> In this Greater India many sacrifice themselves to idols in this way. When they are sick, or involved in any grave mischance, they vow themselves to the idol if they should happen to be delivered. Then, when they have recovered, they fatten themselves for one or two years continually, eating and drinking fat things, etc. And when another festival comes round, they cover themselves with flowers and perfumes, and crown themselves with white garlands and go with singing and playing before the idol when it is carried through the land (like the image of the Virgin Mary here among us at the Rogation tides); and those men who are sacrificing themselves to the idol carry a sword with two handles...and after they have shown off a good deal, they put the sword to the back of the neck, cutting strongly with a vigorous exertion of both hands, and so cut off their own heads before the idol.[63]

In this as in other descriptions Jordanus does not use a single negative word; rather his comparison of aspects of Hindu celebration with Christian celebrations and praise for the Virgin Mary lends it a legitimacy which has its origins in the devotion of the Hindus. Part of Jordanus' description of India and Hinduism came from the development in western Christianity. While the Church had begun isolating certain Christian sects and practices that it did not approve of,

---

[62] Ibid.: 25.
[63] Ibid.: 32–33.

fourteenth-century Christian belief was far more accepting of flamboyant rituals of adoration than the more rigid
Christian structure of post-Reformation Jesuit writing. As
Masuzawa notes, though the church had defined 'pagan'
rituals as non-Christian, even Saint Augustine was willing
to take a more tolerant view of heathens.[64] In contrast the
evangelical missions of the seventeenth century and later
treated idolatry or heathenism or paganism as a distinct
form of religious practice which was looked upon as false
religion.[65] This development meant that Jordanus was not
only willing to believe and accept rituals in non-Christian
lands as comparable to European practices, but that the
Jesuits were more likely to condemn these practices as
'un-Christian'.

By the time of the Jesuit missions the Hindus were
'idolaters' who displayed their ignorance and backwardness in their stubborn adherence to superstitions and ritualistic beliefs. For example, according to Father Martin,

All the *Indians* (to speak in general) worship some Deity;
but alas! How ignorant are they of the true God! Blinded
by their Passions still more than by the evil Spirit, they
form monstrous Ideals of the supreme Being; and you
wou'd scarce believe me, shou'd I name the vile and infamous Creatures to which they pay divine Honours. 'Tis my
Opinion, that no Idolatry among the Antients [sic] was ever
more gross, or more horrid, than that of these *Indians*.[66]

Every letter of the Jesuits contains reference to the idolatrous and superstitious practice of the Hindus followed by
a description of the Jesuits' efforts to convert them to
Christianity. A clear difference of opinion is present in the

---

[64] Tomoko Masuzawa, *The Invention of World Religions* (Chicago
and London: University of Chicago Press, 2005): 48.

[65] Ibid.: 58–64.

[66] Father Martin to Father De Villette. Marava in the Mission of
Madura, Nov. 1709, John Lockman, *Travels of the Jesuits* Vol. 2: 416.

description of Jordanus and a Jesuit priest Father Tachard relating to the polyandrous Nair community of southern India. Jordanus' description of polyandry in the Malabar was focused on property and inheritance:

> In this India never do [even] the legitimate sons of great kings, or princes, or barons, inherit the goods of their parents, but only the sons of their sisters; for they say that they have no surety that those are their own sons, because wives and mistresses may conceive and generate by some one else; but 'tis not so with the sister, for whatever man may be the father they are certain that the offspring is from the womb of the sister, and is consequently thus truly of their blood.[67]

For whatever reason Jordanus focused on property and inheritance in this aspect of Malabar life rather than any judgement about the morality of polyandry. In this manner he noted the custom and shied away from personal comment. This same community was described by Tachard in 1702 as,

> In this Country, called *Malleami,* there are *Castes* as in the rest of *India.* Most of them observe the same Customs; and in particular they all entertain the like Contempt for the Religion and Manner of the *Europeans.* But a Circumstance, that perhaps is not found elsewhere, and which I myself could scarce believe, is that, among these *Barbarians* and especially the noble *Castes,* a Woman is allowed, by the Laws, to have several Husbands.... This Custom, which is somewhat monstrous, as well as many other...are founded on the Religion.[68]

---

[67] Friar Jordanus. *Mirabilia Descripta*: 32.

[68] Father Tachard, Superior-General of the French Mission of Jesuits in the East Indies, to Father De La Chaize. Pondichéry, February 1702, John Lockman, *Travels of the Jesuits* Vol. 1: 168–69.

In contrast to Jordanus, Tachard was clearly appalled at the Malayali custom of polyandry and denounced it. The disjunction in these accounts regarding the ethical and moral aspects of custom came with the rise of European power in India.

An interesting aspect of the Jesuit letters was their status in society. Unlike Jordanus who describes no such ostracism, the Jesuits record their need to present themselves as Indian ascetics in order to avoid ostracism. According to Tachard, 'The Missionaries who were settled in *Caroovepondi*, had resolv'd, at their Entrance into that Mission, to assume the Habit, and lead the Life of the *Sanias Bramins*, or religious Penitents.'[69] In fact this circumstance was so strongly felt that it was not a matter of choice. By the seventeenth century, Europeans had made themselves heartily disliked in India by their complete indifference to the customs of the area. As Father Martin explained,

> The people of *Madura* have no Communication with the *Europeans*, who, by their riotous Excesses, have corrupted all the Christians in *India*.... The Missionaries lead an extremely mortified Life.... They are not known to be *Europeans*; for were the Natives to have the least Notion of this, the Fathers would be obliged to quit the Country.... Several Motives prompt the *Indians* to have the *Europeans* in so much Horror. Great Cruelties have been committed in their Countries; they have been Eye-Witnesses to the most shocking examples of Vices of every Kind....[70]

On one occasion, Father Bouchet, in order to protect the lives of other missionaries, had to admit his own European roots. This was considered to be an extreme step and

---

[69] Father Tachard, Superior of the Jesuit Missions in India, to Count De Crecy. Pondichéry, February 1703. John Lockman, *Travels of the Jesuits*: 481.

[70] Father Martin to Father de Villette. John Lockman, *Travels of the Jesuits*: 5.

only the fact that Bouchet was already well respected in the area made it possible for him to continue working.[71] Among the habits which the Jesuits had to adopt was strict vegetarianism, since eating flesh of any kind would have prohibited social intercourse with the higher castes. They also had to prove their own high caste status by employing Brahmin cooks.[72] Mauduit explained the need to live with such austerities.

I must observe that it is absolutely necessary the Missionaries should lead a Life of the greatest Mortification, in order to win over the Heathens, who would shew [sic] no Regard to the Law of the true God, nor to the Preachers of it, were these to live with less Austerity than their Bramins and Sanias.[73]

Since Jordanus made no mention of any special changes he made in his habits or demeanour, one can assume that he made it a point to respect the customs of each country through which he had travelled, or that his oddities did not offend the local population. By the mid-seventeenth century however, the Europeans had become so confident of their superiority that they flouted the laws of the nations they traded with—eating meat, disobeying the rules of social interaction and etiquette—and consequently became social pariahs. When the Jesuits entered South India their

---

[71] Father Martin to Father le Gobien. Aoor Madura, December 1700. John Lockman, *Travels of the Jesuits*: 459–63.

[72] Father Tachard, Superior of the Jesuit Missions in India, to Count De Crecy. Pondichéry, February 1703. John Lockman, *Travels of the Jesuits*: 481. I use the spelling 'Brahmin' throughout the book to indicate a particular caste among the Hindus, as distinguished from 'brahman' which is often used interchangeably to denote the Upanishadic Universal Soul or Godhead. While the difference in reality lies in pronunciation, I have used a different spelling in order to avoid confusions between the two terms.

[73] Father Mauduit to Father Le Gobien, September 1700. John Lockman, *Travels of the Jesuits*: 9.

first task was to make themselves acceptable members of society, which they could only accomplish by posing as Brahmin ascetics from the north.[74] In fact, Bouchet even took on the name of Periya Sanjivinatha, meaning 'Revered master of spiritual healing'.[75] Since north Indians were fair-skinned, Jesuits could pass for north Indian Brahmins in order to gain an audience with the people of south India. As Dhruv Raina[76] and Ines Županov[77] point out, the custom of *accomodatio* was common among Jesuits who thought that they would not otherwise be able to effect conversions.

In their attempt to fit in with the local population, the Jesuits also made it a habit to court the Brahmins. Interestingly enough, their letters indicate the great contempt which they held for Brahmins as the chief perpetrators of superstition and idolatry, but simultaneously speak of the necessity to court and convert them since they were the religious leaders and one Brahmin convert would surely serve as an example to many other lower castes. Tachard, in his description of the state of the various missions in the south summed up the successes of the missions in terms of the number of Brahmin converts in each

---

[74] Dedication to Vol. 2 by J. B. Du Halde, John Lockman, *Travels of the Jesuits:* 364.

[75] Francis X. Clooney, *Fr. Bouchet's India: An 18th Century Jesuits' Encounter with Hinduism*, (Chennai: Satyam Nilyam Publications, 2005): 3.

[76] Dhruv Raina, 'The Mystery of French Jesuit Manuscripts on Indian Astronomy: The Narratology and Impact of a Late Seventeenth Early Eighteenth Century Project' (paper presented at a workshop on 'Looking at it from Asia: the processes that shaped the sources of history of science.' *Recherches Epistémologiques et Historiques sur les Sciences*, Paris, September 2006).

[77] Županov, *Disputed Mission:* 5. She notes that following Nobili's introduction of the practice of *accommodatio* in India, almost every Jesuit in India chose one or the other side, writing 'opinions' or condemnations, providing arguments for and against this practice. Her work also details the manner in which the practice of *accommodatio* was accomplished in India.

mission. 'Father *de la Fontaine* was extremely fortunate in the very Opening of his Mission....That Father has already baptized a great many *Bramins.*'[78] So as De La Lane wrote to Father Morgues, 'No Sort of People in the World can possibly be prouder then the *Bramins,* stronger Opponents of Truth, or more puffed up with the Ideas of their superstitions and Nobility.'[79] Yet the Jesuits tried their hardest to convert the Brahmins. In his efforts to establish a mission at Carnata, Father Mauduit describes his persuasive words to a group of Brahmins that Indians 'may be in an Error, in imagining that Bruma (Brahma), Wistnou (Vishnu), and Routrem (Shiva), are Gods worthy of Adoration; since that these pretended Deities were only so many vicious, corrupt Men, who were ranked among the Gods, merely by the Flattery of their Fellow-creatures'. Having made this speech on their misconception, Mauduit then recorded their response.

> The *Bramins* list'ned to me very calmly, and without seeming to regard the Contradictions they necessarily fell into, nor the ridiculous Consequences which they were obliged to own resulted from what they said. At last, finding the Attack grow still warmer, their only Refuge was to withdraw without saying a Word. This gives a tolerable Idea of the People of this Country, and shews that the Conversion of a *Bramin* is not so easy a Matter as might be imagined. Few Converts have been made here this Year.[80]

On another occasion, Mauduit recorded his stay at the house of a Brahmin. 'I lay, at *Alcatil,* in the House of a

---

[78] Father Tachard, Superior of the Jesuit Missions in India, to Count De Crecy. Pondichéry, February 1703. John Lockman, *Travels of the Jesuits,* Vol. 1: 487.

[79] Father De La Lane to Father Morgues, Pondichéry, January 1709. *Travels of the Jesuits,* Vol. 2: 387.

[80] Father Mauduit to Father Le Gobien, Carnata, January 1702. *Travels of the Jesuits,* Vol. 1: 423.

Bramin, who daily worshipped the Devil, under the Name and Figure of *Poolear*.[81] Seeing this Idol standing in the Room where I was to lie, I thought proper to throw it upon the Ground.'[82] In a testament to the peaceful nature of the Indians as well as their tolerance of the missionaries, Mauduit recounted that the Brahmin, seeing his idol desecrated the next morning, and a makeshift Altar in its place, left to allow Mauduit to complete his prayers in peace.

> This drew several Persons to the house, which gave me an opportunity of speaking to them concerning God; and of observing, how unhappy they were, in not being acquainted with the Supreme Being, sole Author of all Good. They listened attentively to me, but were not affected, not one of them then discovering the least Desire to turn *Christian*.[83]

Given the rough and ready methods of the Jesuits, it was not surprising that they failed to convert many Brahmins. However they persisted in their efforts to convert Brahmins, deeming this so important that they made many concessions, allowing new converts to maintain their caste purity. In 1702 Mauduit wrote,

> I am to observe that Catechists of a lower Caste, cannot be employed in instructing such *Indians* as are of a higher caste. The *Bramins* and *Shootres,* who are the principal and most extensive Castes, have as much Aversion to the *Parias,* who are under them, than any Prince in *Europe* could entertain for the Dregs of the People. These *Bramins* and *Shootres* would be dishonoured in their native Place, and lose all the Privileges of their Caste, should they listen to the Instructions of a Person whom their Countrymen consider as an abominable Wretch. We therefore are

---

[81] The Elephant-headed deity Ganesha, who is worshipped in the South under the name of Pillayar.

[82] Father Mauduit to Father Le Gobien, Carnata, January 1702. *Travels of the Jesuits,* Vol. 1: 425.

[83] Ibid.: 426.

obliged, to appoint *Parias*-Catechists for the *Parias*, and *Bramin*-Catechists for the *Bramins*; a Circumstance which gives us no little Trouble, it not being easy to procure such, especially of the latter. Nothing is more difficult than to convert the *Bramins*; for these being naturally haughty, and puffed up with Notions of their exalted Birth, and their Superiority over the rest of the Castes, they thence are found less tractable and more strongly attached to the Superstitions of their Country.[84]

It seems that caste barriers were a huge problem in effecting conversions, even among other castes. According to Father De La Lane,

The *Indians* are extremely sober, they never committing any Excess, either in eating or drinking. They are born with a natural Aversion to all Liquors which intoxicate; are very reserv'd with regard to Women...are vastly charitable to the Poor...are of a very mild Disposition; whence nothing shocks them so much as a hasty Temper and Anger. Such being their Frame of Mind, 'tis certain many would then turn *Christians*, were they not afraid of being expelled from their *Castes*.[85]

Considering that society, particularly in South India, func-tioned around the institution of caste, which dictated each person's social, economic and political life, the fear of losing caste is understandable. A person who 'lost caste' effectively lost his whole support system, his social net-work, extended family and even his economic community.

A Person who is expell'd from his Caste is lost to all Refuge or Asylum. His Relations must not hold the least Correspondence with, not even give him so much as a little Fire; and if he had any Children, he never finds an

---

[84] Ibid.: 420–21.
[85] Father De La Lane to Father Morgues, Pondichéry, January 1709. *Travels of the Jesuits*, Vol. 2: 376.

Opportunity to marry them; and thus is forced to either starve, or to enter into the Caste of the *Parias*, which, among the *Indians*, is an Act of the blackest Infamy.[86]

The efforts of the Jesuits to accommodate Indian customs in their efforts at proselytization reached a dead end in the infamous *Rites Malabars*. Jealous of the success that Jesuits claimed to have had in converting peoples in the East, other Catholic orders petitioned the Vatican, based on the conversion of the people of the Malabar region of South India where the Jesuits had effected many conversions by maintaining caste purity. They challenged the Jesuit method of conversion by claiming that a convert who still held on to his previous beliefs and rituals was not a true, believing Christian. Under pressure from these groups, particularly the Dominicans and Franciscans, and despite the pleas of missionaries in India that the allowances made to Indian Christian converts were only meant to be an initial effort to demonstrate the superior religion, the Church ruled in 1744 that such converts were not 'true' converts and that no convert could profess the Catholic faith and still retain his loyalty to customs dictated by Hindu life.[87] From then on, the number of converts to Christianity in India dropped drastically, until the Anglicans began proselytization in a big way in the nineteenth century.[88]

---

[86] Ibid.: 377.

[87] For more information about the Rites see E. Amann, 'Malabares (Rites)'*DTC*, 9: 1704–46. Also see J. Bertrand, *Mémoires historiques sur les missions des ordres religieux et spécialement sur les questions du clergé indigène et des rites malabares d'après des documents inédits.* 2nd edn, (Paris: P. Brunet,1862).

[88] Anglican missionaries targeted lower castes for conversion, offering them an egalitarian society and the possibility of employment in the households of colonial administrators. The history of Christians in modern India reflects the efforts of different groups of missionaries; Southern Indian Christians are pre-dominantly Catholics who were

In spite of these struggles the *Lettres* enjoyed a wide readership. According to Sylvia Murr, the *Lettres Édifiantes* were published when the Jesuits were struggling to maintain their legitimacy in the face of decreasing funds from the Church and the competition of other orders. They were also meant to boost confidence in readers' faith at a time when the Church was under attack from non-believers and the philosophes.[89] As Kate Teltscher notes, the *Lettres* enjoyed wide circulation in part because they were written to persuade individuals to contribute to the cause of proselytization in India and elsewhere.[90]

According to the historian of science R. K. Kochhar, although the spread of the Christian faith was the most important plan of the Jesuits, their activities had a scientific dimension about them also, being the first European men of learning in India.[91] As Kochhar points out, Bouchet was the first person who, having travelled extensively in the southern part of India, was able to produce a reliable map of the peninsula, which the celebrated geographer D'Anville later used as a blueprint for his maps of South India. The Jesuit mission sent by Louis XIV made the first attempt to study Indian languages. These men applied themselves with vigour to the study of the local languages in the south, particularly Tamil and Telegu which were

---

converted by the Jesuits or even earlier. They cling to a caste hierarchy based on their caste in Hinduism prior to conversion, and caste rules, especially relating to marriage, are strictly followed. The Church of North India is Protestant, dominated by Anglican congregations, who willingly gave up their caste status upon conversion since most of them were lower castes anyway.

[89] Sylvia Murr, 'Les conditions d'émergence du discours sur l'Inde au siècle des Lumières, Inde et Littératures', *Purusartha*, 7, (1983): 239.

[90] Teltscher, *India Inscribed*: 80.

[91] Kochhar, 'Secondary Tools of Empire: Jesuit Men of Science in India': 175. Kochhar describes the scientific and geographical studies of various men of the Jesuit Mission in India including Bouchet, Richaud, and Boudier.

spoken by the majority of the area they served. Bouchet was fluent in Tamil and was considered a scholar by his fellow missionaries.[92] They also applied themselves to the study of Sanskrit believing that this would give them a greater understanding of the foundation of Indian religion and cultural traditions. As Tachard described in his survey of the missions,

> Father *Mauduit* applies himself to the *Grandan*, which is the learned Language of the Country. A Jesuit, to make his Ministry still more useful to the *Indians*, must understand their Books writ in that Language; and appear learned in the Sciences professed by their Doctors. The *Bramins*, who set themselves up as the only learned Men in this Country, won't permit such Authors as treat of them to be translated; and are prodigiously jealous of them, from a Persuasion that Learning is the true Characteristic of Nobility.[93]

In studying these languages and writing detailed accounts of their impressions of the Indians they encountered, as well as producing rudimentary grammars, dictionaries and linguistic guides for other missionaries to use, they provided an invaluable service to later generations of Indologists who used these works as their fundamentals to learning about India. For example, a signal service to the study of local languages was performed by Ariel, a missionary in Pondichéry, who had compiled a Tamil grammar and collected a wealth of Tamil manuscripts and sent them to Paris where Charles d'Ochoa organized them. Père Coeurdoux was another missionary in Pondichéry who was

---

[92] David Clines, 'In Search of the Indian Job', in *Vestus Testamentum*, Vol. 33. 4 (October, 1983): 404. Father Martin was an expert in Bengali.

[93] Father Tachard, Superior of the Jesuit Missions in India, to Count De Crecy. Pondichéry, February 1703. John Lockman, *Travels of the Jesuits* Vol. 1: 487.

in touch with Voltaire, Anquetil-Duperron, and other academics, providing them information about Indian culture, history, science, etc.[94] In fact it is no coincidence that until the notion of the academic as a rational man of science became dominant with the Enlightenment, many scholars of India were deeply religious and began their studies on India as part of an effort to understand a 'heathen' religion or to trace the roots of pagan religion.[95]

CONCLUSION

There is no clear image of India which emerges from the fragmentary writings of the early modern period, but there are certain aspects of writings which stand out. The first is the relatively moderate tone which was used to describe Indian religion as compared to the anti-Islamic invective. The second, the intense interest that the Brahmins of India generated. Established as the chief interpreters of religion, they were naturally the first to be consulted on any aspect of religion that travellers were curious about, and equally they formed the first group to be targeted for conversion. In fact this focus on the Brahmins and on caste in India may well be the first 'French' aspect of writing about India. As Kate Teltscher points out, by the mid-eighteenth century, one can talk of specific national images of India in Europe. The Jesuit dedication to 'going native', courting the Brahmins, learning Sanskrit and engaging Brahmins in long theological debates came to be identified as typically French in stark contrast to the writings of the Lutherans and Anglican missionaries who came to India in the eighteenth century.[96] The latter tended to work in North India, completely eschewed the Jesuit practice of *accomodatio* and

---

[94] See Louis Renou, *The Influence of Indian Thought on French Literature* (Adyar, 1948): 2–3.

[95] The most famous example of this kind being Anquetil-Duperron whose life's work on India was dictated by his quest for Judaic origins.

[96] Teltscher, *India Inscribed*: 8, 74–75.

focused on effecting mass conversions among the lower castes. While this was more an accident of history rather than any conscious 'French' action, the readership for these French Jesuits' accounts of India remained primarily French; therefore these accounts informed the French public, particularly the *savants*, about India.[97]

An examination of the writings of French missionaries who visited India points to the efforts of these men to create an image of India for their Western readers. Since they comprised the majority of Europeans who ventured into the country (as opposed to traders who limited themselves to the ports) their writings were virtually the only first-hand accounts of interior regions in India to become available in Europe. When Jordanus was writing in the thirteenth century, notwithstanding the hyperbole to which he was partial in describing fruits which could feed six men and trees of immense proportions,[98] the rare written description of India in the early modern period tended to focus on its difference from Europe. Much of this difference was described in terms of religion, but there were also accounts of the geographical marvels, like the monsoons, which Europeans travelling to the East would have first encountered in India, as well as the different flora and fauna of the area. Jordanus and Pascal also pointed to the fact of idolaters existing in India, but were far more moderate about the religions of the East than may be found in the more extreme rhetoric of the later Jesuits. These issues were relevant to the political context of their writing and it is a fact that after the crusades, an anti-Muslim rhetoric was almost *de rigueur* in all works describing the East. As opposed to Jordanus, later Jesuits were not only

---

[97] Sylvia Murr has commented on the connections between the Jesuits and Enlightenment savants in 'Les conditions d'émergence du discours sur l'Inde au siècle des Lumières, Inde et Littératures', *Purusartha* 7 (1983): 233–84.

[98] Friar Jordanus. *Mirabilia Descripta*: 12–20.

steeped in their own religious fervour, but were also subject to the aggressive economic mission that Europe had launched in Asia, particularly India and China. The Jesuit missions to Asia were corollaries to the steady commercial traffic to the East by the late seventeenth century and the *Lettres* reflect the need to document different aspects of the country in order to provide information about the land and its people. As outlined in the introduction to each volume of the *Lettres*, the Jesuits needed compilation of information in order to better effect conversions, in India, America and China. Yet the availability of their accounts to the reading public meant that these descriptions could be used by secular writers (such as the *philosophes*, who cited the *Lettres* widely as discussed in the next chapter) as well as manuals of information to traders and colonialists to these countries. Many of the missionaries were directly connected to the colonial enterprise, since French ships usually carried at least one missionary on board when they made voyages to India. These men were to provide to the spiritual needs of the French, but once they had established their missions, they also actively converted the native population.

Chapter 2

The 'Sublime' Civilization of India: The Pre-occupation of Philosophes

As India supplies the wants of all the world but is herself dependent for nothing, she must for that very reason have been the most early civilized of any country, and by a like consequence necessarily have had the most ancient form of worship. It is most probable the religion of India was for a long time the same as that of the Chinese government, and consisted only in the pure and simple worship of a Supreme Being, free from any superstition and fanaticism.[1]

By the middle of the eighteenth century, France was a contender for the Empire of India. The French East India Company, which had been created in 1664, was now master of a significant part of southern India, in addition to being a player in the politics of peninsular India. This was a period when the French colonial aims were directed primarily at India and North America. The intersection of missionary work with travel and colonial activity[2] led to a burgeoning study of India among secular *savants* in the mid-eighteenth century. Some scholars now began examining India not as a potential ground for conversion to

---

[1] Voltaire, 'Ancient and Modern History', *The Complete Works of Voltaire*. Edited by Theodore Besterman (Geneva: Institut et Musée Voltaire and Toronto: University of Toronto Press, 1968): Vol. 15, Part 2: 180.

[2] For the history of the early French colonial enterprise in India, see S. P. Sen, *The French in India: First Establishments and Struggle*. (Calcutta, 1947).

Christianity but as a peculiar society extremely different from Europe, which warranted further study. The interest in India was also encouraged by the Enlightenment which sought to look beyond the borders of Europe in its quest for new knowledge. It was in this context that an agenda for defining India in specific terms emerged. In fact, the academic interest in the Orient was one of the defining characteristics of the Enlightenment. One could argue that though the Enlightenment led to a burst of Oriental studies the reverse was equally true and that the discovery of the Orient (particularly India) was a founding pillar of the Enlightenment.[3]

This chapter provides a historical bridge between the thematically 'older' writings of the missionaries and the 'modern' writings of academics.[4] Among the changes that occurred were the individuals who wrote about India and their motives, although this did not necessarily change the image of India in France. The longstanding animosity to Islam continued during this era even though many other aspects of India changed in the French imagination.[5]

---

[3] According to Raymond Schwab, too often we forget that to approach India then seemed like a prerequisite for a profound understanding of humanity. Raymond Schwab, *The Oriental Renaissance: Europe's Discovery of India and the East, 1680–1880* (New York: Columbia University Press, 1984): 14.

[4] I use 'older' in the context of the developing image of India in France to refer to writings which presented a clear binary opposition between East and West in terms of the inferiority of the East. While 'Orientalism' continued in the writings of academics, these were more subtle as compared with earlier writings. Any inferiority of the East was 'proven' as a result of rational, scientific studies, rather than the impressionistic writing of earlier authors. These later writings are therefore called 'modern'.

[5] According to Tomoko Masuzawa, the European feeling against Islam arose from anti-Semitism, since both Muslims and Semites were considered to belong to the Semitic race. Tomoko Masuzawa, *The Invention of World Religions, Or, How European Universalism was Preserved in the Language of Pluralism: Or, How European Universalism*

This chapter is divided into sections which focus on these elements of continuity and change. The first section describes the people who were writing about India and their motives. The second examines the views which continued to command popularity, followed by the conclusion.

ENLIGHTENMENT INDIA: A SHIFT FROM ECCLESIASTICAL WRITING

I focus on the dominant *savant* view of India during the eighteenth-century Enlightenment in France as represented by the writings of the *philosophes*, specifically the work of Montesquieu and Voltaire. These writings constituted a definitive shift from missionary accounts of India. Although missionaries continued to travel to India and produce accounts of their observations and exchanges with the local population, the reading public in France looked to more mainstream works produced by *savants*, when they chose to learn about India. In part this was due to the fact that accounts produced by missionaries were largely preserved as Church records. While scholars eager to learn about India had previously tried to access these sources it was no longer necessary to do so since there was an increasing body of work readily available in personal libraries and larger collections like the *Bibliothèque du Roi*. Moreover the Enlightenment now defined academic and accurate studies as those which were dispassionate and rational, containing none of the religious motives which missionaries had.[6] This was a definite French academic trait and one that was held in great respect throughout the following centuries. The *philosophes'* lens on India made it an

---

Was Preserved in the Language of Pluralism (Chicago: University of Chicago Press, 2005).

[6] As Robert Bartlett puts it, reason or philosophy would thus take the place previously occupied by (what claimed to be) the divine or its representatives. Robert Bartlett, 'On the Politics of Faith and Reason: The Project of Enlightenment in Pierre Bayle and Montesquieu,' *The Journal of Politics*, 63.1 (February 2001): 1–2.

acceptable academic focus and countless Indologists and *savants* of India later credited the work of Montesquieu and Voltaire as among their first introductions to India. Why only Montesquieu and Voltaire? Although Rousseau was a well-known Enlightenment *philosophe* he wrote very little directly about India.[7] While Rousseau undeniably read on the state of politics in the East in order to form his theory of the Noble Savage and the creation of different forms of social contracts in different parts of the world he did not directly refer to India or to Indians. Therefore he has been omitted in this chapter.[8] In addition the *Encyclopédie* of Diderot and d'Alembert[9] was a major achievement of Enlightenment *savants* and contained 685

---

[7] Jean-Jacques Rousseau's best-known work, *The Social Contract* published in 1762, outlined a new political theory of governance based on the belief that man in a pure state of nature is fundamentally good, if uncultured, a 'noble savage' in effect who created a social contract in order to ensure that his freedom and rights were guaranteed. While the individual lost his natural rights by submitting to the general will he ensured that his right to life and liberty were maintained.

[8] In other works, Rousseau demonstrated his knowledge of India. For instance, he refers to an Inquisitor in Goa as an example of religious intolerance in his *Confessions*, Vol. 2 (New York: Blanchard, 1857): 327. He also refers to Jean Chardin's *Voyages de monsieur le chevalier Chardin en Perse et autres lieux de l'orient* (Amsterdam, 1711).

[9] The *Encyclopédie* was the lifetime work of Denis Diderot and Jean d'Alembert who intended to encapsulate all human knowledge in this work. The work was published as 32 initial volumes from 1751–77 with over 70,000 entries provided by a number of authors. The philosophical spirit of the *Encyclopédie* was taken from the Enlightenment emphasis on reason over faith; of observation over doctrine; the authors of the various entries therefore supplied information which was to be based on scientific research and observation rather than religion and doctrine. For more information about the *Encyclopédie* and its impact see, Philip Blom, *Enlightening the World: Encyclopédie, The Book That Changed the Course of History* (New York: Palgrave Macmillan, 2005). Diderot's personal contribution to information about India was in the form of fragmentary writings which never became popular. See Michèle Duchet, *Diderot et l'Histoire des deux Indes: ou, L'écriture fragmentaire* (Paris: A.-G. Nizet, 1978).

entries on India. However, in keeping with the spirit of the *Encyclopédie*, these entries were mostly related to the description of economy, botany, medicine, trades, art, and crafts. The few entries which display personal opinions about the customs and religion of India varied from entries by Voltaire (which reified the opinion he explained in his detailed work on India) to entries by the Chévalier de Jaucourt and Deleyre which continued the older missionary opinion that India was a land where superstition and backward customs abounded.[10] The *Encyclopédie* certainly demonstrated that a plethora of views existed about India in the mid-eighteenth century. However, in the context of the nineteenth century, Indologists seldom used the *Encyclopédie* as a reference for their knowledge about India. Therefore the academic view of India was not influenced by the entries in the *Encyclopédie*. On the other hand, Indologists of all nationalities continued to cite the work of Voltaire and of Montesquieu during the nineteenth century, which makes them relevant to this chapter.

An interesting aspect of the study of India by the *philosophes* was that despite all their protestations about knowledge for its own sake and about the importance of reason, their own view of India was clearly driven by certain agendas. In fact as Raymond Schwab points out, a massive movement to discover and study Oriental texts (a movement he termed the 'Oriental Renaissance') arose due to Enlightenment efforts to find an alternative to the Renaissance in Europe as a source of intellectual and spiritual inspiration.[11] Missionaries had educated *savant* France about the antiquity and religion of India. Now the quest of the *philosophes* to find alternatives to the

---

[10] Denis Diderot and Jean d'Alembert, *Encyclopédie* (Paris, 1765). See for example Deleyre, Vol. 6: 393–401 and Le Chevalier de Jaucourt, Vol. 17: 240–143. Both Deleyre and Jaucourt cited the *Lettres Édifiantes* among their sources.

[11] Raymond Schwab, *La Renaissance orientale* (Paris: Payot, 1950).

Greco-Roman model of antiquity led to a re-examination of India and China.[12] Thus India arrived in the *salons* of Paris and the libraries of the *philosophes*. Virtually every *savant* worth his salt now made it a point to mention his knowledge of India and Indian religion in essays in addition to peppering discussions of humanity, the origin of man and civilization with references to the ancient culture and peoples of India.[13] In particular, Voltaire used the example of India to question the long-held European notion of the Greco-Roman origin of civilization. In fact, as Sylvia Murr, Halbfass and several others note, Voltaire was not interested in India for itself but rather as a vehicle for his theories about the age of the world, origin of man and origin of religion and civilization.[14] Another aspect was the lack of first-hand knowledge. While all accounts of India had previously been written by men who had travelled there, Voltaire's intellectual status in France made him an authoritative voice about India even though he never went there. Although Voltaire aimed at exposing the inherent greatness of India, because he conducted his studies exclusively in France, he perpetuated the theory that Europe was better equipped to study other cultures merely because she possessed their material artifacts. Since the *Bibliothèque Royale* already had

---

[12] Anquetil-Duperron was an early scholar to make this connection. See Siep Stuurman, 'Cosmopolitan Egalitarianism in the Enlightenment: Anquetil-Duperron on India and America,' *Journal of the History of Ideas*, 68.2 (April 2007): 255–78.

[13] All the major French philosophes cited India at least occasionally: Voltaire, Montesquieu, Rousseau and Diderot.

[14] See Sylvia Murr, 'Les conditions d'émergence du discours sur l'Inde au siècle des Lumières, Inde et Littératures', *Purusartha*, 7, (1983), D. S. Hawley, "L'Inde de Voltaire", *Studies on Voltaire and the 18th century*, Vol. CXX (1974), Jackie Assayag, *L'Inde fabuleuse: le charme discret de l'exotisme français XVII–XXe siècles*. (Paris: Éditions Kimé, 1999): 82, Wilhelm Halbfass, *India and Europe. An Essay in Understanding*. (Albany, N.Y.: State University of New York Press, 1988): 58.

an impressive collection of Indic texts,[15] the study of India could be undertaken in the heart of France with no sacrifice as to the academic integrity of the work![16] In fact as Raymond Schwab noted, there were a scant handful of Indologists who actually went to India in the nineteenth century.[17]

---

[15] Once again, the efforts of French missionaries yielded the first extensive library of Indian manuscripts outside of India. By the middle of the eighteenth century the academic interest in India extended to beyond immediate conversion and in 1718 the librarian of the *Bibliothèque Royale*, Abbé Bignon called for missionaries to collect Indic manuscripts and send them to the newly created Oriental section of the library. Felix Lacôte noted the presence of a wonderful collection of Sanskrit manuscripts organized by Père Pons by 1750 at the *Bibliothèque du Roi* which since no one had completely deciphered Sanskrit no one could yet read! See Felix Lacôte, '*L'Indianisme*', *Société Asiatique: Livre du centenaire* (Paris: La Société Asiatique, 1922). In 1739 the first catalogue of Sanskrit, Tamil, and Telegu manuscripts available in France were published as part of the Catalogus Manuscriptorum Bibliothecae Regiae. The catalogue listed 287 works including some of the Vedas, the Epics, Puranas, dramas, poetry, grammars, dictionaries, and works on rhetoric, astrology, logic, philosophy, metaphysics and science. Pons also produced a rudimentary Sanskrit grammar in Latin. See Jean Filliozat, 'La naissance et l'essor de L'Indianisme', *Bulletin de la Société des études indo-chinoises de Saigon*, Vol. 29, Issue 4, (1954): 272.

[16] In fact by the nineteenth century, the European mania for collecting artifacts and original texts from colonies meant that in many situations, better sources were available in the West rather than in the colony! There is an impressive body of work which deals in detail with the implications of this craze for collecting. In particular, see Bernard Cohn, *Colonialism and its Forms of Knowledge* (Princeton: Princeton University Press, 1996) and Carol Breckenridge, 'The Aesthetics and Politics of Colonial Collecting: India at World Fairs', *Comparative Study of Society and History*, 31.2 (April 1989).

[17] Quoting Louis Renou, 'scholarly contact with living India was secured by a small group of Anglo-Indians—Colebrooke, Wilson, and others. It is important to remember that aside from Anquetil-Duperron, and until Emile Sénart in 1887, Foucher in 1895, and Sylvain Lévi in 1897, no major French Indic scholar visited India.' Raymond Schwab, the Oriental Renaissance (New York: Columbia University Press, 1984): 47.

MONTESQUIEU AND THE NOTION OF THE 'ORIENTAL DESPOT'

The earliest work of French philosophes on India was by Montesquieu. Montesquieu's *Persian Letters* (first published in 1721) were a critique of French society ostensibly written by a Persian travelling in France to his friend in the East, encompassing not only the former's impressions of the West but also containing descriptions of 'oriental' society., Building on the success of this work, Montesquieu published his greatest work in 1748, titled *'Esprit de Lois'*. In this he explained the birth and development of different political systems and thereby different laws which prevailed in different parts of the world. This work began with the assumption that the British political system of constitutional monarchy with an element of democracy was the best form of government. Montesquieu's subsequent explanation of other political systems was built upon the fundamental premise that the less a system resembled the British system, the more inferior it was. Montesquieu was not unusual in this view which was very common in the hypercolonial environment of eighteenth-century Europe.[18] His great contribution to the debate was to attribute differences in political systems to climate. Montesquieu provided not only an explanation for the greatness of Europe, but also a legitimate reason for the continued dominance of Europe and of European civilization based on climatic factors. He wrote, for example, that

> People are therefore more vigorous in cold climates.... This superiority of strength must produce various effects; for instance, a greater boldness, that is, more courage; a greater sense of superiority, that is, less desire of revenge; a greater opinion of security, that is, more frankness, less suspicion, policy, and cunning. In short, this must be

---

[18] During the eighteenth century, the colonization of the Americas and India was well under way, resulting in several wars and conflicts between competing colonial powers.

productive of very different tempers. Put a man into a close, warm place, and for the reasons above given he will feel a great faintness. If under this circumstance you propose a bold enterprise to him, I believe you will find him very little disposed towards it; his present weakness will throw him into despondency; he will be afraid of everything, being in a state of total incapacity. The inhabitants of warm countries are, like old men, timorous; the people in cold countries are, like young men, brave.[19]

Not only did Montesquieu state that the physical courage and ability of man sprang from the climatic temperature, but also his moral and ethical sense. So, 'If we travel towards the north, we meet with people who have few vices, many virtues, and a great share of frankness and sincerity. If we draw near the south, we fancy ourselves entirely removed from the verge of morality....'[20]

According to Montesquieu, from this heat in the south, which encompassed the East, one could see the logic behind their peculiar political and legal institutions. He even attributed the state of petrifaction that Western writers typically characterized Eastern societies with having fallen into, to the heat. Under his theory, with the excessive heat sapping one's energy there would be an unwillingness to change, because change involves energy. 'This is the reason that the laws, manners, and customs, even those which seem quite indifferent, such as their mode of dress, are the same to this very day in eastern countries as they were a thousand years ago.'[21]

---

[19] Charles de Secondat, Baron de Montesquieu, *The Spirit of Laws* (London: G. Bell and Sons, Ltd, 1914). Translated by Thomas Nugent, revised by J. V. Prichard. Book XIV: Of Laws in Relation to the Nature of the Climate; part 2: Of the Difference of Men in different Climates. Http://www.constitution.org/cm/sol.htm

[20] Ibid.

[21] Ibid., Book XIV: Of Laws in Relation to the Nature of the Climate, Part 4. Cause of the Immutability of Religion, Manners, Customs, and Laws in the Eastern Countries.

Following from this exposition linking political systems to the climate, Montesquieu popularized the notion that the East was ruled by despots who wielded absolute power over their subjects.[22] His elaboration of the legal systems of the world including that of India was based on the effects of Oriental despotism and the climate on the customs and morals of people.

Montesquieu was not unreasonably harsh about India. He held the view that the climate was responsible for the inferior laws of the Indians and that under the circumstances they could do no better. The peculiarities which the climate brought on were responsible for the contrary nature of the Indians. So for instance the Indians were 'naturally a pusillanimous people...But how shall we reconcile this with their customs and penances so full of barbarity? The men voluntarily undergo the greatest hardships, and the women burn themselves; here we find a very odd compound of fortitude and weakness.'[23] According to Montesquieu, the answer to this paradox was to be found in what he described as 'the principle of Metempsychosis or total inactivity'.[24] Arguing that this principle was responsible for most of the peculiarities of Indian religion, he presented it as the logic behind the customs and manners of India which had remained unchanged for centuries. Even sati could be explained as a result of this indolence. According to him,

> As it inspires men with a certain horror against bloodshed, very few murders are committed in the Indies; and though they seldom punish with death, yet they enjoy a perfect

---

[22] Hence the term 'Oriental Despots'.

[23] Ibid., Book XIV: Of Laws in Relation to the Nature of the Climate, part 3: Contradiction in the Tempers of some Southern Nations. In these passages, Bernier and Tavernier were his sources.

[24] Ibid., Book XXIV: Of Laws in relation to Religion Considered in Itself, and in its Doctrines, part 21: Of the Metempsychosis.

tranquility....On the other hand, women burn themselves at the death of their husbands; thus it is only the innocent who suffer a violent death.[25]

In his *Persian Letters*, Montesquieu included an interesting vignette about the mental indolence of Indians regarding sati. Describing a situation where a new widow was preparing to commit sati merely because she wanted to follow tradition, Montesquieu presented an amusing conversation where a Brahmin urged her to become a sati in order to unite with her dead husband.[26] Upon hearing this, the widow abandoned all plans for sati since she had suffered enough at her husband's hand while he was alive! While this is an amusing account, the ignorance displayed by the widow as to the purpose of sati was presented as the mental inactivity of the East, where one did things, without questioning tradition merely because it was too hot to exert oneself![27] Montesquieu's argument, simplified, was that India, being a hot country, was subject to the lassitude of mind and morals which heat undeniably brought on. The Indians, seeking a rationale to explain their inertia created the principle of Metempsychosis or total inactivity, as a divine philosophy which legitimized their state of inactivity. 'The Indians believe that repose and non-existence are the foundation of all things, and the end in which they terminate. Hence they consider entire inaction as the most perfect of all states, and the object

---

[25] Ibid., Book XXIV: Of Laws in relation to Religion Considered in Itself, and in its Doctrines, part 21: Of the Metempsychosis.

[26] Montesquieu's *Persian Letters* (1721). Translated and annotated by John Davidson (Gibbings and Co: London, 1899) 3 vols. Letter CXXVI http://www.wm.edu/history/rbsche/plp/

[27] Ignorance is a universal phenomenon and in this particular example, there was nothing peculiarly Eastern or climate-driven to explain the widow's actions. In fact, one could argue that since she abandoned her plans for sati once she learned of the outcome, she had broken with tradition.

of their desires. To the Supreme Being they give the title of immovable.'[28]

Montesquieu's understanding of Metempsychosis or the principle of transmigration was incorrect.[29] His references to India concluded with Metempsychosis as the explanation for the customs which any rational Western mind would have found barbaric. He went so far as to explain the Indians' aversion to beef as a result of Metempsychosis.

> The opinion of the metempsychosis is adapted to the climate of the Indies. An excessive heat burns up all the country: they can breed but very few cattle; they are always in danger of wanting them for tillage; their black cattle multiply but indifferently; and they are subject to many distempers. A law of religion which preserves them is therefore more suitable to the policy of the country....The flesh of cattle in that country is insipid but the milk and butter which they receive from them serve for a part of their subsistence; therefore the law which prohibits the eating and killing of cows is in the Indies not unreasonable.[30]

Montesquieu went so far as to write an apologia for certain customs of India which had been criticized by missionaries. For instance, he wrote about polygamy that it

---

[28] Charles de Secondat, *Baron de Montesquieu, The Spirit of Laws* (London: G. Bell and Sons, Ltd, 1914). Translated by Thomas Nugent, revised by J. V. Prichard. Book XIV: Of Laws in Relation to the Nature of the Climate; part 2: Of the Difference of Men in different Climates. Http://www.constitution.org/cm/sol.htm. Book XIV: Of Laws in Relation to the Nature of the Climate, part 5. That those are bad Legislators who favour the Vices of the Climate, and good Legislators who oppose those Vices.

[29] In fact, the principle of Metempsychosis demands just the opposite. Since one's deeds in this life determine one's rebirth in a higher or lower level of being, one must constantly strive to improve so that the end of rebirth can occur with the achievement of *moksha* or unity with the universal Godhead. That alone will end the cycle of rebirth and transmigration.

[30] Ibid., part 24: Of the local Laws of Religion.

was the natural result of the sexual indulgence produced by the hot climate.[31] Even the curious case of the polyandrous Malabar Nairs was explained as the hyper-sexuality of the tropics.[32] The unequal relations between men and women as well as the seclusion of women were also explained as a result of the climate.

> The women should not only be separated from the men by the walls of the house, but they ought also to be separated in the same enclosure, in such a manner that each may have a distinct household in the same family. Hence each derives all that relates to the practice of morality, modesty, chastity, reserve, silence, peace, dependence, respect, and love; and, in short, a general direction of her thoughts to that which, in its own nature, is a thing of the greatest importance, a single and entire attachment to her family.... We find the manners more pure in the several

---

[31] Ibid., Women: Book XVI: How the Laws of Domestic Slavery Bear a Relation to the Nature of the Climate; Part 2: *That in the Countries of the South there is a natural Inequality between the two Sexes.* 'Women, in hot climates, are marriageable at eight, nine, or ten years of age; thus, in those countries, infancy and marriage generally go together. They are old at twenty: their reason therefore never accompanies their beauty....These women ought then to be in a state of dependence; for reason cannot procure in old age that empire which even youth and beauty could not give. It is therefore extremely natural that in these places a man, when no law opposes it, should leave one wife to take another, and that polygamy should be introduced.'

[32] Ibid., Book XVI: How the Laws of Domestic Slavery Bear a Relation to the Nature of the Climate; Part 5: *The Reason of a Law of Malabar.* 'In the tribe of the Naires, on the coast of Malabar, the men can have only one wife, while a woman, on the contrary, may have many husbands. The origin of this custom is not I believe difficult to discover. The Naires are the tribe of nobles, who are the soldiers of all those nations. In Europe soldiers are forbidden to marry; in Malabar, where the climate requires greater indulgence, they are satisfied with rendering marriage as little burdensome to them as possible: they give one wife amongst many men, which consequently diminishes the attachment to a family, and the cares of housekeeping, and leaves them in the free possession of a military spirit.'

parts of the East, in proportion as the confinement of women is more strictly observed....Hence it proceeds that in the empires of Turkey, Persia, of the Mogul, China, and Japan, the manners of their wives are admirable.

But the case is not the same in India, where a multitude of islands and the situation of the land have divided the country into an infinite number of petty states, which from causes that we have not here room to mention are rendered despotic.

There are none there but wretches, some pillaging and others pillaged. Their grandees have very moderate fortunes, and those whom they call rich have only a bare subsistence. The confinement of their women cannot therefore be very strict; nor can they make use of any great precautions to keep them within due bounds; hence it proceeds that the corruption of their manners is scarcely to be conceived.

We may there see to what an extreme the vices of a climate indulged in full liberty will carry licentiousness. It is there that nature has a force and modesty a weakness, which exceeds all comprehension. At Patan the wanton desires of the women are so outrageous, that the men are obliged to make use of a certain apparel to shelter them from their designs.[33]

Thus Montesquieu provided a rationale for the seclusion as well as a warning about the dire consequences of allowing a large measure of freedom to Eastern women. In fact not only did polygamy follow from the hyper-sexuality of the hot climate but also the need for seclusion.

It is not only a plurality of wives which in certain places of the East requires their confinement, but also the climate itself. Those who consider the horrible crimes, the

---

[33] Ibid., Book XVI: How the Laws of Domestic Slavery Bear a Relation to the Nature of the Climate; Part 10: *The Principle on which the Morals of the East are founded.*

treachery, the dark villainies, the poisonings, the assassinations, which the liberty of women has occasioned at Goa and in the Portuguese settlements in the Indies, where religion permits only one wife; and who compare them with the innocence and purity of manners of the women of Turkey, Persia, Hindostan, China, and Japan, will clearly see that it is frequently as necessary to separate them from the men, when they have but one, as when they have many....These are things which ought to be decided by the climate. What purpose would it answer to shut up women in our northern countries, where their manners are naturally good; where all their passions are calm; and where love rules over the heart with so regular and gentle an empire that the least degree of prudence is sufficient to conduct it?[34]

Montesquieu's portrait of India was meant to highlight the inferior civilization, manners, and morals of Indians. His work, however, also maintained that this level of culture and political organization was inevitable given the heat of the tropics. He argued that although the customs and laws of the Indians were barbaric when compared to the West they were suitable for the people they governed. Montesquieu presented India as the territory of the Oriental Despot. In fact his rationale for the prominence of religion in Eastern politics arose from his description of the Oriental Despot. Characterizing the influence of religion in Eastern politics, Montesquieu explained it as the necessary form of checks on the arbitrary power of the Despot.

Though despotic governments are of their own nature everywhere the same, yet from circumstances—from a religious opinion, from prejudice, from received examples, from a particular turn of mind, from manners or morals—it is possible they may admit of a considerable difference....It is proper there should be some sacred book to serve for a

---

[34] Ibid., Part 11: *Of domestic Slavery independently of Polygamy.*

rule, as the Koran among the Arabs, the books of Zoroaster among the Persians, the Veda among the Indians, and the classic books among the Chinese. The religious code supplies the civil and fixes the extent of arbitrary sway.[35]

In effect Montesquieu denied any possibility of self-improvement or progress, which was a powerful argument for European colonizers who used the notion of the backwardness of the East as a justification to colonize and 'civilize'.

VOLTAIRE AND THE VEDAM

Voltaire was the first academic who presented a coherent image of India which was not marked by contradictions. Even Montesquieu was contradictory in his description of India and its customs, at once describing them as weak and cowardly; but also 'mild, tender, and compassionate'.[36] Similarly, while Montesquieu justified the absolute power

---

[35] Ibid. Book XII: Of the Laws That Form Political Liberty, in Relation to the Subject, Part 29: Of the civil Laws proper for mixing some portion of Liberty in a despotic Government.

[36] Charles de Secondat, *Baron de Montesquieu, The Spirit of Laws* (London: G. Bell and Sons, Ltd, 1914). Trans. Thomas Nugent, revised by J. V. Prichard. Http://www.constitution.org/cm/sol.htm. Book 14, Of Laws in Relation to the Nature of the Climate; Part 15. *Of the different Confidence which the Laws have in the People, according to the Difference of Climates....* In contrast again to the tyranny of depots and religion which he described in detail in another section of this work, he also described that, 'Hence their legislators repose great confidence in them. They have established very few punishments; these are not severe, nor are they rigorously executed. They have subjected nephews to their uncles, and orphans to their guardians, as in other countries they are subjected to their fathers; they have regulated the succession by the acknowledged merit of the successor. They seem to think that every individual ought to place entire confidence in the good nature of his fellow-subjects....They enfranchise their slaves without difficulty, they marry them, they treat them as their children. Happy climate which gives birth to innocence, and produces a lenity in the laws!'

of religion in the East as the necessary check to despotic power, he also criticized the same religion which caused fissures in society.[37] Voltaire's was the first work to simultaneously provide a single line of reasoning when it came to explaining the various customs and manners of India and to write positively of a country which was now poised to challenge the great Greco-Roman civilizations of Western antiquity. Thus while Montesquieu only compounded the sense of contradiction which Europeans reading or learning about India had, Voltaire set out to provide a rationale for their actions in terms which were understood by the West.

In stark contrast to Montesquieu's sporadic and critical discussion of India, Voltaire, arguably the most important of the *philosophes*, discussed India at length in his writings.[38] Writing some years after the *Esprit des Lois* had been published and drawn by accounts of the wealth of information that ancient India was credited with, Voltaire was also impressed by the work of British Orientalists such as William Jones, Halhed, and Holwell. Voltaire acquired

---

[37] Ibid., Book XXIV: Of Laws in relation to Religion Considered in Itself, and in its Doctrines; Part 22: *That it is dangerous for Religion to inspire an Aversion for Things in themselves indifferent.* 'A kind of honour established in the Indies by the prejudices of religion has made the several tribes conceive an aversion against each other. This honour is founded entirely on religion; these family distinctions form no civil distinctions; there are Indians who would think themselves dishonoured by eating with their king. These sorts of distinctions are connected with a certain aversion for other men, very different from those sentiments which naturally arise from difference of rank; which among us comprehends a love for inferiors. The laws of religion should never inspire an aversion to anything but vice, and above all they should never estrange man from a love and tenderness for his own species. The Mahometan and Indian religions embrace an infinite number of people; the Indians hate the Mahometans, because they eat cows; the Mahometans detest the Indians because they eat hogs.'

[38] For a detailed discussion of Voltaire's views and constructions of India, see Jyoti Mohan, 'La civilisation la plus antique: Voltaire's Images of India', *Journal of World History*, Vol. 16.2, June 2005: 173–86.

an extensive library of works relating to India.[39] His interest in India found its way into his own writings as well. His primary work on India was *Fragments sur quelques révolutions dans l'Inde and sur le mort du Comte de Lalli* which he wrote as an addendum to his work on *Annales de l'Empire*.[40] In addition, India appeared prominently in his lectures on Ancient and Modern History, on philosophy, and in his letters to other luminaries of the French Enlightenment. Although he never travelled to India he expressed a keen desire to do so in a letter to Paul Gui de Chabonan in 1767.[41]

Voltaire also made frequent references to India in his many operas and plays, many of which were set in an Indian context.[42] He introduced images of India as well as aspects of France's recent relations with India to the people of France through his historical works, plays, and operas. For the first time, there was a sense of a vague, exotic land called India in the French imagination and over the course of the next few decades this land came to acquire certain specific characteristics which defined it as 'Indian'.

Fragments sur l'Inde consists of roughly two sections. One traces the history of French activities in India until the loss of most of the French territories in the subcontinent during the Seven Years War. It deals with the

---

[39] For an exhaustive list of the books in Voltaire's library relating to India, look up D. S. Hawley, 'L'Inde de Voltaire', *Studies on Voltaire and the 18th century*, Vol. CXX (1974).

[40] Voltaire, *Oeuvres Completes de Voltaire: Annales de l'Empire: Fragments sur quelques révolutions dans l'Inde and sur le mort du Comte de Lalli*, vol. 24 (Paris: Imprimérie de la Société Littéraire, 1785–89). (Henceforth 'Oeuvres...').

[41] Voltaire, *Correspondence*, Edited by Theodore Besterman, corr. 13663 (Paris: Gallimard, 1964).

[42] For example, *Zadig et la destinée*,(1747), *Lettresd'un Turc sur les Fakirs et sur son ami Bababec* (1750), *Histoire d'un bon brahmin* (1761), *Le blanc et le noir* (1764), *Aventure indienne traduite par l'ignorant* (1766), *La Princesse de Babylone* (1768) and *Le Taureau blanc* (1774).

establishment, expansion, and decline of French trade in India, from François Martin to Lally. The second part of *Fragments sur l'Inde* is a compendium of all of Voltaire's thoughts and ideas on India which he put together from various articles, letters, and communications regarding the discovery of Hinduism in India. Voltaire was also sufficiently interested in India to include sections on Vedic religion, the Brahmins, and Mughals in his Complete Works.

Here he made an important departure from British Orientalist scholars and provided another key aspect to the *French* representations of India. Jones, Halhed, Holwell, and other Orientalists had focused primarily on ancient India and the so-called Sanskrit texts of Hindu religion.[43] The emphasis was on the strictly theoretical greatness of Indian civilization, one that did not exist in the present. The recovery of ancient texts served to underline this theory of a great, albeit bygone era in India.[44] The works of the ancients demonstrated that India had been a great civilization. Since there were few texts to document the changes which had occurred in India in religion, society, economy and polity from the ancient times to the current

---

[43] Many of these texts which were 'discovered' by Orientalist scholars and sent back to Europe during the course of the eighteenth and nineteenth centuries to be translated by French and British scholars were later discovered to be fakes. In fact Voltaire's primary source about Indian religion and philosophy, the Ezour Vedam, which he described as one of the major theological texts of the Hindus (probably confusing it with the Yajur Vedam) was discovered to be a much later work, of dubious quality and questionable authorship. See Ludo Rocher, *Ezourvedam. A French Veda of the Eighteenth Century* (Philadelphia, 1984).

[44] This was a constant theme of British Indology in India. While ancient India had seen a glorious period, this was now a bygone time and contemporary India was mired in social chaos which provided much of the legitimacy for the colonizing mission. In fact India had sunk to such depths of degeneracy that she had failed to recognize her own great past and it was left to British Indologists to patiently retrieve the old texts and customs. See, for example, James Mill, *The History of British India*. Six vols (London, 1818).

period, academics had to be content with the study of ancient India through its texts, even though modern India was clearly far removed from the prescriptions of the ancient texts. What is significant about Voltaire's work on India was that he appropriated the Orientalist praise for the theoretical framework of Hindu culture based on the ancient texts and applied it to an actual description of the contemporary Hindu. His work on India was in no way meant to represent the *ideal* of Indian culture but, in fact purported to represent the *reality* of eighteenth-century India. This was a marked departure from other works on India, Orientalist or otherwise. The works of Jones and other British Indologists had focused on the translation of ancient Sanskrit texts, and had highlighted the *past* in India's accomplishments whether cultural or temporal. Voltaire argued that where such advanced writing existed there was sure to be some indication of the forward thinking that had produced such writing. He therefore believed that India still had great thinkers and could easily regain her cultural and spiritual greatness since the spirit of the ancients was still present in the contemporary Indian.

Voltaire sought to defend the social and psychological backwardness that Indologists had criticized. He avoided the common themes found in the works of British Indologists which described the 'mildness' of the Indian as 'weakness'. Though he noted the easy conquest of the Indians by numerous invaders, he did not attribute it to the enervation and effeminacy caused by climate, or even mention the fickleness and dishonesty of Indians described so well in later British works.[45] In his representation of

---

[45] The use of adjectives like 'effeminacy' and 'lassitude' was commonly applied to oriental peoples in the eighteenth century, but in the case of India, these took on a new meaning when the British defined certain sections of the Indian people in these terms in the nineteenth century and later, in order to justify the mechanisms of Imperial rule. For an interesting example of this sort and how it was worked into the rubrics of governance, see Mrinalini Sinha, *Colonial Masculinity: The*

India as a 'good' civilization, Voltaire acknowledged that there were undesirable irrationalities and superstitions as well as cruel and barbaric customs like sati. Yet he sought to excuse these shortcomings by comparing these customs with other ancient civilizations revered in the Western world and by attempting to present some sort of explanation for the logic behind these drawbacks.

> The Indians being at all times a trading and industrious people, were necessarily subjected to a regular police; and that people whom Pythagoras visited for improvement, must have enjoyed the protection of wholesome laws, without which the arts are never cultivated; but mankind, even in the midst of sensible laws, have always indulged ridiculous customs. That which constitutes the point of honor and religion among the women, inducing them to burn themselves on the bodies of their husbands, existed in India from time immemorial, and is yet not abolished. Their philosophers throw themselves alive into funeral piles, through excess of fanaticism and vainglory....It would be very difficult to reconcile the sublime ideas which the Brahmins preserve of the Supreme Being, with their superstition and fabulous mythology, if history did not present the same sort of contradictions among the Greeks and Romans.[46]

In this passage Voltaire accepted some of the common criticisms levelled at Indian culture by contemporary writers, mainly missionaries. Yet he attempted to provide some sort of mitigation of sati which had horrified the western world and instantly reduced India to the status of a barbaric backward country. It was no coincidence that he mentioned the self-immolation of Indian male philosophers

---

Manly Englishman' and the *'Effeminate Bengali'* in the Late Nineteenth Century (Manchester: Manchester University Press, 1995).

[46] Voltaire, 'Ancient and Modern History', *The Complete Works of Voltaire*. Edited by Theodore Besterman (Geneva: Institut et Musée Voltaire and Toronto: University of Toronto Press, 1968): 42–43.

and sages immediately following his note on sati. While he did not excuse either custom, the inclusion of males in examples of self-immolation went a long way towards combating the common assumption that Indian civilization was brutal towards its women, sati being a prime example of the low esteem in which women were held. Voltaire's sentence about sages choosing to immolate themselves made two significant points. The first and more obvious point was that self-immolation was not a custom reserved for women but also indulged in by philosophers and sages who were highly respected members of society. The second sought to place sati alongside the self-immolation of sages in pointing to the voluntary nature of the two types of death, rather than the popular descriptions of sati as involuntary suicides by women who were coerced into it by their families. The last sentence of the passage was also an influential defence of Indian customs. In making the reference to the prevalence of superstitions and similar customs of self-mortification among the sages of ancient Greece and Rome, Voltaire basically put Indian culture on par with the ancient civilizations of the West and argued that one could not mitigate the greatness of India based on criticism which could equally be levelled at the cradle of Western civilization.

Attempting also to defend Indians for their customs, superstitions and supposed religious corruption he divided Indians into three categories: the learned Brahmin, keeper of the secrets of ancient learning; the Oriental despot; and the hardworking masses.

The learned Brahmin was the custodian of the ancient religion of India, a noble idea derived from Aryan minds and consisting of a single Godhead and a system of ethics applicable even today.[47] Being responsible for theological ideas, the Brahmins naturally assumed the roles of philosopher and scholar. They taught the West science, astronomy,

---

[47] Ibid.: Vol. 15, part 2: 180.

geometry, and arithmetic, the game of chess, the solar calendar, and the concept of the zodiac. Voltaire wrote, 'The Greeks, before Alexander, travel led to India in quest of science. There the celebrated Pilpay, about two thousand three hundred years ago, wrote those moral fables which have been translated into almost every language of the known world.'[48] In a fictional dialogue between a Jesuit and a Brahmin, intended to demonstrate the achievement of Indian astronomy, Voltaire stressed the notion of the necessity and inevitability of events. The Brahmin claimed that the deaths of kings, the wars in Europe and the current political condition were predicated on the position of the planets.[49] Describing the writings of Arian, Strabo, and Pliny attesting to the scientific and technological development of India as well as Pythagoras' travels in India, Voltaire concluded that the Brahmins were great intellectuals. Ironically these same scientific achievements, including the advanced system of astronomy, were ridiculed in the nineteenth and twentieth centuries as the signs of a superstitious and stagnant society which believed more in the predictions of the stars than in reality.[50]

One can clearly see the defence of Indians in these passages of Voltaire. Ancient Indian civilization was a 'sublime' religion of monotheism and pure worship. Yet modern-day India had degenerated into a corrupt, base form of this praiseworthy ideal. In these passages, Voltaire accepts the charge by missionaries that India was a polytheistic, idolatrous land, yet asserted that this state of affairs was a recent phenomenon, a corruption of a purer state of mind which was brought about by other peoples

---

[48] Ibid., Vol. 13, part 1: 39.

[49] Voltaire, "Dialogue entre un brachmane et un Jésuite sur la nécessité et l'enchaînment des choses", *Mélanges* (Paris, 1961)

[50] See, for example James Mill, *The History of British India*. Six vols (London, 1818).

who, over the course of several centuries had invaded and spoiled the pristine thought of the ancient Indians. Certainly, the concept of the indolent, oppressive, and debauched Oriental Despot arose only with the Islamic invasions as did the description of the passive, superstitious, ignorant masses, oppressed for generations by despots and Brahmins.[51] As Assayag points out, in arguing for the corruption of Hindu thought by the foreign Muslim element, Voltaire was able to argue that the Brahmins had successfully preserved their purity.[52]

These Brahmins...were the peaceable rulers of a mild and discerning people, and were at the same time the chiefs of religion...simple and rational... [and founded on] universal reason....The Brahmins ceased to rule in India long before the time of Alexander the Great...even in their decline, they gave many proofs of that kind of virtue which is compatible with illusions of fanaticism. They continued to acknowledge one supreme God, in the midst of the multitude of subordinate deities, which popular superstition adopted in all countries in the world. Strabo expressly says that, in the main, the Brahmins acknowledge only one God....The seven years of probationership among the Brahmins, and the silence enjoined during that term, were still in force in the time of Strabo. The celibacy to be observed during this novitiate, the abstaining from the flesh of domestic animals, were laws which they never transgressed, and which still subsist among them. They held one God, the creator, preserver and avenger, and believed the fall and degeneracy of man; and this opinion is everywhere to be met with

---

[51] In fact, Voltaire criticized Montesquieu for his stereotypical presentation of the 'Oriental Despot'. According to Voltaire, a 'despotic' regime was far more serious than the rule of Eastern princes, who had been misrepresented by Montesquieu. See *Commentaire sur l'Esprit des lois. Oeuvres completes.* ed. Moland (Paris, 1890), XXX, 409. Cited in Franco Venturi, "Oriental Despotism", *Journal of the History of Ideas*, Vol. 24. 1 (January–March 1963): 135–36.

[52] Jackie Assayag, *L'Inde fabuleuse: le charme discret de l'exotisme français XVII–XXe siècles* (Paris: Éditions Kimé, 1999): 82–83.

among the people of antiquity....Apuleius, Quintus Curtis, Clemens Alexandrinus, Philostratus, Porphyry, and Palladio all agree in their encomiums on the extreme temperance and frugality of the Brahmins, their life of retirement and penance, their vows of poverty, and the contempt they show for all the vanities of this world....Their belief in one God only, for which they are so esteemed by all philosophers, continues with them, in the midst of the numberless idols with which their country abounds, and the extravagant superstition of the common people.[53]

In this passage, as in others devoted to the description of the Brahmins[54] Voltaire provided a vigorous opposition to the Jesuit descriptions of Brahmins as worshipping millions of Gods and believing in every kind of superstition and religious excess. The Brahmin even in decline held to high moral and ethical beliefs and in fact, abstained from following the religion of the masses which thrived on idolatry, polytheism, and superstition.

Much of Voltaire's preoccupation with the greatness of Brahmins and their noble religion sprang from the Enlightenment attack on the Church.[55] By describing their belief in a single Godhead, and the greatest antiquity of their religion, Voltaire sought to prove that the Church's teaching and theology were derivative of Hinduism.[56]

---

[53] Voltaire, *The Complete Works of Voltaire*. Edited by Theodore Besterman (Geneva: Institut et Musée Voltaire and Toronto: University of Toronto Press, 1968): Vol. 15, part 2: 180–83.

[54] For example, the section titled 'The Brahmins, the Veda and the Ezour-Veda' in Voltaire, *Additions a l'Essai sur l'histoire générale &c. Et sur l'esprit & les mœurs des nation [sic] depuis Charlemagne jusqu'à nos jours* (Amsterdam, 1764).

[55] See Robert Bartlett, 'On the Politics of Faith and Reason: The Project of Enlightenment in Pierre Bayle and Montesquieu,' *The Journal of Politics*, 63.1 (February 2001): 1–28.

[56] This challenge to the Church was to become a consistent feature of French writings on India albeit not a very influential school of thought. The nineteenth-century French colonial administrator and prolific writer, Louis Jacolliot for instance wrote several books on the

Voltaire was very interested in the influence of India on Greece,[57] the greatest antiquity of the Indian civilization,[58] the resemblance of Sanskrit to Indo-European languages,[59] the similarity between several Hindu and Catholic customs and therefore, of the originality of Hinduism upon which Christianity was founded.[60] The fact that the Indian civilization pre-dated the Chinese meant that India had taught the Chinese the concept of monotheism.[61] Moreover, the origin of the notion of the single Godhead, of the Sovereign Being, invisible, incomprehensible, formless, creator and conserver, just and merciful, was contained in the Vedam, the Shastah and the modern books of the Brahmins.[62] Thus despite the superstitions and ritual in modern India, the

---

originality of Hinduism and the derivation of Christianity from India. Some of his wider works on this topic include *Christna et le Christ*. (Paris: A. Lacroix et cie, 1874) and *The Bible in India: Hindoo Origin of Hebrew and Christian Revelation* (New York: Carleton, 1870).

[57] Voltaire, *Correspondence* Edited by Theodore Besterman, corr. 13663 (Paris: Gallimard, 1964). Vol. 105. Letter Number 17249.

[58] Ibid.: numbers 8370 and 13548.

[59] Ibid.: number 13702.

[60] Ibid.: numbers 12405, 12763, 18677, and 18756. Many writers have commented upon this aspect of Voltaire's writing on India, including Rocher, D. S. Hawley, and Sylvia Murr, 'Les conditions d'émergence du discours sur l'Inde du siècle des Lumières, Inde et Littératures', *Purusartha*, 7, (1983)

[61] From Voltaire, 'The Ignorant Philosopher', *The Complete Works of Voltaire*. Edited by Theodore Besterman (Geneva: Institut et Musée Voltaire and Toronto: University of Toronto Press, 1968): 277.

[62] *Oeuvres...*, Vol. 19. The actual quotation reads 'Parmi tant d'opinions extravagantes, et de superstitions bizarres, croinons-nous que tous ces païens des Indes reconaissant comme nous un Etre infiniment parfait? Qu'ils l'appellent l'Etre des êtres, l'Être souverain, invisible, incomprehensible, sans figure, créateur et conservateur, juste et miséricordieux, qui se plaît à se communiquer aux hommes pour les conduire au bonheur éternal? Ces idées sont contenues dans le Veidam, ce livre des anciens brachmanes, et encore mieux dans le Shasta, plus ancien que le Veidam. Elles sont répandues dans les écrits modernes des bramins.': 415.

notion of monotheism originated with the Brahmins.[63] The earliest man, called Adimo by the Hindus, was appropriated as Adam in the Old Testament, as was Brahma who became Abraham.[64] The religious significance of a purifying dip in the Ganges appeared as baptism in Christianity.[65] The Hindu pantheon of Vishnu, Shiva, Surya, Varuna, Bhumi, and others were appropriated by the Greeks and Romans and therein into early European religion.[66] In these and other passages Voltaire posed an important challenge to the Church. In the first place, he argued that Christianity, the basis for modern Western civilization and the foundation for the 'civilizing mission' was in fact, based on non-Western ideas and religions. This in itself would have completely destroyed any pretensions that missionaries may have had about converting 'heathens'. Along with the non-Western origins of Christianity was the assertion that monotheism, that great definer of advanced religions, was in fact the contribution of the most polytheistic religion in the world. It says much for the intellect and philosophical maturity of Voltaire that he was able to look beyond the numberless manifestations of Gods in Hinduism and recognize what all Hindus have always acknowledged, the essential oneness of the Divine and the unification of all manifestations of God into a single Godhead.[67] This

---

[63] As the previous chapter indicated, Voltaire was not the first to study the similarities between Christianity and Hinduism; in fact the missionaries as far back as Jordanus had already drawn parallels between the religions and the Jesuits had made detailed theological comparisons between these ancient religions. However, Voltaire was the first to claim the greater antiquity of Hinduism and therefore the notion that Christianity was derived from Hinduism and not vice-versa.

[64] Quoted in _The British Discovery of Hinduism in the Eighteenth Century_, edited by Peter Marshall (Cambridge: Cambridge University Press, 1970): 33.

[65] _Oeuvres…_ Vol. 19: 413.

[66] Ibid.

[67] Interestingly Voltaire used the _Lettres_ for much of his information about the religion and customs of the Indians to challenge the

feature of Voltaire's writing was heavily influenced by the Enlightenment search for pre-Christian intellectual and theological roots. Voltaire was by no means alone in his quest for ancient religions, for non-Western roots of Christianity, or in his belief that being Christian was not proof of being civilized. In no way overtly denigrating the efforts of missionaries in the Orient, and at times even praising their efforts to educate and enlighten Orientals, he nonetheless used fictional dialogues, suggestions as to the intellectual development of India and most of all, the argument that Christianity was derived from the Vedic religion, to build a case against the Church.

MONTESQUIEU AND VOLTAIRE REDUX

In comparing the views of Montesquieu and Voltaire on India, it is interesting to note that although they both used many of the same sources their conclusions were markedly different. It seems logical to conclude therefore that both used their sources selectively to prove their own arguments. Both used the works of ancient Greek writers like Strabo, Pliny and Diodorus as well as the travel accounts and memoirs of men like François Bernier and Jean-Baptiste Tavernier. Both drew extensively on the *Lettres* of the Jesuits, although Voltaire minimized their importance considering them biased. Voltaire, who was writing later on, also used the work of British Indologists like Holwell, Nathaniel Halhed, and Alexander Dow,[68] while

---

Church! Where the Lettres had described superstitions and barbaric practices, Voltaire presented these as evidence of the advanced civilization of ancient India.

[68] See François Bernier, *Travels in the Mogul Empire*. Trans. Archibald Constable (1968), Jean-Baptiste Bernier, John Zephaniah Holwell, *Interesting Historical Events relative to the Province of Bengal and the Empire of Indoustan*, Vol. 2 (1767), Nathaniel Halhed, *A Code of Gentoo Laws, or Ordinations of the Pundits* (1776), and Alexander Dow, *The History of Hindostan* (1768).

Montesquieu had used travelogues and accounts of the colonial enterprise like *Collection of Voyages that Contributed
to the Establishment of the East India Company.*[69] While
Montesquieu used his sources literally, drawing descriptions of Indian customs and manners directly from them,
Voltaire used his sources more critically, interrogating the
validity of their claims. Montesquieu's list of subjects of
India, such as the caste system, sati and the condition of
women, and the peculiar customs of India such as polyandry among the Nairs of the Malabar for instance, almost
seem imported from the *Lettres,* which he used liberally
in his citations.

On the other hand, Voltaire chose to minimize the
information about India which was sent back by missionaries even though he had access to them. It seems that missionary accounts were included in his work only as bridges
to what he perceived as gaps in the knowledge about India
provided by Orientalist scholars. While missionary accounts
naturally tended to harp on the backwardness of India
and the need for conversion, the Orientalists were the
new breed of scholars who glorified Indian civilization. In
effect, Voltaire's choice of sources made his opinion about
India as a highly-developed society a foregone conclusion.
From his sources, Voltaire skilfully created an 'India' that
represented the Enlightenment ideal of an advanced and
accomplished civilization, worthy of emulation in many
ways. In a sense, Voltaire was among the first to write
about India romantically as a land of scenic and utopian
beauty. For the next half century, most acceptable views
of India were presented as romantic visions of a land of
great antiquity and cultural achievement.

---

[69] For example, cited in Charles de Secondat, Baron de
Montesquieu, *The Spirit of Laws* (London: G. Bell and Sons, Ltd., 1914).
Translated by Thomas Nugent, revised by J. V. Prichard. Http://www.
constitution.org/cm/sol.htm. Book XVI, How the Laws of Domestic
Slavery Bear a Relation to the Nature of the Climate, 3. That a Plurality
of Wives greatly depends on the Means of supporting them.

Voltaire constantly emphasized the antiquity of Indian civilization through its ancient learning, arts, literature, and the gradual evolution of the caste system. Debating the relative antiquity of Indian and Chinese civilizations, he finally came to the conclusion that the Indian was the older.

It is probable that the Brahmins existed long before the Chinese had their five kings; and what gives rise to this great probability is, that in China the antiquities most sought after are Indian, and that in India there are no Chinese antiquities.[70]

The other evidence for the superior antiquity of India, according to Voltaire, was the 'Shasta' and the discovery of the 'Ezour-Vedam' which proved, by their theological ideas, to be older even than the Chinese religion.[71] Incidentally, the notion of the 'Shasta' was derived from Holwell who equated it to the Sanskrit 'Shastra' meaning sacred text, while the Ezour Vedam appears to have been some sort of commentary on the Vedas, which Voltaire claimed, was of the greatest antiquity.[72]

This antiquity of Indian civilization gave rise to a unique and sought-after morality.

---

[70] From Voltaire, 'The Ignorant Philosopher', *The Works of Voltaire*, Vol. 18, part 2 (Geneva: Institut et Musée Voltaire and Toronto: University of Toronto Press, 1968): 277. (Henceforth 'Works...').

[71] Works..., Vol. 24: 479. Ludo Rocher has written an excellent monograph on the origins, possible authorship and various recensions of the Ezour Vedam. See Ludo Rocher, *Ezourvedam. A French Veda of the Eighteenth Century* (Philadelphia, 1984).

[72] The first French version of the Ezour Vedam appeared in 1778. Voltaire was presented with a copy by a French official in Pondichéry, a Chevalier de Mondave. The text was supposed to be a translation of an original Veda, made by the missionary Roberto de Nobili although this was later proven false. Voltaire donated his copy to the Bibliothèque Royale at Paris.

Those ancient Brahmins were doubtless as bad metaphysicians and ridiculous theologists as the Chaldeans and Persians, and of all the nations that are to the east of China. But what a sublime morality! According to them life was only a death of some years, after which they were to live with the Divinity. They did not confine themselves to being just towards others, but they were rigorous toward themselves. Silences, abstinence, contemplation, the renouncing of all pleasures, were their principal duties. Likewise, from the sages of other nations, they were to learn what was called Wisdom.[73]

This description of the Brahmins of ancient India was a classic Enlightenment view, one that once again challenged the supremacy of the Christian Church by pointing to traditions of asceticism and notions of self-control, frugality, and discipline in non-Christian cultures. The Brahmin was the antithesis of the corrupt Christian clergy, and the epitome of the new ideal of detachment and meditative living. He was perceived as the living repository of the philosophy of ancient India. Looking for a civilization that pre-dated the Greek, and a link to the theological and philosophical ideas of the ancient Greeks, Voltaire believed that this missing link was India. Drawing upon ancient Greek accounts of India, he described the Indians as

remarkable for their mildness as our northern race for their roughness.... In general, the men inhabiting the south East part of the globe have received from nature gentler manners than we who dwell in the western hemisphere. Their climate naturally disposes them to abstinence from strong liquors and meats, foods which inflame the blood frequently to a degree of madness; and although the natural goodness of their dispositions may have been corrupted by superstition and the repeated irruptions of foreigners, yet all travellers agree that these people have nothing of

---

[73] From 'The Ignorant Philosopher', *Works...*, Vol. 18, part 2: 227.

that petulance and sourness in their nature which had cost so much pains to control in the people of the North.

There being so great a physical difference between us and the natives of India, there must undoubtedly have been as great a moral one. Their vices were in general less violent than ours.[74]

This was in stark contrast to Montesquieu's description of a passive civilization and a country where

The heat of the climate may be so excessive as to deprive the body of all vigour and strength. Then the faintness is communicated to the mind; there is no curiosity, no enterprise, no generosity of sentiment; the inclinations are all passive; indolence constitutes the utmost happiness; scarcely any punishment is so severe as mental employment; and slavery is more supportable than the force and vigour of mind necessary for human conduct.[75]

Voltaire's was an image of an ideal people, who possessed few faults and a sweetness and mildness of disposition which was praiseworthy. What in Voltaire's account was seen as mildness was described by missionaries as 'weakness' and 'insinuating'. Where Montesquieu described the Indians as indolent in contrast to the noble races of the colder North, Voltaire described them as mild, abstinent and possessing far fewer and less offensive vices than Europeans. In this description of India, Voltaire chose to focus only on ancient Greek accounts of thriving trade and industrious people. Following on the great achievements of the ancient Brahmins, he lamented that India, in the current day, practised a degenerate form of the noble 'religion of Brahma'. Science and the arts languished and Brahmins either oppressed the masses and preyed upon

---

[74] 'Ancient and Modern History', *Works...*, Vol. 13, part 1: 179.
[75] Ibid.

their superstitions, or chose to become ascetic and live in solitary contemplation of their great philosophies.[76] Despite his obvious knowledge and use of later writers like Bernier and Tavernier, he did not mention them or their criticism of the superstitions of the common people. In all justice, he tried in all his essays on India to isolate what *he* believed to be indigenous, leaving out all external influence which may have changed Indian civilization. Containing none of the rhetoric which denounced Indians as a class of lazy idlers and drunken degenerates as voiced especially in the missionary accounts of India, Voltaire in fact suggested that many of the current ills of Indian society were imported into India with the constant stream of foreign invasions and were totally unnatural to the disposition of the Indian. Specifically, he suggested that Muslim invasion was probably responsible for this decline[77] and thereby accepted and perpetuated the idea of the Sultanate in India being a dark age. To him, the invasion of the Muslims into India caused a corruption of the pure Hindu mind.

By the time Voltaire came along, the essential elements of the French story of India were already in place. An aspect of French writings on India which was already present by the time of Voltaire was the anti-Islamic sentiment. In this issue, both Montesquieu and Voltaire were united. According to Montesquieu, Christianity was most conducive to a moderate government, and Islam to a despotic government.[78] In fact the *Esprit* can be seen as an opposition of two major forms of civilization, the liberal West and the despotic East, the former characterized by

---

[76] *Works...*, Vol. 15, part 2: 190.

[77] Ibid.: 175.

[78] Ibid., Book XXIV: Of Laws in relation to Religion Considered in Itself, and in its Doctrines, part 3: That a moderate Government is most agreeable to the Christian Religion, and a despotic Government to the Mahometan.

Christianity 'which ordains that men should love each other, would, without doubt, have every nation blest with the best civil, the best political laws; because these, next to this religion, are the greatest good that men can give and receive',[79] the latter by Islam which is a despotic and unfree religion. To this extent, the progression from the works of the missionaries in their anti-Islamic rhetoric, to the secular work of Montesquieu on the hierarchy of political systems and law is clear. Although the subject was entirely new, the opinion was an old one.

As a corollary to the anti-Islamic stance, the sympathetic view of India was a foregone conclusion. While Montesquieu bemoaned the despotic government of the East, including India and China, he wrote of the specific customs of these countries in an apologist tone which explained the reasons for the existence of each of the customs which seemed so barbaric to the West.

Voltaire, while also presenting India as a foil to the negative image of Islam, needed to be more circumspect, since he also posed Brahminism as a good philosophy that could provide much intellectual fodder for Europe and even a model to rival the Greco-Roman model of European antiquity. While on the one hand, Hinduism was theoretically acceptable as a philosophy to many intellectuals in Europe, how was one to account for the many social evils present in India? Having separated the ancient theology of Brahminism from the more contemporary form of Indian religion which Voltaire described as Hinduism (and along the way elevated the former to the level of an omniscient and sublime philosophical concept and its followers to the position of enlightened individuals) it was difficult to separate the ideal from the reality without creating a scapegoat. This scapegoat, conveniently hated and misunderstood by Europeans for centuries, was Islam.[80] Already

---

[79] Ibid., part 1: Of Religion in General.

[80] See for instance the relations between Christian missionaries and Muslims in James Ryan, 'Missionary Saints of the High Middle

misrepresented in Europe, it was easy enough to accept a reductionist view of Indian civilization as having taken a sudden turn downwards as a result of the Islamic invasions. This theory was a powerful sentiment in all French writings on India and echoed what many Hindus in India already felt about the Muslim conquerors thus reproducing and legitimizing a communalist view of history.[81] In fact, Jackie Assayag attributes the Hindu-Muslim conflict presented in plays like La Harpe's *Les brames* to Voltaire's influence.[82]

Ages: Martyrdom, Popular Veneration, and Canonization', *The Catholic Historical Review* 90.1 (2004): 1–28.

[81] The irony of such a process is that Indians had no 'history' before the colonial experience. Therefore 'history' as India came to learn it was solely a product of Western writing and understanding of India's past. Legitimating Indian 'history' came by being viewed through a Western lens, Indians having no sense of 'rational, logical, unbiased history' despite the fact that all of the source material for these Western histories was in fact Indian! The earliest histories which were taught to Indians were naturally written by logical, rational Western historians, who did not allow biases to cloud their judgement. Having concluded, on the basis of faulty and incomplete knowledge that Islam had wrought the downfall of the Hindu civilization, the West accepted this as yet another *fait accompli* for their belief that Islam was a destructive religion. In a vicious cycle of intellectual colonization, this theory was taught to all Indian students who had been brought up to believe in the superiority and rationality of the Western thought process. An excellent account of the creation of communalism is Gyan Pandey, *The Construction of Communalism in Colonial North India,* (Oxford and New York: OUP, 1990). Pandey recounts through a careful analysis of the historical record how the communal past, so long transmitted as an intrinsic part of India's social web, was in reality a creation of the complex processes of nineteenth-century colonialism and the emerging Indian nationalism. This is a good example of how colonialism created a past which did not exist, just as this study seeks to study the many images of India which were created to accommodate the French political and colonial agenda.

[82] Written by La Harpe in 1783, *Les brames* presented many of the key ideas of the Enlightenment, such as the nature of man, development of civilization, the origin of religion and the place of the Oriental Despot within an Indian setting. The tragedy portrayed an Indian Muslim

Tracing La Harpe's beliefs to his preceptor Voltaire, she sees the former's representation of the Muslim tyrant and oppressor as a reflection of Voltaire's belief.[83] Voltaire is an example of how the French created their own understanding of 'India' as a foil for their own agendas. The antecedents of French interest in India, encompassing religious, economic, and political motives were woefully inadequate in terms of presenting a coherent picture of the land and its people. Voltaire was the first secular writer to create a notion of 'India' and what defined 'Indian religion' from the erratic and seemingly unconnected descriptions which had preceded him. Yet, given the vastness of the land and its sheer diversity, Voltaire's image too presented a select idea of India which was fed by the intellectual passions and needs of the day. Voltaire presented India as the land of Brahmins. This land had withstood the onslaught of many foreign peoples and religions that had corrupted its society in many ways but it was essentially Brahminic in thought and composition. In Voltaire's own definition this claim to being 'Brahminical' was basically equated with a Brahminical notion of India. As Bernard Cohn pointed out in his seminal study on *Colonialism and its Forms of Knowledge*, Brahmins as the traditional transmitters of the academic tradition in India were the most forthcoming to Europeans in India as translators, informants, etc., simply because they were by and large the people who *could* communicate with the foreigners. Naturally, the information they provided about Indian customs and religion tended to be very heavily Brahminical rather than influenced by popular

---

ruler as an evil tyrant and his Hindu subjects as suffering under his despotic oppression. See Jackie Assayag, 'L'Inde dans le théâtre des Lumières une tragédie théologico-politique inédite de Jean-François de la Harpe : Les Brames (1783)', *Purusartha* (1998), Vol. 20: 301–25.

[83] Jackie Assayag, *L'Inde fabuleuse: le charme discret de l'exotisme français XVII–XXe siècles* (Paris: Éditions Kimé, 1999): 95.

religion which was seen by the Brahmins as a crude and unsophisticated culture. So the early image of India as Hindu was further refined by its emphasis on a *Brahminic* core and purity as is reflected in Voltaire's writings.[84]

As the foremost *philosophes* of the day, the opinions of Voltaire and Montesquieu carried into a number of projects. In particular, their views about India were identified by specific groups; Montesquieu's were cited as justification for the British colonization of India. As Joseph Lew points out, the model of the 'Oriental Despot' created by Montesquieu was used by the British to justify colonial expansion in India amidst concerns of the enervating

---

[84] In an interesting turn of events, however, the heavy British reliance on Brahmins changed after the Mutiny of 1857. In their push to build a strong and unchallenged Empire in India, the British tried to divide up the loyalties of their Indian subjects by using various theories to justify preferential treatment of different groups, castes, and religions at different times. These theories in turn led to groups of Indians, like Hindus, Muslims and Parsis for example, jockeying for positions within the Raj, in exactly the way the rulers had envisioned, and internalizing the definitions and artificial past that the British had created for them, simply because it suited them, economically and socially, to do so. Historians have studied the creation of 'martial' castes. It is not the subject of this work and in fact requires a separate historical inquiry but I propose that the basis of the present-day caste wars can also be traced to this creation of artificial pasts during the colonial period. During a period when both Indians and British were seeking to benefit from each other, Brahmins were quite willing to be portrayed as learned, erudite, upper caste and privileged. As the nineteenth century progressed however, economic vicissitudes and new processes of caste formation created a distinct and rigid hierarchy (see Nicholas Dirks, *Castes of Mind* (Princeton, NJ: Princeton University Press, 2002)) in place of the previous fluidity and looseness of the caste identity. Lower castes seeking to improve their position and their economic and social status looked around for scapegoats and found it in the upper castes, particularly in the Brahmins, who according to colonial histories, had oppressed the common people for centuries. This was the beginning of a long and bitter battle against the upper castes, especially the Brahmins, which in many ways, defines the socio-political scene of India even today.

effect of the Indian climate on robust British men.[85] As a result his views have frequently been cited in works which examine the British colonial mission and policy in India.[86] Voltaire on the other hand provided no such justification for colonization in India. His views were enthusiastically espoused by Orientalists like William Jones, but otherwise used by French Indologists as representing a view of India uncorrupted by the sordidity of governance.

[85] Joseph E. Lew, 'The Plague of Imperial Desire: Montesquieu, Gibbon, Brougham and Mary Shelley's "The Last Man"', *Romanticism and Colonialism. Writing and Empire, 1780–1830*. Edited by Tim Fulford and Peter Kitson (Cambridge: Cambridge University Press, 1998): 272.

[86] For example, James Mill, in his opus, *The History of British India* (London, 1818) made copious references to Montesquieu to justify British colonial rule in India. Contemporary scholars like Udayon Misra, *The Raj in Fiction: A Study of Nineteenth Century British Attitudes Towards India* (Delhi: B. R. Pub. Corp, 1987) and Thomas Metcalf, *Ideologies of the Raj* (Cambridge: CUP, 1994) have noted the frequent use by British colonial officials and writers, of Montesquieu's model of Oriental Despotism to justify their presence and activities in India.

Chapter 3

The Business of Serious Academics: Indology and the Study of India

India was full of surprise: an original and profound philosophy, a delicate poetry which was at once naïve and all-comprehending, exquisite art, refined morals and a civilization which was older than all others....[1]

The newest group to turn to the study of India was the academics.[2] In some cases these individuals began as religious scholars who then joined academia. In other cases, they turned to India because of the interest that it had generated in the French Enlightenment. Since these scholars eventually devoted themselves almost exclusively to the study of India, presumably with scholarly purpose, I term them the early 'Indologists'.[3] This chapter describes the work of the first such Indologists—Joseph Deguignes, Anquetil-Duperron, and Antoine Chézy. Chézy belongs

---

[1] 'L'Inde réservait donc cette surprise: une philosophie originale et profonde, une poésie delicate, naïve et savante à la fois, un art exquis, des moeurs raffinées, une civilisation antérieure à toutes les autres!'Felix Lacôte, 'L'Indianisme', *Société Asiatique: Livre du centenaire* (Paris: La Société Asiatique, 1922): 220–21.

[2] While Voltaire was arguably very academic, I use the term academic here to demarcate individuals who lived solely by their research and publications and were appointed to academic positions.

[3] I use the term Indology to denote a field where the study of India is accomplished through a textual study of historical works in various Indian languages. An Indologist would be an expert in at least one Indian language. The terms Indology and Indic studies are interchangeable.

chronologically in the nineteenth century but his romantic vision of India which reflected Voltaire's image has led to his inclusion in this section. For the most part the work of scholars on India echoed Voltaire's search for the origins of civilization in India.[4] Assuming that Sanskrit texts were the key to understanding India's Brahminic culture Deguignes, Duperron and Chézy focused on finding original or translated Sanskrit texts and basing their writings and image of India on these. The elements of continuity in the academic image of India thus include the search for Sanskrit, the romantic ideal of India, and the dominance of Paris.

AN ANCIENT CIVILIZATION: SEARCHING FOR SANSKRIT

The first aspect of continuity was the importance of antiquity, and as a result, the focus on Sanskrit. Just as Voltaire had emphasized the value of the Indian civilization because it was the oldest, nineteenth-century scholars followed a search for the oldest texts which represented the civilization of India. The emphasis on antiquity meant that the oldest language, Sanskrit, had to be studied. Unfortunately, Sanskrit had not yet been deciphered. According to Henry Yule, 'The earliest direct intimation of knowledge of the existence of the Vedas, the earliest sacred texts of the Indic Aryans, appears to be in the book called *De Tribus Impostoribus* said to have been printed in 1598, in which they are mentioned. This knowledge probably came through the Arabs. Thus we do not trace back any direct allusion to the Vedas in European books, before the year 1600 or thereabouts. There seems good reason to believe, however, that the Jesuit missionaries

---

[4] The similarity between the work of Voltaire and of Deguignes ends here. The two were opposed in their view of the unity of human history, Chinese history and the history of the Church. See J. G. A. Pocock, *Barbarism and Religion: Narratives of Civil Government* (Cambridge: CUP, 2001): 114–17.

had information on the subject at a much earlier date. St. Francis Xavier had frequent discussions with Brahmins, and one went so far as to communicate to him the *mantra* '*Om śrīnārāyana nāmah*'.[5] In 1559 a learned Brahmin at Goa was converted by Father Belchior Carneyro,[6] and baptized by the name of Manuel. 'He afterwards (with the Viceroy's sanction!) went by night and robbed a Brahmin on the mainland who had collected many MSS, and presented the spoils to the Fathers, with great satisfaction to himself and them.'[7] While Yule's work notes that information about the Vedas existed in Europe from about the end of the sixteenth century, these references continued to be vague. Voltaire popularized the Ezour Vedam which was later discovered to be a fake.[8] The first accurate reference to a Veda occurred in Pierre Sonnerat's late eighteenth-century work.[9] Since Sanskrit had not been deciphered, Enlightenment scholars, including Voltaire, continued to use Arabic and Persian translations of the Vedas, in addition to gleaning some information from the writings of missionaries.

The reason for the inaccessibility of the Vedas seems to have been the unwillingness of Brahmins to translate the

---

[5] 'I salute you oh Lord Narayana.'

[6] The only reference to this missionary appears in Yule's text. However, a Portuguese Jesuit missionary named Belchior Carneiro appears frequently in missions to the Far East. He was a central figure of the Goa inquisition and eventually went on to become the Bishop of Macao.

[7] Henry Yule, *Hobson-Jobson: A Glossary of Colloquial Anglo-Indian Words and Phrases, and of Kindred Terms, Etymological, Historical, Geographical and Discursive*. New edn William Crooke (London: J. Murray, 1903), 961–62. Http://dsal.uchicago.edu/cgi-bin/philologic/getobject.pl?c.2:1:407.hobson. Crooke, who edited this version, mentions that he was unable to locate the actual book in the British Library.

[8] See Voltaire in Chapter 2: 98.

[9] Henry Yule, *Hobson-Jobson*: 962. Http://dsal.uchicago.edu/cgi-bin/philologic/getobject.pl?c.2:1:407.hobson. Sonnerat explained the nature of the Vedas in the works *St. Pierre* and *Chaumière Indienne*.

ancient information of which they were the custodians.[10] Once the colonial enterprises of the eighteenth century began establishing their territorial hold in India there was naturally a greater accessibility to these texts. While the sacred texts were the most prized, since Sanskrit had not yet been deciphered and Brahmins blocked European access to them, European scholars turned to 'secular' literary texts. The first expression of this focus on India was therefore the 'discovery'[11] and translation of ancient Indian literature. The first breakthrough came with the British Indologist William Jones' translation of the ancient Sanskrit poet Kalidasa's famous play, *Shakuntala* from an existing Persian version. Following Jones, there was a spate of translations of Sanskrit texts which had been translated during the Middle Ages into Arabic and Persian. Scholars launched a search to collect the 'original' Sanskrit texts and decipher Sanskrit. Sanskrit had a certain aura in Europe since it was considered the language of the ancients of India. The German Schopenhauer, believed that 'Sanskrit literature will be no less influential for our time than Greek literature was in the fifteenth century for the Renaissance'.[12] This esteem for Sanskrit was partly

---

[10] This reluctance to impart knowledge about their ancient religion can be found described in most of the early works, particularly those written by missionaries, including the *Lettres Édifiantes*.

[11] Interestingly, European Indologists claimed to have 'discovered' the ancient texts of India even though these had been around for centuries and were widely disseminated all over Asia and even parts of the African continent. Islamic writers in particular had translated many of these texts earlier and in fact the first access to Indian texts came to Europe through these Islamic translations. Yet European scholars still looked upon their findings as 'discoveries' based on the argument that the texts that they were studying were the 'original' Indian texts and not adaptations or later versions. This claim in itself was false since the oral tradition of learning in India meant that any written texts were versions of the original which had been committed to writing only centuries after being passed down orally.

[12] Quoted in Raymond Schwab, *The Oriental Renaissance* (New York: Columbia University Press, 1984): 13.

due to the emerging theory that Sanskrit was the language of the early Indo-European or Aryan people who were the ancestors of most of Western Europe. In fact, the earliest scholars of India were philologists who compared the linguistic and philological similarities between Sanskrit and the Indo-European group of languages. Jean Filliozat, the twentieth-century Indologist summed up the significance of India for many scholars of the nineteenth century by pointing out that India was not merely of isolated academic interest, but was in fact the answer to many burning philosophical questions, and provided a view of the human condition.[13] Quoting Max Müller's work 'India, what can it teach us', Filliozat pointed out that India was not merely of interest because of her ancient languages, culture or religions as Müller had described, but because the knowledge of Sanskrit contained the key to knowledge about the ancient Indo-European community. According to Filliozat,

...on the importance of India like [in the] human field. If India imports us [interests us/ occupies us], indeed, it is not only for the value in our eyes or the interest for us of its knowledge, its thought, its institutions, its arts: it is not only because it can teach us something about our ancestral past, owing to the fact that it kept many traces of a [linguistic] community of origin of [between] its Sanskrit with our languages [European]....[14]

---

[13] According to Trautmann, the timing of the comparison between Sanskrit and Germanic languages in the late eighteenth and nineteenth-century can be directly traced to the translation of Sanskrit by Jones, Anquetil-Duperron and others. Thomas R. Trautmann, 'Languages and Nations', in *The Dravidian Proof in Colonial Madras (CA: University of California Press, 2006):* 40–41.

[14] '...sur l'importance de l'Inde comme domaine humain. Si l'Inde nous importe, en effet, ce n'est pas seulement pour la valeur à nos yeux ou l'intérêt pour nous de son savoir, de sa pensée, de ses institutions, de ses arts: ce n'est pas seulement parce qu'elle peut nous apprendre quelque chose sur notre passé ancestral, du fait qu'elle a gardé maintes traces d'une communauté d'origine de son Sanskrit avec nos langues....'

Another reason why Sanskrit was the locus of Indic studies at this time was the reverence which Brahmins had for the language. Once the British were established as the rulers of Bengal by 1767, the Brahmins were the group who most readily acted as interpreters and informants to Europeans, and informed European views about Indian society and culture. As Bernard Cohn points out, even though they were unwilling to part with their knowledge of Sanskrit, their views about the primacy of Sanskrit texts were communicated to the European scholar who came to look upon Sanskritic texts as the definitive guidelines for law, religion, and politics.[15]

Since Sanskrit had not been deciphered, the earliest French academics who studied India had to rely on translations. Among these scholars was Joseph Deguignes. Joseph Deguignes, Arabist and Sinologist was one of the new breed of historians who envisaged a universal history of the world. He set out to study the Indian manuscripts available in Europe in order to fill the gaps which Bossuet, the father of universal history, had left in his seventeenth-century work.[16] Bossuet had ignored the existence of the greater

---

Jean Filliozat, 'La naissance et l'essor de l'indianisme', *Bulletin de la Société des études indo-chinoises de Saigon*, Vol. 29, issue 4, 1954: 1.

[15] Bernard Cohn's chapter on 'The command of language and the language of command', in his book, *Colonialism and its Forms of Knowledge* (Princeton University Press: Princeton, 1996) deals with this issue more thoroughly.

[16] Jacques-Benigne Bossuet was a seventeenth-century French Bishop. Considered one of the greatest orators in French history he wrote his *Discours sur l'histoire universelle* as part of his duties to tutor the Dauphin in 1681. The work was a philosophical treatise where he described God's historical relationship with man in much the same manner as the Old Testament. According to him, the value of such a work was that 'This kind of universal history is to the history of every country and of every people what a world map is to particular maps. In a particular map you see all the details of a kingdom or a province as such. But a general map teaches you to place these parts of the world in their context; you see what Paris or the Ile-de-France is in

part of the globe except for Europe and the limited non-western contacts of the Jews, Greek, and Romans. Unlike the *philosophes* who merely dabbled in academic research, Deguignes extensively read up on his subject. Impatient about learning the language, however, he chose to rely on Arab and Chinese texts about India for his work.[17] He introduced India in his first great work titled *Histoire générale des Huns, des Turcs, des Mongols et autres Tartares occidentaux* which was published in 1756.[18] Deguignes' interest in India was further piqued by his discovery of an Arab version of the Sanskrit text *Amritakunsha* or the Pot of Ambrosia which described the science of levitation, divination, and yoga.[19] He also researched several historical

---

the kingdom, what the kingdom is in Europe, and what Europe is in the world. In the same manner, particular histories show the sequence of events that have occurred in a nation in all their detail. But in order to understand everything, we must know what connection that history might have with others; and that can be done by a condensation in which we can perceive, as in one glance, the entire sequence of time. Such a condensation, Monseigneur, will afford you a grand view' (p. 4).

[17] Deguignes was an Arabist and Sinologist by training. He was a professor of Arabic studies (Syriac) at the *Collège de France*. His interest in India came through his familiarity with various Arabic language texts which had translated Indian texts or had narrated the Muslim conquest of India.

[18] An important aspect of French Indological studies was the active role it played in Anglo-French colonial rivalry. This rivalry was mostly articulated by officials, and later, by scholars. I deal with this aspect of Indological studies later in this chapter. However, it is interesting to note that while in Deguignes' time this rivalry was non-existent, the twentieth-century Indologist Jean Filliozat who was very much involved in the colonial rivalry pointed out that the identification of the Greek reference to Sandrokottus as Chandra Gupta Maurya, which was credited to William Jones, was really the discovery of De Guignes who made this claim as early as 1772.

[19] The following information about the text is via email from Eric Lewis Beverley 'The text is "Amrita-kunda", which would be a pool or tank of nectar/ambrosia. At least that is the Sanskrit name of the text— the Arabic translation was Hauz al-Hayat, I believe. From what I recall, this is an Arabic translation of a Sanskrit mystical text found current

texts written in the medieval period in Persian. He was the first to translate portions of these, and then to use these to produce his own historical articles on India. He furthered his knowledge about India with copious correspondence with a Tamil scholar who was a linguist and spoke French fluently. Maridas Poullé or Maridas Pillai[20] of Pondichéry was a scholar of French and Latin, who had played an invaluable role as intermediary and interpreter to missionaries, voyagers, and scholars alike, from Père Coeurdoux to Le Gentil the astronomer. Pillai was the inspiration for Deguignes' works on India, providing him with a French translation of the *Bhagavatam* which in turn was Pillai's own Tamil version of the *Bhagavata Purana*.[21] From this work came Deguignes' *Réflexions sur un livre indien intitulé Bâgavadam*, which was published in 1777 and firmly placed India within the scope of 'universal history'. Following this work Deguignes also had three other works on India published in 1780 as *Recherches historiques sur la religion indienne et sur les livres fondamentaux de cette religion qui ont été traduits en chinois*. He was able to clearly establish the trade and diplomatic contacts

---

in Northeast India that eventually became a fairly prominent text in the Middle East (and perhaps through there, Europe). The text has also been referred to by Carl Ernst in the context of Muslim mysticism in "Situating Sufism and Yoga", Annemarie Schimmel Memorial Lecture, Royal Asiatic Society, London, 11 December 2003.'

[20] Pillai was one of the few native Pondichériens who not only corresponded regularly with the French but also kept records of his correspondence and his work. Along with the diary of Ananda Ranga Pillai, Maridas Pillai's records form an important narrative of native history.

[21] The reason why Deguignes did not ask Pillai for a Sanskrit version is a mystery. The unpublished papers of Pillai are preserved at the *Bibliothèque Nationale*. The most recent publication of his work is J.B.P. More, *La Civilisation Indienne et les Fables Hindoues du Panchatantra de Mardas Poullé* (Paris, Collection Archéologie et Histoire, De Boccard, 2004) and J.B.P. More, *Bagavadam ouBhāgavata Purāṇa. Ouvrage religieux et philosophique indien traduit par Maridas Poullé de Pondichéry en 1769* (Paris: Éditions Irish, 2004).

between India and China which had led to the exchange of cultural and philosophical ideas and the compilation of Chinese books on Indian religion[22] but he was not the first to establish the link between Buddhism and India. That discovery was made by Eugene Burnouf and is discussed later in the book. The value of Deguignes' work was summed up by Filliozat when he wrote that because of him 'the civilization of India was no longer an enigma that one had no means of deciphering. It took its place among the world's other civilizations, and the science of Indian antiquity found its methodology.'[23] Deguignes' arrival at the study of India via the study of Arabic and Chinese texts also highlights the importance that India had for Enlightenment scholars. I have called him an early 'Indologist' despite his academic specialization elsewhere, solely due to the prominent inclusion of India in his works.

Soon after this initial effort, Anquetil-Duperron undertook the study of India. Born Abraham Hyacinthe Anquetil Duperron in Paris in 1731, he is considered the earliest French Indologist. Originally intended for the Church, he studied at the University of Paris, the *Collège Mazarin* and also with the noted Jansenist scholar Comte Caylus. After his studies he returned to Paris and continued his studies in Hebrew at the *Bibliothèque Royale* when he learnt about the existence of an Avestic manuscript, the *Vendidade Sade*, in Oxford in 1754. By this time Anquetil was convinced that the key to all European culture lay in the early Indo-European works. Even though he was particularly interested in the ancient culture of the Zoroastrians of Persia

---

[22] Chinese travellers, and later on, Buddhist pilgrims coming to study at the great Buddhist universities in India like Nalanda had left accounts of their travels and their descriptions of the customs and people they encountered, as early as the Mauryan period of Indian history in the 3rd century AD.

[23] Quoted in Raymond Schwab, *The Oriental Renaissance* (New York: Columbia University Press, 1984): 152.

from the Avestic works available to him he also formed the theory that Sanskrit was the oldest link to the Indo-Europeans and therefore that the key to all human thought lay in Asia. According to Anquetil, 'Asia is an uncultivated/ unknown land which we other Europeans have neglected. Yet it is where humanity took its source [originated].'[24] He thought that India and the opening of Sanskrit literature to the West could provide a scientific basis for the Bible and even establish the presence of an ancient people to rival the ancient civilization of the Jews. In fact, although Anquetil's works were not published until much later, he wrote in his letters that India could well constitute 'the missing link' between the civilizations of the East and West by providing a common history for all mankind. It is from Anquetil and other such scholars that Voltaire eventually formed the idea that the achievements of an ancient non-Western civilization could rival the Western model of the Greco-Roman civilization.[25]

At the time the West had not yet deciphered Sanskrit. The best that Anquetil could do was to obtain a sample of Sanskrit letters from Oxford. Finding these measures inadequate for his study Anquetil decided to go to India in search of the key to understanding and reading Sanskrit as well as a search for Zoroastrian manuscripts to further research the Near East and Persia. He was engaged by

---

[24] 'L'Asie est une terre inculte que nous négligeons nous autres Européens. C'est pourtant où le genre humain a pris sa source.'Anquetil Duperron, letter dated June 19, 1759 from Surat to Comte Caylus. *Lettres Inédites d'Henri IV et de plusieurs personages célèbres* (Paris: Henri Tardieu, An X (1802)): 222.

[25] Although Anquetil's works were published later than the time Voltaire was writing about India, Voltaire possessed many such views by French adventurers and travellers in his personal library including works by Réne Madec, Abbé Raynal, Thève not, Tavernier, etc. In addition he debated this view in his letters and was informed of scholars like Anquetil by his correspondents. For a complete list of the works on India found in his library see the appendix in Daniel Hawley, 'L'Inde de Voltaire', *Studies on Voltaire and the 18th century*, Vol. CXX (1974).

the *Compagnie des Indes* and arrived in India in 1754. He remained until 1762 when he returned to Paris via England. In this time, he was affiliated with and remained in contact with several societies like the *Académie des inscriptions et belles-lettres*[26] as well as official organizations like the *Bibliothèque du Roi* and the prominent French functionaries in India including the governors of French India. In 1763 the Abbé Barthélemy, a member of the *Académie des Inscriptions* had asked the Père Coeurdoux[27] to collect and compile a list of words and a basic Sanskrit grammar. Although Coeurdoux's efforts did not bear fruit, Anquetil maintained a constant correspondence with him from 1768–75 and was greatly aided in his studies on Sanskrit by this correspondence.[28]

He therefore not only constantly communicated his observations and findings to academics in France but also made the most of his sojourn by means of his well-placed contacts in India. In a sojourn, which was marked by trials including illnesses, heat exhaustion and academic setbacks, Anquetil persevered in his attempt to converse with Parsi high priests and Brahmins in an attempt to learn Persian and Sanskrit and trace the roots of the Judeo-Christian tradition back to India. In a letter to Comte Caylus he

---

[26] Much of Anquetil's work was first published in the *Mémoires* of the *Académie*. At least 17 articles by Anquetil were published in the *Mémoires de l'Académie des inscriptions et belles-lettres* between 1763–85. See Deloche and Filliozat, *Zend-Avesta, discours préliminaire, commentaires et notes J. Deloche, M. et P.-S. Filliozat.* (Paris: Maisonneuve et Larose, 1997): 49–50.

[27] Renou notes that Coeurdoux was one of the first to suggest the link between Sanskrit and the classical languages of the West. Louis Renou, *The Influence of Indian Thought on French Literature* (Adyar, 1948): 2–3.

[28] Coeurdoux and Anquetil corresponded about several topics other than Sanskrit grammar, among which they exchanged the view that Sanskrit was possibly as old as Greek and Latin. *Lettres Inédites d'Henri IV et de plusieurs personages célèbres* (Paris: Henri Tardieu, An X 1802).

described his excitement at being able to converse with some Brahmins as well as his anxiety to recover the Indian texts which would definitively link the ancient histories of India and Greece.[29] According to Deloche and Filliozat, Anquetil grew to hold three strong beliefs about India during his travels in the Indian subcontinent in an extensive and exhaustive search for manuscripts and knowledge. First, despite his personal vicissitudes and hardships in India he began to believe in the essential equality of all races. This belief sprang from his wide knowledge of Oriental texts and his admiration of the level of civilization he had seen in Asia. His belief was also significant since he remained a religious Christian throughout his lifetime, yet ahead of his time was able to perceive the qualities of other peoples without subjecting them to a Eurocentric yardstick of measurement. Second, he grew to love India and Indians. Third, arising from his love for India, he was convinced that the English enterprise in India was fundamentally unfair.[30]

Anquetil also tried to find the key to deciphering Sanskrit. He tried to retrieve the old Sanskrit works in two ways. First, he used a Persian version of the Upanishads and his conversations with Parsi high priests to produce a French translation of the work. In doing so he provided a valuable linguistic channel for retrieving works once thought lost. He proved that ancient works continued to exist in modified forms in other languages and cultures and therefore could be retrieved. For example, he wrote to Caylus during his travels communicating his hope that the Egyptian script could be deciphered using the Indian

---

[29] Letter dated 15 December 1754 from the Orient. Ibid.: 219.

[30] According to Deloche and Filliozat, *Zend-Avesta, discours préliminaire, commentaires et notes J. Deloche, M. et P.-S. Filliozat* (Paris: Maisonneuve et Larose, 1997): 52, Anquetil describes the huge drain of wealth from Bengal following the British victory at the Battle of Plassey as well as the exploitation of that country by Europeans. But the threefold conclusion is the opinion of Deloche and Filliozat, indicating that academic rivalry between the French and English still exists.

script.[31] He also petitioned the Catholic missions for their compilation of Sanskrit letters and received an incomplete Sanskrit vocabulary which was compiled by all the Catholic missions which had worked in India. He used this in conjunction with another dictionary and grammar which was available in the *Bibliothèque Royale* due to Royal direction for compiling a collection of Indian works. As a linguist, he was a thorough perfectionist.

Anquetil continued in his lifetime to harness his scholarship on India to humanism[32] and the study of human nature. He believed that there were essentially two ways to understand humanity: either by studying metaphysics and deconstructing man and his abilities and achievements, or by studying history and examining people in action. He stated in his *Discours Préliminaire ou Introduction au Zend Avesta* that it was the latter course which appealed to him.[33] Anquetil laid out a detailed path by which he proposed to ensure that his work was as historically objective as possible. The precautions he took included providing extensive descriptions of his experiences, attempting to recover as many ancient texts as possible rather than having to rely on later interpretations and interpolations, learning the languages in which the texts were written (Anquetil himself mastered Persian, Sanskrit, Zend, Avestan, and Pahlavi while in India) and undertaking to learn about and observe the people and their country, customs, sciences,

---

[31] Letter dated 15 December 1754 from the Orient. *Lettres Inédites d'Henri IV et de plusieurs personages célèbres* (Paris: Henri Tardieu, An X (1802)): 219. Presumably Anquetil meant the Sanskrit script when he referred to the 'Indian script'. The theory was based on a belief in the interaction between ancient civilizations and cultural exchange which would have led to common practices in culture and language.

[32] I use this term to indicate the belief in the essential equality of all people and the ability of all humans to distinguish between right and wrong based on rational thought.

[33] Deloche and Filliozat, *Zend-Avesta, discours préliminaire, commentaires et notes J. Deloche, M. et P.-S. Filliozat* (Paris: Maisonneuve et Larose, 1997): 5–6.

arts, morals and politics.[34] Halbfass has also commented on Anquetil's determination to study India as dispassionately as possible, citing the latter as writing, 'let us study the Indians as we study the Greeks and Romans—critically, but respectfully, and without ridiculing them'.[35]

Convinced that the key to further knowledge lay in learning the local languages, Anquetil proposed a radical idea. He suggested that the only way to learn about the world was to appoint a number of travelling scholars in different parts of the world. These *académies ambulantes* would then try to gather as much knowledge about the area they were stationed at and bring that knowledge back with them to France. A total of 80 such scholars were proposed to be appointed with two each in Chile, Mexico, Peru and Canada accounting for eight in the Americas; two each in Senegal, Cape of Good Hope, Ethiopia and Cairo accounting for eight in Africa; four each at Marseilles and the port of L'Orient in France to co-ordinate the efforts of all the other scholars, and finally a total of 48 scholars appointed all over Asia, including two each at Constantinople, Baghdad, Isfahan, Delhi, Astrakhan, Tartary, Tibet, Chinese Tartary, Kamchatka, Peking, Canton, Siam, Patna, Bengal, Pondichéry, Surat, Ceylon, Mahé, Pune and Bassora, and four each in the Isles of the Indian Ocean and the China Sea Islands.[36] According to Anquetil,

> Most of the travellers are satisfied to ask the Brahmins (and it is the same process with the ministers of religion in all countries) about the basis of their doctrines, what they believe on this and that; some of them go so far as

---

[34] Ibid.: 7–10.

[35] Wilhelm Halbfass, *India and Europe. An Essay in Understanding.* (Albany, N.Y.: State University of New York Press, 1988): 369. Cited from Anquetil Duperron, *Recherches historiques et géographiques*, appendix: 66.

[36] Deloche and Filliozat, *Zend-Avesta, discours préliminaire, commentaires et notes J. Deloche, M. et P.-S. Filliozat* (Paris: Maisonneuve et Larose, 1997): 66–69.

to procure excerpts from their theological books. The answers, the excerpts, may be accurate, but they might also be analogues of the circumstances, the mind, or even the views of the one asking the questions. The only way to know the truth is to learn the language well, to translate the fundamental works for oneself, and then to confer, book in hand, with the scholars of the country which the materials treat.[37]

By 1771 he published the *Zend Avesta*.[38] In 1786 the first four Upanishads were published as part of Anquetil's *Recherches sur l'Inde*. He proceeded to translate 50 Upanishads from Persian to French and later to Latin. By 1787 he had completed this project and the 50 translations were published in 1801–02 as the *Oupnek'hat*.[39] *Legislations Orientale* was completed and published from Amsterdam in 1778 as well as his contribution to Bernoulli's *Descriptions Historique et géographique de l'Inde* on the history and geography of India.[40] This corpus of work was the foundation for later Indologists' work. In fact, Anquetil's work on the Upanishads was considered so accurate that French Indologists began other translations and interpretations of these only after the 1840s.

Unfortunately, Anquetil did not fare well during the Revolution. Jailed briefly for his religious views during the Terror in 1793 he nevertheless produced and published prolifically until his death. His papers and manuscripts were donated to the *Bibliothèque Nationale* in 1808 and 1837 by the noted Orientalist Silvestre de Sacy and comprised 25 volumes of translations, dictionaries, grammars, and

---

[37] Quoted in Raymond Schwab, *The Oriental Renaissance* (New York: Columbia University Press, 1984): 159–60.

[38] Anquetil-Duperron, *Zend Avesta, ouvrage de Zoroastre* (Paris: N. M. Tilliard, 1771), 3 vols.

[39] Anquetil-Duperron, *Oupnek'hat* (Strasbourg: Levrault, 1801).

[40] Jean Bernoulli, *Description historique et géographique de l'Inde* (Berlin: Impr. de C.S. Spener, 1786–89).

alphabets compiled during his travels.[41] In addition three full volumes of his correspondence make him a valuable and well-documented source for early studies on India. The writing of British and French writers on India in the period following the Enlightenment was remarkably similar. The belief that the origins of Indian thought and civilization lay in the ancient language of Sanskrit meant that British scholars like William Jones, Charles Wilkins, Nathaniel Halhed, and H. T. Colebrooke who were among the first member of the Asiatick Society of Calcutta focused on retrieving literature and laws believed to be the original Sanskrit versions of the ancient period. These British writers were frank admirers of Sanskritic civilization and the Brahmins, whom they understood to be the bearers of the ancient civilization of the Indo-Aryans. In their writings, these British men echoed the Enlightenment image of India popularized by Voltaire to a large extent.

For instance, William Jones drew parallels between the religions of India, Greece, Egypt, Persia and other ancient civilizations based on the anthropomorphic nature of all ancient religions. That their civilization could compare with the other great civilizations of the ancient world was proof of the high sophistication of the ancient Hindus. In a striking comparison with Voltaire's view about the high morality of the ancient Indians,[42] Jones wrote,

> We are told by the Grecian writers, that the Indians were the wisest of nations; and in moral wisdom, they were certainly eminent..., I am not disinclined to suppose, that

---

[41] George Sarton, 'Anquetil-Duperron (1731–1805)', *Osiris*, Vol. 3 (1937): 213.

[42] Although their views were similar, Voltaire posited India as an alternative to the Judeo-Christian tradition, while Jones has traditionally been viewed as conforming to the Mosaic tradition. See Sharada Sugirtharajah, *Imagining Hinduism: A Postcolonial Perspective* (New York: Routledge, 2003): Chapter 1.

the first moral fables, which appeared in Europe, were of Indian or Ethiopian origin.[43]

In addition, Jones also saw the achievements of Hindus in medicine, astronomy, mathematics, science, literature and the arts as proof of the high development of the Hindu mind.

The Hindus are said to have boasted of three inventions, all of which, indeed, are admirable, the method of instructing by apologues, the decimal scale adopted now by all civilized nations, and the game of chess...but, if their numerous works on grammar, logick, rhetorick, musick, all which are extant and accessible, were explained in some language generally known, it would be found, that they had yet higher pretentions to the praise of a fertile and inventive genius.[44]

Despite the common search for Sanskrit texts, the motivation for Jones' work lay in the Anglo-French military rivalry over India. According to Charles Allen, the French, rivals of the British as much in scholarship as in war, had stolen a march by proclaiming themselves leaders of a *renaissance orientale*.[45] Anquetil had been ignominiously removed from India when the British invaded Pondichéry in 1761; he returned to France, laden with at least 200 Indian manuscripts thus underlining France's intellectual superiority in India. In his Zend Avesta, Anquetil criticized the low quality of British scholarship on India prompting a stinging counter-criticism by Jones, who was moved to further scholarship as much by this national rivalry as by his admiration of India. When Jones published his version of the Shakuntala based on Persian versions of the original

---

[43] William Jones, *Asiatick Researches*, Vol. 1 (1789): 258.

[44] Ibid.: 259.

[45] Charles Allen, *The Search for the Buddha: The Men Who Discovered India's Lost Religion* (New York: Carroll & Graf Publishers, 2004 reprint): 43–44.

Sanskrit texts, he became an overnight hero in Britain for redeeming English scholarship. The British popular press stressed the intellectual superiority of Jones over Duperron repeatedly. The common perception that Jones had redeemed English scholarship was captured in an Oxford don Professor Hunt's letter to Jones. 'I have read it (Jones' criticism of Duperron's translation of the *Zend Avesta* and his aspersions on the latter's academic qualifications) over and over again, and think the whole nation, as well as the University and its members, are much obliged to you for this able and spirited defence.'[46]

In 1803 an event of great importance to the future of Indology occurred, which was driven by France's collection at the *Bibliothèque du Roi*. Anquetil had struggled to decipher Sanskrit in the late eighteenth century, but the British scholars in Calcutta finally succeeded. Unfortunately, the hostile relations between England and France at the time meant that it was difficult to share these findings with French scholars. Alexander Hamilton, a British naval official, who was an Indophile and member of the Asiatick Society of Bengal, arrived in Paris in 1803 to study the Sanskrit manuscript collection of the *Bibliothèque Nationale*, when the rupture of the Treaty of Amiens transformed him into a prisoner. He was treated with respect nonetheless and upon the urging of his Parisian friends, he agreed to teach Sanskrit to a small group which consisted of his protector Volney, Langlès, Fauriel, Burnouf senior and the German Friedrich Schlegel. Thus, the secrets of Sanskrit were finally revealed to France.

HERE TO STAY: A PARISIAN MONOPOLY

Despite the tumult of the Revolution, efforts to further Indic studies in Paris continued. At the forefront was the

---

[46] Cited in Garland Cannon, *The Life and Mind of Oriental Jones: Sir William Jones, the Father of Modern Linguistics* (Cambridge: CUP, 1990): 44.

republican Louis-Mathieu Langlès. A well-known Orientalist, he was appointed Professor of Persian languages and literature at the newly founded *École speciale des langues orientales* in Paris in 1795. The *École* was to be attached to the *Bibliothèque Nationale*. While Langlès was fascinated with India, his contribution to Indic studies in France was largely in the realm of translations. Halbfass points out that Voltaire's legacy of using India as a foil against the claims of primacy and exclusivity of Christian revelation continued in the work of Langlès.[47]

By 1801, France had lost even her small *Comptoirs* in India. Occupied by the British during the Napoleonic Wars they were returned only in 1815. There was no more support for the Indian empire in France. Yet attention to penetrating Indic knowledge continued. Indology survived and even flourished during the tumult of the Revolution. Even while the cutting-edge work in learning and translating Indian texts were being undertaken by the British in Calcutta, French academics who were interested in Indology kept up with the latest trends in scholarship. During the Revolution, scholars had kept up with Indic studies through the publications of the *Magazin Encyclopédique*. The *Magazin* did not publish any new research but contained detailed reviews of the Indological work of British scholars (see Table A1).[48] The *Journal des Débats*, created shortly after the first meeting of the

---

[47] Wilhelm Halbfass, *India and Europe. An Essay in Understanding*. (Albany, N.Y.: State University of New York Press, 1988): 58.

[48] Table 1 is a sample of articles published in the *Magazin* in 1795 and 1796. The *Magazin* had replaced several scholarly journals which had suspended publication during the Revolution, including the *Journal des savans[sic], Journal encyclopédique, Journal de Physique, Journal d'Histoire naturelle, Annales de Chymie*, and *Esprit des Journaux*. As the table illustrates the only French contribution that was not a book review was Langlès' bibliography of Indic works in the *Bibliothèque nationale*, but French academics were trying to stay current with Indic works.

Estates General in 1789, also carried articles of interest relating to India during the first Empire(see Table A2).[49] By 1803 Alexander Hamilton had imparted his knowledge of Sanskrit to Parisian academics. This single occurrence gave Paris the edge in Indological studies even though Chézy, the first great French Indologist of the nineteenth century was a self-taught Sanskritist! Once Sanskrit was introduced to Parisian Indologists, a spate of translations of the Indic texts in the *Bibliothèque* were undertaken. By 1805 the Asiatick Researches of the British Indologists at Calcutta[50] was translated and published in French by the *Imprimérie Impériale* as *Recherches Asiatiques, ou mémoires de la Société établie au Bengale pour faire des recherches sur l'histoire et les antiquités, les arts, les sciences et la littérature de l'Asie.* A number of scholars including Langlès, Cuvier, Delambre, and Lamarck contributed to the editing and publication of these translations. Paris was poised to take over from the Indologists in Calcutta as the leader in Indic studies. According to Lacôte, 'Paris, which counted famous orientalists, was designated to become the first center of Sanskrit studies in Europe: if there were not any pandits there, as in Calcutta, one had [there] the famous collection of manuscripts of the Library.'[51] Parisian

---

[49] Table A2 provides a sample of Indic articles in the Journal from late 1803 to early 1805.

[50] The earliest interest in a journal dedicated to Indian studies was the publication of the Asiatick Researches by the Asiatick Society of Bengal, formed by the initiative of William Jones in Calcutta towards the end of the eighteenth century. By the first quarter of the nineteenth century, the Asiatick Society of Bengal was a respected and reputed society and had gained acclaim in the academic world for its efforts towards furthering an understanding of Indian history and civilization. In France, this achievement was duly recognized by the increasing numbers of French academics subscribing and contributing to the journal.

[51] "Paris, qui comptait d'illustres orientalistes, était désigné pour devenir le premier centre d'études sanskrites en Europe: si l'on n'y avait point de pandits, comme à Calcutta, on y possédait la fameuse collection de manuscrits de la Bibliothèque."Felix Lacôte, "L'Indianisme",

Indologists had great pride in the collection of Indic manuscripts held at the *Bibliothèque* and continued to acquire more during the nineteenth century.[52] In 1823 the government agreed to purchase a number of Sanskrit letters for 2000 francs.[53] If for no other reason Paris was the centre of Indological studies outside of India because of the quality and quantity of Indian manuscripts held at the *Bibliothèque*.

Société Asiatique: Livre du centenaire. (Paris: La Société Asiatique, 1922): 220–21.

[52] Jean-Marie Lafont's study of the French officers in the court of various Indian princes during the nineteenth century reveals that they were avid collectors and amateur patrons and archivists of the arts and literature of their kingdoms. Many had written about the histories and cultures of their regions thus contributing greatly to French knowledge of India. Some of these notable French mercenary-savants served at the courts of the Nizam of Hyderabad and the kingdom of Mysore under Hyder Ali and Tipu Sultan like Maistre de la Tour, Loustaunau, Saint-Lubin, de Montigny, Chevalier du Drence, and Benoît de Boigne under the Marathas, Allard, Henri Court and Ventura at the court of Ranjit Singh of the Punjab and Gentil and Claude Martin at the court of the Nawab of Awadh. Most of these men were also high court functionaries and therefore had the material means to accumulate these collections and become patrons of local art and architecture. They also corresponded with scholars in France and initiated hunts for local manuscripts which enriched their own personal libraries as well as collections of Indic manuscripts in France. In 1836, for example, Court and Allard, who were employed in the Punjab under Ranjit Singh and were enthusiastic patrons of local art received a text titled '*Instructions de l'Académie*'. The text was issued by the *Académie des Inscriptions et Belles-Lettres* following the advice of a select committee composed of Walkenaer, Eugene Burnouf, Raoul-Rochette, Fauriel and Langlois all of whom were respected Indologists. The document issued to Court and Allard laid out directions to further archaeological surveys in the Punjab. The *Académie* also asked for maps, site descriptions, and texts of inscriptions, drawings of monuments and bas-reliefs and even the collection of texts which existed in Punjab libraries to be sent as additions to the Indian collections of the *Bibliothèque*. Jean-Marie Lafont, *Indika. Essays in Indo-French Relations, 1630–1976* (Delhi: Manohar, 2000): ch. 3.

[53] L. Finot, 'Historique de la Société Asiatique', *Le Livre du Centenaire*, 1822–1922. (Paris: Société Asiatique, 1922): 12.

As McGetchin points out, most German Indologists had to travel to Paris to study Sanskrit since they possessed no manuscripts of their own, and as in the case of Jules Mohl, eventually became French citizens. Furthermore, German students who were interested in Indic studies flocked to the Parisian pundits Antoine de Chézy, Silvestre de Sacy, Louis Langlès, and Alexander Hamilton. These included eminent Indologists like Friedrich and August Schlegel,[54] Franz Bopp,[55] Jules Mohl[56] and Max Müller.[57] In fact a majority of appointments in Germany to chairs of Indian languages during the early nineteenth century were students of de Sacy. According to Henri Dehérain,

> There is no other country in Europe where he had as many contacts as in Germany. Every university there possessed a chair of Oriental languages. The occupants of these chairs during the first part of the nineteenth Century, with only a few exceptions, were his former students. The list is long:... Bopp [in Berlin] ... Freytag in Bonn, Gottfried Kosegarten in Jena....[58]

---

[54] The Schlegel brothers were the founders of the German school of Romanticism as well as the German school of Indology. August Schlegel held the first Chair of Indology in Germany at Bonn in 1818.

[55] Based on his philological comparisons of Sanskrit, Latin and Germanic languages, Bopp was appointed to the first Chair of Sanskrit and Comparative Grammar in Berlin by 1821. He was among the earliest philologists and attributed much of his inspiration to his Parisian teacher Chézy.

[56] Mohl was to become so attached to Parisian Indology that he would settle down in France and take French citizenship, as well as become the secretary of the *Société Asiatique* by its 25th year.

[57] Müller, easily Germany's most famous Indologist, began his career as Burnouf's student in Paris. Douglas T. McGetchin, 'Wilting Florists: The Turbulent Early Decades of the Société Asiatique, 1822–60', *Journal of the History of Ideas*, Vol. 64, No. 4 (2003): 567.

[58] 'Mais dans aucun pays d'Europe, Silvestre de Sacy n'eut autant de relations qu'en Allemagne. Toute Université y possédait une chaire de langues orientales et de cette chaire le titulaire fut pendant la premiére moitié du XIXe siécle à quelques exceptions près, un de ses

A new Chair of Sanskrit was created at the *Collège de France* in 1815, the first major appointment in Europe. The *Collège* was the pre-eminent school of Indic studies during the nineteenth century. By 1830 the *Ecole nationale des langues orientales*, also called *Langues O* created a chair of Hindustani. In 1868 the *Ecole des Hautes Etudes* at the Sorbonne was founded and soon after a chair of Indian literature was established there, as well as several posts or '*directions d'études*' relating to the study of Indian philology or religion at the *Ecole des Hautes Etudes*.

In 1821 the *Société Asiatique* was formed in Paris. Apart from the Asiatick Society of Bengal which was based in India, this was the first society for Asian studies that had been formed in Europe, the London Asiatic Society only being founded in 1825. Silvestre de Sacy was the first chair in 1822 and the Duc d'Orleans, later king of France was the honorary Chairman. The Duc was an active participant in the *Société*'s meetings and other undertakings, contributing generously of his time and money to the *Société* and often acting as its spokesman in the public sphere where he publicized the activities of the *Société* and its members, stressed the importance of Asia in understanding human history and even asked for subsidies. After he ascended to the throne he subsidized the *Société* from royal funds.[59] In 1823 the *Société* began publication of the *Journal Asiatique*, which again was the premier publication for European Indologists.[60] The Presidents of the *Société* during its first century of existence were a veritable who's

---

anciens élèves. La liste en est longue:... Franz Bopp ... Freytag à Bonn, Gottfried Kosegarten à Iéna....'Henri Dehérain, *Silvestre de Sacy* (Paris, 1938): xxxii. Cited in ibid.: 568. Despite his encouragement of Indology, de Sacy did not publish a single original piece on Indology, which is why he has been omitted in this chapter.

[59] Raymond Schwab, *The Oriental Renaissance* (New York: Columbia University Press, 1984): 82.

[60] See *Société Asiatique, Le Livre du Centenaire (1822–1922)* (Paris, 1922).

who of Indology, including Silvestre de Sacy (1822–29 and again 1832–34), Abel Rémusat (1829–32), Amédée Jaubert (1834–47), Joseph Reinaud (1847–67), Jules Mohl (1867–76), Garcin de Tassy (1876–78), Adolphe Régnier (1878–84), Ernest Renan (1884–92), Barbier de Meynard (1892–1908), Emile Sénart (1908–28) and Sylvain Lévi (1928–35). The majority of these officials were Indologists, as is clear from the above list. After 1935 the presence of French scholars studying the Far East became prominent, but Indologists continued to form a formidable portion of the *Société*. The first 10 years of the journal, the old series, numbering from one to 10 contained mostly translations of Indian texts. The articles included the work of German, British and French Indologists. The journal was published as *Nouveau Journal Asiatique* from 1828 to 1835, after which it was published as *Journal Asiatique, troisieme série*. Since this time, from 1835 to 2009, the journal has been published in a series consisting of 10 years and 20 volumes, with six issues each year, except for 1920 when it was necessary to reduce the number of issues to four. The new series, starting in 1830, listed literature reviews, extracts of originals translated into French, lists of works published or encouraged by the Society, a list of the Society's members (both French and foreign), minutes of the meetings of the Society, death notices, letters to the Editor, reports on bibliographic catalogues and collections as well as advertisements for new works. In addition, the society sponsored the publication of most of the important works on Indology in the nineteenth century, like the translations of Indian texts by Antoine Chézy, Eugene Burnouf and James Darmestetter. As the incumbent president, Sénart remarked during the festivities marking the centenary of the *Société*, 'The annals of our society during this century are the annals of French Orientalism; the Society continues to be a constant inspiration.'[61]

---

[61] 'Les annales de notre Société, pendant ce siècle, sont les annales meme de l'orientalisme française; elle en est l'inspiratrice constant', *Société Asiatique. Les Fêtes du Centenaire* (Paris, 1922): 10.

Meanwhile British scholars at the Asiatic Society of Calcutta continued to study India. The legacy of William Jones' romantic view of India continued with Charles Wilkins' publication of the Bhagavad Gita in 1785. In describing the Bhagavad Gita as the source of all religious revelation for the Brahmins, Wilkins focussed only on the Brahmins of North India, worshippers of Vishnu. Describing them as extremely intelligent and possessing a sophisticated intellect, he also distinguished between the intellect of the Brahmins and the credulous and ignorant masses, whom the former lived off, by playing on their fears and superstitions. Despite the laudatory description of Indian thought, Wilkins also represented the emerging school of imperial administrators (although William Jones also began his study of Indian texts as a result of his belief that it was necessary for improved administration) who judged Hindu thought by its closeness to Western norms of achievement The monotheistic nature of Hindu worship, i.e., the focus of worship being on Krishna, as representative of the Godhead, raised the intellectual achievement of the Brahmins for Wilkins, since they had come close to the western notion of one God and therefore had moved away form the polytheistic nature of anthropomorphic religions.

Other British administrators who took up the study of Indian texts from an interest in administration included Nathaniel Brassey Halhed. Upon studying various Indian legal texts Halhed stressed the extent to which the Hindus had been misunderstood and reduced to idolaters and false believers. He pointed to the very highly developed legal system of the Hindus as proof of their advanced thinking. Reiterating the high level of intellectual achievement, he described the various grammars, of Sanskrit particularly, as evidence of the high cultural, literary and intellectual level attained by the Hindus. The extreme precision and extent of legal provision for the exercise of justice was for Halhed, proof of the complex social structure and civilization of the Hindus.

More important than these contributions to translating Sanskrit texts was the fact that British works were directly aimed at establishing colonial law in India. To that end, scholars like Halhed also recognized that while the Brahmins might claim that authority in India emanated from ancient Sanskrit texts, it was necessary to learn vernacular languages in order to effectively rule the different Indian provinces. French Indologists continued to study Sanskrit texts as the key to understanding India. So the study of Sanskrit as the key to understanding the ancient civilization of India continued to be dominated by Paris.

A CHANGING TIDE: THE END OF ROMANTICISM

Some aspects of the image of India in France continued from the eighteenth to the nineteenth century. But there were other changes taking place, notably in the change from romantic writings to scientific writings. In the first decade of the nineteenth century, Voltaire's romantic view of India flourished beyond the narrow scope of the salon and was incorporated into the *Académie* which had published the work of Deguignes,[62]

---

[62] Deguignes, 'Recherches sur quelques événemens qui concernent l'histoire des Rois Grecs de la Bactriane, & particulièrement la destruction de leur Royaume par les Scythes, l'établissement de ceux-ci le long de l'Indus, & les guerres qu'ils eurent avec les Parthes', Vol. 25 (1759); 'Réflexions sur un Livre Indien, intitulé Bagavadam, un des dix-huit Pouranam ou Livres sacrés des Indiens, dont la traduction a été envoyé en 1769 à M. Bertin, Ministre & Secrétaire d'Etat', Vol. 38 (1777); 'Recherches historiques sur la Religion Indienne, & sur les Livres fondamentaux de cette Religion, qui ont été traduits de l'Indien en Chinois. Premier Mémoire. Etablissement de la Religion Indienne dans l'Inde, la Tartarie, le Thibet & les Isles', 'Recherches historiques sur la Religion Indienne. Second Mémoire. Etablissement de la Religion Indienne dans la Chine, & son Histoire jusqu'en 531 de J.C.', 'Recherches historiques sur la Religion Indienne. Troisième Mémoire. Suite de la Religion Indienne à la Chine', Vol. 40(1780); 'Observations historiques & géographiques sur le récit de Pline, concernant l'origine, l'antiquité des Indiens, & la Géographie de leur pays, avec des recherches sur les principals révolutions de l'Inde', Vol. 45 (1793), *Histoire de l'académie royale des inscriptions et belles lettres* (Paris: Imprimérie Royale).

and Duperron[63] in the eighteenth century.[64] Following in the footsteps of his predecessors, Langlès also viewed India in romantic terms. Another scholar, Louis Langlois, believed that literature was the expression of society.[65] To him, understanding Sanskrit literature was a window to understanding the nature of Indians, especially since the unchanging nature of the customs and traditions of India and Indians were captured by their writers.[66] Based on the study of translated Sanskrit literature, Langlois described the Indian as gentle, tranquil, pacifist, and moderate, occupied with his destiny and religion more than with politics or laws. He was a stranger to progress, change and the movement of civilization looking instead for monotony, triumph over passion and over the bodily needs by recourse to philosophy and conquering emotions.[67]

The last great romantic Indologist of the nineteenth century in France, Antoine Chézy[68] was also the first French Indologist of note in the nineteenth century. A student of Silvestre de Sacy who taught Persian at the *Collège*

---

[63] Anquetil-Duperron, 'relation abrégée du voyage que M. Anquetil- Duperron a fait dans l'Inde pour la recherche et la traduction des ouvrages attribués à Zoroastre', Vol. 1762, 'Mémoire dans lequel on établit que les livres zends déposés à la Bibliothèque du roi le 15 mars 1762' May 1769 (part 1), Jun 1769 (part 2), 'Observation sur trois cartes...', 1776.

[64] The *Journal de Savants* was the leader in publishing articles about India. Between 1665 and 1797, when the journal was suspended during the Revolution, the articles published on India equalled 162, gallica.bnf.fr.

[65] Louis Langlois, *Monumens Littéraires de l'Inde ou Mélanges de literature sanscrite* (Paris, 1827): 3.

[66] Ibid.

[67] Ibid.: 4.

[68] Born at Neuilly in 1773, Chézy was originally prepared to follow his father's profession as an engineer. In 1799, however, Chézy succeeded in obtaining a post in the oriental department of the national library.

de France, he began his academic profession as a scholar of Persian. But soon, Chézy was drawn to Indic studies after reading Kalidasa's *Shakuntala* which had been translated into various languages and had undergone many academic interpretations after William Jones' first work on the play. Caught up in this great Indic wave, Chézy decided to make the shift from Arabist to Indologist. Yet afraid that this shift in interest would annoy his teacher, Chézy studied Sanskrit on his own in secret even though Alexander Hamilton had acquired a sizable student following in Paris by this time. Without either a grammar or a dictionary Chézy mastered Sanskrit by surrounding himself with the mass of Sanskrit manuscripts available at the *Bibliothèque Nationale*. He pored over the early seventeenth- and eighteenth-century attempts at putting together grammars, and added to that knowledge with the latest publications of the Asiatick Society of Bengal. Based on this study he managed to learn the language and publish his best-known work in 1830. This was his translation of the Shakuntala, the play which had inspired him to pursue Indic studies. Chézy's work was a breakthrough for Indic studies because he had managed to acquire and translate the play directly from the Sanskrit, without the need for a Brahmin to translate or act as an intermediary. Thus, even though the Brahmins were still recalcitrant, Europeans could now access Sanskrit texts. According to Filliozat,

> The 'Essay Informing of Grammar' preserved at the Library of the King was thus not without playing a meritorious part in the beginnings of Indianism in allowing for the first time, a European to [be] initiated to Sanskrit without the help of a pandit, before the time when the printed [Sanskrit] works thanks to the pandits could make initiation relatively easy.[69]

---

[69] 'L'<<essai informe de grammaire>> conservé à la Bibliothèque du Roi n'a donc pas été sans jouer un rôle méritoire dans les débuts

This was a first for Indic studies and set the tone for subsequent standards of Indology. Jean Reynaud commented on the importance of Chézy's work when he noted that 'For several years almost all the progress made in France toward an understanding of the Sanskrit language and its treasures has resulted from the work of a single man: Chézy.'[70] Following Chézy's work there was a scramble to learn Sanskrit and to translate 'original' Sanskrit texts rather than relying on other translations. Chézy's work had demonstrated the enormous gulf that existed between the linguistic, poetic, and literary quality of the original and the translated Arabic or Persian version. More than ever, Chézy's translation of the Sanskrit play underlined the high literary quality of the language and therefore of the people who had used it. From now it became a point of academic integrity to use original texts rather than using later versions of popular literary works, or relying on contemporary interpretations. This endeavour literally opened up the ancient literary canon to the West, both in terms of massive manhunts to uncover copies of original texts as well as analyses of these texts. In 1832, the well-known liberal scholar Jean-Denis Lanjuinais completed a French translation of the *Bhagavad Gita* directly from Sanskrit. Soon Vedic studies led to studies of Hinduism and Vedism, as well as exploring the linkages between ancient religions. Chézy's translation set off a chain of studies in comparative philology and the historical links between ancient civilizations. Although he was not as prolific as some of his counterparts

---

de l'indianisme en permettant pour la première fois à un européen de s'initier au sanscrit sans le secours d'un *pandit*, avant le temps où les travaux imprimés grâce aux pandits pouvaient rendre l'initiation relativement facile.'Jean Filliozat, 'Une grammaire sanscrite du XVIII siècle et les débuts de l'indianisme en 'rance', *Bulletin de la Société des Études Indochinoises*, 29.4, (1954): 276.

[70] Quoted in Raymond Schwab, *The Oriental Renaissance* (New York: Columbia University Press, 1984): 94.

like Burnouf,[71] Chézy devoted himself to teaching,[72] and his importance, both as an individual and an academic, is memorialized in a biographical article written by his first teacher, Silvestre de Sacy in the *Mémoires de l'Académie de belles-lettres et inscriptions.*[73]

During Chézy's brief lifetime, an important shift occurred in the study of India. This shift was a move to study Indic literature in a more precise, scientific fashion. In a controversy that erupted within the *Société Asiatique*, French Orientalists became divided into two camps: the Florists or those who romanticized the Orient and focussed on the style and flourish of Oriental literature and the anti-Florists who wanted to rely entirely on direct translations from Oriental texts and do away with romanticism.[74] The rift within the Society was obvious enough to be mentioned in the various journals of the day. For instance, the *Revue Brittanique* noted the rift between those members of the Society it termed 'Whigs' and the group who opposed them, and warned that the journal was in danger

---

[71] Burnouf complained to M. Bopp that 'Mr. [de] Chézy, as you ought to know, says that he will publish everything and publishes nothing.' ('Mais M. Chézy comme vous devez savoir, dit qu'il publiera tout et ne publie rien.') Burnouf to Bopp, 14 November 1825 letter. Cited in Douglas T. McGetchin, 'Wilting Florists: The Turbulent Early Decades of the Société Asiatique, 1822–60', *Journal of the History of Ideas*, Vol. 64, No. 4 (2003): 569.

[72] Bopp wrote to A. W. Schlegel on 13 February 1825 with resignation: 'There's not much to expect out of de Chézy; perhaps his students will accomplish more.' Cited in McGetchin: 570.

[73] Silvestre de Sacy, *Notice sur la vie et les ouvrages de m. de Chézy, lue à la séance publique de l'Académie des inscriptions et belles-lettres, du 14 août 1835* (Paris, Impr. de C. Eberhart, 1835).

[74] Douglas T. McGetchin, 'Wilting Florists: The Turbulent Early Decades of the Société Asiatique, 1822–60', *Journal of the History of Ideas*, Vol. 64, No. 4 (2003): 565–66. The controversy has also been referred to in L. Finot, 'Historique de la Société Asiatique', *Le Livre du Centenaire, 1822–1922* (Paris: Société Asiatique, 1922).

of closing since the members who opposed the Whigs were publishing their work in other journals.

> It is said that there does not exist a perfect harmony between the members of the Asiatic Society... this schism, indeed, is extremely prejudicial to the interest of the newspaper; distinguished orientalists are to insert their productions [publications] in other collections, and, inter alia; in the collection of the Memoires of the Geographic Society.[75]

Among the prominent Indic Florists were Chézy, Langlois and de Tassy. The early years of the *Société Asiatique* were dominated by them. The Florists emphasized the romantic, aesthetic, and poetic element of the East rather than precise translations, characteristics which led to their derision as 'philologer-poets'.[76] Naudet, describing Chézy as the archetypal Florist, wrote of him as

> of a gentle and melancholy nature, with an elegant and classical imagination, was above all in love with the forms of poetry of that language [Sanskrit] that appeared to be an emanation of Eden. Because of his desire to be systematic, or the desire to attract an audience to this unknown literature more easily, he only showed its beauty adorned in gauze and embroidery. He applied himself to transposing

---

[75] 'On dit qu'il n'existe pas une harmonie parfaite entre les membres de la *Société Asiatique*...ce schisme, en effet, est fort préjudiciable aux intérêt du journal; des orientalistes distingués sont insérer leurs productions dans d'autres recueils, et, entre autres; dans la collection des mémoires de la Société de Géographie.''Littérature orientale', *Revue Brittanique*, Vol. 17 (March–April 1828): 277–78.

[76] 'philologues poètes' F. E. Schultz, 'Sur le grand Ouvrage historique et critique d'Ibn-Khaldoun, appelé: Kitab-ol-iber we diwan-ol moubteda wel khaber, etc.',*Journal Asiatique* 7 (1825): 218. Cited in Douglas T. McGetchin, 'Wilting Florists: The Turbulent Early Decades of the Société Asiatique, 1822–60', *Journal of the History of Ideas*, Vol. 64, No. 4 (2003): 570.

these strange and gigantic figures into proportions and French structures of design, substituting an artificial ideal for an actual ideal.[77]

The faction opposing the Florists wanted a more rigorous, scientific examination of texts. By the mid-1820s the disagreement had become personal[78] with the established Florists seeking to exclude the anti-Florists from positions in the *Société Asiatique*. In 1826 the president of the *Société Asiatique*, de Sacy, advocated the position of the Florists by suggesting the exclusion of anti-Florists from the *Journal Asiatique*. In response, the anti-Florists voted to replace the Florist Garcin de Tassy with the anti-Florist Burnouf as assistant secretary of the *Société*. Chézy was furious and his ire was noted by Burnouf who wrote 'This excited a rage by the de Chézy party which expressed itself in every means possible and which truly causes me quite a fright.'[79] The serious

---

[77] 'douce et mélancolique *[sic]* nature, *[sic]* imagination élégante et classique, s'était épris surtout des formes et de la poésie de ce langage qui lui semblait une émanation de l'Éden; et, soit esprit de système, soit désir d'attirer plus facilement son auditoire à cette littérature inconnue, il n'en montrait les beautés que parées de gaze et de broderies, et il s'appliquait à ramener aux proportions et au dessin de la physionomie française ces étranges et gigantesques figures, substituant un idéal artificiel à l'idéal véritable.' Joseph Naudet, *Notice Historique sur MM. Burnouf, Pere et Fils* (Paris, 1854): 27. Cited in McGetchin: 568–69.

[78] Chézy was a particular target for the anti-Florists, with Schlegel calling him the 'remora of the Sanskrit ship'. Felix Lacôte, *'L'Indianisme'*, in *Le Livre du Centenaire (1822–1922)*, ed. Société Asiatique (Paris, 1922): 221–22; Finot writing almost a hundred years later derided Chézy as well. 'Then in 1833, M. de Sacy made a funeral eulogy for Rémusat and [de] Chézy, whom he called "the two colossi of Asian studies". [de] Chézy, a colussus!' ('Encore en 1833, M. de Sacy, faisant l'éloge funèbre de Rémusat et du Chézy, les appelle'ces deux colosses des études asiatigues". Chezy, un colosse!') Loius Finot, 'Historique de la Société Asiatique', *Le Livre du Centenaire*: 17.

[79] 'Cela a excité dans le parti Chézy une rage qui s'exhale par tous les moyens possibles et qui vraiment me cause quelque effroi.' Eugène

dissension almost led to the dissolution of the *Société* by 1828. In 1852 Jules Mohl noted that the *Société* had narrowly 'escaped the great danger of internal dissension'.[80]

By 1829 the older generation of Florists who held the executive positions in the *Société Asiatique* were beginning to relinquish their hold over the *Société*. De Sacy retired and Chézy left the helm of the *Journal Asiatique*. The anti-Florist Abel Rémusat replaced Sacy as the president of the *Société* and Burnouf became the Secretary. The death of Chézy in 1832 was the last blow to the Indic Florists who had no more well-connected teachers.

The victory of the anti-Florists led to the domination of this group within the *Société* and *Journal Asiatique*. As Douglas McGetchin points out, although individual Florists like Langlois and Lanjuinais continued in their romantic focus, the institutional shift from romanticism to scientific examination was made in the years of the Florist controversy.

In the early years of the nineteenth century, the image of India in France and in Britain was of an ancient civilization which had proved its intellectual and philosophical greatness through the corpus of Sanskrit Brahminic literature. Despite the actual situation of India being a land of frequent military warfare as the British sought to expand their empire, the presentation of India in scholarly works and popular operas alike was of a romantic, lyrical civilization summed up in Chézy's starting flourish to the inaugural issue of the *Journal Asiatique*: 'The Greek muses would today make homage to their sisters on the banks of the Ganges and suspend for a moment the scholarly harmony

---

Burnouf's letters to Christian Lassen on 4 April and 8 May 1826, quoted in Finot, 'Historique de la Société Asiatique', *Le Livre du Centenaire*: 16–17. Cited in McGetchin: 573.

[80] Jules Mohl, *Vingt-sept Ans d'histoire des etudes orientales: Rapport faits à la Société Asiatique de Paris de 1840 à 1867*. 2 vols (Paris: Reinwald, 1879–80), Vol. I: 450.

of the lyre to give room to the sounds, perhaps a little delicate, of the Indian lute.'[81]

The next chapter opens up a new era in French Indology. Reflecting on Florist works like Chézy's as 'erotic and emotional rubbish',[82] the anti-Florists like Jules Mohl and Burnouf inaugurated the nineteenth-century quest for empiricism in the field of Indology. Yet the shift meant significant changes to the trajectory of Indic studies in France and, as a result, the image of India in France.

In addition, articles on geography, theology, mythology, and fables, articles on Egypt, China, the Middle East, Ancien colonies and the Indian Ocean carried many references to India. Letters to the editor also included reflections on articles pertaining to India.

---

[81] Antoine Chézy, 'L'Ermitage de Kandou', *Journal Asiatique*, July 1822, Vol. 1: 3.

[82] Douglas T. McGetchin, 'Wilting Florists: The Turbulent Early Decades of the Société Asiatique, 1822–60', *Journal of the History of Ideas*, Vol. 64, No. 4 (2003): 569.

Chapter 4

The Era of Empiricism and the Rise of Philology

For me, Gentlemen, I think, to the honor of scholarship, that work of the erudite men who devoted their life to the study of India will not be sterile for the old story of this country. I have the hope that the meeting of, as well of efforts, will finish some day by rebuilding the most brilliant and perhaps the richest literary history as people can offer to the curiosity and the admiration of Europe.[1]

With the eclipse of the Florists a new era of Indology dominated by empirical, scientific comparisons began. The harbingers of this change were Eugene Burnouf, Abel Rémusat, and Jules Mohl. Many of the anti-Florists were keenly interested in the natural sciences and wanted to bring a similar accuracy to their work on linguistics. Accordingly, the period from 1835 to 1855 saw an increased focus on philology. In return, natural scientists like Cuvier noted the impact that linguistics had on their studies. Cuvier specifically noted the contribution that French Indic linguists

---

[1] 'Pour moi, messieurs, je pense, à l'honneur de l'érudition, que les travaux des hommes savants qui ont dévoué leur vie à l'étude de l'Inde ne seront pas stériles pour l'histoire ancienne de ce pays. J'ai l'espérance que la réunion de tant d'efforts finira quelque jour par reconstruire la plus brillante et peut-être la plus riche histoire littéraire qu'un peuple puisse offrir à la curiosité et à l'admiration de l'Europe.' E. Burnouf, 'Discours sur la langue et la littérature sanscrite, prononcé au Collège de France', *Journal Asiatique*, Series 2, Vol. 11, January–June 1833: 264.

had made through their work on the 'sacred books of the Hindus' to help open up human history.[2] This chapter looks at the new beginning that Indology and the image of India in France made in the nineteenth century with the advent of comparative philology. Indology was funded primarily by the government in France. The major institutions of Indology, the *Collège de France* and the Sorbonne, were both supported financially by the government. In addition, the major vehicles of Indological publications were financially supported by the Government. The *Journal de Savants* was (and is) the journal for the *Institut Française*, specifically the *Académie des Inscription et Belles-Lettres* which was (and is) the Humanities group within the *Institut*. Additionally, the *Société Asiatique* and its journal, the *Journal Asiatique*, was funded by the *Académie des Inscription et Belles-Lettres* since its inception in 1822. As Schwab points out, the close relationship between the *Société Asiatique* and the restoration government of Louis Philippe was common knowledge, with the latter being a generous patron and even holding the position of Honorary Chairman of the society. The prestigious position of Orientalism in French academia was cemented by the fact that the 'Orientalist group' constituted (and continues to constitute) one of four informal groups comprising the *Académie des Inscription et Belles-Lettres*. By the early nineteenth century, all higher education in France was funded by the government, with teachers and professors being state employees. The connection between the fortunes of Indology and the interests of the State, particularly in research institutions like the *Collège de France*, Sorbonne, and the *Académie des*

---

[2] Georges Cuvier, *Discours sur les révolutions de la surface du globe; et sur les changemens [sic] qu'elles ont produits dans le règne animal* (Paris, 1825): 3. Quoted in Douglas T. McGetchin, 'Wilting Florists: The Turbulent Early Decades of the Société Asiatique, 1822–60', *Journal of the History of Ideas*, Vol. 64, No. 4 (2003): 574.

Inscription et Belles-Lettres are undeniable. According to Schwab, 'These [Oriental] studies were important to the State...by quieting national memories.'[3] France in the mid-nineteenth century was still smarting from her military loss to England in the previous century. According to Jennifer Pitts, the Restoration government, in an effort to recapture France's prior glory as well as to prove itself an adequate replacement for Napoleon, sought without success to rebuild the empire in India, Indochina and West Africa.[4] In this context, France's shifting colonial interests (to North Africa and South East Asia) meant that Indology was no longer politically useful. The status of Indology therefore became precarious by 1840. In order to preserve itself, the discipline needed to appeal, if not to popular demand, then at least to immediate intellectual needs, such as the need for increased Buddhist studies in response to France's expanding colonial empire in the Far East. These were the changes which took place in Indology during the period 1835–55 and they were reflected in the image of India in France.

THE NEW PHILOLOGY

The major change which had occurred in Indology was the view of scholars on how to go about studying India. The older school of romantics, which focused on the achievements of Sanskritic culture, was now eclipsed by scientific academics who put aside the content of the writings as being representative of hyperbole and focused instead on grammar, syntax, and the comparison of languages. The era of philology was inaugurated in Indic studies, important for the links it demonstrated between Sanskrit and

---

[3] Raymond Schwab, *The Oriental Renaissance* (New York: Columbia University Press, 1984): 82.

[4] Jennifer Pitts, *A Turn to Empire: The Rise of Imperial Liberalism in Britain and France* (Princeton: Princeton University Press, 2005): 165–66.

other languages of antiquity. By the third decade of the nineteenth century, scholars who had been looking for clues to the origin of the Indo-European stumbled upon the linguistic affinities between the classical languages of the West and many of the languages of the East, especially Sanskrit and Avestic. As Burnouf put it, 'the common relationship of the dialects of Europe... and which presented the more striking analogies with Greek, Latin and the Germanic and Slav dialects.... it is the Sanskrit of the Brahmins.'[5] These contributions to the study of man and history made philology valuable. According to Burnouf, 'The family ties which link it [Sanskrit] with the idioms of erudite Europe are undeniable, and this result, most singular of those was obtained in this day [through] philology, is also most obviously demonstrated.'[6] He saw the similarities between Sanskrit, Greek, Latin, and the Germanic and Latin languages. But unlike Voltaire and the earlier Florists, Burnouf cautioned against using comparative philology to build theories about the relative antiquity of civilizations and the notion that India was the source for the Greek and Roman cultures. In 1840 he wrote in his translation of the Bhagavat Purana, 'I don't need to point out that I found here absolutely no trace of Greek or Christian ideas where the Indian works in which up to now such ideas have supposedly been positively identified.'[7]

---

[5] 'la parenté commune des dialectes de l'Europe...et qui présentait les analogies les plus frappantes avec le grec, le latin et les dialectes germaniques et slaves...c'est le Sanskrit des Brahmanes..." E. Burnouf, "Discours sur la langue et la littérature sanscrite, prononcé au Collège de France', *Journal Asiatique*, Series 2, Vol. 11 (Jan–Jun 1833): 253–54. Burnouf also describes the philological similarity between Sanskrit and Avestic which led to the hypothesis of the Aryans or Indo-Europeans possibly hailing from north-west India.

[6] 'Les liens de parenté qui l'unissent aux idiomes de l'Europe savante sont incontestables, et ce résultat, le plus singulier de ceux qu'ait obtenus de nos jours la philologie, est aussi le plus évidemment démontré.'Ibid.: 254.

[7] Quoted in Raymond Schwab, *The Oriental Renaissance* (New York: Columbia University Press, 1984): 134.

By 1826 a breakthrough occurred with the publication of a joint work by Eugene Burnouf and Christian Lassen titled *Essai sur le Pali*. In the words of Joseph Naudet,

> E. Burnouf proposed a more virile and more serious object; he wanted to seek the traces of the filiation of people, the family ties between the East and the Occident, and the hereditary titles of European races, conserved in the analogies of the signs of their thought; to disentangle and promulgate the laws of decomposition of the originating idioms in the old languages and the modern languages, to find finally by/through grammar, the great epochs of the history of the human family.[8]

Therefore, a scholarly interest in discovering the linguistic origins of different people was already becoming popular. In the case of India, the close study of languages, particularly of Sanskrit, was related to the search for the origins of Indo-European or Aryan languages. As Naudet points out, Burnouf's work was an important milestone in the linguistic comparison of Indo-European languages and therefore of the Indo-European people.

Based on the linguistic similarities between the dramas which had been written in a common language called Prakrit and dated to the early centuries AD in India and Sanskrit, Burnouf and Lassen were able to prove that the former was a vernacular, vulgar form of the more refined Sanskrit. Furthermore, there were linguistic and philological similarities between Prakrit and another vernacular

---

[8] 'E. Burnouf se proposa un objet plus viril et plus sérieux; il voulut rechercher les traces de la filiation des peuples, les liens de parenté entre l'Orient et l'Occident, et les titres héréditaires des races européennes, conservés dans les analogies des signes de la pensée; démêler et promulguer les lois de décomposition des idiomes originaires dans les langues anciennes et dans les langues modernes, retrouver enfin par la grammaire les grandes époques de l'histoire de la famille humaine.' J. Naudet, 'Notice historique sur MM. Burnouf, père et fils', *Mémoires de l'Académie des inscriptions et belles-lettres*, Vol. 20, no. 1 (SD): 309–10.

called Pali in which most of the Indian Buddhist texts were composed. By a rigorous process of comparison and dating, Burnouf and Lassen were able to conclusively prove that Pali had Sanskrit origins. Linguistic studies looked at the different versions of texts and analysed the changes in syntax and grammar making it possible to date the different recensions of a text, and interpret the differences in presentation and storyline as the result of the historical process. Since many texts were written late in the historical period, relying on oral transmission for preservation, the written text could offer valuable clues about the material culture of the time, as well as changes which occurred in religion like the expansion of the pantheon and the development of new sects.[9] Indologists rely on this method to the present day, with the most popular studies having being performed on the highly prolific epics, the Ramayana and Mahabharata. According to Burnouf,

> Man is however not forgotten in the other productions of the religious spirit of India, and the great Epics which recall the heroic history of the Brahmins and of the warlike caste [and] show it to us in the milieu of a society which combines the most advanced refinements of civilization [and] naivety of primitive manners.[10]

---

[9] Some examples of such articles include E. Burnouf, '*Analyse et Extrait du Devi-Mahatmyam, fragment du Markandeya-Pourana*', *Journal Asiatique*, Series 1, Vol. 4 (Jan–Jun 1824); Auguste Schlégel, 'Observations sur la critique du Bhagavad-Gita, insérée dans le Journal Asiatique', *JA*, Series 1, Vol. 9 (Jul–Dec 1826); and Baron G de Humboldt, 'Mémoire sur la séparation des mots dans les textes sanscrits', *JA*, Series 1, Vol. 11 (Jul–Dec 1827).

[10] 'L'homme n'est cependant pas oublié dans les autres productions de l'esprit religieux de l'Inde, et les grandes épopées (*sic*. Possibly Epics) qui retracent l'histoire héroïque des Brahmanes et de la caste guerrière nous le montrent au milieu d'une société qui allie aux raffinements de la civilisation la plus avancée (et) la naïveté des moeurs primitives.' E. Burnouf, '*Discours sur la langue et la littérature sanscrite,*

In his inaugural lecture to the *College de France*, Burnouf stressed the study of Indian history as a result of the philological study of Indian languages. He emphasized the advantage of being able to date and situate events in Indian history chronologically by studying the development and evolution of Sanskrit and its dialects, particularly Pali and Prakrit.[11] In terms of history-writing, Burnouf introduced the chronological timeline into Indic studies with his clear demarcation of the Vedic and Buddhist eras. According to Naudet, 'E. Burnouf clarified these questions in a new day [of Indic studies], and, by determining the relative times of Brahmanism and Buddhism, he introduced an element of chronology into the history of India, which seems to be unaware of real divisions of time.'[12] As a direct result of the linguistic and philological methods of comparison which were favored by Burnouf, Indologists were able to create an understandable chronological timeline for India in the place of the eighteenth-century image of India as being in a spaceless, timeless continuum, where religious belief, custom and ritual were ostensibly practised as they had originally been conceived of hundreds of years ago with no change or rupture. So rather than speak of a vague concept of India, scholars now traced the historical changes and progress of Vedic, post-Vedic, and Buddhist India.

---

prononcé au *Collège de France*', *Journal Asiatique*, Series 2, Vol. 11 (Jan–Jun 1833): 258.

[11] Ibid.: 266–67 and passim.

[12] 'E. Burnouf éclaira ces questions d'un jour nouveau, et, en déterminant les époques relatives du brahmanisme et du bouddhisme, il introduisit un élément de chronologie dans l'histoire de l'Inde, qui semble ignorer les divisions réelles du temps.' J. Naudet, 'Notice historique sur MM. Burnouf, père et fils', *Mémoires de l'Académie des inscriptions et belles-lettres*, Vol. 20, no. 1 (SD): 321. Also see J. Barthélemy Saint-Hilaire, *Eugene Burnouf. Ses Travaux et sa Correspondence.* (Paris, 1891): 44.

BUDDHISM AND ITS INDIAN ORIGIN

In his lifetime, Burnouf published seven monographs, 18 articles in the *Journal des Savants*, and a total of 36 articles and miscellaneous items in the five series of the *Journal Asiatique*. A master linguist, he published in Zend, Cuneiform, Sanskrit, Pali, and Nepalese languages. But his greatest achievement was the association of Buddhism with India. With Burnouf's debut work the origins of Buddhism in India were discovered and a huge period in Indian history hitherto forgotten now opened up to Western study.

Once the Pali Buddhist canon had been translated, Burnouf decisively established the great antiquity of these texts thereby proving that Buddhism had originated in India. Burnouf also demonstrated the common link between the Northern and Southern traditions of Buddhism[13] and the Great and Little traditions.[14] Although the work bore the imprint of two scholars, Burnouf was almost solely credited with the findings. Lassen went on to carry out notable work on Pali but Burnouf shot to fame as the man who had discovered a new religion of great antiquity. In doing so he was able to open up the entire Buddhist canon to scholars who had been searching in vain for the origins of Buddhism in the Far East.

---

[13] As Buddhism spread in Asia, the followers found themselves in disagreement about the practice of the religion. The basic divisions were the Northern or Mahayana school of Buddhism which became popular in China, Japan, Korea, Tibet and Mongolia, and Southern or Theravada Buddhism which became the norm in Southeast Asia—Thailand, Burma, Cambodia and Laos. Tibetan Buddhism which is also practised today and incorporates a great deal of Tantra, developed much later and largely independent of these two schools due to its geographical isolation.

[14] After the death of Buddha, the followers of Buddhism split into two schools based on disagreements about the level of austerity to be practised. The teachings of the Buddha were split into two main traditions, or 'vehicles', which were the Little or Hinayana and the Great or Mahayana. The lay followers of the Buddha tended to follow the former, which largely consisted of precepts meant for everyday living, while the monks followed the more rigorous Mahayana tradition.

Burnouf also opened a new chapter in the history of India by focusing attention on the Buddhist period. No longer was the interest of scholars solely on the Vedic period of Indian history. With Burnouf's *Essai...*, Buddhism and the Buddhist canon opened the way for a shift in Indic studies in France to the post-Vedic period. Burnouf undoubtedly also provided a greater service to Indian history than he realized. With the philological discovery of Pali and its connection to Sanskrit, historians now began to look more closely at the post-Vedic period as a real historical era, rather than a blur between the Aryan period of Indian history and the Islamic invasions of the medieval period. The Buddhist era, as it was termed, now attracted the attention of scholars who discovered the existence of Republics and Empires, like the Mauryan empire, and discovered that northern India had an evolved system of monarchy and self-governing republics.[15] Continuing on

---

[15] Unfortunately the exigencies of colonial rule dictated that the myth of the Oriental Despot be perpetuated and this period of Indian history, together with Kautilya's *Arthashastra*, remained the preserve of Indic scholars. In India's nationalist tradition too, the unfortunate reliance on the myth of the 'Golden Age' of Vedic Aryanism (see, for example, the revisionist history proposed by Uma Chakravarti, in her essay 'Whatever Happened to the Vedic Dasi?', in *Recasting Women. Essays in Colonial History,* edited by Kumkum Sangari and Sudesh Vaid (Delhi: Kali for Women, 1989) which raises the issue of the forgotten dasas and dasyus while Hindu Nationalists like Dayanand Saraswati of the Arya Samaj were propagating the myth of the Golden Age of Vedic Aryanism. What is significant here is that Indian nationalists built upon this creation of French Indologists to argue that Indians belonged to the Aryan race and therefore should free themselves from British colonial rule. (I discuss this creation of Aryan India by French Indologists and anthropologists in detail in Chapter 5) This meant that Indians too neglected this period of Indian history until the reform of the historical syllabus in post-Independence India. In schools and colleges of modern India, the study of the post-Vedic and Buddhist period, as it is called, now stimulates a discussion on the continued achievements of India, in stark contrast to the colonial histories which portrayed the history of post-Vedic India as a dark age which continued until the colonial period.

his discovery, Burnouf traced the spread of Buddhism to Nepal, Sri Lanka and beyond through the Pali canon.

In 1844 Burnouf published *Introduction à l'histoire du Buddhisme Indien*, the first great French scholarly monograph on Buddhism which established the Indian origins of Buddhism, emphasized a textual approach to Eastern religions, and made Buddhism into an object of western scientific knowledge.[16] By 1852 he had completed a work on the Lotus Sutra. Burnouf was single-handedly responsible for turning the focus of Indic studies in France from Hinduism to Buddhism. French schools created a specific degree in Buddhist studies due to his work.[17] The numbers of Indologists focusing on Buddhism and the numbers of manuals of Buddhism written for erudite and common readers alike increased exponentially. For example, from its founding in 1822 until 1825, the *Journal Asiatique* published only three articles on Indian Buddhism out of a total of about 30 articles focusing on India. After the popularization of Burnouf and Lassen's *Essai...*the number of articles on Indian Buddhism jumped to 10 articles out of a total of 63, in the period 1827–36; a jump from 10 per cent to almost 16 per cent. Thereafter, studies on Buddhism continued to be published in the journal at a steady pace until the number jumped once again towards the end of the

---

Unfortunately, this discussion, introduced in Independent India, comes too late to rectify the damage done both by colonial historians as well as Indian nationalist historians determined to create a 'Golden Age' for India. In a sense this represents the 'colonization of knowledge' wherein India's past was first interpreted and then appropriated by her colonial masters, and then taught to Indians themselves. The result of such a process was that most erstwhile colonies internalized the same discourses of 'western progress' and 'eastern decadence' that they were trying to resist, primarily through the education of a new westernized middle class. This middle class was responsible for the recycling of colonial knowledge back into their own societies.

[16] Lee Irwin, 'Western Esotericism, Eastern Spirituality, and the Global Future', *Esoterica* III (2001): 1–47.

[17] Schwab, *The Oriental Renaissance*: 111.

FIGURE 4.1: ARTICLES ON INDIA BY TOPIC: *JOURNAL DES SAVANTS*, 1817–99

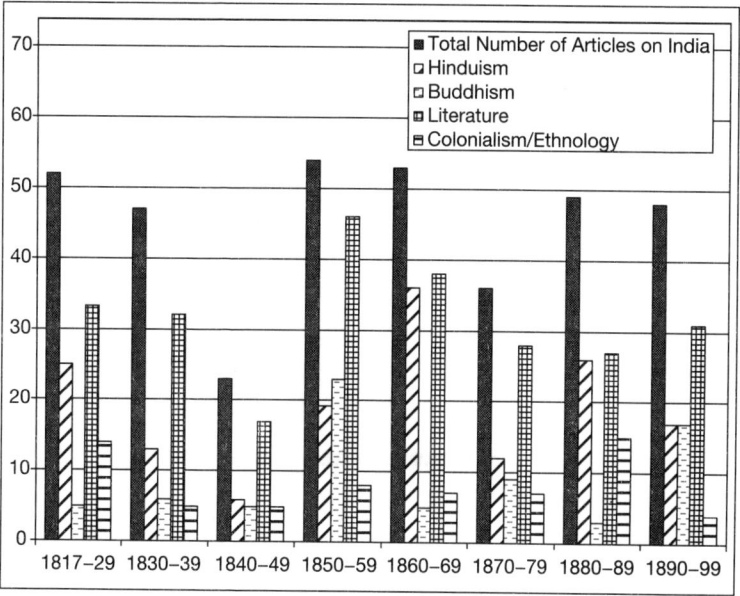

century.[18] The articles on India in the *Journal des Savants* exhibit a similar pattern.[19] The image of India in French academia had definitely changed.

TASSY AND THE STUDY OF INDIAN ISLAM

Another aspect of Indology which shifted was the view of Islam. While older writers had described Islam in India in critical terms, while simultaneously acknowledging its formidable presence in the subcontinent, Indologists in the nineteenth century completely ignored it. Only two major scholars made Indian Islam their focus among a plethora of French Indologists during the long century, an unusual omission for a group which studied the Indian past so assiduously. In most cases, Islam was acknowledged to be an

---

[18] I examine the later popularity of Indian Buddhism in Chapter 6.
[19] See Tables A3, A4, A5 at the end and Figures 4.1 and 4.2.

FIGURE 4.2: Articles on India by topic: *Journal Asiatique*, 1822–1902

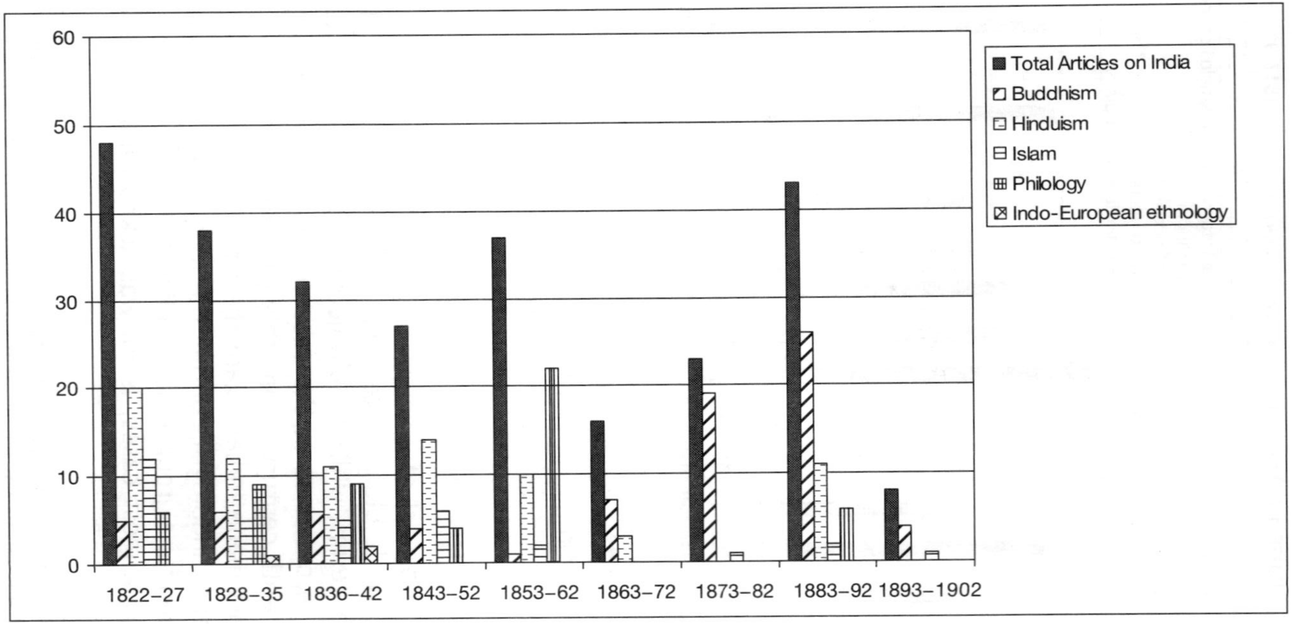

Legend:
- Total Articles on India
- Buddhism
- Hinduism
- Islam
- Philology
- Indo-European ethnology

X-axis categories: 1822–27, 1828–35, 1836–42, 1843–52, 1853–62, 1863–72, 1873–82, 1883–92, 1893–1902

Y-axis: 0, 10, 20, 30, 40, 50, 60

important influence in the subcontinent, but Indologists focused on Sanskrit. Burnouf's only reference to Islam was in the context of historicizing India's past. Noting that the study of documents had revealed that India had remained the same from the descriptions in the epics to the Muslim invasion of the eleventh century, according to Burnouf, 'Thus, being pressed on numerous and decisive documents, the historian will recognize the ancient India of the Mahâbharata and Râmâyana, in India such as it appears to us at the beginning of the eleventh-century AD, to the time of the Moslem invasion.'[20] So while Islam was not necessarily described in disparaging terms by Indologists it simply did not figure in the works of most Indologists. For the most part therefore, Islam in India was ignored. However, the rare reference to Islam in India was usually in the vein of disparagement. For example, even though Garcin de Tassy focused his study on Indian Islam, he noted that the fanaticism common to Islam, and especially the antagonism between Shi'as and Sunnis, had been watered down by contact with Hindu tolerance. According to him, 'The Indian tolerance came to decrease Moslem fanaticism in India. There Sunnites and Shiites do not have this animosity between them which divides the Turks and the Persians; they usually live in good relations and share, with a few exceptions, in the same religious holidays.'[21] Earlier than

---

[20] 'Ainsi, s'appuyant sur des documents nombreux et décisifs, l'historien reconnaîtra l'Inde antique du Mahâbharata et du Râmâyana dans l'Inde telle qu'elle nous apparaît au commencement du onzième siècle de notre ère, au temps de l'invasion musulmane.'Ibid.: 265.

[21] 'La tolerance indienne est venue diminuer dans l'Inde le fanatisme musulman. Là Sunnites et Chiites n'ont point entre eux cette animosité qui divise les Turcs et les Persans; ils vivent ordinairement en bonne intelligence et prennent meme part, à peu d'exceptions près, aux memes fêtes religieuses.'Garcin de Tassy, 'Mémoire sur quelques particularités de la religion musulmane dans l'Inde, d'après les ouvrages hindoustani', *Nouveau Journal Asiatique* (August 1831): 90.

Tassy, Langlès had already expressed this same opinion in stronger terms.

It was there [that] the term of the wars and the persecutions [were] caused by the outraged ambition and the zeal of the Arabs for their religion: because idolatry had its martyrs. This persecution ceased only little by little: the softness of the climate and the character of the Indians made the successors of these Arabs and Mughals lose, in continuation [time], the species of fanaticism that their predecessors [had] expressed.[22]

Thus, even though Tassy belonged in the camp of the Florists the older antagonistic view of Islam expressed by the romantic writers of the previous century was now giving way to a more neutral, incisive opinion. The new generation of scholars from the 1840s expressed their opinion of Islam in India, not by what they wrote about Islam, but rather by choosing *not* to focus on that aspect of India.

The exclusion of studies on Islam in India is an interesting aspect of French Indology, especially in the context of their claim to be the leading Indic scholars in the world. A rare academic who focused on Indian Islam, Garcin de Tassy noted the irony in the exclusion of this aspect of India when he pointed out that in contemporary India, regional languages (particularly Hindustani which was a hybrid language borrowing from Hindi and Urdu) was far more in use than dead and elite languages like Sanskrit. In particular, the fact that this language along with Indian Islam, was

---

[22] 'Ce fut là le terme des guerres et des persécutions causées par l'ambition et le zèle outrés des arabes pour leur religion: car l'idolâtrie eut ses martyrs. Cette persecution ne cessa que peu à peu: la douceur du climat et le caractère des Indiens fit perdre, dans la suite, aux successeurs de ces Arabes et Moghols, l'espèce de fanatisme que leurs prédécesseurs manifesté....' L. Langlès, 'Notice sur l'Indoustan, tirée des manuscrits de la Bibliothèque nationale', *Magasin Encyclopédique*, Vol. 16 (1795): 43–44.

practised by some twenty million people in North India alone, made the subject worthy of attention.

The religion of the Hindus generally draws the attention of the savants who deal with India, and of the travellers who, after having traversed the beautiful provinces of them [Hindus], communicate the fruits of their research to the public. It is not thus [with] Muslim culture in India, which was nevertheless during several centuries the religion of the Government of most of the peninsula on this side [of the] Ganges subjected to the sceptre of [the] Mogol [Mughal], and which is professed still today by several sovereigns of this vast region, and by twenty million individuals of which the number increases every day. The savants spoke little about it; also one is generally unaware of what, precisely, is the state of this religion, [and] its characteristics. This lack of positive data is especially felt by those who want to read the Hindustani and Persian works/writings in India, and decipher the inscriptions of the Moslem monuments of this beautiful part of the world... [in order] to partly fill the gap is why I announce, I undertook work that I submit today to the friends of India.[23]

---

[23] 'La religion des Hindous attire généralement l'attention des savans qui s'occupent de l'Inde, et des voyageurs qui, après en avoir parcouru les belles provinces, communiquent au public les fruits de leurs recherches. Il n'en est pas ainsi du culte musulman dans l'Inde, qui fut néanmoins pendant plusieurs siècles la religion du Gouvernement d'une grande partie de la presqu'île en deçà du Gange soumise au sceptre du Mogol, et qui est encore aujourd'hui professée par plusieurs souverains de cette vaste contrée, et par vingt millions d'individus dont le nombre s'accroît tous les jours. Les savans en ont peu parlé; aussi ignore-t-on généralement quel y est précisément l'état de cette religion, quelles en sont les particularités. Ce manque de données positives se fait surtout sentir à ceux qui veulent lire les ouvrages hindoustani et persans écrits dans l'Inde, et déchiffrer les inscriptions des monumens musulmans de cette belle partie du monde...Pour remplir en partie la lacune que je signale, j'ai entrepris le travail que je soumets aujourd'hui aux amis de l'Inde....' Garcin de Tassy, 'Mémoire sur quelques particularités de la religion musulmane dans l'Inde, d'après les ouvrages hindoustani', *Nouveau Journal Asiatique* (August 1831): 81–82.

In 1829 the *Imprimérie royale* had published a Hindustani language manual which also contained copies of some Hindustani texts. By the late 1830s this was complemented by Garcin de Tassy's *Histoire de la littérature Hindoue et hindoustanie*, published initially by the Asiatic Society of London in 1839 and 1847 which also broadened the scope of Indic studies to include works written in the popular dialects of North India, which had remained outside the scope of Sanskritic and Buddhist scholars. Interestingly, despite the craze for Indological work in Paris, Tassy's work was published by the London Asiatic Society rather than the *Société Asiatique* of Paris.[24] A quote from the Asiatic Journal, published in the *Revue Brittanique*, noted that the French had chosen to study Indian languages like Sanskrit and Pali as opposed to the British, who had chosen contemporary languages like Persian and Turkish which would allow them to maintain diplomatic relations in the region. In effect the French took charge of India's past and the British of India's present.

Eastern literature has made fast progress in France for a few years; the savants do not limit themselves any more to the languages necessary for diplomacy and trade, such as Persian, Turkish or Arabic; they embrace in their studies the faded Sanskrit, Chinese, Georgian... research which they deliver on the history and the philology of the East are [contained in the] collections of the Journal Asiatic, the Journal des Savants and some other periodic writings, which can give [us] an idea of the importance of their work.[25]

---

[24] In fact the majority of Tassy's sources were works commissioned by British administrators. The major source material was compiled using works by full-time employees of the Fort William College at Calcutta, which had been established as a training ground for young officers of the East India Company. Tassy's work came to be used primarily as a local guide by British administrators.

[25] 'La littérature orientale a fait en France de progrès rapides depuis quelques années; les savants ne se bornent plus aux langues nécessaires

Correspondingly Tassy also made another huge contribution to Oriental work by compiling the *Mémoire sur des particularités de la religion Musulmane dans l'Inde d'après les ouvrages hindoustani* and the *Notice sur les fêtes populaires des Hinduous d'après les ouvrages hindoustani*. Both works were initially published as articles in the *Journal Asiatique*[26] and the former was later published as a book. These were catalogues of the festivals, customs, and religious celebrations of Hindus and Muslims as described by contemporary writers of Hindi and Urdu which became very important to British colonial officials in India.[27] Tassy patiently compiled an extensive selection of works in Hindi (which was the language of ordinary Indians, especially in the rural areas of Northern India), Hindustani (which was derived from Urdu and Persian and was very elegant, being spoken mainly by the Muslim elites), Urdu and Dakkhani (which was a version of Urdu spoken by

---

pour la diplomatie et le commerce, tels que le persan, le turc ou l'arabe; ils embrassent dans leurs études le sanskrit, le pali, le chinois, le géorgien.... Les recherches auxquelles ils se livrent sur l'histoire et la philologie de l'Orient sont recueils dans le *Journal Asiatique*, le *Journal des Savants* et quelques autres écrits périodiques, qui peuvent donner une idée de l'importance de leurs travaux.' 'Littérature orientale en France', *Revue Brittanique*, Vol. 17 (March–April 1828): 377.

[26] Garcin de Tassy, 'Mémoire sur quelques particularités de la religion musulmane dans l'Inde, d'après les ouvrages hindoustani', 3 articles, *Nouveau Journal Asiatique* (August 1831).

[27] In fact, the efforts of French scholars who studied aspects of Indian life and culture which were relevant but not fashionable seem to have been sidelined by the Parisian intelligentsia while receiving a warm reception from the British who were only too glad to have help in their colonial enterprise in India. An example of this type is the copious use of French academics' translations of works by Indian Islamic writers from Persian, Urdu, Dakkhani, and Arabic into French, by Elliot, *The History of India, as Told by Its Own Historians. The Muhammadan Period*. Ed. John Dowson (London: Trubner Company, 1867–77). The series was greeted with great acclaim since it professed to present India's history as told by natives, untouched and uninterrupted by the British.

Muslims in Southern India). It included the many genres of prose and poetry, a presentation of the complexity of composition and the elegance of expression on these works. An important aspect was the inclusion of the works of women poets and authors. The huge three-volume work contained extracts of the works of all the authors listed there as well as short biographies.

In terms of academic oversight, there could be two possible explanations for the exclusion of Indian Islam from the mainstream of French Indology. The first and most convincing was that since the French chose to highlight only the Sanskritic culture of India, Islam was simply out of the purview of French Indology. This reasoning points to French Indologists making clear choices about which aspects of India to highlight and which to ignore, thus demonstrating the artificial process by which images of India were constructed. Despite their claims to be rational, scientific scholars, French Indologists only *wanted* to see and present India in terms of her ancient and Sanskritic civilization.

The second possibility is Jean Marie Lafont's reasoning that due to the methodical nature of French academics, Islam was treated as a different academic field, with different principles governing its study and a different administrative structure established for its study.[28] As Tassy realized, Indian Islam had acquired a syncretic nature that was entirely unique in the Islamic world. Centuries of coexistence with Hinduism had led to certain hybrid religious

---

[28] According to Lafont, a combination of the dominance of Arabic and Persian studies from 1699 onwards at the *École des Jeunes de Langues* as well as the 'systematic nature' of the French was responsible for the lack of attention paid to Muslims in India, at least until Garcin de Tassy was appointed as the first to hold the newly created Chair of Hindustani in 1828. However, this does not explain the lack of interest in Muslim India which continued throughout the nineteenth century. Jean-Marie Lafont, *Indika. Essays in Indo-French Relations 1630–1976* (New Delhi: Manohar, 2000): 43.

ceremonies which borrowed heavily from the Hindu culture of lavish feasts and pageantry.

I thus will describe, according to the works which I have
just indicated, the proper festivals in Moslem India and
also the solemnities used in Persia or even among all
Moslems, but [also] what distinguishes India from the particular ceremonies. I will speak about some superstitions
practised by the Moslems [of India] born of contact with
the Hindus; I will give finally the Biography of several very
famous Moslem saints of India, but [who are] unknown out
of its limits.... What [is] especially striking in the external
worship of the Moslems of India, is the deterioration which
it underwent to take the indigenous aspect. They are
these additional ceremonies and these uses [are] not very
[much] in conformity, or contrary with the spirit of Coran,
but which were established imperceptibly by the contact
of the Moslems with the Hindus.... Indeed the worship of
Mahomet was too simple for a country where an allegori-
cal religion and idolatry which speaks to the directions and
imagination dominates, rather than with the spirit and to
the heart.[29]

---

[29] 'Je vais donc décrire, d'après les ouvrages que je viens
d'indiquer, les fêtes propres à l'Inde musulmane et aussi les solennités
usitées en Perse ou même dans tout le monde musulman, mais que
distinguent dans l'Inde des cérémonies particulières. Je parlerai de
quelques pratiques superstitieuses nées du contact des Musulmans avec
les Hindous; je donnerai enfin la Biographie de plusieurs saints musulmans très-célèbres dans l'Inde, mais inconnus hors de ses limites....Ce
qui frappe surtout dans le culte extérieur des musulmans de l'Inde,
c'est l'altération qu'il a subie pour prendre la physionomie indigène. Ce
sont ces cérémonies accessoires et ces usages peu conformes ou con-
traires à l'esprit du Coran, mais qui se sont établis insensiblement par le
contact des Musulmans avec les Hindous....En effet le culte de Mahomet
était trop simple pour un pays où domine une religion allégorique et
idolâtre qui parle aux sens et à l'imagination plutôt qu'à l'esprit et
au coeur...'Garcin de Tassy, 'Mémoire sur quelques particularités de
la religion musulmane dans l'Inde, d'après les ouvrages hindoustani",
Nouveau Journal Asiatique (August 1831): 87–88.

For a scholar of Islam, the variation in Indian Islam would have been a matter of great academic interest. Tassy studied the contrast between practices which 'conformed' to Middle Eastern Islam and to the Koran, and those which went against the 'spirit of Muhammad and the Koran', but formed an essential part of Indian Islamic practice. He also analysed the transformation of Islam as a result of Hindu contact. Yet his works were mentioned only in footnotes by French scholars of Islam.[30] In contrast, the French studied the origins of Sanskritic Buddhism in India, but also engaged with the development of Buddhism in China and the Far East.[31]

One must remember that the French *Comptoirs* in India were inhabited by a minority of Muslims. As the judicial records as well as the state registers indicate, the primary concerns in French India were related to inter-caste disputes.[32] Therefore, the possibility that academic foci

---

[30] Works like E. de Neveu, *Les Khouans: Ordres religieux chez les musulmans de l'Algérie* (Paris: A. Guyot, 1846) which was an early text, compared to the burst of French scholarship on Islam post-1848 which deal with the varieties of Islam. According to George Trumbull (NYU), there are only passing references to Indic Islam. Email communication.

[31] From the *Journal Asiatique*, there were a number of articles which dealt with the links between India and Buddhism in the Far East, including several articles by British scholars. For example, M.B.H. Hodgson, 'Notice sur la langue, la littérature et la religion des Bouddhistes du Népal et du Bhot ou Tibet', 2 articles, Series 2, Vol. 6 (July–December 1830); H.H. Wilson, 'Notice sur trois ouvrages bouddhiques reçus du Nepal', Series 2, Vol. 7 (January–June 1831); M. Klaproth, 'Table chronologique des plus célèbres patriarches et des événemens remarquables de la religion bouddhique; rédigée en 1678 (traduite du Mongol), et commentée', Series 2, Vol. 7 (January–June 1831); Théodore Pavie, 'Examen méthodique des faits qui concernent le *Thien-tchu* on l'Inde', 3 articles, Series 3, Vol. 8 (July–December 1839).

[32] Jean-Claude Bonnan, *Jugemens du tribunal de la chaudrie de Pondichéry, 1766–1817*. 2 vols (Pondichéry Institut Français de Pondichéry, 1999). Bonnan has compiled the records of the Chaudrie or Choultry court of Pondichéry. Among the dozens of cases heard, the majority related to issues of privilege between different castes. In most cases, the court deferred to local custom, rather than a rigid adherence

were at least indirectly influenced by colonial ambitions cannot be ignored. In the case of India, colonial agendas may be read into what was *not* studied, rather than what was.

SCHOLARS HAVE PRACTICAL CONSIDERATIONS TOO

While the end of the Florist debate meant that India was studied more scientifically in the spirit of the nineteenth-century quest for empiricism and science, it also meant that institutional Indology was marginalized. The political and financial repercussions of the 1830 Revolution meant that universities were starved of funding, affecting Indic studies. As McGetchin points out, the *Société Asiatique* suffered from a lack of members and funds between 1833 and 1840.[33] Mohl echoed the financial deprivation of Indic studies in his 1846 report to the *Société*.[34] According to McGetchin, by adopting a more exacting scholarly agenda, the non-Florist scholars eventually cut themselves off from a more popular intellectual culture. Thus even if the scientific scholars had purged their Florist colleagues from positions of power in the *Société Asiatique* by shifting to a method less accessible outside the university, they began to lose the *Société's* popular appeal.[35] He points out that literary taste in France still tended to lean towards the florid and romantic, and by distancing themselves from

---

to French or even 'Hindu' law. The *Etat Civil*, or Civil Registry of the French *Comptoirs* which recorded births in French India from 1824 (prior to this the Registry only contained records for the mixed race *Topas*, Hindu converts to Christianity and the French) also substantiates the fact that the majority of natives in French India were Hindus.

[33] Douglas T. McGetchin, 'Wilting Florists: The Turbulent Early Decades of the Société Asiatique, 1822–1860', *Journal of the History of Ideas*, Vol. 64, No. 4 (2003): 576.[34] Quoted in Raymond Schwab, *The Oriental Renaissance* (New York: Columbia University Press).

[34] Mohl, *Vingt-sept Ans*, 2 vols (Paris: Reinwald, 1879–80), Vol. 1: 204. Cited in McGetchin, 'Wilting Florists': 577.

[35] Ibid.

this tradition of eloquence, the *Société* made it harder to procure popular and institutional support for itself.

Popular references to India came partly through the works of Edgar Quinet's *Génie des Réligions*,[36] Michelet's *Bible de l'Humanité*,[37] Victor Hugo's *Orientales*, Etienne Jouy's plays (*Les Bayadères* and *Tippo-Sahib*), Philarète Chasles and Joseph Méry's short stories, Lamartine, Vigny and Leconte de Lisle's poems, Théophile Gautier's novels, Flaubert's writings and Baudelaire's art.[38]

Schwab uses the example of Balzac's literary character, Louis Lambert, to highlight the continued belief among literary circles in Paris, that India was a romantic and ancient nation. He imbued in Lambert the phrases 'smiling images of blissful love', 'the Bible...[was] part of the traditional history of the antediluvian peoples who had shared a universal history' and the belief that the Greeks had borrowed their civilization 'both from the Hebrew Bible and the sacred texts of India'.[39]

---

[36] Edgar Quinet titled the chapter on India the 'Oriental Renaissance' in his *Genie des religions* published in 1841. He compared the ancient Hindu texts to the Iliad and Odyssey and the role of early translators like Anquetil to the great poets and scholars of the West.

[37] See Jules Michelet, *Bible de l'Humanité* (Paris, 1864). In this work Michelet incorporated a great deal of Indian thought and philosophy which he had spent the preceding decades in learning and understanding. His deep interest in Indic studies was a continuing vein which grew with his friendship with Burnouf as well as his explorations into natural history and law. In fact his fascination with Indian literature and thought as well as his increasing dependence on it to interpret his life can be seen in his later works, both historical and literary, which not only include his interpretation of Indian thought but also his indebtedness to it.

[38] Raymond Schwab, *The Oriental Renaissance* (New York: Columbia University Press, 1984). Also see Richard Anderson, *India in Romantic and Parnassian French Poetry* (New Haven, 1950), Jean Biès, *ittérature française et pensée hindoue des origines à 1950* (Paris: C. Klincksieck), 1973. Reprint 1992; and Jean Lahor, *L'Influence de la pensée religieuse indienne dans le romanticisme et le Parnasse* (Paris: AG Nizet), 1962.

[39] Ibid.: 104.

Thus, on the one hand the popular literary conception of India as a land of romance and bliss continued to be propagated. Among the Indian words which Rémusat noted in French romantic literary vocabulary and in nineteenth-century French dictionaries were 'rajah', 'pariahs', 'sutras', 'kshatriyas', 'nabob', 'avatar' and 'bayadère'.[40] On the other hand serious scholars like Burnouf continued to warn against romanticizing the Orient. In the preface to the Bhagawata Purana he noted that 'Philosophical fragments...should not be confused with dogmatic passages, and one should not seek in them what we in the West understand, strictly speaking, as philosophy....'[41]

According to McGetchin the lack of popular reception to the changed study of India led to the decline of Indic studies in France at a time when German Indology was at its height. He cites Lacôte, 'The Burnouf school, aging among unfavourable circumstances and the indifference of the public powers, was not able either to form a new generation or to deliver what one expected of them.'[42] As a result, Indic studies in France 'dozed for twenty years'[43] and 'the entire university organization put itself in opposition to any adept recruited by Sanskrit studies.'[44] Yet Schwab points out that in the period 1825–69 the *Revue Brittannique* published 20 articles on the religions of India and China.[45] Similar articles were published in the *Revue Européene, Correspondant* and *Revue de Paris.*[46] The *Revue des Deux Mondes* actually saw a steady increase in Indic articles from 26 in 1829–39 to 29 in 1840–49 and

---

[40] Ibid.: 107.
[41] Quoted in ibid.: 461.
[42] Felix Lacôte, 'L'Indianisme', *Le Livre du Centenaire (1822–1922)*, ed. Société Asiatique (Paris, 1922): 229–31. Quoted in McGetchin, 'Wilting Florists': 579.
[43] Lacôte, 'L'Indianisme': 232. Quoted in McGetchin: 579.
[44] Lacôte, 'L'Indianisme': 231. Quoted in McGetchin: 580.
[45] Schwab, *La Renaissance orientale*: 100.
[46] Ibid.

37 in 1850–59.[47] The *Encyclopédie des gens du monde, Dictionnaire de la conversation, Encyclopédie du XIX siècle* and the *Dictionnaire universel d'histoire et de géographie* contained several articles and entries on India and Indic scholars.[48] Schwab has also noted the popularity of books with Indian themes in Lorenz's *Catalogue de la Libraire,* and Brunet's *Manuel du Librairie.*[49] What seems more likely in the light of Schwab's evidence is that a shift took place in Indic studies away from Brahminic texts.

Burnouf's work had already highlighted the importance of Indian Buddhism as the source of Far Eastern Buddhism. Yet Buddhism was not as important in the study of Indian history, offering at best a brief philosophical interlude to the staunchly held Brahminic beliefs.[50] It is possible then that Indologists struggling for institutional support viewed the French colonial empire in Indo-China as the answer to their quandary. Through a study of Indian Buddhism, they could support the practical aims of France by furthering an understanding of Indo-Chinese Buddhism, and simultaneously ensure their own academic relevance.

As Penny Edwards points out, the school of Buddhist Studies which emerged in Europe during the early nineteenth century found its initial inspiration in India and remained dominated by Indologists well into the 1900s.[51] Masuzawa notes the particular importance of the French

---

[47] See Table A5.

[48] Schwab, *La Renaissance orientale*: 101.

[49] Ibid.: 100–101.

[50] See Romila Thapar, *Asoka and the Decline of the Mauryas* (Delhi: Oxford University Press, 1960) and Akira Hirakawa and Paul Groner, *A History of Indian Buddhism: From Sakyamuni to Early Mahayana* (Delhi: Motilal Banarsidass, 1996).

[51] Penny Edwards, 'Taj Angkor: Enshrining *l'Inde* in le *Cambodge*', Paper presented at 'Indochina', India and France: Cultural Representations, University of Newcastle upon Tyne, Newcastle, England, 5–7 September 2003: 11.

school of Indology in the recovery of Buddhist texts.[52] Scholars agree that the breakthrough in the study of Buddhism began when the British East India Company servant, Brian Hodgson, gifted tens of Buddhist texts and documents in Sanskrit to the Asiatic Society of Calcutta, the Royal Asiatic Society in London and the *Société Asiatique* in Paris. As Masuzawa notes, the first two societies did not pay much attention to this gift, preferring to continue their focus on Sanskritic texts of Hinduism.[53] Since Buddhism had virtually died out in India, and Britain was more occupied by the task of learning about India, this neglect makes sense. For France however, the urgency of the colonial enterprise in Indo-China at this time made these texts a most opportune discovery for learning about Indo-Chinese and Chinese religion.

Following in Burnouf's steps, the study of Buddhism in France focused solely on the retrieval of texts and the reconstruction of textual Buddhism which formed the foundation for the elaboration of Buddhism as a religion. As Max Müller noted in 1862, while Burnouf acknowledged the importance of Buddhist texts and literatures in Tibet, Mongolia, China and Ceylon, he insisted that the 'original' and 'purest' form of Buddhism was contained in the Sanskrit corpus sent by Hodgson from Nepal, the remaining being corruptions of the original.[54] As Masuzawa points out, in the judgement of the scholars, the actual on-the-ground manifestations of Buddhism were subjects more suitable for the attention of missionaries, casual observers, and travellers chronicling foreign curiosities, than for serious-minded philologists who should dedicate their labour first to the reconstructions of 'original Buddhism' and

---

[52] Tomoko Masuzawa, *The Invention of World Religions* (Chicago: University of Chicago Press, 2005): 125.

[53] Ibid.

[54] Cited in ibid.: 125–26.

subsequently to the study of its historical developments.[55] Insisting that the scientific approach to the study of Buddhism involved the use of verifiable texts, Buddhism was reconfigured within the European imagination[56] and projected onto the colonial present of Indo-China as being solely Indic in origin and as deriving all its purity from Indic texts on Buddhism.[57] As Lamairesse noted,

> Descended from the high plateaus of Asia, the Aryan race populated all the Occident, conquered India and Persia, acted by this one [similarly] on the Semites, and finally, by India, printed its seal [left its mark], in all [of the] Far East. Today Aryan civilization goes up towards [returns to] its cradle; the Slavic, English, and French ones [races], inserted each day more narrowly [colonizing the interior] in Central Asia and the Chinese empire; it is thus for us of most interest to know the current result of the action and the influence of the religions resulting from the Indian Aryans on these countries [Far East]; and the key of this influence is especially [found] in the life of the Çâkyamouni Buddha.[58]

In turn this led to an interest in India's influences globally including South East and East Asia. Felix Lacôte noted

---

[55] Ibid.: 126.

[56] Ibid.

[57] Edwards, 'Taj Angkor': 12. Also, see Donald Lopez, *Curators of the Buddha: the Study of Buddhism under Colonialism* (Chicago: University of Chicago Press, 1995).

[58] ' Descendue des hauts plateaux de l'Asie, la race Aryenne a peuplé tout l'Occident, conquis l'Inde et la Perse, agi par celle-ci sur les Sémites, et enfin, par l'Inde, imprimé son cachet, à tout l'Extrême-Orient. Aujourd'hui la civilisation Aryenne remonte vers son berceau; les slaves, les Anglais, les Français, inséré chaque jour plus étroitement dans la Haute-Asie et l'empire Chinois; il est donc pour nous le plus haut intérêt de connaître le résultat actuel de l'action et de l'influence sur ces countrées des religions issues des Aryens de l'Inde; et la clef de cette influence se trouve surtout dans la vie du Bouddha Çâkyamouni.'Ibid.: 23.

that the French were among the leaders in trying to link Indian influences in Asia, especially in Indo-China.[59] He cited the efforts of Etienne Aymonier who stressed the extent to which India had influenced Indo-China, from the use of Sanskrit by the Indo-Chinese royalty to the heavy Brahminical influence in the bas-reliefs of Angkor, as well as the Sanskritist and Sinologist Edouard Huber. Lacôte noted also that the *École Française d'Extrême-Orient* founded in 1899 and based first in Saigon and later in Hanoi was an important institution for studies on India and Indo-China.[60] As Louis Finot points out, Emile Sénart was a leading scholar in the domain of Asian studies, and that '... he exerted a dominant influence on the foreign relations of French orientalism and our scientific enterprises in Asia'.[61] According to Finot, Sénart was instrumental in the establishment and growth of the EFEO.

> But the happy influence of Mr. Sénart was especially felt in Indo-China. He had formerly been interested in the Aymonier mission and the deciphering of the Sanskrit inscriptions brought back by this voyager. When Mr. Doumer resolved to create the *Ecole Français d'Extrême-Orient*, Mr. Sénart was the first to open it by his design and, with his friends Auguste Barth and Michel Bréal, the charge to realize the EFEO.[62]

---

[59] Lacôte, 'L'Indianisme': 245–46.

[60] In fact the EFEO was initially proposed as a society to study Indian history, to be called the History Society of Chandernagore. The importance of Indo-China in French colonial history led to the reconfiguring of the Society as an institution which would study both India and Indo-China.

[61] '...il exerça une influence prépondérante sur les relations extérieures de l'orientalisme français et sur nos enterprises scientifiques en Asia.' L. Finot, 'Necrologie. Émile Sénart', *Bulletin de l'École Française d'Extrême Orient*, 1928, Vol. 28: 343.

[62] 'Mais surtout en Indochine que s'est fait sentir l'heureuse influence de M. Sénart. Il s'était jadis intéressé à la mission Aymonier et au déchiffrement des inscriptions sanskrites rapportées par ce voyageur.

Émile Sénart, a leading Indologist completed his life of the Buddha which laid emphasis on the Indian tradition of royalty. The work titled *Essai sur la légende du Buddha* was published in 1875 in *Asiatick Researches*. He also studied Buddhist inscriptions in India and in Indo-China. Following Sénart, Louis de La Vallée Poussin wrote on popular Buddhism and the yogic and tantra derivations of Buddhism which were practised in Nepal, Tibet and the Far East.

The work of later Indologists like Bergaigne and Barth's *Inscriptions sanskrites de Campâ et du Cambodge* also merged the Indic and Indo-Chinese interests. Louis Finot, prominent Indologist and first president of the EFEO declared in his inaugural address that the EFEO would study the part of Indochina which owed its monument, its customs and its culture to India.[63] By 1928 French scholars had begun the publication of *Bibliographie Bouddhique*, a primary French source for Buddhist studies of all types.

Finot also pointed out that the lack of academic interest in French Indo-China made it an easy target for Orientalists from rival European nations underscoring the close connection between scholarship and colonialism and urging greater academic focus on Cambodge.[64] Despite the scholarly focus on the colonial influence of India in South East Asia, the French government did not similarly stress this 'Indian' heritage of Indo-China in popular representations of colonialism. It was left to British academics to mention this aspect of Indo-China's past. I have looked at this issue elsewhere.[65] The logical explanation of this discrepancy

---

Lorsque M. Doumer résolu de créer l'Ecole Français d'Extrême-Orient, M. Sénart fut le premier à qui il s'ouvrit de son dessin et qui eut, avec ses amis Auguste Barth et Michel Bréal, la charge de le réaliser.' Finot, 'Necrologie. Émile Sénart',: 344–45.

[63] Edwards, 'Taj Angkor': 5. Cited from Paul Doumer, L'Indochine française (Paris: Librairie Vuibert, 1930): 270–74.

[64] Ibid.: 6.

[65] Jyoti Mohan ' "I Thought India was French": The Images of India at the Exposition Universelle, Paris 1931', *Francophone Postcolonial Studies*, 3.1 (Spring/Summer 2005). Also see Edwards.

can be found in the exigencies of colonial history and in the unfortunate but inevitable influence of colonial policy and rivalry on scholarship.

Whether academics inspired colonial projects or were inspired by them remains unclear. However, their work mirrored the development of the colonial project and ideology. For instance, the articles of the *Journal Asiatique* clearly indicate that the dip in Indic subjects came at the mid-century when France was actively colonizing Indo-China.[66]

In yet another example where academic and political aims combined, the French Ministry of Public Education funded a mission by Delaporte to India in 1876 to study the relationship between Hindu and Cambodian art. Soon after Delaporte published an account of his journey[67] and emphasized the similarities between the height of the Khmer Kingdom and the brilliant Indian empires. He also stressed the duty of France in reviving 'the marvellous past of these people'.[68] Certainly, French interest in Buddhism became doubly significant with colonial expansion in the Far East.

BRITISH PREOCCUPATIONS

While French Indologists continued studying India almost exclusively from Sanskrit texts, the British had moved to practical considerations of understanding contemporary India and Indians. Tassy's work on Indian Islam, was useful

---

[66] See Table A4.

[67] Louis Delaporte, 'Rapport fait au Ministre de la Marine et des colonies et au minister de l'Instruction Publique, des cultes et des beaux arts, par M. Louis Delaporte, sur la mission scientifique aux ruines des monuments Khmers des l'ancien Cambodge", *Journel Officiel de la republique Française*, Vol. 6, No. 90.

[68] Edwards, 'Taj Angkor': 5. Cited from Louis Delaporte, *Voyage au Cambodge: L'Architecture Khmer* (Paris: Librairie ch. Delagrave, 1880): 159, 337–38.

both for its study of Indian Muslims who were a substantial portion of India's population, as well as its contribution to the understanding of vernacular literature. Similarly, the neglect of Buddhism stemmed from the fact that at least in India, Buddhism had virtually died out.

Instead British writers looked to the history of India as a window into a contemporary understanding of the country. The production of colonial histories was part of a colonizing apparatus, which privileged the narrative of the colonial historian and justified the existence of the colonial state. The first and most important process was the appropriation of native histories and the voices of natives. Histories could only be claimed to be rational and legitimate if written by a member of the civilized, colonizing classes, who set out, ostensibly to make sense of the chaotic, disordered past that faced them in the mission of civilizing 'natives'.

Once this task of appropriation was complete, the historian set out to construct a 'history' from the mass of tradition, superstition, legend, and myth that confronted him in the colony. The appellation of 'history' to his work meant that the task was undertaken in the spirit of academic, rational, and scientific inquiry. The historian's task was to separate the wheat from the chaff, thereby privileging certain sources and aspects of his material over others. As Thapar points out, historical interpretation can therefore become a two-way process, where the needs of the present are read into the past, and where the image of the past is sought to be imposed upon the present.[69]

The process of historical interpretation was aimed at the explanation of certain phenomena in the Indian past. Therefore, there was no 'total' history of the colonial past. In the first place the different political interests operating within the EIC set the foundation of the Raj on competing interpretations of the Indian past. This basic layer of

---

[69] Romila Thapar, *The Past and Prejudice* (New Delhi, 1975): 1.

historical exploration was followed by a far more nuanced and sophisticated discourse which was used to bolster the growing administrative and state apparatus. Indian history, assimilated thereby to the history of Great Britain, would henceforth be used as a comprehensive measure of difference between the peoples of these two countries. Politically that difference was spelled out as one between rulers and the ruled; ethnically, between a white *Herrenvolk* and blacks; materially between a prosperous Western power and its poor Asian subjects; culturally between higher and lower levels of civilization, between the superior religion of Christianity and indigenous belief systems made up of superstitions and barbarism, all adding up to an irreconcilable difference between colonizer and colonized.[70]

All claimed to be writing their histories 'from the earliest times' thus leading the reader to believe that the subject had no history before the historian gave it a voice. Thereby India had no history before the beginning of the historical chronicle.

As Guha points out,

> ...the substitution of Indian culture by colonialism was completed in two successive movements—the abolition of the historic culture of the Hindus followed by the supersession of that of the Muslims. Taken together, these two movements amounted to a deletion of the entire pre-colonial past of our people who were then compensated for that loss by the gift of a new history—a foreshortened history with the colonial state as its subject.[71]

Also they tended, when discussing religious developments in India, to conflate the state with religion. Thus divisions of history were the Hindu period, Buddhist period,

---

[70] Ranajit Guha, *Dominance Without Hegemony. History and power in Colonial India* (Cambridge, Mass, 1997): 3.

[71] Ibid.: 79.

Mohammedan period, and finally the British period. As Gyan Pandey points out, this production of politico-religious states tended to play out in colonial historical narratives as explanations of Hindu-Muslim violence and communal antipathy with no regard to time, space and political experiences of people.[72] Colonial history was emptied of all contextual narrative except the linear progression of the Indian state from a state of anarchic, religious rivalry to the superior, secular qualities of the 'just British state'. In this exercise of political legitimacy, the British created stereotypes of ethnic groups as 'quarrelsome' or as 'weak', 'fanatic', 'martial', etc., also thereby setting the stage for an official policy of exclusivism, and patronage of certain groups to the antagonism of others. The colonial state, through this production of 'history' was thus also setting the stage for a successful tenure as the only neutral presence by furthering a policy of division.

British histories were set by the political and professional background from which authors wrote. Each constructed his own image of India, which sometimes conflicted with each other. Yet the focus on different aspects of Indian past tended to dovetail neatly into a grand explanation of the legitimacy of the colonial state through the superiority of the civilizing mission and the record of colonial rule as a civilizing force.

Among the widely-read histories of India were the works of Edmund Burke and James Mill. A conservative defender of British politics, Edmund Burke nevertheless viewed the Empire and its practices of rule with deep reservations. Foremost in impeaching Warren Hastings, Burke openly admitted to the moral and political excesses of the British EIC officials. Primarily concerned with communities that were threatened, he recognized India as a political community of individuals with a history, tradition and

---

[72] Gyan Pandey, *The Construction of Communalism in Colonial North India* (Delhi, 1990).

social structure of their own. He also admitted that these institutions had been fractured by the British seeking their own personal enrichment. Burke was really concerned about India also because of the moral impact he saw as rebounding on England itself: in his opinion the decayed morals of men such as Warren Hastings were bound to be detrimental to social order and cohesion in Britain. Burke tended to view the Indian past as dark, but unlike most of his contemporaries and successors in Indian affairs, he admitted that this view of the Indian past could be a result of his own ignorance and lack of comprehension rather than an indictment of the backwardness of India and therefore a reason to deny them political self-determination. Burke saw India as possessed of a system of law, society and government that was ideal; the result of centuries of development and possessed of all the checks and balances needed. While British justice needed to be applied to India, this was to ensure that plunder and mis-rule no longer took place. India had to be governed according to Indian experiences and tradition lest the fabric of Indian society be destroyed.

The first real 'historian' of India, James Mill, never visited India, yet his *History of India* started the flood of historical works on India. Written from a political-philosophical point of view, Mill was writing a rationalistic, utilitarian history[73] and therefore saw no good in India's past achievements.

---

[73] Mill has traditionally been portrayed as a classic utilitarian by historians like Eric Stokes, *The English Utilitarians and India* (Michigan: Clarendon Press, 1959); Gautam Chakravarty, *The Indian Mutiny and the British Imagination* (Cambridge: Cambridge UP, 2005); and Uday Singh Mehta, *Liberalism and Empire: A Study in Nineteenth-century British Liberal Thought* (Chicago: University of Chicago Press, 1999). However scholars like Jennifer Pitts, *A Turn to Empire: The Rise of Imperial Liberalism in Britain and France* (Princeton: Princeton University Press, 2005) have expressed their doubt that Mill was guided strictly by Utilitarian ethics in his portrayal of India, positing instead that he was motivated more by imperial ambition for Britain.

Applying his own conceptions of civilization to judge India, he found only the worst forms of priestly despotism and superstition. The political and legal systems too were despotic and Indian law was too vague to provide any relief. Religion was solely the power of the Brahmins and consisted of useless and harmful ceremonies rather than the morality of ideas of improvement. The social system and the state of education were dismal. India was in an inferior state of civilizational development. Hindu society lacked a sense of historicity, development, and progress and was hence backward, savage and based on myths. Without modern tools, art, sculpture and architecture were too ornate and yet inferior to the West. A slight but passing improvement came with the Muslim invasions of India, which injected some sense of historicity into India, a belief in one God and political unity; yet Muslim India continued to be despotic and therefore the character of the people and essential Indian venality remained unchanged. The real development of India could only occur under the superior civilizing influence of the British.

Another group of British writers were military historians, who focused essentially on political histories, accounts of battles, and the transference of political power. In most of these accounts, the state of society appeared only when it was fundamental to an understanding of statecraft. This group was among the first writers of 'Indian' history. The dominant theme in most of their writings was a description of the chaotic political structure and weakened military apparatus of native kingdoms, which justified the colonial conquests of these areas.

Joseph Davey Cunningham joined the East India Company's army and went out to India as a cadet at 16. His experiences and interest in Sikh affairs was published in 1849 as the *History of the Sikhs*. The work was based primarily on official records, personal observations, and narratives like the *Adi-Granth*, *Dabistan-i-Mazahib* and the

Siyar-ul-Mutakherin for the period before colonial inter-action. Describing India as being in a state of universal resentment, peasant against their masters, aristocracy against rulers, Cunningham described the internal politics of the Sikhs, the canny rule of Ranjit Singh and the rea-sons for the Anglo-Sikh wars after his death. Ultimately however, Cunningham saw the alleviation of problems in the establishment of a good English administration and the spread of Christianity.

Grant Duff, inspired by the friendship of Elphinstone and his experiences as Political Agent at Satara, wrote a *History of the Marathas*. This was his only historical work and did not see any revisions or subsequent editions after its first publication in 1826. While the work had great merit in being a pioneer effort in recording information about regional kingdoms in India, Duff was criticized for his dreary prose, omission of certain historical events, and factual errors. The reason for these may lie in the use that Duff made of his sources. Despite trying to be as scientific as possible, Duff used primary documents in the archives of the Raja of Satara, other documents and especially land records held by other nobles, eyewitness accounts of bat-tles and significant political events, and Hindu and Muslim chroniclers rather than local Maratha chroniclers. While Duff believed that this body was the most historically true literature available, there were several biases—of official sources, of eyewitnesses, of the Hindu and Muslim chroni-clers in favour of or against certain social groups, in their narration of events, etc. Ultimately however, the work was meant to justify the imperial mission, in the light of the chaotic infighting among the Maratha princes.

As opposed to French writings, British writings on India tended to focus essentially on socio-economic and socio-political issues—who owned the land, how was the wealth from the land shared between the proprietors and the state and finally on the relationship of power and property at the local level.[74] These constituted the first historical writings on India. Later on, extended political narratives were developed as the state apparatus expanded. In all these needs of the ruling state, the distance between the colonizers and the natives ensured that accurate information about these issues was not available. Therefore history was a convenient alternative; by researching the past of India administrators hoped to understand local structures of economy and power. In doing so however, they brought with them traditions of European history-writing, political philosophies and the discipline of a Western academic subject which produced a very different kind of knowledge that they sought to understand.[75] In doing so they also tended to privilege certain types of narratives like written accounts, while dismissing oral narratives, and local legend.[76]

CONCLUSION

By the middle of the century, the image of India in French academia had shifted, but subtly. While Parisian academics continued to drive the trends in Indology and the search for Sanskrit manuscripts representing an ancient civilization continued, the older romantic view of India was now replaced by an incisive, scientific tone, which was sometimes critical of contemporary Indian foibles. Rather than writing lyrically about the literature of India, scholars now stressed factual, scientific knowledge in terms of grammatical and philological data. The move from romance to science also threw attention on other periods of Indian history, such as the Buddhist period, leading to critical comparisons of Brahminic religion

---

[74] Guha, *Dominance Without Hegemony*: 160–61.

[75] Ibid.: 163.

[76] Retrieving these histories has been a modern phenomenon. See Gyan Prakash, *Bonded Histories: Genealogies of Labour Servitude in Colonial India* (Cambridge: Cambridge University Press, 2003).

with Buddhism. No longer were Brahmins seen as representative of Indic greatness. They did however continue to dominate French impressions of India but for other reasons. As I will investigate in the next chapter, the Brahmins of India were considered great, not because of their literary and cultural accomplishments, but because they were considered to be 'Aryan'. According to Burnouf, the Brahmins represented a great *era* of creativity and accomplishment for Indian civilization. As a group the Brahmins did not necessarily warrant the highest praise, since they built a religion which relied on the blind credulity of the people they governed. '...Because the Brahmins requested too much from easily credulous peoples to which they gave laws....'[77] The importance of India and of the Brahmins of India lay in their philosophy, laws, and literature. These, in turn, were representative of a greater human spirit which demanded the attention of scholars worldwide. According to Burnouf, 'It is India, with its philosophy and its myths, its literature and its laws, which we will study in its language. It is more than India, Gentlemen, it is a page of the origins of the world, the primitive history of the human spirit, that we will try to decipher together.'[78]

As the romance of India waned, the results of comparing a civilization which was as different from Europe as night to day led to the colonializing of *knowledge*, a process whereby Western standards meant that different

---

[77] '...Parce-que les Brahmanes avaient trop demandé à la crédulité facile des peoples auxquels ils ont donné des lois....' E. Burnouf, 'Discours sur la langue et la littérature sanscrite, prononcé au Collège de France', *Journal Asiatique*, Series 2, Vol. 11 (January–June 1833): 263–64.

[78] 'C'est l'Inde, avec sa philosophie et ses mythes, sa littérature et ses lois, que nous étudierons dans sa langue. C'est plus que l'Inde, messieurs, c'est une page des origines du monde, de l'histoire primitive de l'esprit humain, que nous essaierons de déchiffrer ensemble.'ibid.: 272.

was often seen as inferior. Indologists no longer focused on what the Brahmins of India claimed to have done or written. Rather, they analysed the language, which was ostensibly more reliable, since it did not contain the human element of error. Through an analysis of syntax and grammar, Indologists could now study not only the evolution of language (Sanskrit), but also account for changes within the language in terms of the 'degeneration' of India.

In addition, institutional support for Indology declined and it was distanced from popular Orientalism in France. Indologists thus turned to comparative studies of India with Asia, particularly the Buddhist comparison between India and Indo-China, which greatly aided the French colonial understanding of the latter. In this manner the colonial agenda was tied closely to the careers of Indologists.

Another manner in which Indology changed was through its espousal of the scientific method. Since the sciences had become so popular by mid-century in France, Indology needed to reconfigure itself in terms of physical science. The next stage in the image of India in France was thus spearheaded by anthropologists. With anthropology, new notions of race and the importance of physical markers of progress, rather than older notions of cultural or linguistic markers redrew the image of India.

Chapter 5

The Glory of Ancient India Stems from her Aryan Blood: The Development of 'Scientific Anthropology' in Relation to India

A Dr Paterson of Calcutta, having examined the skulls of a number of Hindus concluded that the skull of an average Hindu man aged thirty years was comparable to the skull of a fifteen year old European boy. Therefore, if one believes that the volume of the skull is an indicator of the intelligence of the individual, it is not impossible to understand why a mere 30,000 Europeans have successfully conquered this huge nation of 40 million Hindus.[1]

The problem was that colonialism was founded on a basic contradiction: on the one side was a rhetoric proclaiming that the colonized possessed the capacity to become civilized, while on the other was a political and economic agenda that depended on exclusiveness and the myth of racial purity.[2]

By the middle of the nineteenth century the rapidly growing enterprise of imperialism had established its position in the intellectual lives of European nations. European colonialists

---

[1] *Revue Britannique*, Vol. 4, (January–February 1826): 402.

[2] Anne Maxwell, *Colonial Photography and Exhibitions. Represent-ations of the 'Native' and the Making of European Identities* (London and New York: Leicester University Press, 1999): 3. Maxwell is referring to all Western colonial projects—British, French, German, Dutch and American.

now justified their dominance and continued exploitation of colonies in terms of their natural superiority and their duty as advanced civilizations to civilize other, lesser cultures. The merging of this need to justify imperialism with the emerging discipline of anthropology inevitably led to the use of 'scientific data' in the form of anthropometric measurements to prove conclusively that colonies were peopled by inferior races who needed the 'benevolent' rule of their colonial masters. This chapter follows the development of India as a specific racial entity[3] from the middle of the nineteenth century, as reflected in the work of Louis Rousselet, Arthur Gobineau, Paul Topinard, and Gustave le Bon. In fact, the decline in the number of articles on Indian history and philology in the mid-nineteenth century was matched by an increase in the number of anthropological articles on India.[4]

The first section of this chapter provides the context for nineteenth-century anthropological writings about India. The second section looks at the opinion of Paul Topinard regarding the position of India in a hierarchy of men, followed by sections on Gobineau, Rousselet and Le Bon. Thus the study of anthropology is contextualized in the example of India.

THE STUDY OF MAN

The scientific study of other people in the early part of the nineteenth century was undertaken by men who called themselves ethnologists. The work consisted mostly of

---

[3] I use 'race' in this project to define a category which was socially constructed to include a group of people who supposedly represented specific physiological and mental characteristics. On the other hand, the modern category of ethnicity, used to specify a group of people with specific common backgrounds such as history, culture, language, etc., is a more accurate way of categorizing people, even though many 'ethnicities' can, and invariably do overlap.

[4] See Tables A6, A7, A8 and Figures 5.1, 5.2 and 5.3.

'natural histories' of man, which became the examination of non-European peoples.[5] Various models of human development emerged out of these ethnological accounts, some privileging the notion of development through association with 'superior' cultures and others arguing that levels of development were determined by heredity.[6] The most common division between ethnologists was between the monogenists who believed that all humans had a common ancestry and therefore could achieve the same level of civilization[7] and the polygenists who insisted that different human races developed independently, based on intrinsic genetic factors.[8] According to the polygenists the level of

---

[5] Eighteenth-century ethnologists who contributed a good deal to later conceptualizations of race include the naturalists Georges-Louis Leclerc, Comte de Buffon and Carolus Linnaeus. They were followed in the nineteenth century by Georges Cuvier and Saint Simon.

[6] A comprehensive study of early ethnological and anthropological figures and institutions is Martin Staum, *Labeling People. French Scholars on Society, Race and Empire, 1815–48* (Montreal and Kingston: Mc Gill's-Queen's University Press, 2003).

[7] The most famous of the monogenists were Linnaeus, Buffon, Cuvier, and Quatrefuges. These men held that all men originated in a single region based on the Biblical or Adamic story of Adam and Eve. The differences between men in the current time were solely a result of environmental factors. Although the monogenists accepted that different species or races of men were not equal in ability, the fact that there was one single point of origin meant that, at least theoretically speaking, given the right conditions, lower races could evolve to the level of superior races. See John Haller, 'The Species Problem: Nineteenth-century Concepts of Racial Inferiority in the Origin of Man Controversy', *American Anthropologist*, 72 (1970): 1319–29. Another interesting aspect of the monogenist group was that many of them were naturalists. John Greene, 'Some Early Speculations on the Origin of the Human Species', *American Anthropologist*, 56 (1954): 31–41.

[8] Influential polygenists were Paul Broca and Saint Simon, who pointed out that even in the Bible there was reference to many groups of men, clearly distinguished from other groups by their physiology as much as their intellect. The polygenist notion that different species of men evolved separately meant that race theorists now had a scientific theory to back up their claims that different races were immovable in

development of a culture, defined in terms of literary, social, and cultural accomplishment, reflected the capacity of each race.

Accounts of India during this time were primarily ethnological. In fact, many of the members of the *Société Ethnologique* established in 1831 and devoted to the subjective study of races and peoples, were Indologists like Garcin de Tassy and Burnouf.[9] Reflecting the general intellectual trend to become more scientific, French ethnology gave way to ethnography by the middle of the century, where authors interspersed narratives of festivals and cultural observations with sweeping statements as to the level of 'civilization'. The works examined in this chapter—Gustave le Bon's *Les Civilisations de l'Inde*, and Louis Rousselet's *L'Inde des Rajahs*—belong in this category. In the case of India these ethnographic accounts placed the various races on a hierarchical ladder which was based on parallel anthropological[10] studies which focused

---

their capability. Therefore by association, the racial hierarchy of man could not be voided by education or association of inferior races with superior races.

[9] Among the founder members of the *Société Ethnologique* was Garcin de Tassy who was also the Vice-President of the Society in 1843. Historians like Jules Michelet and other Indologists like Eugène Burnouf, Baron Eckstein, Jules Mohl, and several members of the *Société Asiatique* were active members too.

[10] According to Staum, the French physician Cabanis was among the first to use the word 'anthropology' in French. See Staum, *Labeling People*.: 14. The *Société des Observateurs de l'Homme*, established in 1799, was the world's first anthropological society. The members included physicians, chemists, explorers and linguists, several French *ideologues*, and influential race theorists like the polygenist Georges Cuvier and the monogenist Lamarck. At this point, 'anthropology' signified primarily the use of biological or physical criteria to study man, as opposed to the cultural and linguistic criteria used by ethnologists. Among the early anthropologists in France were Paul Broca and his followers. See Francis Schiller, *Paul Broca: Founder of French Anthropology, Explorer of the Brain*. (Berkeley: University of California Press, 1979).

on categorizing human races on a civilizational and developmental hierarchy based on race.[11] By the mid-century, the polygenist theory was driving anthropological studies. The notion that race (defined in physiological rather than linguistic or cultural terms) was a determining factor in the capacity of people to progress was established.[12] Studies on race provided validation to the colonial civilizing mission since the white race was now indubitably superior to other races. As Martin Staum points out, the collection and classification of species and objects in the nineteenth century was not an inherent impulse of the mind, but often directed toward a specific purpose.[13] For example, the *Société Géographique de Paris,* founded in 1821, was primarily interested in seeking knowledge during its early years. In 1860, the society had 300 members. By 1881 the number had swelled to 2,000 and the proliferation of a number of provincial geographical societies by 1881 added 9,500 new members. This period of interest in overseas territories also coincided with a growing nationalism in Europe, particularly in France. By 1871 the geographical society's aim had shifted to promote the civilizing mission, an agenda that was emphasized in reports by the secretaries of the various geographical societies during the 1870s.[14] Maxwell also points to the fact that between the 1867 Paris Exposition Universelle and the next exhibition in 1889, the attention of the Parisian academy had shifted towards anthropology.

---

[11] As Staum points out, the physical criteria for classifying men triumphed over cultural criteria by 1850. Staum, *Labeling People*: 8. These physical criteria looked at anthropometric measurements, cranial and nasal indices and other physiological criteria like height, and limb length to compare different races with the 'norm' or dominant group of Europeans: 7.

[12] Maxwell, *Colonial Photography and Exhibitions*: 39–40.

[13] Staum, *Labeling People*: 7.

[14] See Henri Brunschwig, *French Colonialism 1871–1914: Myths and Realities.* (New York, Washington, London, 1964): 24.

Correspondingly, the focus on the exhibitions was on 'live' displays of people and cultures, rather than displays of the Orient.[15]

India first caught the attention of anthropologists because she had a diverse racial composition. Nearly every pure and mixed race was represented in the larger subcontinent. Therefore comparisons between races and studies in relative intelligence, ability, and civilization of races were made easy in India since there were so many races existing side by side. Unlike other comparisons of races where climate, language and even history were variables and therefore could be cited as the cause of difference, racial hierarchy could clearly be proved by studying India, since Aryans, Mongoloids, Dravidians and Negrito races had developed their different cultures and civilizations within the same climatic and historical conditions. By studying India, anthropologists tried to prove that the crucial element in determining the physical and intellectual ability of people was not their history or climate but their racial make-up.

Before long, the practice of making qualitative statements about 'superior' and 'inferior' races had crept into anthropology. The rise of anthropology coincided with the mid-century imperialistic expansion which sought to legitimize colonization as the effort by superior people to civilize inferiors. Racial hierarchies now validated colonial beliefs that Europeans, particularly the Caucasian race which had descended from the Indo-European or Aryan race, was superior to the Asian, African, Aboriginal, and Native American races whom they had conquered. This was the era of 'scientific racism'. The fact is that these uses for race were a nineteenth-century development and one that dovetailed neatly with the era of Imperialism. The studies on race and the subsequent creation of hierarchies were

---

[15] Maxwell, *Colonial Photography and Exhibitions*: 16.

artificial constructs, meant to support specific agenda.[16] The sheer extent of academic imagination in these hierarchies is easily demonstrated in the case of India. Although India was frequently cited in studies on race in the nineteenth century, the categories and their characteristics continually shifted to correspond to prevailing colonial agenda.

Early Indologists and travellers had remarked that the sheer diversity of India made it nearly impossible to demarcate its inhabitants into clear and distinct categories, whether of race or other descriptors. They preferred to focus on linguistic and historical similarities which were clearer than physiological traits in a country which was marked by racial intermixing for centuries. For example, in an article published in the *Nouveau Journal Asiatique* in 1828 (before the craze with racial hierarchies took centre-stage) Burnouf examined the context of the usage of the words Drâvida and Tamil.[17] 'On [of] thirty words taken among the principal geographical names of the country that the Hindus call Drâvida desha, seventeen were found to belong to the dialect tamoul [Tamil], and nine to Sanskrit; four only are of a doubtful origin.'[18] In a total of 30 references to the word '*Drâvida*' (from ancient texts like Ptolemy's *Geography* to modern texts like Buchanan's account of India[19] and the accounts of missionaries in the

---

[16] Many recent monographs have examined the construction of race in the colonial enterprise. In the French case, some important works include Patricia Lorcin, *Imperial Identities: Stereotyping, Prejudice and Race in Colonial Algeria* (St. Martin's Press: New York, 1999).

[17] Eugene Burnouf, 'Seconde lettre à M. le Rédacteur du Journal Asiatique, sur quelques dénominations géographiques du Drâvida ou pays des Tamouls', *Nouveau Journal Asiatique*, Vol. 2 (October 1828).

[18] 'Sur trente mots pris parmi les principaux noms géographiques du pays que les Hindous appelant *Drâvida desha*, dix-sept se sont trouvés appartenir au dialect tamoul, et neuf au sanscrit; quatre seulement sont d'une origine douteuse.' Ibid.: 275–76.

[19] Francis Buchanan, *Journal of Francis Buchanan* (Asian Educational Service: New Delhi, 1989 reprint).

Lettres Édifiantes, including both indigenous texts and European accounts) Burnouf concluded that 17 were to a linguistic region, *Drâvida,* or the Tamil-speaking people. Nine references defined *Drâvida* as Sanskrit-speaking people, where the *Drâvida* people were Aryan Brahmins who had migrated to the Southern peninsula and spoke Sanskrit as opposed to the locals who were lower castes and spoke Tamil.[20] The Brahmins were Aryan invaders from the North and therefore brought their own language, Sanskrit, with them.[21] This usage of *Drâvida* did not refer to a race since the Southern Brahmins were also presumably Aryans, but rather distinguished the Southern Brahmins as a sub-branch of the Indo-Aryans, and called *Drâvida* due to their geographical location. The indigenous people, who were dark-skinned and spoke a different language, Tamil, were conquered by the Aryans and incorporated into the Aryan social hierarchy as *Sudras.* They were called '*Tamiler*'. 'It is that the caste of Shoûdras, or the last of all in the Brahmanic hierarchy, constitutes the primitive population of the southernmost end of the peninsula; it is that it is them who, strictly speaking, are called Tamiler, in opposition to the Drâvida Brahmins.'[22] The last four of the references Burnouf examined were of doubtful origin.

---

[20] Eugene Burnouf, '*Seconde lettre à M. le Rédacteur du Journal Asiatique, sur quelques dénominations géographiques du Drâvida ou pays des Tamouls*', *Nouveau Journal Asiatique,* Vol. 2 (October 1828): 256–59. This is the traditional explanation for the mythology of the Sage Agastya and his voyage south of the Vindhyas. Agastya's journey indicated the southward movement of Aryan Brahmins into the peninsula. Many South Indian Brahmin families even today trace their antecedents to Agastya thus claiming to hail from the Aryans.

[21] Once again, the heavy influence of Sanskrit in the dialects of Tamil, Telugu, Malayalam, and Kannada which are spoken by the Brahmins of these regions is pointed to as proof of the Sanskritization and Aryanization of the South. See M. N. Srinivas, *The Cohesive Role of Sanskritization and other Essays* (Delhi: OUP, 1989).

[22] '*C'est que la caste des Shoûdras, ou la dernière de toutes dans la hiérarchie brahmanique, constitue la population primitive de l'extrémité*

In other references to the word *Drâvida* Burnouf noted the various geographical meanings the term had come to represent, including the peninsula of India south of the Vindhya Mountains and the Coromandel coast: references which became popular by the time of the Muslim invasion and early European penetration.[23] Burnouf also noted the changing boundaries of the areas comprising the *'Drâvida'* region, including Canara, Karnataka, Malabar, and the Coromandel Coast; and the shifting definitions of these areas as topographic sub-divisions, linguistic and political boundaries over the course of several centuries.[24] The important thing to note was that nowhere did *'Drâvida'* or even *'Tamil'* equate to a racial definition. Burnouf's lithographs of 'Indian types' also similarly stressed the difference in clothing styles far more than physical differences (see Image 5.1). At least until the 1840s India was not a part of racial hierarchies. Statements about the achievements of India or the lack of thereof, were based on Western interpretations of language and literature rather than assumptions about the 'racial capabilities and limitations' inherent in the races of India. By the middle of the nineteenth century this focus on literature and philology changed to a specific focus on the races of India and theories which explained the past and present in India as a direct result of racial tendencies and capabilities.

---

méridionale de la presqu'île; c'est que ce sont eux qui, à proprement parler, sont appelés *Tamiler*, par opposition aux Brahmanes *Drâvida.'* Eugene Burnouf, *'Seconde lettre à M. le Rédacteur du Journal Asiatique, sur quelques dénominations géographiques du Drâvida ou pays des Tamouls'*, *Nouveau Journal Asiatique*, Vol. 2 (October 1828): 258–59.

[23] Ibid.: 246.
[24] Ibid.

IMAGE 5.1: Types of inhabitants of Pondichéry in 1832

Source: Narayani Gupta, 'The Citizens of French India: the issue of cultural identity in Pondicherry in the XIX century', in *Les relations historiques et culturelles entre la France et l'Inde XVII- XXsiècles.* 2 volumes. Sainte-Clotilde, 1987.

TOPINARD AND THE ANTHROPOMETRIC METHOD

Despite the lack of evidence for constructing racial categories in India, by 1859 French anthropologists had shifted to studying races on comparative, anatomical lines and Burnouf's philological approach was left behind as arelic of an older, less accurate method of studying races. Paul Broca, who founded the *Société d'Anthropologie de Paris* in 1859, was the proponent of a new method of studying man called 'scientific anthropology'. Broca was one of the pioneers of the new method of anthropometric measurement as a means to document the differences between races. Broca outlined his method and theory in several articles published in the *Bulletin de la Société de l'Anthropologie.*[25] While Broca was clear that the results of his method could not be used to argue for a racial hierarchy, his students, notably Paul Topinard and Gustave le Bon, were convinced that the results of the new anthropometry could explain why Europe was superior to the rest of the world.[26] The result of this new method was that anthropologists now began looking for 'specimens' which would measure up to their preconceived categories of race rather than taking a random sample of the population and allowing the data to dictate the result. Paul Topinard, for example, argued that the development of various parts of the brain was determined by race, and that an examination of cranial development and cultural 'progress' could define the intellectual and mental capabilities of each race.[27] He conducted a survey of cranial measurements of different races and concluded that the African Negroes had a brain capacity of 1400 cc, the Negroes of Oceania a brain of 1450, the yellow races a brain of 1500 and the whites a brain of 1550,[28] thus sug-

---

[25] See, for example, *Bulletin de la Société de l'Anthropologie.* Paul Broca, 'Sur le volume et la forme du cerveau suivant les individus et suivant les races', Vol. 2: 139, and 'Sur les proportions relatives du bras, de l'avant-bras et de la clavicule chez les nègres et les Européens', Vol. 3: 162.

[26] Most scholars agree that Broca himself was not a proponent of racial hierarchies. However, many of his statements indicate that he believed very strongly in the intellectual limitations of race. For instance, in 1866, Broca wrote in a dictionary article on 'Anthropology': Never has a people with dark skin, woolly hair, and a prognathous face (jutting jaw, receding forehead) been able to spontaneously elevate itself to civilization....' Paul Broca, 'Anthropologie', from *Mémoires d'Anthropologie* 1 (Paris: Reinhalt, 1871): 33. Cited in Staum, *Labeling People.*: 179. Paul Topinard represented the official position of French anthropology in his textbook, *L'Anthropologie.* (Paris: Reinwald and Cie, 1876).

[27] Paul Topinard, *L'Anthropologie* (Paris: Reinwald and Cie, 1876). Chapters 15–17 and passim.

[28] Paul Topinard, *Science and Faith.* Translated by Thomas McCormack (Chicago: Free Press, 1899): 304–5. S. J. Gould has argued that such measures of 'intelligence' are flawed by their tendency to

gesting the existence of a racial hierarchy in intellect and development.[29] He further elaborated on this racial hierarchy by defining civilizational development in terms of religious development (from fetishism to animism to polytheism and then to monotheism), social organization (savage hordes to tribes to clans and then classes), and achievements (such as architectural ruins or monuments). Within these parameters of development the blacks were at the lowest level. According to Topinard, 'the characteristic of all the black races is the inaptitude to rise by their own 'efforts.'[30] Next in the racial hierarchy were the yellow races which were capable of achievement of varying levels. These races were capable of attaining average civilizational development like the Dravidians of India, or even relatively high development like the Aztecs and Peruvians of South America and the Chinese. According to Topinard, 'The characteristic of the yellow races is a certain quickness in apprehending the means of satisfying the immediate needs of life and of rendering existence agreeable, but they have little initiative, do not know how to raise themselves to higher planes and seem prone to immobilization.'[31] The white races were the highest in terms of civilizational development and included the culture of the Vedic Aryans of India. He summed up the white races thus: 'The characteristics of the white races are a remarkable aptitude for developing by their own independent efforts or for

---

categorize knowledge into measurable entities. See S. J. Gould, *The Mismeasure of Man* (New York: W.W. Norton & Co, 1981).

[29] The natural corollary to these ideas was the birth of Aryanism which held that the Aryan race was the most developed; and the theory of eugenics or the selective breeding of 'developed races'. In the French case, the Aryan theory also contributed to the rise of Gallicism which was an aggressive form of French national pride based on a common racial heritage in the late nineteenth century.

[30] Paul Topinard, *Science and Faith*. Translated by Thomas McCormack (Chicago: Free Press, 1899): 206.

[31] Ibid.: 207.

assimilating the empirical results of others, their ever-increasing need of comfort, their vigorous and comprehensive cerebral activity and their spirit of initiative....'[32] Topinard further observed that all races might progress if favoured by circumstances of location (topographical and climactic serendipity, the presence of abundant food as well as the freedom from invasion and the presence of peaceful and advanced neighbours to emulate), and brilliant leaders who spurred progress and needs which provided the stimulus for material and intellectual development. Nevertheless all races did not possess the same aptitude or initiative to progress and Topinard noted that leaders were lacking among the blacks, scarce among the yellow races and common in the white races.[33]

Topinard's application of racial principles to define progress was clear in the Indian context in his work, *L'Anthropologie*. In this work, he defined the Hindu type as best represented by the Rajputs and most of all by the Brahmins of Mathura, Thaneswar, and Banaras. According to him, 'The Hindu type is not any more represented in the Indies [than] by Radjpouts and especially by the most venerated Brahmins of Mattra, Bénarès and Tanessar in Hindoustan.'[34] In his work on Science and Faith[35] he described the Aryans in India as dividing society into four classes according to the Code of Manu. These were the *Brahmins* or priests, the *Kshatriyas* or warriors, the *Vaiçyas* or husbandmen, merchants and artisans, and the *Shudras* or servants. The aim in this classification was to prevent a mingling of the conquering Aryans with the Dravidians and consequently the absorption of the former

---

[32] Ibid.: 208.

[33] Ibid.: 208.

[34] 'Le type hindou n'est plus que faiblement représentée aux Indes par les Radjpouts et surtout par les Brahmanes les plus vénérés de Mattra, de Bénarès et de Tanessar dans l'Hindoustan.' Paul Topinard, *L'Anthropologie*: 481.

[35] Paul Topinard, *Science and Faith*.

into the lower ranks of Vedic society. The first caste
was composed of pure Aryans, the second of the Aryans
and Dravidians who had intermixed and the other two
of Dravidians. The black aborigines were excluded from
the four-fold classification, which were mentioned in the
Vedic texts, and consequently bore the name of Pariahs,
a term invented only later.[36] Afterwards the castes continued to be modified and numerous intermediary castes
were created within each caste.[37] Topinard quoted the
Census of 1881 as saying that the total number of castes
in India was 2,500.[38]

According to Topinard, castes in themselves were not
an evil. But in the case of closed castes, as were found in
India and Egypt, where the caste or corporation became
the social unit/entity and submerged the individual entity
within the corporate identity, there could be no sense of
liberty. Consequently such people became submissive and

---

[36] While the notion of the 'Aryan invasion' itself has been challenged in recent times, the caste system was sometimes explained as
a process by which the Aryan conquerors of North India assimilated the
indigenous peoples whom they vanquished. Since the Aryans remained
in the North for a substantial period of time, and the Rig Veda, which
contains the earliest reference to the caste system, was composed in
the North, it is probable that the Aryans were unfamiliar with the aborigines when the caste system evolved. Subsequently, they did interact
with the aborigines in central, east, and south India and, unable to
place them in the existing four castes, created the *pariah* caste which
was the lowest. Over centuries of history, the *pariah* caste came to
include offspring of some inter-caste marriages, as well as newer groups
which the Aryans conquered.

[37] The basic four divisions were the castes. Each caste was further
divided into jatis, primarily representing specific trades and occupations. Over the years the number of jatis proliferated into several hundred. Even though French academics would have been aware of the
difference between 'caste' and 'jati', they continued to write only in
terms of 'caste'. Interestingly Indians themselves use 'caste' and 'jati'
interchangeably; the strict separation of the two terms occurs only in
academia.

[38] Ibid.: 201–2.

social development suffered. The antagonism between class and individual was central to the continued development of a society.[39] It was this aspect of development or the lack of development which had played a role in the decline of Indian civilization.

The change between the the race-neutral study of Burnouf and the racial context of Topinard is clearly demonstrated in the latter's use of Rousselet. Louis Rousselet had travelled in India from 1863 to 1868 and written extensively of his travels and experiences. His essays were published in *Revue d'Anthropologie* and in *La Tour du Monde*. Rousselet collected all his essays and published them *as L'Inde des Rajahs. Voyage dans l'Inde centrale et dans les présidences de Bombay et du Bengale* (Paris: Hachette, 1875). Rousselet was highly regarded in anthropological circles[40] and many leading anthropologists, including Topinard, used his data on India in their works.

Among the essays that he contributed, Rousselet's anthropological writings on the races of India were published in the *Revue d'Anthropologie*. His writing focused primarily on the racial composition of the various tribes and peoples of India much in the same style as other ethnographic writings of the time. Rousselet described the different tribes that he came across in terms of height, cranial measurements, and mental and cultural achievements. In his detailed descriptions of the different tribes and castes of India, Rousselet did categorize them racially as Aryan, Turanian and Dravidian, as well as combinations of these. His writings contained none of the critical descriptions of

---

[39] Ibid.: 203.

[40] In 1872 he was appointed a lifelong member of the *Société d'Anthropologie de Paris,* and the title of '*Voyageur dans l'Inde, archéologue*' was bestowed upon him. He continued to have a distinguished career and in 1878 was appointed the secretary to the section of Anthropological Sciences at the Universal Exposition in Paris. For more information about Rousselet see Patrick Chézaud, *Louis Rousselet et l'image de la culture de l'autre* (Saint Pierre de Salerne: G. Monfort, 2005).

'inferior' and 'superior', 'inability' of certain races to progress beyond a racially determined level that Topinard and
other anthropologists stated clearly. Although he used the
accepted anthropological language of the time to describe
his findings, he eschewed ranking the various peoples of
India. Even though other anthropologists were experiment-
ing with various methods of depicting the differences in
racial characteristics, Rousselet's lithographs show a clear
and consistent use of the same type of features for all the
different people he encounters in the Indian subcontinent
(see Images 5.2–5.5). The images he provides in his articles
and his book are more ample and attractive than the text,
which often becomes a compilation of his travels. The title
of his articles and his book which prominently feature the
'races' of India, along with the images he provides thus
form a powerful image of India. The difference between
the work of Rousselet on races of India and that of other
anthropologists like Topinard is in the latter's creation of
racial hierarchies.

IMAGE 5.2: Bayadère

Source: Louis Rousselet, L'Inde des Rajahs. Paris: Hachette, 1875.

IMAGE 5.3: Jeweller

Source: Louis Rousselet, L'Inde des Rajahs. Paris: Hachette, 1875.

IMAGE 5.4: The Maharana of Udaipur with the English Resident. Note the remarkable similarity in their features as well as the weaponry. The fact that the former is seated indicates his centrality and dominance in the image.

Source: Louis Rousselet, L'Inde des Rajahs. Paris: Hachette, 1875.

IMAGE 5.5: Samboe-Sing *(SIC)* THE MAHARANA OF MEWAR
Source: Louis Rousselet, L'Inde des Rajahs. Paris: Hachette, 1875.

Rousselet's work was used by many subsequent
authorities on anthropology, including Topinard, although
the former's neutral statements about race were used
to define a racial hierarchy by the latter. Topinard cited
Rousselet as an important source for his information about
India and the racial composition of India in his work on
L'Anthropologie (Paris, 1876). Yet while Rousselet's articles on the Central Indian tribes were full of ethnographic
descriptions, Topinard appropriated these descriptions to
a racial hierarchy of India, citing the tribes of Rousselet's
descriptions as examples of lower races in India. Based
on his understanding of Rousselet, Topinard divided the

population of South India into black, Mongol, and Aryan.[41] According to Topinard, the blacks in India were the tribal groups such as the *'Bhils, Mahars, Gonds,* and *Khonds* who possessed a primitive character, black colour, and short stature'.[42] Contrasted to this was Rousselet's original description: '[The] Bhils are in general of a medium height; though missing the elegant shapes of the Aryan Hindu, they are much more robust; their force and their agility are sometimes surprising.'[43] The Mongol race, which belonged primarily to Central Asia was also found in the North East [Assam for example] and North West of India, as well as intermixed with the indigenous Dravidian population of the Tamils and Jats.[44] The third and most recent race in India was also the most important in India, because of their numbers as well as their quality, the Aryan race.[45] He described the Aryans as 'The Brahmins of the banks of Ganga, says Mr. Rousselet, have the high, developed front [forehead], the oval face, the perfectly horizontal eyes, the nose projecting, hooked and slightly thick at the end, but framed by delicate nostrils. They are white, but are more or less bronzed by the sun of these climates. Their black hair appears abundant.'[46] Elsewhere in the

---

[41] Paul Topinard, *L'Anthropologie*: 481. Topinard was using Rousselet's articles from Revue d'Anthropologie, specifically 'Tableau des races de l'Inde centrale et de l'Inde septentrionale' *Revue d'Anthropologie*, Vol. 2 (1873) and Vol. 4 (1875).

[42] Ibid.

[43] 'Les Bhils sont en général d'une taille moyenne; quoique manquant des formes élégantes de l'Hindou-Aryen, ils sont beaucoup plus robustes; leur force et leur agilité sont quelquefois surprenantes.' Louis Rousselet, 'Tableau des races de l'Inde centrale et de l'Inde septentrionale' *Revue d'Anthropologie*, Vol. 2 (1873): 60.

[44] Paul Topinard, *L'Anthropologie*: 481.

[45] Ibid.

[46] 'Les Brahmanes des rives du Ganga, dit M. Rousselet, ont le front haut, développé, la face ovale, le yeux parfaitement horizontaux, le nez saillant, busqué et légèrement épais à l'extrémité, mais encadré par des narines délicates. Ils sont blancs, mais plus ou moins bronzés

work, Topinard notes the presence of blue-eyed, 'white' types in India, as described by Rousselet, Prichard, Davy and Frasier. 'One finds [them] in India, notably among the Kattees, who sometimes have "clear hair [blonde?] and blue eyes" [Prichard and L. Rousselet]....The Bisahuris of Rampoor, not far from the sources of the Ganges, often have "very fair skin, though burned by the sun, blue eyes, curly hair and beards of clear or red colour" [Frasier].'[47]

In addition Topinard divided the Negroids in India into the 'true Negroid which could be traced back to mentions in the Mahabharata as inhabiting the South and were represented by the Andaman tribes',[48] and the Australian type represented by the *Bhils, Gonds, Khonds, Mahars, Varalis, Mundas, Yanadis* and the *Maravars* of the Coromandel coast, *Todas* of Nilgiri, *Kurumbas, Irulas* and other tribes of the Ghats and Deccan.[49] Topinard even noted the existence of the bust of a black of the Tasmanian type born in Pondichéry examined in 1875 at the Anthropological laboratory and present in the collection of Paul Broca.[50] The hierarchical racial development which was absent in Rousselet was clear in Topinard's work. While Rousselet preferred to describe the customs of many tribes as 'primitive' and used 'inferior' very sparingly, Topinard's description of various

---

par le soleil de ces climates. Leur système pileux noir paraît abundant.' Paul Topinard, *L'Anthropologie*: 481.

[47] 'On en trouve dans l'Inde, notamment chez les Kattees, qui ont quelquefois les <<cheveux clairs et yeux bleus>> (Prichard et L. Rousselet)...Les Bisahuris de Rampoor, non loin des sources du Gange, ont souvent <<le teint très-blanc (*very fair*), quoique brûlé par le soleil, les yeux bleus, les cheveux et la barbe bouclés et de couleur clair ou meme rouge>> (Frasier)' Ibid.: 477–78.

[48] Ibid.: 529.

[49] Ibid.: 536. Interestingly, Topinard points out that the tribes of central and south India as well as tribes of Australia spoke the Dravidian group of languages, thus providing further anthropological proof of the inferiority of the Dravidians. See Tony Ballantyne, *Orientalism and Race: Aryanism in the British Empire* (New York: Palgrave MacMillan, 2002).

[50] Ibid.

human races was almost exclusively in terms of 'superior' and 'inferior'. Broca and Topinard were only beginning to apply theories of race to the relative development of people. Most of their work was suggestive at best, especially in the context of India. Moreover they were unclear about how to define race in India. A select group of intellectuals transformed race into a pernicious weapon in the aid of colonialism. The most famous of these was Arthur de Gobineau.

GOBINEAU AND RACE

Among the most visible works on racial theory in the nineteenth century was the Comte de Gobineau's *Essai sur l'inégalité des races humaines*. Gobineau's ideas influenced the German school of anthropology more than it did the French,[51] but his ideas were certainly a window into the literary and scholastic treatment of France's various colonies, being cited by many major scholars of the day, like Ernest Renan as well as the outspoken anti-Semite, Edouard Drumont. Gobineau argued that political systems, governments, and regimes did not determine the quality of a civilization. Nor did conquest, since this was a superficial imposition, and did not change any racial characteristics or the accident of geography. Defining 'civilization' as 'a state of relative stability, where the mass of men try to satisfy their wants by peaceful means, and are refined in their conduct and intelligence',[52] all civilizations were not equal, and this was the central quest of his work, to discover why, given the existence of these conditions in different civilizations, there was still a wide variance in the quality of civilizations.

---

[51] Frank H. Hankins, *The Racial Basis of Civilizations* (New York and London: A. Knopf, 1926).

[52] Arthur de Gobineau, *The Inequality of Human Races*. Translated by Adrian Collins (New York: H. Fertig, 1967): 91.

He concluded that the only variable being race, there was a fundamental intellectual and moral capacity for each race that determined civilizational development and which only miscegenation could alter. This capacity was different and therefore measurable on a scale of superior to inferior for all human races. This scale, based on cranial measurement and moral and material achievement of races in their purest form, proceeded with the whites declining to the yellow race and finally the blacks at the bottom. Translated to the Indian case, Gobineau described the Hindus as having reached great heights of intellectual and metaphysical achievement but fundamentally lacking in material desire and therefore material accomplishment.[53] Moreover, this achievement had been accomplished in the early stage of the development of Hindu civilization, when the Aryan race was at its purest. Gobineau argued that a civilization was strongest when the blood or race of its founders was purest, and that degeneration occurred with inter-racial unions and the weakening of inherent racial qualities.

According to him,

The world of art and great literature that comes from the mixture of blood, the improvement and ennoblement of inferior races—all these are wonders....Unfortunately, the great have been lowered by the same process; and this is an evil which nothing can balance or repair... the Brahmins of primitive India...give us a higher and more brilliant idea of humanity, and were more active, intelligent and trusty... than the peoples, hybrid a hundred times over, of the present day.[54]

---

[53] Ibid. Gobineau divided races into those dominated by the 'male' principle of material desire (*purusha*) and headed by the Chinese civilization; and those dominated by the female principle (*prakriti*) of 'intellectual current' and headed by the Hindus (86–87) who chose to focus their entire energy on philosophical and theological ideas to the detriment of material progress (91–92).

[54] Ibid.: 209.

To Gobineau race mixing was the cause for the downfall of Indian civilization. When the conquering Aryans decided to mix with the indigenous blacks, they allowed the many characteristics of the blacks, including their lack of judgement and reason to cloud the naturally intelligent Aryan mentality.[55] In the present day and despite its noble origins Brahminism was in complete decline and decadence, riddled with absurd superstitions, theological complications and a lack of great men to guide it. This was, Gobineau argued, solely a result of the influx of black and yellow blood into the original Aryan blood, to such an extent that it was impossible to tell a high-caste Brahmin from a lower caste anymore. In all cases of culture and life this perversion and degeneration of the white race in India meant that India was incapable of withstanding the superior white races of Europe.[56] In fact, he continued, the races which continued to withstand English power in India and all other foreign invasions were the races which were still more or less Aryan, like the *Rajputs, Sindhis, Rohillas,* and other people of the North-West borders of India.[57] The Aryan family was the most noble, intelligent, and energetic of all races. In India, the Aryans had a high sense of morality, philosophy, grand institutions of family and politics, and a total superiority of personality over the black tribes which inhabited the area. The caste system was a reflection of Aryan superiority. He pointed out that the Indian notion of beauty was described in terms of the typical Aryan physiognomy—fair skin, oval face, and muscular and graceful appearance. The descriptions of great

---

[55] Comte de Gobineau, *Essai sur l'inégalité des races humaines* (Paris: Librairie Firmin-Didot, second edition, 1884), Vol. 1: 397.

[56] Ibid.: 446. Also see Wilhelm Halbfass, *India and Europe. An Essay in Understanding* (Albany, N.Y.: State University of New York Press, 1988): 139.

[57] Gobineau, *Essai:* 447, 449. Ironically these areas were peopled in the nineteenth century by Muslims (modern-day Pakistan) who in the case of Algeria were classified as savages.

heroes and Gods in Indian literature always conformed to this ideal of beauty, which in turn was the appearance of the higher castes, which were more Aryan than the lower castes.[58] The Indian term for caste, 'varna' also meant colour. Although he noted that ethnographically speaking the system of dividing society according to race was a fiction since all castes had been penetrated by the local black races, he maintained that the importance of caste for the Indians lay in the importance of maintaining race purity.[59] All over the world, however, the dilution of Aryan blood caused the degeneration of the race. Due to this complete ethnic disorder which had occurred with particular violence in India, Gobineau predicted that the civilization of India could never regain its former majesty and glorious culture.[60]

Gobineau was the most vociferous of race thinkers. His theory of scientific racism had various agendas and India's place in these was incidental at best. For instance, according to Halbfass, Gobineau used India to argue against the liberal democratic ideals of the French Revolution, the kind of progress which Marx was promoting in his argument that racial ability was fixed and that the white race was

---

[58] Gobineau's pronouncement was typical of the simplification of Indian religion. In reality the Gods of the pantheon were of different colours, which may have represented their affiliation to the natural elements or to other aspects of their personalities. For example, while Indra the God of lightning was fair, Agni, the God of fire was described as being of a reddish hue. The God Vishnu, who is touted as being representative of the original 'Aryan' race is dark blue and is described as being handsome but exceedingly dark in the most human of his avatars, that of Rama and of Krishna. This aspect of his colour is often overlooked by those who, like Gobineau, looked for references to race in the Hindu pantheon, and pointed to the existence of the dark Shiva, who represented the expansion of the Aryan religion to include elements of indigenous, tribal beliefs.

[59] See Gobineau, *Essai*: 396.

[60] Ibid.: 447–48.

pre-eminent.[61] But his theories were echoed in the growing anthropological interest in India and were reflected
in the consistent number of articles and items of interest
about India which were published in the prominent anthropological journals available in Paris by the late nineteenth
century, including the *Revue d'Anthropologie*, which was
published by Paul Broca, and the *Revue d'Ethnographie*.[62]
The more prominent works included some articles by
travellers, articles by Broca and other anthropologists on
topics directly pertinent to India, or on topics related to
race where India was a crucial part of the popular theory
of Aryan migration from the Caucasus. According to Leon
Poliakov, '...however they were transmitted, Gobineau
merely systematized in a very personal way ideas which
were already deeply rooted in his time.'[63]

LE BON AND INDIA

The piecemeal anthropological statements on India and the
tentative ethnographic work of Rousselet were surpassed
in the late-nineteenth century by a magnum opus on India.
In 1886, Firmin Didot published an all-encompassing ethnographic work on India by Gustave Le Bon, comprising
over 700 pages of text and hundreds of photographs, lithographs and etches, and titled *Les Civilisations de l'Inde*. A
student of Paul Broca, Le Bon was a controversial anthropologist who continued to have an acrimonious relationship

---

[61] Wilhelm Halbfass, *India and Europe*: 139.

[62] From 1890 onwards the *Revue d'Ethnographie* and *Revue
d'Anthropologie* were merged to form the popular anthropological journal, *L'Anthropologie*, of which Paul Topinard was a prominent founder
member and contributor. The journal published a fairly constant amount
of news in the form of book reviews, scholarly opinions, and articles
concerning developments in Indian anthropology, including the efforts
of French and British anthropologists. See Figures 5.1–5.3.

[63] Leon Poliakov, *The Aryan Myth: A History of Racist and
Nationalist Ideas in Europe*. Translated by E. Howard (New York: Basic
Books, 1971): 233.

with his fellow anthropologists and even with his one-time teacher throughout his lifetime. Many of his differences with other anthropologists, notably Broca, sprang from the fact that Broca believed in strict scientific anthropology, as verifiable by data and anthropometric measurements, while Le Bon believed that ethnological study in terms of culture, language and religion, was as useful to anthropology as anthropometry.

In the context of India, however, Le Bon's conclusions were not markedly different from the views of other anthropologists. Often quoted in contemporary works of the period, Le Bon seems to have been forgotten by modern scholars of India who find it difficult to trace references to him. That said one must closely analyse his work on India because it mirrored the traditional French view of India as a land of spirituality, which had been produced over the course of the nineteenth century in many ways. Le Bon provided, in some ways, a grand summary of the French image of India at the end of the nineteenth century. His work drew on most of the known and available literature on India at the end of the nineteenth century, including translations of Indian texts as well as works by other ethnologists, geographers, historians, and Indologists. His work demonstrated the enduring image of India, which was painstakingly created by the primarily Parisian academic elite during the course of the nineteenth century and the recovery of 'India' as a great example of civilization.

On the other hand, Le Bon was also influenced by prevailing theories of colonial administration and in fact, was a notable participant in many debates on the nature of colonial assimilation.[64] His work on India reflected the debate in France on colonial policy between the propo-

---

[64] A highly vocal participant in the debate on assimilation at the Colonial Congress of 1889, Le Bon was among a minority of those who vigorously resisted assimilation. Since Le Bon believed that races could improve themselves by contact with superior races, he argued that

nents and opponents of assimilation and the emerging idea of association in colonial rule. A firm believer in anthropology and the capabilities of people based on their racial heritage, Le Bon was an influential and outspoken opponent of the idea that inferior races could uplift themselves through association with superior races.[65] For Le Bon, the capability of each race was already decided and available for academic examination through the civilization it had produced. Race determined intelligence and this intelligence gave rise to the cornerstones of civilization.

While in the previous century India had always been thought of as a land with a homogenous culture, inhabited by a single race that possessed a single culture, art, and religion, studies in the nineteenth century had proven that this was really not the case. India was really a diverse milieu of peoples, languages, religions, and cultures, in fact a whole world in miniature.[66] However, the theme of a single homogenous race representing 'India' was inextricably woven into Le Bon's work.

Le Bon divided the main Indian racial types into four: Negroid, the Yellow races, Turanian and Aryan. The caste system, which to Le Bon was a reflection of this four-fold racial mix consisted of the more or less pure Aryan type, the Brahmin, the Rajput type or the Aryan-Turanian mix which was the Kshatriya, the Turanian or the Vaiçya and the Shudra who represented the amalgamation of the Turanian and local aboriginal races.[67]

---

assimilation would undermine the Empire. I discuss the French debate on assimilation in more detail in the conclusion.

[65] For a detailed examination of le Bon's position on this issue, see Martin Deming Lewis, 'One Hundred Million Frenchmen: the "Assimilation" Theory in French Colonial Policy', *Comparative Studies in Society and History*, Vol. 4.2 (January 1962).

[66] Gustave le Bon, *Les civilizations de l'Inde* (Paris: Ernest Flammarion. 1900): 77.

[67] Ibid.: 78.

Narrating an anthropological history of Indian race, Le Bon began with the assumption that the earliest inhabitants of India were blacks of the Negrito type who inhabited the centre and the blacks of the Australian type who lived in the south and west. These people lived as savages in the mountains of Central India in the first example, in the region known as Gondwana, and the Australian blacks lived in the South, in the mountains of the Nilgiris.

The mountains bounding India on the north, northwest and northeast and the seas, which protected India from invasion from the south, southwest and southeast meant that India remained fairly undisturbed in terms of racial intermixture for a long time. However, there were two sets of peoples who managed to penetrate the Indian subcontinent. The first were the Turanians who originated in Turkestan and represented the yellow race. They entered from the Brahmaputra valley and fanned out into two branches. The first settled in the Ganga valley and the second continued south to Bengal. The result of the intermixture of the Turanians and Negritos of India resulted in the Proto-Dravidian race that in turn evolved into the Dravidians or Tamils of south India. The dominant Turanian influence in terms of physical features was clear in the inhabitants of Assam, Tibet, Nepal, and Bhutan. The natives of Bengal and Orissa also displayed marked racial features of the yellow races.

The second racial invasion was of the Aryans who entered India through the northwest and settled primarily in the north of India. Their mixing with the Turanian element in the north accounted for the emergence of the *Kshatriya* caste while the pure Turanian element became the *Vaiçya* caste according to Le Bon. The southern part of India remained more or less proto-Dravidian or Kolarian, after the Kolar region.

In his description of the people inhabiting various geographical regions of India, he painstakingly listed the various tribes (*Chibalis, Paharis, Gaddis, Kulus, Gujars*) and populations of the Western Himalayas (*Ladakh, Balti, Dardistan, Kashmir*); Nepal (*Gurkhas* and *Newars*), Bhutan and Sikkim. Then he moved to Assam, inhabited by the *Abors, Michmis, Singpos, Nagas, Garos*, and *Khasias*. Most of these people were described as being predominantly part of the yellow race. Southward to the Ganga Valley he listed the result of the racial mix of Aryans, Turanians and proto-Dravidians as the populations of Awadh, Bengal, and Bihar, including the tribes of the *Malers* and *Santals*. The Punjab was described as the land of the *Pathans* who approached the closest 'pure Aryan' racial type, then the *Jats, Dogras, Sikhs* and the *Rajputs* who came from the mix of Aryan and Turanian blood. Sindh and Rajputana included the tribes of the *Bhils* and *Minas* who represented the Negrito element. The populations of Gujarat and Kathiawar were too mixed to allow for a racial categorization. The races of central India included the *Marathas* of Maharashtra, who represented the Turanian element, the Kolarian people of the Konkan, the *Nairs* on the Malabar coast, and the Negrito tribes of the *Todas, Irulkas, Kotas, Kurumbas* and *Vadagas* of the Nilgiri hills, the Gondwana tribes of the *Gonds, Bhils* and the Chotanagpur/Orissa area of the *Kols* and *Khonds*. The primitive tribes of the South included the *Kaders* in the Annamalai hills, *Shanars* of Travancore and Cape Comorin, *Kanikhars, Nayadis* of Calicut and Pulicat and the *Kolars* of Madurai and Coimbatore.

Each of these peoples was described in terms of their racial mix, and their customs, culture and religion. Thus while Le Bon stated at the outset that there were no pure races left in India in anthropological terms, he described the 'races of India' ethnologically as possessing all the characteristics of anthropological races, because his discussion of the culture of each 'race' was intended to describe their mental and intellectual capacity, as well as their physical attributes. The descriptions were further cemented by numerous illustrations of each 'racial type'. Le Bon concluded that India was composed of four main racial groups:Kolarian, Dravidian, Turano-Aryan, and Tibetan. These were secondary races but possessed distinct physical and mental characteristics.[68] Le Bon blurred the line between 'race' and 'peoples' by attributing both with hereditary physical and mental characteristics. This confusion was more pronounced in his work on *Lois Psychologiques* where le Bon used the terms 'race' and 'people' interchangeably. As Nye points out, the use of race now could be used to provide:

> a total explanation of the history of man and of the modern world itself. By providing a 'scientific' explanation of race which was based on psychological and character traits, but which had the concrete durability and hereditary transmissibility of physical characteristics, Le Bon could avoid the worst pitfalls of the 'caliper' race thinker whose data was so often conflicting. His more flexible definition, though it clearly took its initial inspiration from the body-mind analogy, could be used to explain psychological differences arising between social classes, linguistic groups and broad culture types and still retain the word 'race' which the nineteenth century understood so well and which clearly favored the power of 'blood' over education. The integrity and uniqueness of race, class, language and culture, which were themselves so much the psychological extension of a people's hereditary apparatus, were dominant themes in a Europe experiencing the pangs of a growing nationalism and class consciousness: the invention of a flexible definition of 'race psychology' was Gustave Le Bon's own small contribution to these movements.[69]

After having discussed the physical characteristics of Hindus, Le Bon moved to the mental features of these

---

[68] Ibid.: 87.

[69] Robert Allen Nye, *An Intellectual Portrait of Gustave LeBon: A Study of the Development and Impact of a Social Scientist in his Historical Setting* (PhD Thesis, University of Wisconsin, 1969): 135–36.

diverse peoples. The mentality of the Hindus was no less diverse than their physical traits. So while the Rajputs were fair, tall and well-built, tribal populations were represented as semi-savages, dark, short, half-naked, and unkempt (see Images 5.6–5.8). Similarly there were extremes of bravery like that of the *Rajputs* existing with the cowardice of the *Bengali*, as well as the honesty of the mountain people of Rajmahal and the lying treachery of others.[70] Yet, despite these various mentalities there was a certain 'Hindu' mentality which had formed over the centuries and that generally speaking, allowed for a characterization of the mentality of the Hindu as a determinate racial entity.[71] The three major factors which accounted for the mentality of the Hindu were the caste system, the political regime of caste and village being the primary political entities and the paramount importance and all-encompassing nature of Hindu religion. These in sum accounted for the nature and mentality of the Hindu. The caste system prevented the Hindu from developing any other identity outside of his caste and meant that loyalties of region and nation were ignored in the all-encompassing identity of one's caste. Moreover the nature of the caste system as a corporate entity with its age-old privileges and unchanging nature took away all sense of initiative and energy from the individual who knew that his innovations in work or talents outside of his hereditary occupation would go unnoticed.[72]

---

[70] Gustave le Bon, *Les civilizations de l'Inde*: 178. His pronouncements about the different races will be familiar to scholars of the British theory of martial races. For an excellent monograph on the actual result of the racial categorization of Indians, see Mrinalini Sinha, *Colonial Masculinity: The 'Manly Englishman' and the 'Effeminate Bengali' in the Late Nineteenth Century* (Manchester: Manchester University Press, 1995).

[71] Ibid.: 179.

[72] Ibid.: 608.

IMAGE 5.6: The Caption Reads 'Minas: A Half-Savage Tribe in Rajputana'
Source: Gustave le Bon, *Les Civilisations de L'Inde*. Paris: Firmin Didot, 1887.

IMAGE 5.7: The Caption Reads 'Savages of Chota Nagpur'
Source: Gustave le Bon, *Les Civilisations de L'Inde*. Paris: Firmin Didot, 1887.

IMAGE 5.8: Rajput warriors. Note the more sophisticated weapons (swords) that they carry as opposed to the primitive weapons of the dark-skinned and Negroid featured Minas and Chota Nagpur tribes, in addition to their half-clothed, semi-civilized aspect opposed to the fairer Rajputs with their more chiseled features.

Source: Gustave le Bon, *Les Civilisations de L'Inde*. Paris: Firmin Didot, 1887.

The lack of ambition on the part of the Hindu arose both from the knowledge that his growth was dictated more by his position within his caste rather than his achievements, as well as the fact that the self-sufficient nature of the village limited economic growth. The overarching nature of Hindu religion which dictated obedience to higher castes without the possibility of individual growth as well as the prohibitive injunctions regarding economic or social radicalism meant that the Hindu gradually became submissive and timid. As a result Le Bon summed up the mentality of the Hindu as:

> As a general rule, the Hindu is weak, timid, crafty, insinuating, and dissimulating to the highest degree. His manners are flattering and importunate; he is entirely deprived of ideas of patriotism. Centuries of tyranny [have] habituated him to the idea that he must have a Master, and provided that this Master respects the laws of his caste and his religious beliefs, the Hindu is resigned in advance to undergo all his will, and finds happiness if one leaves him about the handful of rice which he needs to live. The Hindus form a soft, patient population, absolutely resigned to their fate. Their defects [all the] more striking, for a European... are indolence, the absence of precaution and the still larger absence of energy.[73]

As a result of these characteristics, Le Bon concluded that while the average Hindu was not inferior intellectually to the average European, he was still condemned to be servant and never master.

Gustave Le Bon's magnum opus about India contained many inaccuracies, inconsistencies, and stereotypes.

---

[73] 'En règle générale, l'Hindou est faible, timide, rusé, insinuant et dissimulé au plus haut degree. Ses manières sont adulatrices et importunes; il est entièrement dépourvu d'idées de patriotisme. Des siècles de tyrannie l'ont habitué à l'idée qu'il doit avoir un maître, et pourvu que ce maître respecte les lois de ses caste et ses croyances religieuses, l'Hindou est résigné d'avance à subir toutes ses volontés, et se trouve heureux si on lui laisse à peu près la poignée de riz dont il a besoin pour vivre. Les Hindous forment une population douce, patiente, absolument résignée à son sort. Leurs défauts les plus frappants, pour un Européen...sont l'indolence, l'absence de prévoyance et l'absence plus grande encore d'énergie.'Ibid.: 186. Le Bon's choice of words itself is interesting in its contradictory approach. Describing the Hindu initially as weak and timid, he later uses the adjectives gentle and patient. This contradictory description may be found in many works of the time, both French and British. See for instance the contradictory explanations of the 'Aryan village' in India in Sir John Phear, *The Aryan Village in India and Ceylon* (London, 1880).

Yet no one seems to have analysed his work far enough to point out these problems. Instead Le Bon was used as a reliable reference about Indian life, customs and peoples not only by European travellers to India, but also respected and noted scholars writing about India. A clear indication of the direction in which race studies in France had progressed from the time of Rousselet to Le Bon can be seen by comparing the lithographs of Rousselet with the photographs of 'racial types' which Le Bon brought back with him from his voyage in India. Rousselet's images used standard features for a gamut of occupations (which would have meant different castes as well); a dancing girl would have belonged to a lower caste,[74] a jeweller to the trading caste[75] and a ruler to the warrior caste.[76] Even the lithograph of the English Resident with the Maharana of Udaipur shows both in terms of similar build, features, and physiology.[77] In fact the seated position of the Maharana indicated his superior social standing. The only variation in Rousselet's lithographs is in the skin colour. While Le Bon used this feature as an indicator of caste, Rousselet does not, representing both the *bayadère* (lower caste) and Maharana as darker skinned.[78]

Based on a desire to capture his 'subject' at his most exotic, Le Bon's images built a racial hierarchy for India which was far more succinct than and just as forceful as his hundreds of pages of description. He used physiology, colour, and material apparatus to distinguish the inferior races of India. In his depiction of the savages and semi-savages of central India for instance, he presents a classic European conception of a savage as semi-clothed with long unkempt hair, and possessing primitive weapons like

---

[74] See Image 5.2.
[75] See Image 5.3.
[76] See Image 5.5.
[77] See Image 5.4.
[78] Compare Images 5.2 and 5.5.

the bow and arrow.[79] In addition a closer look at the image of the Minas reveals the presence of a bottle (presumably alcohol) as well as a pipe (presumably an opium pipe) emphasizing the relationship of the inferior race with inferior morals.[80] Le Bon had definitely 'staged' his subjects to support his writing.[81] In the photos that he collected, Le Bon emphasized the difference between the dark-skinned tribes who belonged to inferior races and the fair-skinned Rajputs and Brahmins of North India[82] by contrasting the latter's fair skin colour, facial structure and clothing with that of the tribes. Le Bon also highlighted the difference between the Brahmins of southern India with their exaggerated ritual marks, semi-nakedness and dark skin, and the fair, well-built Aryan Brahmins of the North.[83] As Anne Maxwell points out, anthropologists could use photographs to make anatomical comparisons needed to racially classify and rank human subjects on an evolutionary scale by the 1880s. While ostensibly scientific, the photographs that

---

[79] See Images 5.6 and 5.7.

[80] See Image 5.6.

[81] This was a common aspect of early ethnographic images. The 'staging' of images meant that the natives were presented as if in their 'natural environment' thus defining their material additions, clothing, and other accoutrements as intrinsic to their level of culture and development. See Ellen Strain, 'Exotic Bodies, Distant Landscapes: Touristic Viewing and Popularized Anthropology in the Nineteenth Century', *Wide Angle* 18.2 (1996): 70–100; James Ryan, Picturing Empire: Photography and the Visualization of the British Empire (Chicago:University of Chicago Press1998); Elizabeth Edwards, Anthropology and Photography, 1860–1920 (New Hampshire: Yale University Press, 1994); Paul Landau, 'Empires of the Visual: Photography and Colonial Administration in Africa', *Images and Empires: Visuality in Colonial and Postcolonial Africa,*edited by Paul Landau and Deborah Kaspin (Berkeley and Los Angelos: University of California Press, 2002); and Christopher Pinney, Photography's Other Histories (co-edited volume with Nicolas Peterson) (Durham NC: Duke University Press, 2003).

[82] See Images 5.9 and 5.10.

[83] See Image 5.9.

Brahmane du Mysore.

IMAGE 5.9: CAPTION READS 'BRAHMAN OF MYSORE'. NOTE THE DARK SKIN OF THE SOUTHERN, 'DRAVIDIAN' BRAHMIN AS OPPOSED TO THE FAIR NORTHERN, 'ARYAN' BRAHMIN. ALSO NOTE THE EXCESSIVE EXOTICISM IN THE FIRST IMAGE WITH THE NUMEROUS RITUALISTIC MARKS AND THE SEMI-NAKEDNESS OF THE MYSORE BRAHMIN, AS OPPOSED TO THE MORE CIVILIZED LOOKING, FULLY CLOTHED UDAIPUR BRAHMIN.

Source: Gustave le Bon, *Les Civilisations de L'Inde.* Paris: Firmin Didot, 1887.

IMAGE 5.10: CAPTION READS 'HINDU PANDIT OF UDAIPUR'

Source: Gustave le Bon, *Les Civilisations de L'Inde.* Paris: Firmin Didot, 1887.

anthropologists developed around this time also served a political purpose by confirming that some peoples were less evolved than others and would therefore benefit from imperial control.[84]

Le Bon's images merely reinforced his writings. Based on his study of India he made assertions about the nature of caste and religion which echoed the statements of British administrators in India. Since Le Bon greatly admired the British and their empire this is not surprising. Yet his pronouncements about race in India were unparalleled in British scholarship. His position about India was widely read in France and therefore influenced the image of India in late nineteenth-century France to a considerable extent. While fallacies about the caste system, like its immutability, its presence as the sole identity of Indians and its tyrannical position had already been repeated in endless French operas of the day,[85] Le Bon's text now added a racial dimension to the French lens on India.

In particular, Le Bon added to the Aryanism of the mid-century by looking closely at the elements of 'Aryan' culture in India. Despite his considerable criticism of contemporary Indian culture and society, he held that the only worthwhile institutions which still existed in modern India were part of her Aryan heritage. For instance, he noted that the one institution in India which came close to assuring the average person rights in the midst of the tyranny of religion and despots was the *Panchayat* or the assembly of elected peers in each village; an institution which Le Bon traced to Aryan origins.[86] The *Panchayat* system was an elected assembly of peers who tried all disputes and cases involving petty theft and crime in the village. This was the first court of appeal and most disputes and cases

---

[84] Anne Maxwell, *Picture Imperfect. Photography and Eugenics, 1870–1940* (Brighton and Portland: Sussex Academic Press, 2008): 21.

[85] Such as Délibes' *Lakmé*, and Roussel's *Padmavati*.

[86] Gustave le Bon, *Les civilizations de l'Inde*: 676.

were usually resolved at this level. The *Panchayat* system was mostly prevalent in the North of India.

Another institution of Aryan origin, which according to Le Bon began as an admirable system of division of labour as well as a means by which the racial components of Vedic society could be identified was the caste system. If one was to compare the Aryan with any other race of antiquity the former would come out superior, in terms of mentality, intellect and physicality.[87] A few years after he had published his work on India, Le Bon's theories of race crystallized into a hierarchy of intelligence in anthropological races, proceeding downwards from the white races to the yellow and the black. The main feature of the white race was its superior intelligence and thereby its capacity to grow through education, invention and culture. While all races may choose to raise themselves through external achievement their psychological capacity limited their level of attainment. Thus, a black or yellow race may never be as great as a white race. 'They are capable of the rudiments of civilization, but solely the rudiments.'[88] Moreover, while the inferior races were possessed of a uniformity of intelligence, the variation of intelligence between individuals of the white race was the norm. It was this variation of intelligence which gave rise to different civilizations.[89]

An interesting feature of French race theory as it applied to India was the inability of scholars to come to any sort of consensus about which Indian races were 'Aryan'. Variously defined as the *Rajputs* or the North-Western tribes, *Pathans* or even the Banaras Brahmins,

---

[87] Ibid.: 284.

[88] 'Elles sont capables de rudiments de civilisation, mais de rudiments seulement.' Gustave le Bon, *Lois psychologiques de l'evolution des peuples* (Paris, Librairie Félix Alcan, 11th edition, 1913): 25.

[89] Ibid.: 26 and passim, chapter 3, 'Hiérarchie psychologique des races'.

French scholars described these races as possessing nobler mental and physical traits than their Dravidian or Turanian brethren. While the British concluded that the great Aryan potential of India had long been diluted by inferior racial blood, the French thought otherwise.[90] As the studies examined in this essay demonstrate, the French anthropologists while lamenting the dilution of Aryan blood among the peoples of India, yet defined certain tribes and races in terms such as 'more or less pure Aryan' (Gobineau), and 'pure Brahminical Aryans along the Ganges' (Topinard). Yet there was no agreement as to what constituted the 'pure Aryan'. While Topinard described the Brahmins in Banaras as Aryan, Gobineau lamented that the dilution of Aryan blood made it impossible to distinguish physically between a Brahmin and a lower caste. Rousselet described the Rajputs as Aryan, while Le Bon described them as having a large element of the Turanian in them. Anthropologically there was a huge gap between French scholars as to what degree of racial elements could pass for a 'pure race'. Yet the description of Aryan India was an inevitable part of all their works. Even with the variance as to which races and

---

[90] The British attitude towards the Aryan question in India is well summed up in Joan Leopold's 'British application of the Aryan theory of race to India', in *English Historical Review* 89.3 (1974). As Leopold points out, the British while agreeing that the Aryans had once created a great civilization in India, argued that races in contemporary India were too mixed to talk about any pure 'Aryan' blood existing. Instead the dilution of Aryan blood in the Indian subcontinent meant that the modern Indian could never reach that state of Aryan greatness again. Other detailed studies on the Aryan issue in India and elsewhere include Tony Ballantyne, *Orientalism and Race. Aryanism in the British Empire* (New York: Palgrave, 2002) and Thomas Trautmann, *Aryans and British India* (Berkeley and LA: University of California Press, 1997). Trautmann also pursues the issue as it was taken up by Indian nationalists as proof of the greatness of Indian civilization and the capacity of India to progress. Hindu nationalists, in particular, used the Aryan theory to argue that Indians were quite capable of ruling themselves without British domination.

tribes were Aryan, there was still an agreement that certain races of India continued to be Aryan. Le Bon accepted that modern races were the product of racial intermixing and therefore called them 'historical races' rather than 'anthropological races'.[91] Yet, he too described certain races of India as Aryan, thus blurring the line between his categories of 'historical' and 'anthropological' races.[92] The important thing was that the races which were described as being 'Aryan' were usually credited with the ability to withstand British rule (see Image 5.11). The British on the other hand described 'martial races of India' as those who had remained loyal to them during the Mutiny of 1857.[93]

For French scholars, the common ground between India and France lay in their shared Aryan ancestry, which Norman Britain could not share. The diffusion theory of civilization, which was extremely popular at the time, held that civilization was spread through the world by the migrating Aryans, and described the migration of various streams of Aryans from the Caucasus region to different parts of the world. The branch of Aryans who arrived in India was obviously linked to other branches that had migrated to Europe and elsewhere. This explained the high cultural achievements of the Vedic civilization of India

---

[91] Gustave le Bon, *Lois psychologiques de l'evolution des peoples* (Paris, Librairie Félix Alcan, 11th edition, 1913): 4, 173–77.

[92] Despite Le Bon's allowance that anthropologically speaking, 'pure' races no longer existed, he managed to obscure the line between his definition of historical and anthropological races, to assign to superior 'historical' races the same physiological features as superior anthropological races. In terms of its application to the Indian context, Le Bon's work is clearly a call for the superiority of aspects of Indian civilization because of its Aryan element.

[93] For more work on the British construction of 'martial races' of India, see Pradeep Barua, 'Inventing Race. The British and India's Martial Races', in *The Historian* 58.1 (1995); Tony Ballantyne, *Orientalism and Race. Aryanism in the British Empire* (New York: Palgrave, 2002); and Thomas Trautmann, *Aryans and British India* (Berkeley and LA: University of California Press, 1997; New Delhi: Yoda Press, 2004).

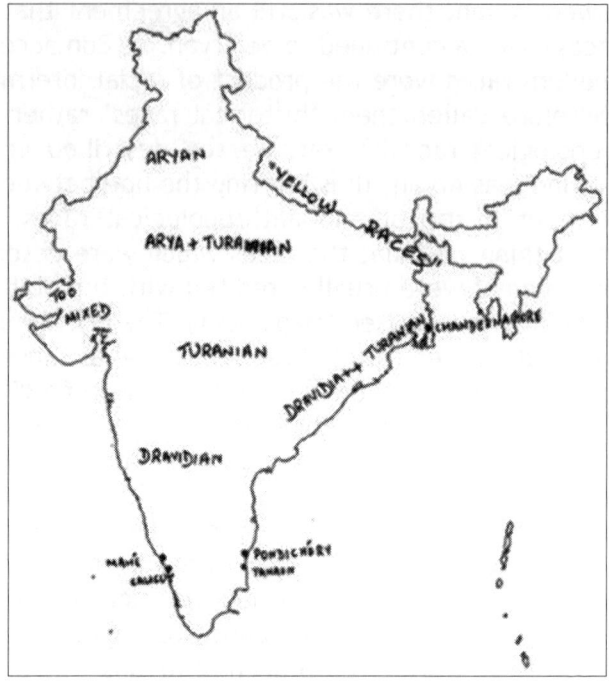

IMAGE 5.11: THE RACIAL MAP OF INDIA. THIS MAP CONSTITUTES A VISUAL READING OF THE 'RACES OF INDIA' AS DESCRIBED BY GOBINEAU, TOPINARD AND LE BON.

and the linguistic affinities between Sanskrit and other Indo-Germanic languages.[94] Since the Aryans were the

---

[94] The Indus Valley Civilization which effectively put an end to the claim that the Aryans were the first highly developed people in India was not discovered until the early twentieth century. Harappa and Mohenjo-Daro, the two great cities of the Indus Valley civilization were only unearthed in 1925, and along with them the discovery of an advanced technological and cultural society which had existed several hundred years before the Aryans' advent in India was the biggest blow to the theory that only the Aryans possessed the inherent capability to produce advanced civilizations, since the Harappan peoples were clearly not Aryan. Interestingly enough, for all their efforts to rank among the foremost Indologists, the French did not study the Indus Valley civilization much, leaving both the historical and archeological finds to the British.

forefathers of modern Indians, they came from the same racial stock as the Europeans. The superior civilization of the Aryans in India was already proven in terms of the institutions they had created such as the caste system, as well as the advanced religion and philosophy that they had produced in the form of Brahminism. In its core therefore, India was Aryan. She had degenerated over centuries due to the invasions of foreigners, particularly the Muslims. But her Aryan ancestry meant that she had the capability to throw off the decline of centuries and assume her place among the advanced countries of the world once more.

By the mid-nineteenth century, race was an important characteristic of India. Specifically, India was home to the Aryan race which explained the heights of civilization attained by the ancients who had been glorified in the work of Voltaire. The presence of the inferior Dravidian race and centuries of inter-mixing provided a cautionary tale of the dangers of race mixing. The history of India, from her glory days of Aryan civilization, to her position as an inferior society colonized by Britain, was a perfect example of the theory of racial hierarchy and the resulting downfall of a superior race as a result of diluting their pure blood. Anthropologically speaking, India could provide an all-encompassing example of racial theory. Leon Poliakov's seminal work on Aryanism in Europe also points to the importance of India in the creation of the myth of Aryan supremacy. According to Poliakov the importance of India as the home of the Aryans only declined with the emergence of Germanic Aryanism.[95]

BRITISH AND ARYAN INDIA

The father of the theory that Sanskrit was the original language of the Indo-Aryans was William Jones. That said,

---

[95] Leon Poliakov, *The Aryan Myth: A History of Racist and Nationalist Ideas in Europe*. Translated by E. Howard (New York: Basic Books, 1971).

the British did not set much store by the Aryan blood of contemporary India. To them, Aryans had indeed accomplished great intellectual and philosophical levels in the ancient period, but the dilution of their race over centuries of inter-marrying with inferior races had left them corrupt and incapable of ruling themselves. Unlike the French and German school of Indologists who posited a possible return to greatness if India embraced her Aryan past once again, the British theory justified in large part by the need to rule India, held that the once great capability of the Indo-Aryan was non-existent in the present time, simply because there were no extant, pure Aryans left in India.

As Joan Leopold points out, British explanations of India's inferiority were based on Lamarckian notions of the environment, which in India were considered physically enervating and morally sapping; the admixture of Dravidian blood and institutions, history and the influx of Mongoloids, Muslims, and Dravidians into pure Aryan blood and the notion that in India, the Aryans exhibited an arrested growth.[96] The combination of these factors was applied in theories of rule to justify British rule which would provide Indians with the necessary institutions and civilization needed to develop. On the other hand, the essentially Aryan roots of India also meant that a combined Orientalist and Anglicist method be used in Indian government and reform.

Thus, the modification of the theory that Indo-Aryans were the originators of the Indo-Europeans argued that the historical inferiority of India validated British colonial rule. In fact, Le Bon certainly held this view. For some, the racial equality and thereby a greater respect for, and fairer treatment of Indians was the key to preventing any

---

[96] Joan Leopold, 'British Applications of the Aryan Theory of Race to India, 1850–70', *English Historical Review*, 352 (July 1974).

repeats of the 1857 Mutiny.[97] Similarly, Henry Maine's studies of the Aryan institutions and its remnants in India were
meant to combat British prejudice against India by pointing
to common roots.[98] Yet the official position was to ignore
this ostensible claim by Indians to equality. As Thomas
Trautmann has demonstrated in his work on Aryans and
British India, the Aryan race theory was mostly propagated
by romantic Indologists like William Jones, in the eighteenth century.[99] In the nineteenth century these voices
in Britain were rare. Instead, officials focused on retrieving evidence of the dominance of inferior races like the
Dravidians, in present-day India.[100] The use of the Aryan
race theory was limited to civilians, especially missionaries
who hoped to show that Christianity was the natural Aryan
corollary to the degraded religion of idolatry in India.

The need for an overview of Indians was certainly
felt in order to strengthen rule, and particularly to avoid
a repeat of the 1857 Rebellion. So, the government insti-
tuted a Census, which collected information relating to
race. The Census Commissioner, Herbert Risley was pro-
foundly influenced by Topinard's anthropometric method
and instructed his juniors to collect data about the nasal
and cranial indices of different groups in India. The result
of this process was the institutionalization of the caste
system, which is discussed in the next chapter.

---

[97] Fredric Farrar, *Families of Speech* (London 1870); Samuel
Laing, *Lecture on the Indo-European Languages and Races* (Calcutta,
1862); and *India and China, England's Mission in the East* (London,
1863).

[98] Henry Maine, *Village Communities in the East and West*
(London, 1871): 12 and passim.

[99] Thomas R. Trautmann, *Aryans and British India*.

[100] Thomas Trautmann, *Languages and Nations. The Dravidian
Proof in Colonial Madras* (Berkeley: University of California Press, 2006;
New Delhi: Yoda Press, 2007).

FIGURE 5.1: Comparative graph of article content among articles on India, *Journal Asiatique*, 1822–1902

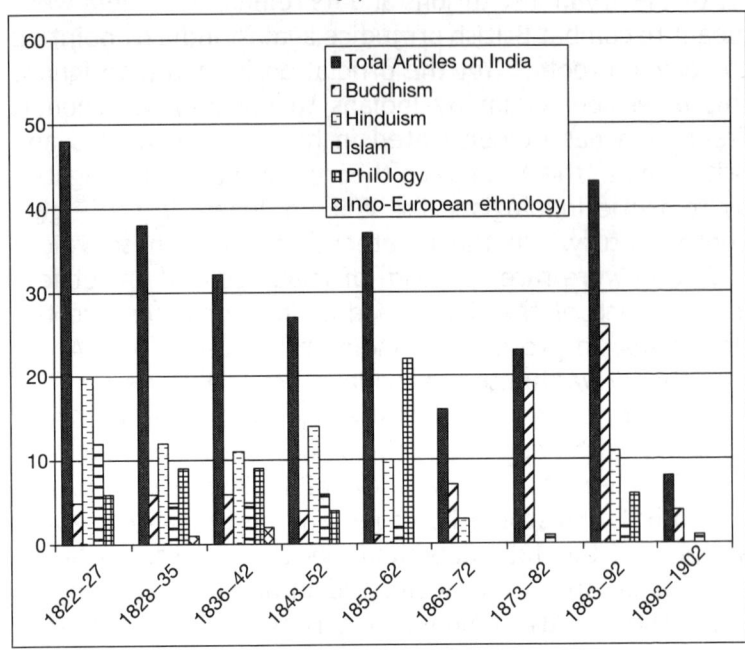

FIGURE 5.2: Comparative graph of article content among articles on India, *Bulletins de la Société d'anthropologie de Paris*, 1822–1902

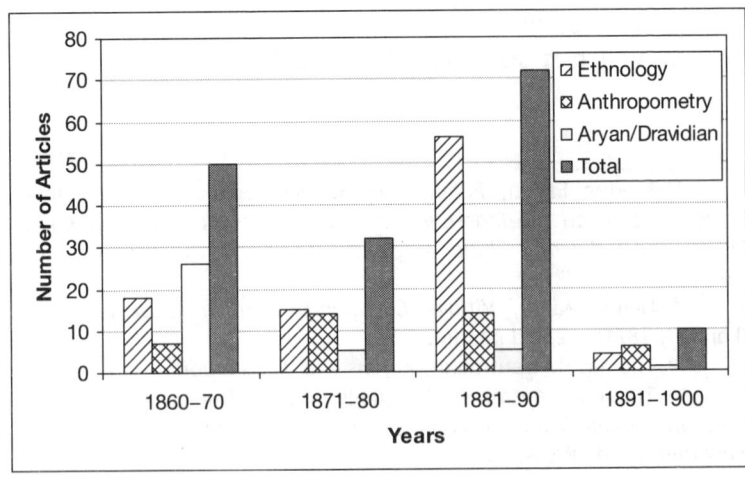

FIGURE 5.3: COMPARATIVE GRAPH OF ARTICLE CONTENT AMONG ARTICLES ON INDIA, *JOURNAL ASIATIQUE*, *REVUE D'ETHNOGRAPHIE*, *REVUE D'ANTHROPOLOGIE* AND *BULLETINS DE LA SOCIÉTÉ D'ANTHROPOLOGIE DE PARIS*, 1860–1900

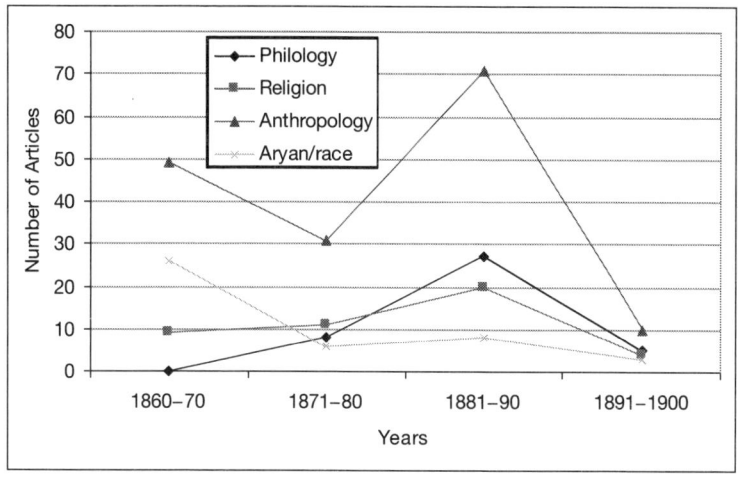

CONCLUSION

Through the efforts of Topinard, Gobineau and Le Bon, India became an intrinsic part of nineteenth-century anthropology. As Poliakov points out, even the father of French anthropology, Paul Broca, who followed the tradition of physical anthropology laid by the work of Cabanis, 'thought of the Aryan theory as very probable, even regarding the use of the term "Aryan races" as perfectly scientific....'[101] By the time Le Bon's most popular works on crowd psychology had been published[102] the theory of scientific racism was perfectly accepted even among

---

[101] Leon Poliakov, *The Aryan Myth*: 257.

[102] Gustave Le Bon is best known for his works on mob psychology, and his academic position was as a psychologist too. See Gustave le Bon, *Lois psychologiques de l'evolution des peoples* (Paris, Librairie Félix Alcan, 11th edition, 1913). Yet as Robert Nye's work on Le Bon shows, his later works on psychology were drawn primarily from his research in India and North Africa. See Robert Allen Nye, *An Intellectual Portrait of Gustave LeBon*.

academics. Poliakov notes that 'the popular works of Gustave le Bon on collective psychology and the racial soul show how rapidly these theories of racialism could spread and be used in the practice of racism.'[103]

The primary lesson to be learned from India was the danger of racial mixing. As these scholars pointed out, the regions in India which had adhered closely to their 'Aryan' roots and institutions had maintained a higher level of culture and achievement despite the overall degeneration of Indian civilization. No one seems to have pointed out the inconsistencies in their definition of 'Aryan' and the extent of the achievements of the Aryan race. By the mid-century, colonialism had allied itself with race to argue that Europeans were eminently qualified to civilize Asia and Africa by virtue of their 'Aryan heritage'. While Germany was the leader in Aryan studies, French scholars were not far behind in using polemic to disguise the gaps and inconsistencies in their studies. In fact, Poliakov's work on the Aryan Myth is notable for the number of French scholars who contributed to the growth of the theory of a pre-eminent Aryan race.[104] In the process, the systematic studies of Burnouf who warned against loosely comparing Western culture with Eastern religion or philosophy were ignored.

The academic and popular journals of the day reflected the hold that anthropology, and by extension race theory, had over both the institutional and the popular culture. Traditional Indological publications like the *Journal Asiatique* and the *Journal des Savants* presented a decline in the number of articles on India (compensated for by the increase in articles on Indo-China and Africa).[105]

---

[103] Leon Poliakov, *The Aryan Myth*: 285.

[104] Ibid.

[105] For instance, in 1863–72, the number of articles on India was at its lowest: 16 during the nineteenth century. Correspondingly the number of articles dealing with French interests in the Far East and Islamic world increased to 103! *Journal Asiatique*. Gallica.bnf.fr. Accessed on 26 September 2008.

The same decade witnessed the popularity of articles on Indian race and anthropology with the *Bulletins de la Société d'anthropologie de Paris* registering a total of 50 such articles in 1860–70.[106]

For Indologists, race theory was too persuasive and pernicious to ignore. If they were to survive they would have to adapt to the changing focus on India. So, while they continued focusing on textual translations, they took the lessons learned from anthropology and applied it to Indology. In the last quarter of the nineteenth century, the image of India was recast yet again, this time to reflect the urgency of race.

---

[106] See Image 5.3.

Chapter 6

Recasting India in French Indology: Hinduism and the Caste System

> In sectarian India at present, and since the appearance of foreign proselytizing religions, caste is the express badge of Hinduism. The man who is a member of a caste is a Hindu; he who is not, is not a Hindu. And caste is not merely the symbol of Hinduism; but, according to the testimony of all who have studied it on the spot, it is its stronghold. It is this, much more than their creeds, which attaches the masses to these vague religions, and gives them such astonishing vitality.[1]

The influence of anthropology on Indic studies had begun by the mid-century. Indologists who continued to look to language and culture for comparisons between civilizations were in danger of becoming completely superfluous to French academia.[2] In order to secure their survival they adapted their studies to larger national academic interests. Another means to ensure survival and continuity was to embrace the anthropological studies which defined race in physiological rather than linguistic terms. This chapter looks at the result of these shifts for the image of India. When Indologists combined traditional philological studies with newer anthropological theories they recast India in

---

[1] Auguste Barth, *The Religions of India*. Translated by Rev. J. Wood (London: Kegan Paul, Trench Trübner and Co, 1891). Third Edition, preface: xvii.

[2] See Chapter 4.

terms of the caste system. They also created a hybrid religion called Hinduism to explain the inconsistencies they saw in India.[3]

The new Indology was the effort of a handful of scholars. Auguste Barth, Emile Sénart, Sylvain Lévi, and Julien Vinson rescued Indology in France and restored it to a pre-eminent position in academia. This chapter follows the new image of India created by French Indologists in terms of caste, racial divisions, and Hinduism.

CASTE AND THE 'RACIALIZATION' OF INDIA

As the previous chapter has shown, studies on race were grounded in the Indian context through the institution of caste. According to Sénart, the word 'caste' arose from the Portuguese understanding of the social divisions they encountered among the Indians.

...the Portuguese were not long in noticing that they were divided into a great number of hereditary, closed sections, being characterized by the specialty of their occupations. They were superimposed in a kind of hierarchy, the higher groups kept with a superstitious care of [precluding] any bringing together with the groups considered [to be] humbler. It is to these sections that they gave the name of *castes*.[4]

---

[3] The French did not invent the term Hinduism. Instead they adopted this term in the late nineteenth century to explain the degeneration of Brahminism due to the influence of foreign (particularly Islamic) incursions and the consequent mixing of races.

[4] '...les Portugais ne tardèrent pas à remarquer qu'elles étaient divisées en un grand nombre de sections héréditaires, fermées, se distinguant par la spécialité de leurs occupations. Elles se superposaient en une sorte de hiérarchie, les groupes plus élevés se gardent avec un soin superstitieux de tout rapprochement avec les groupes réputes plus humbles. C'est à ces sections qu'ils donnèrent le nom de *castes*.' Emile Sénart, 'Les castes dans l'Inde: Le Présent', in *Revue des Deux Mondes* (1 February 1894): 596.

While early century scholars had described the caste system in detail and included the rights and duties of the four castes, the addition of race by the mid-century meant that each caste was now correlated to a race. Generally speaking, Brahmins and warriors (*Kshatriyas*) were of Aryan ancestry, while the third caste of *Vaiçyas* was of mixed blood. The lowest caste of workers or *Shudras* as well as the *Pariahs* or untouchables were a combination of the lowest races—Negroid and Mongoloid.

The use of caste as a measure of the racial make-up of India was first used by the British, who sought to categorize Indians into various castes in the wake of 1857, each caste defined as possessing certain fixed characteristics.[5] French colonial administrators in India found that much of their experience centred around caste too. In southern India and particularly in the *Comptoirs*, conflicts within the native community usually arose around issues of caste privilege, more so than the conflicts of religion which came to characterize British India. In 1871, M. Esquer, who was president of the Pondichéry Tribunal on caste conflicts, wrote a controversial tract on the nature and effects of the caste system in India.[6] Witness to the multiple conflicts which occurred between caste, reinforced by the work of British officials in similar positions, Esquer naturally saw caste as a divisive entity which reinforced the tyrannical oppression of a Brahminical caste to the compete neglect and absence of a sense of patriotism and nationalism.[7] In a sentiment repeated throughout his work, Esquer wrote,

---

[5] See for example the exhaustive surveys of William Crooke, *The Tribes and Castes of the North-Western Provinces and Oudh*. 4 vols (1896); Sir Denzil Ibbetson, *Punjab Castes*. (1883); and Herbert Risley, *The People of India*. Second edn (1915). For an excellent study on how these works affected the construction and perception of India, see Nicholas Dirks, *Castes of Mind* (Princeton University Press, Princeton NJ, 2001).

[6] A. Esquer, *Essai sur les castes dans l'Inde* (Pondichéry 1871).

[7] Ibid., Chapters 3 and 5, passim.

Among the sixty million inhabitants who populate these vast regions, the word of nationality did not have any sense [meaning]: this multitude, in which each individual [is] vegetated, insulated and parked in his caste, as in an insuperable barrier, does not ask any more but to cultivate their rice, to plant their tobacco or their indigo, to supervise the maturity of their sugarcanes, [and] to incline [prostrate] themselves in front of [the] Brahmins, [and] to venerate the higher castes.[8]

Most French writers agreed with Esquer about the divisive aspects of the caste system. For instance, the geographer and savant Vivien Saint-Martin published his own critique of Esquer along with his theory on the caste system.[9] Saint-Martin claimed to be knowledgeable not only about the geography of the subcontinent but also about the history

---

[8] 'Parmi les soixante millions d'habitants qui peuplent ces vastes contrées, le mot de nationalité n'avait plus de sens: cette multitude, dans laquelle chaque individu végétait, isolé et parqué dans sa caste, comme dans une barrière infranchissable, ne demandait plus qu'à cultiver son riz, qu'à planter son tabac ou son indigo, surveiller la maturité de ses cannes à sucre, s'incliner devant les Brâhmes, vénérer les castes supérieures....' Ibid.: 10.

[9] Vivien de Saint- Martin. 'Compte rendu de l'Essai sur les castes de l'Inde par M. Esquer, président du tribunal de Pondichéry', *Bulletin de la Société de géographie* (November 1872): 534–42. Saint-Martin, born in 1802, was arguably the most famous geographer of the nineteenth century. Immortalized in the Jules Verne's novel, *In Search of the Castaways or the Children of Captain Grant*(1867–68. See Chapter 7). Saint-Martin had an illustrious academic career which included authoring the *Nouveau Dictionnaire de Géographie Universelle* and becoming *président honoraire* of the *Société de Géographie de Paris*. Although he never visited India, he was considered an expert nonetheless and published three *Mémoires sur la géographie de l'Inde*. These were the *Etude sur la géographie grecque et latine de l'Inde* (Paris 1858), *Etude sur la géographie et les populations primitives du Nord-Ouest de l'Inde, d'après les Hymnes védiques* (Paris 1859) and *Etudes de géographie ancienne et d'ethnographie Asiatique* (Paris, 1850), Vol. 1. A fourth work which was to take up the geography of Southern India—though promised and referred to in the third—was unfortunately never published.

of ancient India (through his exploration of the ancient texts of India on historical geography) and social institutions like caste. While challenging Esquer on the historical origins of the system, Saint-Martin accepted that Esquer's treatment of the current state of the caste system, of the position, duties and responsibilities of each caste, particularly those in the South were detailed.[10] Saint-Martin also applauded Esquer's treatment of the three views of caste: 'vue historique...vue social...vue philosophique...'.[11]

Esquer's work integrated the Aryan view into the study of the caste system in India. According to Esquer, the conquering Aryans created 'India' the moment they invaded the Gangetic plains and defeated the indigenous inhabitants or *dasyus*.[12] Esquer waxed long on the historical origin of castes, which he traced to the beginning of Brahminism. When 'les membres de la blanche famille Aryenne' descended upon the indigenous *dasyus* of India, the resulting contact meant that the latter accepted the superior culture and civilization of the Aryans by centring their thought on two key concepts, the transmigration of souls and the caste system.

> We said then how these new Masters of India, giving up their primitive beliefs, to assimilate part of the beliefs of the conquered races, substituted new religious and philosophical dogmas to them, worked out a new social constitution, and created a civilization, strange and imposing at the same time, whose two essential components were the dogma of the transmigration of the souls and the system of the castes.[13]

---

[10] Ibid.: 536–37.

[11] 'Historical view...social view...philosophical view....'Ibid.: 535.

[12] A. Esquer. *Essai sur les castes dans l'Inde* (Pondichéry 1871): 481.

[13] 'Nous avons dit ensuite comment ces nouveaux maîtres de l'Inde, abandonnant leurs croyances primitives, pour s'assimiler une partie des croyances des races conquises, leur substituèrent de nouveaux dogmes

In Esquer's estimation, the noble Aryans could not have thought of such a restrictive and limiting system of social classification. Therefore, Esquer, having examined a number of 'ancient texts' such as the *Manusmriti* and Sanskrit plays like the *Meghaduta,* concluded that the illness of caste came upon Indian society through its exposure and susceptibility to Brahminical oratory.[14] According to him while the origin of the caste system was an admirable notion, the manner in which it evolved to become hereditary and rule-bound meant that all individual freedom was crushed under Brahminical tyranny.

> The division of the castes is, one can affirm boldly, a masterpiece of legislation: this system, at the origin, was admirably adapted to the climate of India and to the native practices characteristic of its inhabitants... the system of the castes, undoubtedly, [was] devoted to a disastrous inequality; but it gave to the new society a fixed position [stability], favoured the increase in population and the creation of the richnesses [wealth], and permitted a great philosophical, literary, political and industrial rise.... But, and there was their great error, the legislators ignored human nature, by declaring that their organization could not be modified... human authority is primarily circumscribed by the imprescriptable rights of freedom, [without it] it becomes usurpation and tyranny... the Brahminic spirit, which inspired this regime of inequality, was really the antipode [of the] Christian spirit.[15]

---

religieux et philosophiques, élaborèrent une nouvelle constitution sociale, et créèrent une civilisation, étrange et grandiose à la fois, dont les deux éléments essentiels étaient le dogme de la transmigration des âmes et le système des castes....' Ibid.: 482.

[14] Ibid., Chapter 5.

[15] 'La division des castes est, on peut l'affirmer hardiment, un chef-d'œuvre de législation: ce système était, à l'origine, admirablement adapté au climat de l'Inde et aux habitudes natives et caractéristique de ses habitants...Le système des castes, sans doute, consacrait à une inégalité funeste; mais il donnait à la société nouvelle une assiette

Disagreeing with Esquer that the origins of caste could be found in the Brahminical orthodoxy which followed the Vedic period, Saint-Martin noted that the division of society was a common feature of many ancient societies. What was remarkable about India was the vigour with which caste had eclipsed virtually any other social order and asserted itself as the basis on which Indian society, economy, polity, and even religion derived authority. According to Saint-Martin,

India is not, with much near, the only region of the world where the division of the castes was introduced. One can say that nature deposited the germ within all human society, from the most negligible and most rudimentary associations, to the highest organizations in the historical and philosophical hierarchy. The largest nations, most famous and most glorious in old or current times, recognized them under various names and under more or less absolute conditions; but nowhere are they developed in such an encompassing and complete, deep manner, as in India. Nowhere did they become as here the single base of the political, religious and civil society, the fundamental institution from which all the remainder derives and to which all is referred.[16]

---

fixe, favorisait l'accroissement de la population et la création des richesses, et permettait un grand essor philosophique, littéraire, politique et industriel...Mais, et c'est là leur grande erreur, les législateurs ont méconnu la nature humaine, en déclarant que leur organisation ne pourrait être modifiée...L'autorité humaine est essentiellement circonscrite par les droits imprescriptibles de la liberté, elle devient usurpation et tyrannie...L'esprit brâhmanique, qui a inspiré le régime de l'inégalité, a été vraiment l'antipode de l'esprit chrétien....'Ibid.: 74–75.

   [16] 'L'Inde n'est pas, à beaucoup près, la seule contrée du monde où la division des castes se soit introduite. On peut dire que la nature a déposé le germe au sein de toutes les sociétés humaines, depuis les associations les plus infimes et les plus rudimentaires, jusqu'aux organisations les plus élevées dans la hiérarchie historique et philosophique. Les nations les plus grandes, les plus célèbres et les plus glorieuses dans les temps anciens ou actuels, les ont reconnues sous différents noms et

His disagreement with Esquer lay in the latter's view of the historical origins of the system. 'This view brings us back to the purely historical side of the question of the castes on which M.Esquer, as I said, does not show as much decision as one could wish.'[17] Unlike Esquer, who had suggested that the caste system had evolved in the period of Brahminical orthodoxy, Saint-Martin suggested that the germ of the caste system was contained in the Vedic period itself and in fact, in all human societies. According to Saint-Martin the Brahminical contribution to the system was to make it hereditary and inviolable, to impose all manner of regulations as to the interaction and mobility between castes and the equation of caste with a divinely ordained system of hierarchy.

> The distinction of the castes as I said, was in [a] germ [germinant form] within the Vedic tribes, as it is at the bottom of all human society. It is its indelible and hereditary character, it is its insuperable limit, it is its religious dedication and divine institution, which marked it [as] so deeply sealed in the Brahminic constitution, and gave him [the brahmin], on the destiny of the Hindu people, an influence that the same social fact, with various degrees of development, had with no other people.[18]

---

dans des conditions plus ou moins absolues; mais nulle part elles sont développées d'une manière aussi éntendue (*sic*- entourer ?), aussi complet, aussi profonde que dans l'Inde. Nulle part elles ne sont devenues comme ici la base unique de la société politique, religieuse et civile, l'institution fondamentale d'où tout le reste dérive et à laquelle tout se rapporte.' Vivien de Saint-Martin, 'Compte rendu de l'Essai sur les castes de l'Inde par M. Esquer, président du tribunal de Pondichéry', in *Bulletin de la Société de géographie* (Nov 1872): 534.

[17] 'Cette vue nous ramène au côté purement historique de la question des castes sur lequel M.Esquer, ainsi que je l'ai dit, ne montre pas autant de décision qu'on pourrait le désirer.' Ibid.: 537.

[18] 'La distinction des castes je l'ai dit, était en germe au sein des tribus védiques, comme elle est au fond de toutes les sociétés humaines. C'est son caractère indélébile et héréditaire, c'est sa limite

According to Saint-Martin, the particular development of caste in India was 'the result of the conquest... the historical and social expression at the same time of the control of an ignorant, coarse race, [with] limited faculties, [and] without organization policies, by an infinitely more developed race and [with] much higher physical and intellectual faculties.'[19] While regrettable from a moral standpoint, it was undeniable from a physiological viewpoint that there were races which possessed nobility, strength and were born superior to other races which were inferior from all angles to the former and therefore must be subordinate to them.[20] In India too the caste system was demarcated not merely on the basis of physique, but also on colour; the first three castes were fair and the last was dark.[21] There were thus two clear races: 'a conquering, dominant race and a conquered, enslaved race.'[22]

The Aryan antecedents of the system were reinforced in Emile Sénart's work on India.[23] Sénart held that the caste

---

infranchissable, c'est sa consécration religieuse et d'institution divine, qui l'ont marquée d'un cachet si profond dans la constitution brahmanique, et lui ont donné, sur la destinée du peuple hindou, une influence que le même fait social, à différents degrés de développement, n'a eu chez aucun autre peuple.' Ibid.: 537.

[19] 'le résultat de la conquête... l'expression historique et sociale à la fois de l'asservissement d'une race ignorante, grossière, de facultés bornées, sans organization politiques, par une race infiniment plus développée et de facultés physiques et intellectuelles très-supérieures.'Ibid.: 537–38.

[20] Ibid.

[21] Ibid: 539–42.

[22] Ibid: 539. 'une race conquérante et dominatrice, une race conquise et asservie.'

[23] Emile Sénart, born at Rheims in 1847, studied at the Universities of Munich and Goettingue where he got interested in studying India. Sénart's prolific work as a scholar alone makes him noteworthy among the ranks of French Indology. Not content with studying only literary texts, or inscriptions alone, Sénart re-set the bar for scholars of India in terms of the qualifications and quality of scholarship. He had, by

system sprang from a common Aryan heritage of Greek, Roman and Indian pasts which held family, clan, and tribe as the basic social units, each with its own rules of social contract and behaviour. He based his assumption about the origin and common heritage of the caste system on linguistic comparisons of the term for tribe in Rome, *gens* or *curia*; family in Greece, *phratria, phyle*; and the extended family or caste in India, *gotra*. He interpreted the meaning of the word for caste in Sanskrit, *jati*, as race.[24] According to him, 'Caste is, in my opinion, the normal prolongation of the old Aryan institutions, modeling itself through the vicissitudes that the medium [caste] prepared them [Aryans] which they met in India.'[25]

Sénart's position was a middle ground between Esquer and Saint-Martin. In his assessment of the contemporary practice of caste, Sénart pointed out that the system included the categorization of certain castes belonging to the Aryan race, and of furthering the inferiority

---

the end of his long career, published three types of works dealing with India. The first body was that of translation. Sénart had translated Sanskrit and Pali works like the Pali grammar of *Kacchayana* in 1871, the *Bhagavadgita* from the Sanskrit in 1922, and the Buddhist text, the *Mahavastu,* between 1882 and 1897. The second corpus consisted of epigraphic translations, of Asokan, Indo-Bactrian and Buddhist inscriptions into French. The last, and possibly the richest contribution to Indology, were a series of works on Indian art, history, and religion. These works included a work on the Gandhara school of sculptures in 1906, on Asoka and Buddhism in 1889, on Indian theatre in 1891, on the caste system in 1894, on the origins of Buddhism in 1907, and on Buddhism and Yoga in 1900. So, in the course of a long and rich career Sénart managed to become as complete an expert as possible on ancient as well as contemporary India, applying his scholarship and theories derived from studies of ancient texts and inscriptions to contemporary institutions like the caste system, economy and religion.

[24] Emile Sénart, 'Les Castes dans l'Inde: Les Origines', *Revue des Deux Mondes* (15 September 1894): 326–32.

[25] 'La caste est, à mon sens, le prolongement normal des antiques institutions âryennes, se modelant à travers les vicissitudes que leur prépara le milieu qu'elles rencontrèrent dans l'Inde....' Ibid.: 344.

of the lower castes by grouping them as belonging to the Dravidian race. According to Sénart, the four major castes could be divided into two groups: the three upper castes who corresponded to the 'Aryas'—the upper born, 'twice-born' or 'dvija'; and the Shudras or lower caste, which was excluded from the ceremonies which allowed the upper castes to take their place in society. The explanation for this division, according to Sénart, lay in the Aryan conquest of the indigenous people of India and the inevitable tensions between the two races. 'Between Aryas and Coûdras, there is certainly in the beginning an opposition of race, that it is more or less absolute.'[26]

In a summary of his work on caste, Sénart presented the following image: the Aryans, upon their entry into India, were already divided into an aristocratic class, a priestly class and 'the rest of the Aryans [who] were merged in a single category, in the midst of which the various groups operated in their own autonomy'.[27] As the invading Aryans successfully subdued the 'dark-skinned race of inferior civilization',[28] they strengthened the divisions between the various classes to preserve their own exclusiveness and purity; absorbing the conquered people into the lowest strata of their society. As Aryan ideas penetrated the indigenous civilization, simultaneously, continuing expansion meant that the original Aryan ties of family were weakened.

In time, two facts emerged: admixture, only half acknowledged, occurred between the races, and the Aryan ideas of purity gained more and more ground amongst this hybrid

---

[26] 'De l'Aryas à Coûdras, il y a certainement à l'origine une opposition de race, qu'elle soit plus ou moins absolue.'Emile Sénart, 'Les Castes dans l'Inde: Le Passé', *Revue des Deux Mondes* (1 March 1894): 109.

[27] Emile Sénart, *Caste in India. The Facts and the System.* Translated by Sir Denison Ross (London, 1930): 209.

[28] Ibid.

population and even amongst the purely aboriginal peoples. From thence arose two categories of scruples, the
categories of which were multiplied according to the varying degrees of impurity either of descent or occupation.
While the ancient principles of family life were perpetuated, the grouping factors were diversified—that is to
say, function, religion, vicinity, and so forth, side by side
with the primitive principle of consanguinity, behind which
they more or less conceal themselves. The groups grew
and overlapped. Under the double influence of their own
traditions and of the ideas they borrowed from Aryan civilization, the aboriginal tribes themselves, in proportion as
they renounced an isolated and savage life, accelerated
the influx of new sections. Caste came into existence.[29]

As Sénart pointed out, the theoretical injunctions
regarding the working of the caste system and the caste regulations of the Law Books of ancient India (*Dharmasastras*)
like the *Manusmriti*, the codes of Vasishtha and Yagnavalkya
notwithstanding, the system never in fact, existed in so
pure a form as the texts lead one to believe.[30] The Law
Books were essentially collections of customs and usage,
which were constantly evolving. While the system was
premised upon the working of four tiers each with the right
to practise only certain occupations, men constantly chose
varied occupations within each caste, and in the late nineteenth century, there were more than 800 castes and sub-
castes present in India.

He pointed out that the manner in which caste was
practised in India, including rules about marriage, occupations, and social intercourse between castes, indicated
that caste could not be equated with the European notion
of class. Moreover, it was not as stagnant or as rigid as it
had been portrayed. Caste was a tool of social organization

---

[29] Sénart, *Caste in India.*: 210–11.
[30] Emile Sénart, 'Les Castes dans l'Inde: Le Passé', *Revue des Deux Mondes* (1 March 1894): 94–105.

and not a religious construct. It was also a useful organization for the exercise of authority and jurisdiction in the
face of nebulous political authority. As Sénart pointed out,
castes were constantly evolving, disintegrating, and form-
ing, and as such were a fact of everyday life in India rather
than a religious characteristic. According to him,

> Let us disregard some definitely lower racial populations,
> isolated by geographical circumstances and [by] history,
> secondly by numerical importance: on the whole India
> appears to us, not like a simple collection of individu-
> als, but like an agglomeration of corporative units. The
> number, the name, the characters, [and] the function vary
> ad infinitum....[31]

Moreover, the authority of family, of the village as a spatial
unit continued to be important, as did competing divisions
of left- and right-hand castes, multiple sub-castes within
the four major castes and the rules regarding the social
intercourse between these sub-castes.

This development of the notion of caste as an unchanging entity was a result of the Western effort to study
the anthropological and racial composition of India. Yet
as Risley's copious efforts on cataloguing the nasal indices, and cranial measurements of the members of various
castes showed, races in India were too mixed to divide the
caste system into different races. As Sénart pointed out,
the only certain knowledge about caste was that it had
evolved, possibly from a simpler system of occupational

---

[31] 'Faisons abstraction de quelques populations décidément infé-
rieures par la race, isolées par les circonstances géographiques et par
l'histoire, second par l'importance numérique: l'Inde tout entière
nous apparait, non pas comme une simple collection d'individus, mais
comme une agglomération d'unités corporatives. Le nombre, le nom,
les caractères, la fonction en varient à l'infini....' Emile Sénart, 'Les
Castes dans l'Inde: Le Present', *Revue des Deux Mondes* (1 February
1894): 600.

classes during the Vedic period, into a complicated and hereditary system during the period of the Epics and Brahmanas in order to assimilate the indigenous peoples. 'Caste is the framework of all brahminic organization. It is to come to brahminism that the aboriginal populations are constituted as castes, accepting the strict rules of the caste.'[32] What most scholars failed to see was that the system, created in order to maintain social organization, had undergone several evolutions—from class to caste, the process incorporated different occupations, as well as a need to distinguish different races.[33] To see the caste system as an unchanging system was therefore a great mistake. The maturity and tempered judgement of this monograph was unprecedented in French works on India.

Another important contributor to ideas of caste was the Indic philosopher Célestin Bouglé who wrote several essays on the caste system. Bouglé saw the essence of caste as consisting of three tendencies—repulsion, hierarchy, and hereditary specialization.[34] Pointing out that the European system, even at the height of feudalism, was never as airtight about these three tendencies as India, Bouglé adhered to the French school of scholars who saw the system as specific to India.[35] This was an important criticism to the many anthropologists like Gobineau and Le Bon who sought a link between the social systems of

---

[32] 'La caste est le cadre de toute l'organisation brâhmanique. C'est pour venir au brâhmanisme que les populations aborigènes se constituent en castes, acceptant les règles strictes de la caste.' Emile Sénart, 'Les Castes dans l'Inde: Les Origines', *Revue des Deux Mondes* (15 September 1894): 326.

[33] Emile Sénart, 'Les Castes dans l'Inde: Le Passé', *Revue des Deux Mondes* (1 March 1894): 121.

[34] Célestin Bouglé, *Essays on the Caste System*. English translation by D. F. Pocock (Cambridge, 1971): 9.

[35] The most respected scholars of caste studies continue to be French. Louis Dumont's *Homo Hierarchicus*, published in 1950 is the model of caste that contemporary scholars refer to.

the Indo-Aryans and the Aryans of Europe. While Bouglé noted that the Indian system of caste was also particularly noted for the enormous influence and power accorded to the priesthood [the Brahmins], the race theorists like Gobineau ascribed this power and thereby the degeneration of the system of caste from an admirable social construct to a repressive institution to the influx of non-Aryan blood.

The study of caste by French Indologists conclusively proved that India was a racially diverse country. The element of unanimity lay in the origins of the system. The caste system in ancient times had been the product of the invading Aryans. Its division of society into occupational strata was a common enough aspect of most other societies such as Egypt, Greece and Rome. In theory, it represented an admirable ideal. In its earliest and simplest form, therefore, the caste system represented the capacity of the Aryans to organize themselves into efficient groups. The Indologists went on to say that the institution of caste in contemporary India was a divisive force and an example of degeneration. The degeneration of the system had occurred due to the influx of non-Aryan races into the lower echelons of the system, leading to the formation of an oppressive, tyrannical system.

The French study of caste at the turn of the century was important for several reasons. The first was the confluence of Indology with anthropology. In the study of caste, one can clearly see the unity of the race theories of anthropologists with the traditional philological and literary studies of Indologists. At its core, the argument ran thus: the system of caste as conceived by the ancient Aryans was a superior one that had none of the hereditary restrictions or tyranny of the Brahmins. This theory could be proved by the superior literature of the day. The latter-day degeneration of the system could be studied through literature, and the degeneration of the noble language of Sanskrit proceeded side-by-side with the degeneration of the Aryan race in India as they incorporated more and more non-Aryans into their society. According to Sénart,

The classical language of India is distinguished from cognate languages by a striking peculiarity. The finite verb finds small place in the sentence; the thought is unfolded in long, compound phrases, often very ambiguously related. Instead of a solid syntactic construction in which the design is perceptible and the stresses stand out of themselves in clearly defined clauses, the sentence boasts no more than a loose structure in which the constituent parts of the thought, merely juxtaposed, are lacking in relief. The religious beliefs of India are scarcely ever presented in positive dogmas. In the vague outlines of an imperfectly defined pantheism, opposition and divergences rise for a moment only, then sink back into the shifting mass. Contradictions are quickly resolved in a conciliatory syncretism which weakens schisms, and all differences are cloaked by a convenient orthodoxy. Nowhere is there categoric doctrine, consistent and uncompromising. On the social plane, an analogous phenomenon appears in the caste system. Everywhere is the same spectacle of plastic impotence.[36]

The ambiguity of Brahminical Sanskrit was mirrored in the need to incorporate, through religious syncretism and contradictory doctrine, the various indigenous people of India into the Aryan society. The language and dogma which increasingly became more complex was a reflection of the Aryan need to incorporate the ideologies of the locals whom they conquered, without losing their own ritual and social superiority. Just as the crisp verses of the Rig Veda gave way to the philosophical conundrums of the Upanishads, the society of the Aryans was becoming more complex with the integration of the local inhabitants at the lower levels of the caste system. Thus, caste was merely a symbol of the larger degeneration of Indian society due to the racial mixing that occurred.

---

[36] Sénart, *Caste in India.*: 218–19.

Second, the study of caste was harnessed to the late-century civilizing mission. For instance, Esquer's view was a classic colonial view of the degeneration in Indian society and the ameliorating and civilizing effects of colonial rule. His whole work consisted of a denunciation of the tyranny of caste and an enumeration of the colonial attempt, both British and French, at ameliorating the ill effects of caste. Note however that the greater success and tolerance of the French could perhaps explain the acceptance of French rule in the *Comptoirs* as opposed to the Great Revolt of 1857 in the British-ruled areas of India.[37] In a fairly typical chapter detailing the efforts of the French government in the *Comptoirs* to diminish the evils of the caste system, Esquer wrote,

In taking charge of the populations whose fate was abandoned by the treaties of 1815, France was to think of improving their material wellbeing, at the same time as [being] the moraliser: it was a second means, effective and practical, of civilization, which it was to use in the interest of its Indian subjects.[38]

In particular, Esquer pointed to the effects of western education in breaking the stronghold of caste in addition to missionary activities.

A second mode of action, more effective and more practical than the preceding, is employed with success by the friends of India for raising its populations to the height of modern ideas and civilization; this means, surer and less dangerous than the preaching of Christian ideas... is

---

[37] Bouglé, *Essays on the Caste System*, Chapter 6.

[38] 'En prenant la charge des populations dont le sort lui était abandonné par les traités de 1815, la France devait songer à améliorer leur bien- être matériel, en même temps qu'à les moraliser: c'était un second moyen, efficace et pratique, de civilisation, dont elle devait user dans l'intérêt de ses sujets de l'Inde.' A. Esquer. *Essai sur les castes dans l'Inde* (Pondichéry 1871): 353.

education, the initiation of the masses to [the] arts and [the] sciences of the Occident.[39]

The bulk of the later chapters of the tract (which was published as an independent tract by a government press in Pondichéry) related to the French effort to cope with, and break out of the caste stronghold in the *Comptoirs*. Even Saint-Martin and Sénart expressed their reservations about the positive qualities of caste in contemporary India, both noting the attempts of colonial governments to break the stranglehold of caste.[40] According to Sénart,

> In practical life...the Hindu genius rarely shows itself capable of organization—that is to say, of measure and harmony. In the caste, it has exhausted all its efforts in maintaining and strengthening a network of closed groups, without common action or mutual reaction, recognizing in the long run no other motive-power than the unchecked authority of a sacerdotal class, which has constituted itself the people's sole director. Under the levelling rule of Brahminism, the castes move as the episodes jostle one another haphazardly in the vague unity of an epic narrative. It is enough that an artificial system theoretically masks their incoherence.[41]

Even though Sénart managed to strike a neutral note in most of his work, noting the distance between the theoretical injunctions of caste and the actual practice of it,

---

[39] 'Un second mode d'action, plus efficace et plus pratique que le précédent, est employé avec succès par les amis de l'Inde pour élever ses populations à la hauteur des idées et de la civilisation modernes; ce moyen, plus sûr et moins dangereux que la prédication des idées chrétiennes...est l'éducation, l'initiation des masses aux arts et aux sciences de l'Occident.' Ibid.: 425.

[40] Vivien de Saint-Martin. 'Compte rendu de l'Essai sur les castes de l'Inde par M. Esquer, président du tribunal de Pondichéry', in *Bulletin de la Société de géographie* (November 1872): 542.

[41] Sénart, *Caste in India*: 219–20.

he too succumbed to the frustration of most Europeans when faced with this mass of contradictions.

The work of Sénart and Bouglé represented a new, more nuanced image of India as possessing both positive and negative elements. This was a radical departure from previous works which were either completely laudatory or scathing denunciations of Indian civilization. In fact, the tempered judgement of these scholars meant that India could be viewed as an evolving society. Breaking away from the notion of India being a 'timeless' or 'stagnant' society, the work of Sénart and Bouglé, among a small group of Indic scholars in this period, heralded the realization of historical and social progress through centuries of existence.

CASTE AND RACE

The link between the anthropological studies of mid-century and caste studies of the late century was the focus of the racial origins of caste. Despite a general agreement that caste in India possessed more negative, limiting prescriptions than positive aspects, the origin of caste and its subsequent development was always treated in reference to the racial history of India. This development proceeded side by side with more obvious racial comparisons. A common enough development in the mid-nineteenth century was the inclusion of India in various works on Aryans, such as Adolphe Pictet's 1859 work on *Origines Indo-européenes ou les Aryas primitives*.[42] While some of these works were essentially linguistic and philological comparisons of various Indo-European languages, many

---

[42] Pictet was a student of Burnouf at the *Collège de France*. As early as 1815 Adolphe Pictet had posited the link between the Aryans and the Celtic peoples of Europe in *De l'affinite des langues celtiques avec le Sanscrit*. Pictet was awarded a prize from the Institut de France for this work in 1856, demonstrating the enormous popularity of this theory of Aryan origin.

also made dangerous claims about the origins and abilities of different races. An example of this kind of race theory becoming the most prominent aspect of Indian study is a work by François Lenormant titled *Manuel d'histoire de l'Orient jusqu'aux guerres Médiques* and published in 1859 in the form of a syllabus[43] which included 50 pages on the Aryan societies and extended bibliographies of Indic works as representations of the work that the Aryan intellect had produced such as sections of the *Bhagavad Gita*, *Bhagavata Purana*, *Lalita Vistara* and *Manusmriti*. These works extolled the Aryan genius. Not surprisingly, the *Journal Asiatique*, which was a good indicator of trends in Indology, published an increased number of articles relating to Indo-European philology in the period 1853–62.[44]

In the late nineteenth century, the noted Tamil scholar Julien Vinson published a series of articles which demonstrated that the inherent abilities of races were indeed reflected in their linguistic and cultural accomplishments. Vinson focused on the Dravidian race of southern India. By 1886, he was appointed Professor of Hindustani and Tamil languages at the *Langues O*, as successor to Garcin de Tassy. In 1878, Vinson and Abel Hovelacque collected a number of articles they had authored and previously published in journals like the *République française*, *Revue d'anthropologie*, *Revue de Linguistique* and *Revue ethnographie* into a book titled *Études de linguistiqe et d'ethnographie*.[45] Vinson

---

[43] Raymond Schwab, *The Oriental Renaissance* (New York: Columbia University Press, 1986): 125. François Lenormant (1837–83) was a French Assyriologist and archaeologist. As early as 1867 he had turned his attention to Assyrian studies; he was among the first to recognize in the cuneiform inscriptions the existence of a non-Semitic language, now known as Akkadian. The inclusion of India in this work was incidental to theories that the Aryans had originated in India but it is clear through this and other works of the day how central race theory was to all branches of knowledge at this time.

[44] See Tables A5 and A6 in the Appendix.

[45] Abel Hovelacque and Julien Vinson. *Études de linguistiqe et d'ethnographie* (Paris, Reinwald and Co., 1878).

described the relative inferiority of the southern peoples of India, who belonged to the Drâvida race. Unlike Burnouf, who had attempted to demonstrate that 'Drâvida' could not be equated to a specific race, Vinson studied the achievements of the Dravidian race of southern India. He classified the Dravidian languages of India as relatively inferior since they possessed a simple grammar and easy phonetics. According to him, 'Dravidian grammar is of a remarkable simplicity... [its] phonetics does not offer serious difficulties.'[46] These included Tamil, Telinga [Telegu], Malayala [Malayalam] and Canara [Kannada]. Vinson had worked extensively on the similarities of the Dravidian languages of India and the Basque languages of Europe, both of which displayed a similar disregard for the concept of 'God' and reflected this in their word structure. Vinson speculated that since the synonyms for 'God' in Dravidian languages were prince, king, and master; this reflected the introduction of the concept of 'God' only by the Aryans. His conclusion was that '...there does not exist any purely Dravidian word which indicates the idea of God...many of these words [can be used] equally [for] "prince, king, master, God"....This belief of God was one of the first effects of the civilization brought to the south of India by the Aryas.'[47] The Dravidians had no knowledge of religion or spirituality before their contact with the superior Aryans. 'I thus believe that, before the arrival of Aryas in Dravida, the inhabitants of these beautiful regions were completely atheistic savages.... Dravidians, before being in contact with the Indian branch of Aryas, probably did not have any religious idea.'[48] He further pointed out that there were

---

[46] 'La grammaire dravidienne est d'une remarquable simplicité... La phonétique n'offre point de difficultés sérieuses',Ibid.: 62.

[47] '...il n'existe pas de mot purement dravidien qui exprime l'idée de Dieu...beaucoup de mots signifient également <<prince, roi, maître, dieu>>...Cette croyance a dû être l'un des premiers effets de la civilisation apporté dans le sud de l'Inde par les Aryas.'Ibid.: 86.

[48] 'Je crois donc que, avant l'arrivée des Aryas dans le *dravida*, les habitants de ces belles contrées étaient des sauvages

no metaphysical concepts in the Dravidian languages unlike the complex metaphysical works of the Aryans, or indeed the cultural pastimes of the latter.

> The Dravidian vocabulary indicates a very great moral inferiority; one does not find original words for the great metaphysical entities: in spite of the so-called unanimous consent of the people, there was not, in the Dravidian country, before the arrival of the Aryas, 'God', or 'soul', or 'church', or 'priest'...it is true that they did not have the advantage of 'books', of 'writing', of 'painting', of 'grammar'....[49]

By the twentieth century, the equation of 'Dravidian' to a specific racial subtype was complete. A clear example of this is Gaston Courtillier's *Les Anciennes civilizations de l'Inde*. Courtillier began his work by placing the subjects, not in the traditional geographical milieu, but by describing the races to be found in the different parts of the subcontinent. He described the Dravidians as the original and oldest inhabitants of India in the Deccan. According to him,

> The study of races retraces the origins and the progress of this settlement: it is in the archaic country of [the] Dekkan where one finds the most ancient samples of the present inhabitants of India... .It is to the prehistory also, that [one can create] the installation [or hierarchy] of an ensemble of people united by certain ethnic affinities as

---

completement athées...les Dravidiens, avant de se trouver en contact avec la branche indienne des Aryas, n'avaient probablement aucune idée religieuse.'Ibid.: 87.

[49] 'Le vocabulaire dravidien indique une infériorité morale très-grande; on ne trouve point de mots originaux pour les grandes entités métaphysiques: en dépit du soi-disant consentement unanime des peuples, il n'y avait, dans le pays dravidien, avant l'arrivée des Aryas, ni <<dieu>>, ni <<âme>>, ni<<église>>, ni <<prêtre>>; il est vrai qu'il n'y avait pas advantage de <<livre>>, d'<<écriture>>, de <<peinture>> ou de <<grammaire>>....'Ibid.: 64.

by the language and that one is [ac]customed to name Dravidians.[50]

He described the original inhabitants in terms of their physiognomy—short statured and dark; they followed old customs, were mostly tribals like the Munda tribes of Chota Nagpur and the Santals of Bengal and Bihar and had a certain linguistic and cultural affinity. Moreover, their affinity to the Negroid or black races was certain although their original home was uncertain.[51]

Yet India was esteemed as the land of the Vedic Aryans. If the Dravidians had been incorporated into Aryan society and had adopted Aryan religion, how could one explain their backwardness? In addition to the opposition of the superior Aryan race and the inferior Dravidian race within India therefore, Indologists created a new 'Hindu' identity.

BARTH AND THE 'HINDUIZATION' OF INDIA

The term Hindu could be employed in multiple contexts and encompass diverse beliefs and practices as a catch-all phrase that was purposely vague. The origin of the term 'Hindu' was itself obscure, lending itself to geographical and cultural/linguistic affiliations. The term seems to have become popular after the Islamic invasions of the eighth century, when the Muslim invaders referred to the inhabitants of India or 'Hind' as 'Hindus' and the land itself as 'Hindustan', the land of the Hindus. However, since the

---

[50] 'L'étude des races retrace les origines et les progrès de ce peuplement: c'est dans le pays archaïque du Dekkan qu'on trouve les plus anciens échantillons des habitants présents de l'Inde....C'est à la préhistoire aussi que remonte l'installation d'un ensemble de peuples unis par certaines affinités ethniques comme par la langue et qu'on a coutume de nommer Dravidiens.' Gaston Courtillier, *Les Anciennes civilizations de l'Inde* (Librairie Armand Colin: Paris, 1945). Third edition: 7.

[51] Ibid.

peninsula was excluded in the extent of 'Hindustan', the southern people continued to be referred to in various terms, including the geographical label of 'Dekkani'. When the European infiltration of India was complete, and particularly after the British conquest of India, the ancient boundaries between 'Hindustan', and the southern kingdoms were erased and the giant subcontinent was unified as 'India'. It is at this time, in the mid to late nineteenth century that the line between the terms 'Indian' and 'Hindu' were blurred. Eventually, in place of the term 'Indian', to indicate a geographical affiliation, academics began using the term 'Hindu' to indicate anyone in the subcontinent who was not a Muslim, Christian, Jew or Parsi.

In particular Indologists tried to situate the racial history of India within the history of caste and the development of Vedic Aryanism into Brahminism, and eventually into Hinduism. The choice of this hybrid term, 'Hinduism', made it easier for scholars to explain the multitude of contradictions in India as well as the reason for the uneven development of Indian civilization, the development of tyranny and superstition, explanation for the backward, savage aspects of Indian religion.

In tracing the evolution of religion, French scholars once again focused on the Vedic texts as representing the purest thoughts of the Aryans, which were subsequently diluted and degenerated through contact with the indigenous peoples of India. The first major contribution towards the study of 'Hinduism' as a composite Indian religion was made by Emile Sénart. In conjunction with his work on caste, Sénart held that the Veda of the Aryans held the key to all Indic thought. According to him, 'Under the eternal Veda fermented the popular cults, under the authoritarian Shastras, the heresies and controversies; under the dead language of the grammarians, the living idioms [dialects] of the people....'[52] Proceeding from this assumption, Sénart

---

[52] 'Sous le Veda éternel fermentent les cultes populaires; sous les çastras impérieux, les hérésies et les controverses; sous la langue morte

studied Buddhism as originating in the tenets of existing Hinduism. '...the Buddha theory [Buddhist theory], whose superhuman features bind and are harmonized in the unity of an older cycle.'[53] According to him the speculative/ philosophical aspect of Buddhism was already contained in the Upanishads, the Epics[54] and the concepts of death (*mrityu*),[55] temptation (*Mâra*, the Buddhist Satan and lord of the senses),[56] and meditation as found in the six schools of Yoga. Sénart's conclusion was that Gautama was an ascetic who practised the kind of Yoga which had already been achieved by the Bhagavatas in the Mahabharata.[57] He did incorporate certain individual teachings to Buddhism, but his greatest success lay in his personal reputation and ability to communicate with crowds.

Gautama was a yogin formed [from] among the practices of a Yoga which was finished as a religious sect, [in] the worship of Vishnu-Krishna, in a form [of] whom [the] Bhâgavatas of [the] Mahâbhârata offer a neighboring [close] type to us, though more definite and more advanced. Undoubtedly, he [Gautama] professed certain particular doctrines; especially, he exerted a personal prestige which seems to have been powerful.[58]

---

des grammairiens, les idiomes vivant du peuple....' L. Finot, 'Necrologie. Émile Sénart", *Bulletin de l'École Française d'Extrême Orient* (1928), Vol. 28: 338.

[53] '...le Bouddha théorique, dont les traits surhumains se lient et s'harmonisent dans l'unité d'un cycle plus ancien.'Emile Sénart, 'Origines Bouddhiques', in *Conférences faites au Musée Guimet* (Paris, 1907): 129. Also see L. Finot, 'Necrologie. Émile Sénart', *Bulletin de l'École Française d'Extrême Orient* (1928), Vol. 28: 337.

[54] Emile Sénart, 'Origines Bouddhiques', in *Conférences faites au Musée Guimet* (Paris, 1907): 116–20.

[55] Ibid.: 125–28. 'Le Mrityu- Pâpman brâmanique est antérieur au Ma- Kâma du bouddhisme': 128.

[56] Ibid.: 121–29.

[57] Ibid.: 125–38.

[58] 'Gautama fut un yogin formé parmi les pratiques d'un Yoga qu'achevait en secte religieuse le culte de Vishnou-Krishna, sous une forme dont les Bhâgavatas du Mahâbhârata nous offrent un type voisin

In effect Gautama's achievement was the popularization of forms of mediation and life which already existed
in Hinduism. Buddhism, therefore, while repudiating
Brahmanical orthodoxy, also depended, at its core, on
the fundamental practices of Vedism. 'More or less dete-
riorated and deformed, a certain Vishnouite heritage sur-
vives, carried in the Buddhist currents.'[59] For Sénart the
history of Hinduism was the history of the development of
Aryan thought in India, and the vicissitudes it faced due
to the admixture of other thought systems professed by
the pre-Aryan people of India. Historian Ronald Inden also
describes the development of the theory that the Aryan
Brahmins had conceived a philosophy that was far superior
to that of the indigenous people of India. The subsequent
racial mixing, over centuries, of Aryans and the indigenous Dravidians is what spawned the religion of popular
Hinduism, with its myriad Gods and popular saints.[60]

Sénart and Sylvain Lévi[61] created a renaissance for
Buddhist studies in India. For some time since Burnouf,
Buddhist scholars had focused on Buddhism in the Far
East, in part due to the French colonial interest in Indo-
China. In the last decade of the nineteenth century, however, Sénart and Lévi produced a huge number of articles
on the Buddhist origins in India, leading to a renewed
interest in India among French colonists. Sénart's thesis
about Buddhism was that it was inherently Hindu in

---

quoique plus défini et plus avancé. Sans doute, il professait certaines
doctrines particulières; surtout, il exerçait un prestige personnel qui
semble avoir été puissant....' Emile Sénart, 'Origines Bouddhiques', in
Conférences faites au Musée Guimet (Paris, 1907): 156.

[59] 'Plus ou moins altéré et déformé, un certain héritage vishnouite
surnage emporté dans les courants bouddhiques.' Ibid.: 138.

[60] Ronald Inden, *Imagining India* (Oxford: UK; Cambridge, Mass.,
USA: Basil Blackwell, 1990): 117–22.

[61] Lévi was the last great French Indologist of the nineteenth century, whose prolific writing spanned religion, literature, and history,
although his greatest scholarly accomplishment was the production of a
dictionary of Buddhism.

thought and practice. This was a radical departure from the earlier writings of Burnouf and his followers, who had treated Buddhism as a popular reaction to the tyranny of the Brahmins. By closely analysing the legend of the Buddha, Sénart concluded that the essentials of the personality of the Buddha far pre-dated Buddhism itself and in fact, were culled from existing traits of various Hindu Gods. Furthermore, according to Sénart the core of the personality was inherited from myths of existing Gods and heroes.[62] The addition of an intensely mystical element lent itself easily to a new movement, since it drew upon existing injunctions rather than exhorting a radical break from traditional religion. Sénart also reasoned that if these divine types actually were composites of earlier ideas, the ideas within Hinduism were probably older than scholars had earlier believed them to be.[63] Sénart thus reified both the superior thought of Buddhism and of Vedic literature.

On the other hand, Sylvain Lévi justified the focus on Brahminism and Brahminic religion in India by pointing to its ability to withstand all challenges and still emerge dominant. According to Lévi, Brahminism had succeeded in drawing attention to itself as the authentic expression of religious feeling in India, in preference to its rivals.[64] Since Brahminism had proved its strength in maintaining its superiority, it warranted, in his view, a scientific study based on literary and epigraphic history. In a triumphant tour of India and Japan in 1897, sponsored by the French Ministry of Education (*Ministère de l'Instruction Publique*), Lévi, the first French Indologist in a century to actually

---

[62] Emile Sénart, 'Origines Bouddhiques', in *Conférences faites au Musée Guimet* (Paris, 1907): 141 and passim.

[63] Ibid.: 147 and passim.

[64] Sylvain Lévi, *La Science des religions et les religions de l'Inde* (Paris, 1892): 3. 'Le triomphe écrasant du brahmanisme semble le désigner à nos premières recherches, de préférence à ses rivaux malheureux, comme l'expression la plus authentique du sentiment religieux dans l'Inde'.

visit India, emphasized the importance of Sanskrit studies. Recounting his travels in India and his journey to Nepal to discover the Sanskrit roots of Buddhism, Lévi provided the *Académie* with only a truncated version of his longer report to the Ministry. Describing his journey in Japan, focusing specifically on the Sanskrit Buddhist texts he had found and studied in Japan, Lévi voiced his conviction that the Académie would not be interested in a longer account of his journey in Japan.[65] Tracing from the pure form of the Rig Veda, Lévi saw the spirit of Indian religion contained therein.[66] It was the manifestation of the varied intellectualism that pervaded Indian religion in the form of the Brahmanas, Sutras, and Upanishads. According to Lévi,

> They are not only necessary to supplement the religious history of India; they contain [therein] almost the whole germ [notion of Indian religion], and the most beautiful result of Indianism will be to find the origin of the infinitely varied manifestations where the intellectual life of India poured forth.[67]

The twin reform sects of Buddhism and Jainism were merely different manifestations of this spirit yet constituted a 'moment of rupture'[68] and were therefore important to the development of Indian religion. The development of Brahminism proceeded through the centuries with the gradual incorporation and transformation of popular

---

[65] 'Rapport de M. Sylvain Lévi sur sa mission dans l'Inde et au Japon' in *Mémorial Sylvain Lévi*. By Sylvain Lévi, Eli Franco, Louis Renou (Motilal Banarsidass: Delhi, 1996): 266. Originally published in Comptes rendus de l'Académie des Inscriptions et Belles- Lettres, 1899: 71–92.

[66] Ibid.: 164.

[67] 'Ils ne sont pas seulement nécessaires pour compléter l'histoire religieuse de l'Inde; ils la contiennent presque tout entière en germe, et le plus beau résultat de l'indianisme sera d'y trouver l'amorce des manifestations infiniment variées où s'est épanchée la vie intellectuelle de l'Inde.' Lévi, *La Science des religions et les religions de l'Inde*: 4.

[68] Ibid.: 5.

beliefs, moulded by political conquests, changing social life and the rise of a priestly class which claimed to inherit the religious mantle of India.

Brahmanism was formed gradually by the transformation of popular beliefs under the slow action of convergent forces. The progress of conquest, the modifications of social life, the advent of a sacerdotal caste, substituted a new religion for the former worships by unperceivable degrees; the change was a long time completed when/before it became apparent. The reform of Jina and the reform of Buddha were born, on the contrary, on a determined day, of an individual thought and a conscious will; one and the other felt in one moment of rupture....[69]

Lévi disagreed with Sénart about the origin of reformist doctrines, holding that Buddhism and Jainism were the products of individual thought and of a voluntary conscience of objection to popular religion. He noted, however that over time, both Buddhism and Jainism degenerated and lost their popularity in India, Buddhism finding a new home in the Far East. Once again Indologists may have disagreed about the relative merits of various religions and doctrines in India, but the conclusion that the most enduring and notable civilization had been provided by the Vedic Aryans was upheld.

Sénart and Lévi may have disagreed on minor issues with regard to the origin of Buddhism, but both of them emphasized the continuity of Indian thought. Rather than

---

[69] 'Le brahmanisme s'est formé graduellement par le transformation des croyances populaires sous la lente action de forces convergentes. Le progrès de la conquête, les modifications de la vie sociale, l'avènement d'une caste sacerdotale substituèrent par d'imperceptibles degrés une religion nouvelle aux cultes antérieurs; le changement était depuis longtemps achevé lorsqu'il devint apparent. La réforme du Jina et la réforme du Buddha sont nées, au contraire, à jour déterminé, d'une pensée individuelle et d'une volonté consciente; l'un et l'autre ont senti en un moment de rupture....'Ibid.

the episodic movements presented by earlier scholars, they sought to present the development of Indian thought and religion as a series of interconnected movements, in no way and at no time sealed from other philosophical influences. For instance, both emphasized the varied and eclectic nature of Hinduism as a religion. Unlike other religions Hinduism never progressed in a linear fashion.[70] Therefore one cannot describe the history of Hinduism as Vedism, Buddhism, Brahminic Hinduism, and so forth. At any time a number of competing philosophies and religious practices co-existed and were accepted within the broad framework of a 'Hindu' religion.[71] According to Lévi, 'Hinduism is a convenient designation to include the innumerable worships that, referencing itself [sic] to a variety of divinity, have nevertheless these common characters recognized as the basis of the Brahminical orthodoxy....'[72]

The Indologists of this time were not influenced by any lyrical views of India, but they seem to have been moved by the contemporary representation of social ills in India— caste, poverty, and superstition. Their work was aimed at discovering the origins of Indian thought and philosophy so that they could better effect a cure for contemporary ills. Notwithstanding his view of ancient India as 'la terre des prestiges',[73] or a 'veritable Eden',[74] or even of his notion that the religion of India was the result of the genius of the Brahmin, Lévi pointed out that in the modern period it was

---

[70] Emile Sénart, *'Origines Bouddhiques'*, in *Conférences faites au Musée Guimet*. (Paris, 1907): 131 and passim.

[71] Ibid.

[72] 'L'hindouisme est une designation commode pour englober les cultes innombrables qui, s'addressant à une diversité de divinités, ont néanmoins ces caractères communs reconnus comme la base de l'orthodoxie brahmanique....' 'Aux Indes' in *Mémorial Sylvain Lévi*. By Sylvain Lévi, Eli Franco, Louis Renou (Motilal Banarsidass: Delhi, 1996): 166. Originally published as the introduction to *Aux Indes, Sanctuaires*, (1935).

[73] Lévi, *L'Inde civilisatrice*: 9.

[74] Ibid.: 15.

due to the efforts of European scholars that the history of India had been retrieved from the 'geography of the fantastic' that was the production of the ancient Indians.[75] Moreover, according to Lévi, India's problems were not merely those of knowledge and history but were in fact, the immediate problems of life and of the starving millions of India: of gross inequalities imposed by tyrannical rulers and priests on the mass of passive Indians.[76]

This colonial view of India, which integrated anthropological views of Aryans as well as criticism of modern India, was best approached by Auguste Barth in his magnum opus on the religions of India.[77] Barth's great contribution to Indology was his popularization of 'Hindu' for the Indian civilization. He was the first to focus attention and bring all his professional and personal influence to bear upon this new 'Hindu' image of India which contained all the inconsistencies and weakness of Indian civilization in its history and development.

According to Barth, the Vedic literature was already marked by a complicated theology. Far from being the work of a pastoral Aryan people, who collated their beliefs into the Rig Vedic hymns, Barth held that the Rig Vedic literature was,

> pre-eminently sacerdotal, and in no sense a popular one.... Neither in the language nor in the thought of the Rig-Veda have I been able to discover that quality of primitive natural simplicity which many are fain to see in it. The poetry it contains appears to me, on the contrary, to be of

---

[75] Ibid.: 30. Also see Sylvain Lévi, 'Les parts respectives des nations occidentales dans les progrès de l'Indianisme', *Scientia* (January 1924).

[76] Ibid.

[77] Auguste Barth, *The Religions of India*. Translated by Rev. J. Wood (London: Kegan Paul, Trench Trübner and Co, 1891). Auguste Barth was born in 1834 and inducted into the *Académie* for his works on Sanskrit translations and on Indian religion, primarily Hinduism. By the time of his death in 1916 he was a reputed and respected Indologist whose primary claim to fame came from his editing of the *Bulletin de Religion*.

a singularly refined character and artificially elaborated, full of allusion and reticences, or pretensions to mysticism and theosophic insight; and in the manner of its expression is such as reminds one more frequently of the phraseology in use among certain small groups of initiated than the poetic language of a large community.... In all these respects the spirit of the Rig-Veda appears to me to be more allied than is usually supposed to that which prevails in the other Vedic collections, and in the Brahmanas.[78]

Yet the Rig Veda contained the core of the common Aryan beliefs of nature-worship, which were common to all Aryan societies.[79]

Barth's argument continued the notion that ancient Aryan thought was the manifestation of a superior people. However, he broke with the Indic tradition of seeing this great thought reflected in the Rig Veda. Barth's argument was that the corruption of Aryan thought had begun even in the period of the Rig Veda. This corruption was due to the intermingling of Aryan races with the indigenous races of India. So, for instance, while he cited the lack of evidence to argue concretely for the exchange of ideas between the Aryans and the indigenous people, he suggested that the Rig Veda itself indicated the beginning of a priestly class asserting itself in the face of indigenous challenges. Since the Rig Veda was the sacred liturgy of a select group of priests, Barth held that:

I am therefore far from believing that the Veda has taught us everything on the ancient social and religious condition of even Aryan India, or that everything there can be accounted for by reference to it. Outside of it I see room not only for superstitious beliefs, but for real popular religions, more or less distinct from that which we find in it....We shall perhaps find that, in this respect also, the past did not differ so

---

[78] Ibid., preface: xiii.
[79] Ibid.: xxi.

much from the present as might at first appear, that India has always had, alongside of its Veda, something equivalent to its great Civaite and Vishnuite religions, which we see in the ascendant at a later date, and that these anyhow existed contemporaneously with it for a much longer period than had till now been generally supposed.[80]

These religions, popularly referred to as Neo-Brahminic religions which had been seen as emerging in the same period of Buddhism and Jainism were therefore, according to Barth, of earlier origin, even though their popularity occurred later.[81] Moreover, the kernel of the Neo-Brahminic religions of Vishnu and Shiva lay in the belief systems of the pre-Aryan peoples of India, in their emphasis on idol-worship and fertility cults. According to him,

The sectarian or neo-Brahminic religions, which we embrace under the general designation of Hinduism, and which are at the present time professed by about 180,000,000 people in British India, Nepal, Ceylon, Indo-China, the Sunda Isles, at the Mauritius, at the Cape and as far as the West-Indies (according to the Census of 1872)... do not form a whole as homogenous as ancient Brahminism, still less Buddhism and Jainism.... They constitute a fluctuating mass of beliefs, opinions, usages, observances, religious and social ideas, in which we recognize a certain common ground principle, and a decided family likeness indeed, but from which it would be very difficult to educe any accurate definition. At the present time, it is next to impossible to say exactly what Hinduism is, where it begins, and where it ends. Diversity is its very essence, and its proper manifestation is 'sect'....[82]

The essence of Hinduism, according to Barth, was the amalgamation of Aryan and indigenous beliefs. In

---

[80] Ibid.: xv.
[81] Ibid.: xvi.
[82] Ibid.: 153–54.

Hindu worship therefore, we find elements of popular religion side by side with the remnants of Vedic gods. 'Alongside of the great sectarian divinities and their personal surroundings, their wives, fathers, mothers, sons, brothers, and servants, we meet with the ancient gods of Brahmanism, Agni, Indra, Varuna, etc., powers that have fallen mostly into decay, but which survive in what remains of the ancient ritual, especially in the domestic ceremonies.'[83] While Barth was careful with regard to the extent of Aryan and non-Aryan assimilation of beliefs he was categorical about the inferior nature of non-Aryan worship. According to him, the religions of the aboriginal peoples of India,

> survive in fact under two forms: either in the condition of popular superstitions, which resemble what they are elsewhere; or, as among the tribes which have remained more or less savage, in the condition of national religions to some extent inoculated with Hindu ideas and modes of expression. These religions, in their turn, if we analyse them, are resolvable, on the one hand, into those beliefs and practices of an inferior type, having relation to idol or animal worship, such as we find in all communities that are uncivilized, and, on the other hand, into the worship of the divinities of nature and the elements, such as personifications of the sun, heaven, the earth, the mountains—that is to say, of systems of worship which are not essentially different from those which we meet at first among the Hindus.[84]

Furthermore, the remnants of such aboriginal people were to be found to a far greater extent in the south of India, where, 'Each several district, especially in the Dravidian South, has besides its own local deities, which have been identified in the main with the general types of Hinduism,

---

[83] Ibid.: 252–53.
[84] Ibid., preface: xix.

but rarely to the extent of being absolutely confounded with them.'[85]

Barth's view of Hinduism while on the one hand providing a nuanced study of the mingling of Aryan and non-Aryan elements to explain the system of belief prevalent in contemporary India also gave voice to the belief expressed by Vinson that the inferior people were to be found primarily in the southern regions of the subcontinent.

Like the ancient religion, Hinduism, then, has its excommunicated races; but alongside of those who are thus repudiated by it there are some which repudiate it in their turn—we mean the tribes in a more or less wild state, which represent, the majority of them at least, the first tenants of the soil before the arrival of the Aryans. In Hindustan and the north of the Dekhan the great body of these tribes has become indistinguishably blended with the victorious race. In the South they have also adopted the Aryan culture and religion, preserving, however, their languages, which are different forms of the Dravidian, radically distinct from the Sanskrit. It is a question which is not yet ripe for solution, how far they in turn have been able to infect their conquerors with their own ideas and customs. It is probable, however, that some at least of the goddesses of the Hindu religions which sanction the sacrifice of blood are of Dravidian origin.... The most interesting and best known are those of the aborigines of the Dravidian race. They have as their common character the adoration of divinities connected with the elementary powers and the earth, mostly female and malignant, the worship of ghosts and other mischievous spirits, which they seek to appease by bloody sacrifices and orgiastic ceremonies which recall the Shamanism of the tribes of Northern Asia....Many of these practices have left traces among all the Dravidian population, even among those that are most thoroughly assimilated....[86]

---

[85] Ibid.: 253.
[86] Ibid.: 286–87.

While not excusing the Indic Aryans of creating a rigid and limiting religious and social system, Barth also suggested that the impetus for much of the 'backward' and 'pagan' rituals in Hinduism may have been the Dravidian element. As a result, Barth concluded that the Hindu religion was in decline, being besieged moreover, by the rational processes of science, industry, administration, police, and sanitary regulation. While Hinduism had consistently met and resolved all challenges to its authority through perpetual reform, each of these had been transient and liable to corruption.[87]

In the work of Barth, the term 'Hindu' came to apply not only to religion but, in fact, to a race of people. By the end of the nineteenth century, it was an accepted fact that notwithstanding India's chequered Aryan past, the current people of India were too racially mixed and therefore too philosophically mingled to single out specific groups as 'Aryan' or 'Dravidian'. The term 'Hindu', referring as it did, to centuries of racial intermixing, now came to be used to define the Indian people. In any case, anthropologists were concluding that there were very few 'pure' biological races left, instead using examples of historical or national races. India was therefore peopled by the 'Hindu' race.[88] This appellation could be used as a positive term to signify some aspect of Vedism or Aryanism; or it could also be used as a pejorative term to indicate a stagnant thought process or even as an example of 'oriental tyranny'.

THE BRITISH AND THE USES OF CASTE

Unlike the French theories that the mixing of castes had created so much racial mixing in India that only a term

---

[87] Ibid.: 290.

[88] The use of 'Hindu' to indicate a race is especially clear in nineteenth- and early twentieth-century America, where South Asians were referred to as 'Hindu' or 'Hindoo' regardless of their religious affiliation.

like 'Hindu' could be used to explain the inconsistencies and paradoxes present in India, the British needed to move away from this philosophical discussion of doctrine and actively integrate categories of caste and race into their government.

In contrast to these explanations of caste as an evolving organism, British uses for caste were to create dangerous dissensions within Indian society. The government soon became involved in the issue of caste, with the introduction of the Census. The first India Census of 1871–72 divided the population on the basis of caste, with built-in assumptions about social hierarchy following the caste hierarchy with the Brahmins at the top of the caste pyramid. Surveys in Bengal, Mysore, Bombay, Madras and the United Provinces used caste as the primary unit of classification. Occupations were classified on the basis of caste as well. The Census was meant to catalogue every aspect of Indian life, and the development brought about by British rule. It included statistics on roads and rails, on agricultural and commercial production, on education, of hospitals and medical facilities, on sanitation, on jails, etc. In the process, statistics were compiled also of the sections of the native population actively involved in these activities:natives involved in agriculture, manual labour, trade and commercial activity were catalogued as well as castes that seemed to have a high percentage of criminal members. This project snowballed into an official ethnographic project cataloguing the castes and tribes of India. As Goodwin Raheja suggests, the exercise also utilized discourses of consent; by cataloguing the languages, castes, and ethnic divisions in India, the official enterprise was portrayed as one which was being carried out with the consent and participation of the subjects, even though the writings of Edgar Thurston and other ethnographers clearly stated otherwise.[89]

---

[89] Gloria Goodwin Raheja, 'The Illusion of Consent. Language, Caste and Colonial Rule in India',*Colonial Subjects. Essays on the Practical*

The Decennial Census of 1881 continued this system. The total population of British India was divided into three broad categories of Brahmins, Rajputs and 'other castes', which included agricultural castes, artisans and village servants, merchants, etc.

Under the influence of a growing proliferation of views about the origin and nature of the caste system among Western scholars, the 1891 Census gave up caste-based classifications. The nature of caste as a social or religious institution was questioned in favour of a theory of occupationally-based castes. The case for this classification had been strengthened by writers like William Crooke, Denzil Ibbetson and John Nesfield, whose researches in Punjab and the Northwest Provinces had concluded with the theory that caste had originated as an occupational division of the population.

In 1882, William Plowden, Census Commissioner for India, suggested that a list of castes and occupations be compiled for each district along with a description of the peculiarities of each. The Government of India, while interested in the project, did not invest any money, leaving it to the discretion of state governments to invest in the project. Only the Bengal Government, pointing out that new communication, travel and education was changing much of the traditional structure of Indian society, suggested that Risley be employed for two years, in 1884, to undertake this project. The survey developed and a number of correspondents for particular cases were appointed. In addition, efforts by anthropological societies were made to extend the study to other provinces.

The 1891 Census divided 60 subgroups of the Indian population into six occupational categories: agricultural and pastoral, professional, commercial, artisans and village servants, vagrants and other races, and indefinite

History of Anthropology, Edited by Peter Pels and Oscar Salemik (Ann Arbor: University of Michigan Press 1999).

titles. Caste was used only to explain long-term changes for an occupational group. The succeeding confusion was immense. The clear dichotomy between a caste and its occupation, even of various occupations within a single caste, made for some very mixed and inaccurate results.

Finally, Crooke's study on the Northern tribes was published and in 1901, Curzon's government allocated money for a comprehensive ethnographic survey of the customs of the tribes and castes of India. Each province was in charge of its own survey under a Superintendent of Ethnography, who, a government servant, was allocated an extra allowance of 160 pounds sterling per annum for undertaking this project in addition to his usual duties. He was to correspond with district officers, who obtained information from people who were familiar with the religion, customs and traditions of particular castes and tribes, and put these informants in touch with the Superintendent. The Superintendent was then to provide these informants with a questionnaire of general questions. The scope of this survey included ethnography and anthropometry.

The result of the ethnographic survey was the production of several tomes on the castes and tribes of South India, Bombay, United Provinces, Rajputana, Central Provinces, Punjab and the North West Frontier Province, Assam, Burma, Cochin, Mysore and Travancore. Simultaneously, the appointment of W.W. Hunter as the Director-General of the Imperial Gazetteer in 1877 began the investigation of the statistical composition by caste, of the military, police, land, market activity, re-inforcing the Survey's conclusions about the innate criminal, martial, intellectual or menial tendencies of certain castes. The results of such exercises in caste composition and analysis were actively utilized in recruitment to the army, clerical divisions of the government, the passing of laws outlawing certain castes and tribes as 'criminal', etc. According to Dirks,

Throughout the nineteenth century, the collection of material about castes and tribes and their customs, and the specification of what kinds of customs, kinship behaviours, ritual forms and so on, were appropriate and necessary for ethnographic description, became increasingly formalized and canonical. Gradually the institutional provenance of caste expanded, affecting the recruitment of soldiers into the army (particularly after the Great Rebellion), the implementation of legal codes applicable on caste lines, the criminalization of entire caste groups for local police purposes, the curtailment of the freedom of the land market when excessive amounts of land were thought to be sold by 'agricultural' to 'merchant' groups, and the assessment of the political implications of different colonial policies in the area of local administration in caste terms.[90]

The next section looks at the manner in which the conflation of caste and race was used to further French and British theories about India.

The Census Commissioner for the 1901 Census, Herbert Risley, was a firm believer in anthropometry as an indicator of race, human development and social status. Caste, which had been increasingly conflated with race theories in the past few decades, was now made the basis of the census. Higher castes were presumed to be descended from the Indo-Aryans and therefore their anthropometric measurements were correspondingly more developed. The downward scale of race followed the pattern of the Aryan at the top, followed by the Dravidian, Mongoloid and African. The anthropometric measurements of nasal and cephalic measurements of different castes were now correlated with the race that they were shown to originate from. The result was shown to be the present social hierarchy of India, whereby the Aryan and Aryan-descended castes were the highest castes followed by the Dravidian, Mongoloid and African castes.

---

[90] Nicholas Dirks, *Castes of Mind* (Princeton: Princeton University Press, 2000): 44–45.

According to Risley, the Purusha Sukta hymn was only a later manifestation of an originally Iranian derivation of the caste system based on a division of society into priests, warriors, cultivators and artisans. The main conclusions of Risley's ethnological study were:

1. There were seven major Indian physical types, of which only the Dravidian was indigenous.
   These types were Indo-Aryan, Mongoloid, Turko-Iranian, Aryo-Dravidian, Mongolo-Dravidian and Scytho-Dravidian.
2. The main reason for such an intermixture were India's natural barriers, which made it difficult for women to accompany invaders, who resorted to unions with indigenous women.
3. The only exception to this intermixture seems to have been the Indo-Aryans who managed to retain their racial purity to a large extent.
4. The social grouping of Indians occurred both as tribe and caste—there were three types of tribes and seven types of castes.
5. Both of these groups, tribe and caste, were divided into endogamous, exogamous and hypergamous groups.
6. A large number of the exogamous groups were totemistic.
7. Castes could be classified on the basis of social precedence but no scheme of classification would hold for the whole of India.
8. The Indian caste theory, possibly derived from Persia, had no factual foundation but was universally believed to be a fact.
9. The origin of caste could only be the subject of conjecture and not fact.

In making these statements about the nature of caste, Risley was simultaneously denying that India had progressed beyond a primitive form of social organization, and attributing to the prevalence of caste, the widespread belief in superstitions, and outdated rituals. Here was the height of the colonial constriction of caste as proven beyond doubt, to demonstrate India's backward social development and corresponding lack of infrastructure to survive in a modern world, without the tutelage of a Western power.

Risley's conclusions about the nature of caste prompted him to comment on the role of caste in the social and political life of India. Contrary to notions that caste was breaking up, he pointed out that caste ties in India remained as strong as ever. It prevented the formation of a unified nationalism and democracy. Factors prompting a nationalistic feeling, like a community of origin, common language, common political history, common religion or ties by intermarriage lacking due to caste divisions, national sentiment in India tended either to not be there or to produce dissension rather than cohesion. According to Risley, the existence of any little national feeling in India was due to the common intellectual tradition and communication caused by the introduction of English, and the unity provided by a single colonial government and common system of laws. While Risley acknowledged that it was not impossible for a number of castes to form a common national attitude, citing the Marathas as an example, he also claimed that this was a long and frustrating process, which would constantly be impeded by caste.

Interestingly enough, these theories of racial hierarchy were internalized by Indian writers, especially the indigenous elite.[91] The echo of Risley, Thurston and Crooke is clear in works such as B. S. Guha's *An Outline of the Racial Ethnology of India* (Calcutta, 1937), 'Professor Tagore', in lectures to the Anthropological Society of London in 1863

---

[91] Sumit Guha, 'Lower Strata, Older Races, and Aboriginal Peoples: Racial Anthropology and Mythical History Past and Present', *Journal of Asian Studies* 57.2 (May 1998).

and 1868, as well as Rajendralal Mitra's contributions to the same society in 1869, Anatha Krishna Iyer, *Lectures on Ethnography* (Calcutta, 1925), Ramaprasad Chanda, *The Indo-Aryan Races* and M. M. Kunte's *Vicissitudes of Aryan Civilization in India* (Bombay, 1880). In addition the application of these theories' skewed accounts of legendary and heroic origins of races, in terms of clashes between Aryans and indigenous peoples, the description of tribals as jungle peoples and semi-savages appears in the works of many early historians.[92] This construction of the *adivasis*, tribals and aborigines has been attacked by several scholars as well, making not only for contentious debates within the public sphere but also in the academic sphere, since no discussion of caste can be separated from social hierarchy.[93] As Guha points out, 'the archaeological record offers little support for the mythic history of clashing races that took shape when the brown sahibs and white sahibs sought to escape their fears about the instability of social hierarchy by giving it a biological basis and projecting it into the past....'[94]

Based on the Censuses, the two most obvious uses of caste and race were to define certain castes as 'criminal'

---

[92] V. Raghaviah, *Nomads* (Secunderabad, 1968), which carried prefaces by the president, vice-president and other political officials; D. D. Kosambi, *An Introduction to the Study of Ancient Indian History* (Bombay, 1956), who used the racial hierarchy to argue for the technological development in pre-historic India, R. C. Majumdar, and Romila Thapar, who classified the 'Aryan invasion' as the last in a series of racial influxes in India. She has subsequently changed her views.

[93] G. S. Ghurye, *The Scheduled Tribes* (Bombay, 1963); Andre Beteille, 'The Concept of Tribe with Special Reference to India', *European Journal of Sociology* 27.2; Binay B. Chaudhuri, 'The Myth of the Tribe', *Calcutta Historical Journal* 16 (1994); K. Sivaramakrishnan, 'Unpacking Colonial Discourse: Notes on Using the Anthropology of Tribal India or an Ethnography of the State', *Yale Graduate Journal of Anthropology* 5 (1993).

[94] Ranjit Guha, *Dominance without Hegemony* (Cambridge, Mass: Harvard University Press, 1998): 438.

castes, and specific races as 'martial' races. Military handbooks were usually compiled by serving members of the
military, theoretically an expression of first-hand experience of the martial qualities of the different racial groups
of natives serving in the British Indian army. The aftermath
of 1857 and the policy of recruiting specific castes and
ethnic segments of the native population into the army was
clearly reflected in the creation of martial backgrounds and
qualities which eminently suited their employment in the
army. As Pradeep Barua points out, the physical qualities
of the 'martial' races were measured by the anthropomet-
rical measurement of the skull, the breadth of the shoul-
ders and the physical build; accordingly Pathans, Dogras,
Punjabis and other ethnic groups which came closest to
the 'Indo-Aryan type' were recruited.[95] Another measure
of martial quality was the degree of loyalty; once again
the Sikhs and Gurkhas, owing to their loyalty during the
Revolt of 1857, were lauded as possessing superior martial
qualities.

The handbooks for the Indian army were published
from the end of the nineteenth century well into the
twentieth century and were circulated among officers of
the army as sources of knowledge about the qualities and
mannerisms of their native troops. Handbooks on Pathans,
Gurkhas, Dogras, Sikhs, Rajputs, Marathas and other 'martial races' were abundant among literature of this sort.
The handbooks relied heavily on British histories of India,
ethnographic accounts, like those of Risley, Ibbetson, and
Thurston, and official sources like Gazetteers, census
reports, and intelligence reports to construct an elaborate

---

[95] Pradeep Barua, 'Inventing race: The British and India's Martial
Races' *Historian* 58.1 (Autumn 1995). Similar policies were put into
effect in other British colonies. See Timothy Parsons, 'Wakamba
Warriors are Soldiers of the Queen': The Evolution of the Kamba as
a Martial race, 1890–1970', *Ethnohistory* 46.4, (Fall 1999), Marjomaa
Risto, 'The Martial Spirit: Yao Soldiers in British Service in Nyasaland
(Malawi), 1895–1939' *The Journal of African History* 44.3 (2003).

martial heritage for the races they described.[96] The 'martial races' were shown to be possessed of a long lineage of fighting and brave ancestors. They also possessed innately martial natures, based on their willingness to fight, their loyalty and their physical stamina. In the process, other groups who had been traditionally recruited were marginalized.[97]

All of these ideas were compiled into a book by George MacMunn, titled *The Martial Races of India*. MacMunn traced the martial background of each group, their performance in combat, and their behaviour within the unit, including their relations with other ethnic groups, their social skills, and their loyalty to officers. In a testament to the longevity of such theories, certain groups within modern Indian society continue to join the military as a proof of their 'martial' heritage.[98]

Far more destructive was the 'criminalization' of certain castes and tribes. These groups were described as having innate tendencies to crime, and these tendencies were reinforced by religious and cultural sanctions. As the work of Máire Ní Fhlathúin indicates, this development was a characteristic of the British colonial administration, and one that had no resonance in the work of French colonial writers of previous centuries.[99] The government committed

[96] Mary Des Chene, 'Military Ethnology in British India', *South Asia Research*, 19.2 (1999).

[97] Philip Constable, 'The Marginalization of a Dalit Martial Race in Late Nineteenth- and Early Twentieth-century Western India', *Journal of Asian Studies* 60.2 (May 2001).

[98] As Heather Streets demonstrates, these groups were often socialized to believe that they were of 'martial' stock. Heather Streets, *Martial Races: The Military, Race and Masculinity in British Imperial Culture, 1857–1914* (Manchester: Manchester University Press, 2004).

[99] Fhlathúin points out that while Jean Thévenot noted the prevalence of murders and dacoits in certain regions of India, he did not ascribe these crimes to any specific section or group of society. Máire Ní Fhlathúin, 'The Travels of M. de Thévenot through the Thug Archive', *Journal of the Royal Asiatic Society*, Third Series, Vol. 11. 1 (2001).

to rehabilitate all such castes and tribes, with death and imprisonment as a last resort. While missionaries devoted themselves to saving the souls of these criminal castes,[100] the government undertook police and military campaigns against them.[101] A famous example of such a group was the Thuggees. Described as religious fanatics who committed senseless murders in the name of religion, the Thugs were broken up into their caste components.[102] The outlawing of Thuggee and subsequent incarceration of all Thugs meant that the government hunted for members of castes which were among the Thuggee organization. In the process, many individuals who belonged to castes which were prominent among the Thugs, but may themselves not have practised it, were jailed. Similar reports were compiled for Dacoits in the Central Indian jungles. Books like William Sleeman's *Rambles and Recollections of an Indian Official* (1844) which described Thuggee and Sleeman's suppression of it in detail, and Meadows Taylor's *Confessions of a Thug* which was written as a biography of an imprisoned thug, but was entirely fictional, reinforced the belief that criminality was inherent in certain castes, just as other castes were possessed of martial qualities, commercial propensities, intellect and the like.

The official verdict on criminal castes was provided by Frederick Mullaly, a senior police officer in the Madras

---

[100] The Salvation Army was very active in this area. See Rachel J. Tolen, 'Colonizing and Transforming the Criminal Tribesman: The Salvation Army in British India', *American Ethnologist* 18.1 (1991).

[101] Andrew J. Major, 'State and Criminal Tribes in Colonial Punjab: Surveillance, Control and Reclamation of the "Dangerous Classes"', *Modern Asian Studies* 33.3 (1999).

[102] For the colonial construction of Thuggee, see Kim A. Wagner, *Thuggee: Banditry and the British in Early Nineteenth-century India* (Basingstoke: Palgrave Macmillan, 2007), Parama Roy, 'Discovering India, Imagining Thuggee', *The Yale Journal of Criticism Volume* 9.1 (Spring 1996) and Mary Poovey, 'Ambiguity and Historicism: Interpreting Confessions of a Thug', *Narrative* Volume 12. 1 (January 2004).

presidency.[103] Appointed the first honorary superintendent of ethnography for the Madras Presidency, his work
on criminal castes and tribes had each group described in
separate chapters, with the historical background and an
explanation of the origins of their criminal practices, their
customs and rituals, and the kinds of crimes committed by
each group. Mullaly's work proved to the British that criminal castes were not limited to specific regions of India.

Yet as issues surrounding the 'criminal' nature of
these castes continue to plague modern India and prevent
any social cohesion, the creation of British knowledge
about Indian caste was indelibly implanted in India. These
castes continue to be persecuted as a result of their 'criminal tendencies'.[104] More importantly, the government of
India has taken on the mantle of the British in insisting
on using 'caste' as the central category for the modern
Census system.[105]

Finally, caste was used as a powerful argument by
British missionaries to point out the oppression of Hinduism.
By equating caste and Hinduism, missionaries overlooked
the practice of caste by Muslims, Jews, Christians, and even
Parsis in India. For instance, Alexander Duff, an outspoken
Scottish missionary, held that caste was both a social and a
religious institution that effectively held Indians back from

---

[103] Frederick Mullaly, Notes on Criminal Classes of the Madras
Presidency, Madras, 1892.

[104] For example, Dilip D'Souza, 'De-Notified Tribes: Still 'Criminal'?'
Economic and Political Weekly, Vol. 34, No. 51 (1999); Susan Abraham,
'Steal or I'll Call You a Thief: "Criminal" Tribes of India', Economic
and Political Weekly, Vol. 34, No. 27 (1999); Meena Radhakrishna,
'Colonial Construction of a "Criminal" Tribe: Yerukulas of Madras
Presidency', Economic and Political Weekly, Vol. 35, No. 28/29 (2000);
P. K. Bhowmick, 'Rehabilitation of a "Denotified Community": The
Ex-Criminal Lodhas of West Bengal', Royal Anthropological Institute
Newsletter, No. 44 (1981).

[105] Laura Dudley Jenkins, 'Another "People of India" Project:
Colonial and National Anthropology', Journal of Asian Studies, Vol. 62.4
(2003).

achieving any real equality. He wrote a tract titled, *What is Caste: How is a Christian Government to Deal with it?* Another missionary, Robert Caldwell was an example of the correlation and confusion between the concepts of race and caste. While admitting that most converts were from lower castes, Caldwell saw this as a result of the natural degradation, which the caste system imposed upon them and from which they were eager to escape. Caldwell thus opened up the caste system as an imposition of the Brahmins on the lower castes, who were eager and willing to escape from the confines of their lowly status. He also put forward a theory of increased Sanskritization; according to Caldwell, the Brahmin caste was the most Sanskritized caste, and in effect, an Aryan intrusion into Dravidian life in the South. The Sanskritized castes were most resistant to change because they held the highest positions in the caste system. On the other hand, the lower castes, who were originally Dravidians who had been inducted into the lower rungs of the Aryan caste system, were more amenable to conversion. Caldwell's views, while purporting to support the lower castes in south India against what he believed was an Aryan Brahmin tyranny, opened up new controversies about the racial status of Aryan and Dravidian. Caldwell's lower castes in south India were aghast that he would term them a Dravidian and therefore, an inferior race. While Caldwell held that Dravidian culture, in its history, language and literature was as highly evolved as Aryan culture, he also described Dravidian religion as being of the more primitive form, relying on witchcraft, superstition and animal and plant worship. The contradiction in his argument placed the Dravidian in an ambiguous position vis-à-vis a linear scale of human development. Moreover, while Caldwell despised the Brahmins, he also viewed the rare Brahmin convert as the supreme achievement since it signified a true conversion in terms of theology and not merely an escape from the confines of a restrictive institution.

Even missionaries who served in native kingdoms echoed this sentiment. Samuel Mateer described the caste system as the greatest detriment to progress.[106] He regarded caste as the external manifestation of Hindu religious doctrines, based on the 'divine' origin of caste sanctions regarding occupation, social status, marriage, social intercourse and rituals. Mateer described caste as

> separates the people into many different classes throughout the whole of India. Each caste is supposed to be as distinct from others as are the various species of animals, such as the horse, the ox or the ass. Those who belong to the highest caste enjoy extravagant privileges, and are almost worshipped as gods, while the lowest are regarded as degraded almost below the level of the beasts of the field.[107]

He viewed caste as obstructing even basic human kindnesses such as hospitality and kindness to one another. Ironically Mateer's description of caste as a barrier to common courtesies was in stark contrast to other writers of travelogues and descriptive accounts which praise the Indian sense of hospitality. Despairing of the higher castes, particularly the Brahmins and the Nayars of Travancore, from ever renouncing their ill-gotten caste privileges, Mateer also provided a 'humane' look at the ill-use of caste in matters of legal status, inheritance and property issues.

The Christian mission in Travancore, according to Mateer, had wrought limited but remarkable improvements in breaking through the prejudices of caste among those who had been converted to Christianity. Describing the efforts of the missionaries at education, particularly at female education, Mateer also attributed the rise of

---

[106] Samuel Mateer, *Native Life in Travancore* (London, 1893), *'The Land of Charity': A Descriptive Account of Travancore and its People* (London, 1871).

[107] Ibid.: 27.

a new class of native teachers, doctors and professionals to Christianity and the freedom from caste. Conversion also greatly improved the manners and morals of natives, since it freed them of caste prejudices, idolatry and rigid dogmas. They were educated in the Christian manner to become honest, upright members of the Church.

Mateer regarded caste as far more insidious than a result of Hinduism. He noted that native Christians and Syrian Christians in Travancore, as well as Muslims in the area had held on to their caste status over the centuries and were recognized as belonging to different castes even by the Government of Travancore until the efforts of the Christian missionaries persuaded the renunciation of caste status by Christian converts. More than eschewing a Hindu philosophy of life, conversion of Christianity was seen by missionaries as leading to a material and moral emancipation from the restrictions of the caste system.

CONCLUSION

By the end of the nineteenth century the image of India had undergone much change. From a land of Brahminic spirituality and philosophy, the image of India had first been challenged by the discovery of Buddhism and subsequent reform movements. Then in the mid-century studies on race indicated that the subcontinent, far from being an Aryan land, also possessed inferior races who had infected the Aryan mind with degenerate concepts of inequality and rigidity. In fact, Inden points to the European theory of the medieval decline of Hinduism as the result of the belief of the 'lower race or lower layer of the human mind'... gaining 'the upper hand over the higher'.[108]

In response to the race studies, French Indologists at the turn of the century designated a new term, 'Hindu', to

---

[108] Inden, *Imagining India*: 122.

refer to the result of the Aryan-Dravidian mixture, both in terms of a race of people as well as their thought processes and civilization. The hallmark of this 'Hindu' civilization was its dependence on caste and ritual. In comparison with the romantic view of the Florists of the early century, French Indologists now held that India, despite her Aryan past, indeed justified the need for a civilizing mission in her current state. In the French case, this evolving image of India came to be represented as two schools of study. Indologists based in Paris continued to focus their studies on Sanskrit texts, and, by extension, the study of North, primarily Aryan, India. While accepting that India in the present was a decayed civilization, the implication of a once-advanced Aryan civilization was clear. The suggestion therefore, that given the right circumstances, possibly the right tutor, India could once again achieve a praise-worthy civilization, was made repeatedly in works such as Sylvain Lévi's writing about the European contribution to the recovery of India's glorious past.[109]

The British on the other hand used the category of caste as a useful tool to divide and separate the people of India not only for easier administration but also to ensure that internal dissension would overcome any desire to be independent of colonial rule. Their use of caste to define specific 'martial' and 'criminal' castes and tribes was an ingenious mode of divide and rule.

Apart from the difference in the construction and use of categories like caste and race between British and French writers, colonial theories of superior and inferior caste and race were internalized by Indians more than any other creation of colonial knowledge. For instance, in understanding their own past and writing Indian history, Indians from the late nineteenth century used the same categories of race and caste to describe themselves, thus

---

[109] Sylvain Lévi, 'Les parts respectives des nations occidentales dans les progrès de l'Indianisme', *Scientia* (January 1924).

converting the colonial interpretation[110] of these identities into self-fulfilling prophecies of exclusive and competing castes and of superior/inferior races which continue to haunt modern India to the present day. For instance, there were three major areas into which caste discussion among Indians fell. One was to regard it as a divisive, social evil, a negation of Indian nationhood. This was the 'incubus theory', and was popularized by social reformers like M. G. Ranade, R. Raghunatha Rao, T. V. Vaswani, Rao Bahadur M. Audinarayana Iyer, C. Sankaran Nair and other members of the National Social Conference. These men recognized the importance of caste in Indian life but pushed for radical reforms within the system. A more extreme version of the reform movements came with the anti-Brahmin movements of the early twentieth century, like E. V. Ramaswamy Naicker's Self-Respect Movement, founded in 1925. Naicker called for a repudiation of all Aryan values and organizations, including the caste system, as a manifestation of Brahmin tyranny. While some of the reformers visualized a casteless, egalitarian society in India's future, most of them pressed for immediate social reforms especially with regard to educational opportunities, social restrictions of caste and political representation. It is important to understand that these men had internalized the colonial discussion of caste as representing race, a theory that was emphasized by French scholars more than the British, even though all 'scientific evidence' proved that in the modern period, there could be no such conclusion about specific castes representing different races.

In discussing the nature of caste, it is impossible to ignore B. R. Ambedkar's indictment of the caste system as an oppressive, exploitative regime, which needed to be wiped out from India. Well known for his efforts to uplift the Untouchable castes and his

---

[110] Among scholars who have discussed the notion of caste as a colonial construct is Dirks, *Castes of Mind*.

disapprobation of the *chaturvarna*, as it was understood in India, I include here a series of excerpts from Ambedkar's tract on the Annihilation of Caste:

> Hindu society as such does not exist. It is only a collection of castes. Each caste is conscious of its existence. Its survival is the be-all and end-all of its existence. Castes do not even form a federation. A caste has no feeling that it is affiliated to other castes except when there is a Hindu-Moslem riot. On all other occasions each caste endeavours to segregate itself and distinguish itself from other castes. Each caste not only dines among itself and marries among itself but each caste prescribes its own distinctive dress.[111]

Ambedkar accused higher castes of deliberately keeping lower castes economically and culturally deprived. Demonstrating that caste sanctions were imposed by appeals to religious scriptures, he called for an entire overhaul of the religious and social system of India.

> The effects of caste on the ethics of the Hindus is simply deplorable. Caste has killed public spirit. Caste has destroyed the sense of public charity. Caste has made public opinion impossible. A Hindu's public is his caste. His responsibility is only to his caste. His loyalty is restricted only to his caste. Virtue has become caste-ridden and morality has become caste-bound. There is no sympathy for the deserving. There is no appreciation of the meritorious. There is no charity to the needy. Suffering as such calls for no response. There is charity but it begins with the caste and ends with the caste. There is sympathy but not for men of other castes.[112]

The second theory regarding caste was the 'golden chain view' which regarded caste as varna, an ideology of spiritual order and moral affinity and a rallying point for

---

[111] B. R. Ambedkar, *The Annihilation of Caste* (Bombay, 1936): 26.
[112] Ibid.: 37.

the regeneration of the nation. Proponents of this view included Dayanand Saraswati and Tilak. Tilak saw caste standards as divinely mandated, while Saraswati saw caste as the basis for an ordered Hindu society, while simultaneously allowing for spiritual and sacral access to all. The theory that caste was a means of ordering Hindu society was also popularized by members of societies like the Manava Dharma Sabha and the Prarthana Samaj. While the members of these groups pressed for social reform within the caste system, they nevertheless saw the institution as essential to Indian nationhood.

The third view was of caste as an 'idealized corporation', where caste equated with jati, was a concrete ethnographic fact of Indian life. The proponents of this view included the organizers of Maratha and Rajput movements, valourizing Kshatriya values, and extolling the 'natural' attributes of courage, strength and character of Kshatriyas. They essentially equated caste with racial identity, taking their cue from British and French ethnographies which defined the castes in terms of belonging to Aryan, Dravidian and aboriginal races.

Modern anthropologists, sociologists and historians who study caste have refuted the different assertions that caste was the sole social identity of Indians[113] or that it was rigid, or fixed in its hierarchy[114] or in fact that caste

---

[113] Brenda Beck, *Peasant Society in Konku. A Study of Right and Left Sub-castes in South India* (Vancouver: University of British Columbia Press, 1972); Niels Brimnes, *Constructing the Colonial Encounter. Right and Left Hand Castes in Early Colonial South India* (Richmond, Surrey: Routledge, 1999).

[114] McKim Marriot, *Caste Ranking and Community Structure in Five Regions of India and Pakistan* (Poona: Deccan College Monograph Series, 1960); Gloria Goodwin Raheja, *The Poison in the Gift: Ritual, Prestation and the Dominant Caste in a North Indian Village* (Chicago: University of Chicago Press, 1988); Robert Hardgrave, *The Nadars of Tamilnad. The Political Culture of a Community in Change* (Berkeley: University of California Press, 1969).

had proved to be an impediment to progress.[115] Instead the only 'truth' about the caste system was that its significance in ordering the lives of Indians varied greatly, and so did notions of purity-impurity, and dominant-subordinate with respect to the institution. In some circumstances caste was not the predominant identity of Indians, thus allowing for a plurality of identities, each assuming primacy in specific circumstances.[116]

While Indologists merely pointed out that India had once possessed a great (Aryan) civilization, popular histories took this notion one step further. Not only did these histories clearly state that France, and not Britain, was the proper nation to guide India back to civilization, but by providing a more understandable impression of India to the interested individual than the scholarly philological and philosophical monographs of Indologists, they constituted a far more permanent addition to France's 'colonial memory'. In addition, they demonstrated the dissemination of scholarly images of India to the reading public. Building on the work of Indologists, historians in France wrote about India in diverse and sometimes contradictory terms.

---

[115] Milton Singer, *When a Great Tradition Modernizes* (New York: Praeger, 1972); Karen Leonard, *Social History of an Indian Caste: The Kayasths of Hyderabad* (Delhi: South Asia Books, 1978); Frank Conlon, *A Caste in a Changing World. The Chitrapur Saraswat Brahmans, 1700–1935* (Berkeley: University of California Press, 1977); Mattison Mines, *The Warrior Merchants: Textiles, Trade and Territory in South India* (Cambridge: CUP, 1984).

[116] Susan Bayly, *Caste, Society and Politics in India from the Eighteenth century to the Modern Age* (Cambridge: CUP, 1999).

Chapter 7

Writing Histories, Creating 'India'

'It is the centre of Asia, of Asia, mother of the world, of this antique fatherland of nations; from Asia, the most vast of three parts of the old continent [world] and oldest [to be] populated, that spread the first germs of civilization with which the human species is honoured: it is there that the first empires arose, the nations most famous for their population, their magnificence and their riches [wealth]; it is there that half-savage Europeans went to seek laws, luxury, the fine arts; it is [from] there that they drew all their systems of philosophy, all their moral codes: but it is there too that liberty and civilization are irreconcilable; that the peoples seem born for servitude; that the type of absolute authority and passive obedience increases from age in [to] age from the origins of human society.'[1]

---

[1] C'est du sein de l'Asie, de l'Asie mère du monde, de cette antique patrie des nations; de l'Asie, la plus vaste des trois parties du vieux continent, et la plus anciennement peuplée, que se sont répandus les premiers germes de la civilisation dont s'honore l'espèce humaine: c'est là que s'élevèrent les premiers empires, les nations les plus célèbres par leur population, leur magnificence et leurs richesses; c'est là que les Européens demi sauvages allèrent chercher des lois, le luxe, les beaux-arts; c'est là qu'ils puisèrent tous leurs systèmes de philosophie, tous leurs codes de morale: mais c'est là aussi que la liberté et la civilisation se montrent inconciliables; que les peuples semblent nés pour la servitude; que le type de l'autorité absolue et de l'obéissance passive remonte d'âge en âge jusqu'à l'origine des sociétés humaines. Collin de Bar, *Histoire de l'Inde ancienne et moderne de l'Indoustan* (Paris: Le Normant, Imprimeur-Librairie, 1814): introduction, i–ii.

This chapter examines the histories of India which were available to the French public at the end of the nineteenth century. In particular, the most accessible historical information came from school textbooks. The themes presented in these works reinforced with vigour (and often without proof) the images of India which had been constructed by French Indologists, and also the popular notion of India which was presented in the press. The chapter serves as a reminder that academics too were men of the world, and susceptible to the influence of powerful rhetoric which they then carried over into their academic works. The division between the academic and the popular images of India in France, therefore, became ever more blurred towards the end of the nineteenth century.

Histories of India written by the French were relatively few in the nineteenth century in keeping with the French preoccupation with the linguistic and religious aspects of India. Yet the few histories that did get published were influential disseminators of the academic view of India and helped shape French popular opinion about India. Additionally, histories contained composite images of India as opposed to monographs which closely studied single aspects of India. Historians read up on all the available monographs and summarized the opinions contained as one flowing narrative. In effect histories are good mirrors of the kind of ideas that were being created in more isolated academic disciplines like Indology.

There is evidence to suggest that the constructions of India by academics and colonial officials percolated to the masses, even though India, unlike Algeria and Indochina, never really formed a prominent part of the cultural landscape in France. Certainly, many Indologists like Sénart and the archeologist and art historian Jouveau Dubreuil, were key advisors for committees dealing with the large colonial Expositions of the late nineteenth and early twentieth centuries.[2] The impact of these Expositions has been studied in many monographs as well as in the next chapter.[3] Their visual impact cannot be underestimated. In the case

_____

[2] For instance, Jouveau-Dubreuil was the brain behind the Indian exhibit at the *Section Retrospective* in the *Musée des Colonies* during the *Exposition Coloniale de Paris* of 1931. See *Rapport Général de Exposition Coloniale Internationale de 1931, présenté par Gouverner Général Olivier* (Paris: Imprimérie Nationale, 1933), Vol. 5, part I: 134.

[3] See, for instance Patricia Morton, 'National and Colonial: the Musée des colonies at the Colonial Exposition Paris 1931',*Art Bulletin* LXXX, number 2 (June 1998); Patricia Morton, *Hybrid Modernities: Architecture and Representation at the 1931 Colonial Exposition, Paris* (Cambridge Mass. and London, England: The MIT Press, 2000); Wendy Shaw, 'Stylizing the French Sudan', Jusûr, 9 (1993); Burton Benedict,'International Exhibitions and National Identity',*Anthropology Today*, Vol. 7.3 (June 1991); Carol Breckenridge,'The Aesthetics and Politics of Colonial Collecting: India at World Fairs', *Comparative Study of Society and History*, 31.2 (April 1989); Thomas August, 'The Colonial Exhibition in France: Education or Reinforcement?', *Proceedings of the Sixth and Seventh Annual Meetings of the French Colonial Historical Society* (1980/ 82), *Images et Colonies: iconographie et propagande coloniale sur l'Afrique française de 1880 à 1962*, edited by Nicholas Bancel, Pascal Blanchard et Laurent Gervereau (UNESCO,); Tony Bennett, 'The Exhibitionary Complex', *New Formations* 4 (Spring 1988); Elizabeth Ezra, 'The Colonial Look: Exhibiting Empire in the 1930s', *Contemporary French Civilization* 19.1 (1995); Herman Lebovics, 'Donner à voir l'Empire colonial: l'exposition coloniale internationale de Paris en 1931', *Gradhiva*, no. 7, (hiver 1989–1990); Patricia Mainardi, 'The Double Exhibition in Nineteenth Century France', *Art Journal* 48.1, (Spring 1989); Jacques Marseille, *L'Age d'Or de la France Coloniale* (Paris: Éditions Albin Michel, 1986); Christopher Miller, 'Hallucinations of France and Africa in the Colonial Exhibition of 1931 and Ousmane Socé's Mirages de Paris', *Paragraph* 8.1; Timothy Mitchell, 'The World as Exhibition', *Comparative Study of Society and History*, 31.2 (April 1989); Jean-Claude Vigato, 'The Architecture of Colonial Exhibitions in France,'*Daidalos* 15, (March 1986); Gwendolyn Wright, 'Tradition in the Service of Modernity: Architecture and Urbanism in French Colonial Policy, 1900–1930', *Journal of Modern History*, Vol. 59.2 (1987); Gwendolyn Wright, *The Politics of Design in French Colonial Urbanism* (Chicago: Chicago University Press, 1991); Sami Zubaida, 'Exhibitions of Power', *Economy and Society* 19.3 (August 1990).

of India, while the work of Parisian Indologists may not have interested the masses of rural French, their opinions and theories were certainly present in the staging of countries at Expositions, and also in the school textbooks which became part of a uniform educational curriculum after the Revolution. Moreover, India was used as an example to demonstrate theories of race and the degeneration of civilization caused by racial intermixing. Therefore, despite the relative marginality of India to nineteenth-century French public life it is instructive to look at the role that India played in creating French images of self, as a colonizer and in conceptualizing scholarly theories (such as Scientific Racism) which would have an immense impact on the world (through the theories of Aryanism and Gallicism).

Arguably an equally effective means of looking at the extent to which academic work of creating images of India percolated to the common French boy and girl is to examine the school textbooks of the era. Indeed, as Raymond Schwab points out, the inclusion of India in the repertoire of contemporary ideas depended on two vehicles: books and oral exposition.[4] In particular history textbooks by Victor Duruy and the team of Isaac and Malet presented an image of India to French schoolchildren, beginning in the sixth grade, which contained elements of anthropology and the new Indology which have been discussed in the preceding chapters. This chapter focuses on the themes which these history textbooks contained in reference to India. The different sections of the chapter discuss the elements highlighted with reference to India: Aryanism, and the Anglo-French colonial rivalry.

School textbooks were written according to the prescribed curriculum of the day.[5] In France the curriculum

---

[4] Raymond Schwab, *The Oriental Renaissance* (New York: Columbia University Press, 1984): 125.

[5] In fact, each textbook contained an outline of the official curriculum for its subject as part of the foreword. This tradition continues today.

changed every now and then, but the manner in which India was portrayed remained by and large the same over the large period of time spanning the middle of the nineteenth century to the first quarter of the twentieth. The two most prescribed sets of history textbooks were written by famous French historians Victor Duruy, Albert Malet, and Jules Isaac who did not have any special expertise in most of the areas they wrote about. They were primarily historians of France and were appointed to write history textbooks in a series which would span the earliest to modern times in world history. Being academics, they used scholarly texts to form their histories. The inclusion of their works represents the impact that the small group of Indic specialists had on a larger intelligentsia. The best-known textbooks were written first in the mid- and later nineteenth century, by Victor Duruy, and in the early twentieth century, by the team of Albert Malet and Jules Isaac. Duruy's textbook covered the pre-colonial period of Indian history while Isaac and Malet focused on the contemporary period. Specifically, Duruy's history texts discussed India in two works. *Histoire de l'Orient* was meant for the eleven-year-old sixth graders who were beginning the study of history for the first time.[6] The book followed the format laid out by the official programme of 28 January 1890, which defined the Orient as consisting of Egypt, the Chaldeans, Assyrians, Israelites, Phoenicians, Medes, and Persians. The other work was *Histoire des Temps Modernes depuis 1453 jusqu'a 1789*, which dealt with the colonial period.

The texts written by Isaac and Malet which I refer to include *L'Orient et La Grèce*, which followed the official curriculum of 1931 and was meant for sixth graders. It was presumably prepared to replace Duruy's older text. The comparison of Duruy's *L'Orient* and Isaac and Malet's

---

[6] The study of history and geography for a period of three hours each week was included as part of the curriculum for the sixth grade.

L'Orient is therefore interesting for the changes which occurred in the description of India between 1890 and 1932. The other texts written by Isaac and Malet: *XVII & XVIII siècles, XIX siècle*. *Histoire contemporaine, 1815–1920* and *Cours abrégé d'histoire* refer to India in the context of colonial rule, making for a comparison of Duruy's *Histoire des Temps Modernes* and Isaac and Malet's work.

DURUY AND ARYANISM

Victor Duruy, French historian and statesman was born in Paris on 11 September 1811. The son of a workman at the factory of the Gobelins, he was at first intended for his father's trade but succeeded in passing brilliantly through the *École Normale Supérieure*, where he studied under Michelet, whom he accompanied as secretary in his travels through France. By 1836 at the young age of 24 he was teaching at the *École Normale*. Ill-health eventually forced him to resign and poverty drove him to undertake to write an extensive series of school textbooks which first brought him into public notice.

He devoted himself with ardour to secondary school education even while his career as a historian took off. He continued to write textbooks while holding a Chair in the *Collège Henri IV* at Paris for over a quarter of a century. Already known as a historian for the two volumes of his *Histoire des Romains* (1843–44), he was chosen by Napoleon III on 23 June 1863 as the new Minister of Education.[7]

---

[7] In this position, he displayed incessant activity and a desire for broad and liberal reform which aroused the bitter hostility of the clerical party. Among his measures may be cited his organization of higher education *(enseignement special)*, his foundation of the *conferences publiques*, which have now become universal throughout France, a course of secondary education for girls by lay teachers, and his introduction of modern history and modern languages into the curriculum both of the *lyceés* and of the *collèges*. He greatly improved the state of primary education in France and proposed to make it compulsory and free. From 1881 to 1886, he served as a member of the *Conseil*

As a historian Duruy aimed in his earlier works at a graphic and picturesque narrative which was meant to make the study of and interest in history, popular. He made several efforts as Minister of Public Instruction to introduce Indian history into the French secondary school syllabus although these efforts did not bear fruit. However, Duruy, who began writing history textbooks prior to his appointment to the ministry to supplement his income, included as much Indian history as he could in his textbooks.[8] It is important to note the continued link in France between the Indic enthusiasts and the academic establishment. His textbooks published by Hachette became known as *'Les Duruys'* and educated many generations of French school children.[9] However, the content of his textbooks also spoke of an agenda charged with the intellectual theories of the period. Specifically, Duruy focused on the ancient period of Indian history and therefore echoed many of the images which Indologists of the mid-nineteenth century wrote about—images of India as a land of caste, the home of the Aryans, etc.

The most significant aspect of Duruy's work on India related to the incorporation of race, specifically Aryanism. Since the focus of Indologists and anthropologists in the mid-century was on constructions of race in India, Duruy's stress on Aryanism reflected the extent to which these

---

Superieur de l'Instruction Publique. In 1884, he was elected to the Academy in succession to Mignet. He died in Paris on 25 November 1894.

[8] Schwab, *The Oriental Renaissance*: 125.

[9] Sandra Horvath, Victor Duruy and French Education, 1863–1869. PhD Thesis, Catholic University of America, (1971): 69. As David Finkelstein and Alistair McCleery point out in *An Introduction to Book History* (Routledge: NY, 2005): 89,French publisher Louis Hachette who had begun publication in 1826 in Paris successfully and shrewdly won the right to publish school textbooks by the 1860s thus transforming the scale of his company into France's largest publishing house. In this context, the close link between the government and Indology can once again be seen in the number of Indological works published by Hachette.

images were disseminated down to the school system. From his theory of the Aryan origins of India, Duruy expanded his understanding to include the notion of India as a land of philosophical and spiritual attainment if not of any tangible material accomplishment. The Aryan mind had given India religions which could be compared in theory to Christianity in its organization and core values. Aryans had also invented the caste system which had begun as an admirable social division. In these explorations Duruy wrote only about an ancient India as timeless as it was imaginary and dominated by the spirit of the legendary Aryan race.

In his research on French history Duruy had come to the conclusion that there were many parallels between ancient India and Gaul. According to him, the Celts/Gauls originated from the plains of Central Asia making them the kin of the Indo-Aryans and part of the larger Indo-European family. The Gauls continued to maintain their Asiatic origins in their religious practices and worship of anthropomorphic Gods of nature, even though they had diverged from the original customs, such as the pre-eminence of a priestly/sacerdotal caste and the use of a language which had much in common with Sanskrit. According to him,

> The Celts extended and multiplied on this vast territory, not keeping, in testimony of their Asiatic origin, some of the religious dogmas of the East, [like] perhaps the organization of a sacerdotal caste, and an idiom which, [though] more distant than Greek and Latin from Sanskrit, the sacred language of the Brahmins of India, is attached however by close links, and reveals the relationship which linked the Celts or Gallic [people] to the big family of Indo-European nations.[10]

---

[10] 'Les Celtes s'étendirent et multiplièrent sur ce vaste territoire, ne gardant, en témoignage de leur origine asiatique, quelques-uns des dogmes religieux de l'Orient, peut-être l'organisation d'une caste sacerdotale, et un idiom qui, plus éloigné que le grec et le latin du sanscrit,

His interest in India therefore stemmed from a belief that the Gauls and the early Indo-Aryans were related. This translated into a thorough examination of the Aryan influence in India. Chapter Two of Duruy's work on the East titled *'Les plus anciennes sociétés'*, defined the two major racial components of the white race as the Semites in southwest Asia and Africa, and the Aryans or Indo-Europeans in the rest of Asia and Europe, who had migrated from their original home northwest of the Indus and established colonies in all parts of the world.[11] These Aryans were, he claimed, the parent race of the Hindus, Medes, and Persians in the Orient, the Hellenics in Asia Minor, Greeks, Italians, Celts, Germans, and Slavs in Europe. In his estimation, the racial affinities of the large Indo-European family were contained in their languages, which in the nineteenth century were seen as continuing to have similar vocabularies and grammar, all of which could be traced to Greek and Latin, which in turn were parents to Sanskrit, the parent language of the Indian Brahmins which itself was possibly derived from a language spoken by the ancient Aryan tribes. This was Duruy's paean to the work of Burnouf and his students who had emphasized the importance of philology. According to him,

> The relationship of the Hindus, Medes, and Persians, of the East, of Pélasges and the Hellenes, in Asia Minor, Greece and Italy, of the Celts, Germans and Slavs [people], in the north of the Euxin Sea, Haemus, and the Alps, was noted by the grammatical analogies of idioms and the resemblance of the roots in the essential words. Thus, Greek and Latin are linguistic sisters, [and] both [are] close relations of Sanskrit, the sacred language of the Indian Brahmins,

---

la langue sacrée des brahmes de l'Inde, s'y rattache cependant par des liens étroits, et révèle la parenté qui unissait les Celtes ou Gaulois à la grande famille des nations indo-européennes.'Victor Duruy, *Histoire de France*. 2 volumes (Paris, 1866): 21.

[11] Victor Duruy, *Histoire de l'Orient* (Paris, 1890): 12.

and perhaps derived from a older language which all the Aryan tribes spoke at the foot of the plateau of [the] Pamir, before their dispersion.[12]

Continuing his praise for the fundamental precepts of Indian society Duruy noted that political and religious organization was governed by the Laws of Manu, which he compared to the Pentateuch of Moses as reflecting the same fundamental truths about the origin of the earth and human institutions like family and social hierarchy. According to him,

...because this book claims to expose, after [like] a revelation, the genesis of the world, the sacerdotal or levitic institution, precepts for the individual, the family and the city; duties of the prince and the castes, civil and military organization, criminal and religious laws. All is summarized in two rules: for society, the subordination of the castes; for the individual, physical, and moral purity.[13]

Since the common belief in the nineteenth century was that Christianity was the expression of civilization, the comparison of the *Manusmriti* and the Pentateuch was an important admission as to the equal advancement of

---

[12] 'La parenté des Hindous, des Mèdes et des Perses, à l'orient, des Pélasges et des Hellènes, dans l'Asie Mineure, la Grèce et l'Italie, des Celtes, des Germains et des Slaves, au nord du Pont-Euxin, de l'Haemus et des Alpes, a été constatée par les analogies grammaticales des idiomes et par la ressemblance des racines dans les mots essentiels. Ainsi le grec et le latin sont des langues sœurs, toutes deux proches parentes du Sanskrit, la langue sacrée des brahmanes indiens, et peut-être dérivées d'une langue plus ancienne quel toutes les tribus aryanes parlaient à pied du plateau de Pamir, avant leur dispersion.' Ibid.

[13] '...car ce livre prétend exposer, d'après une révélation, la genèse du monde, l'institution sacerdotale ou lévitique, les préceptes pour l'individu, la famille et la cité; les devoirs du prince et des castes, l'organisation civile et militaire, les lois pénales et religieuses. Tout se résume en deux règles: pour la société, la subordination des castes; pour l'individu, la pureté physique et morale.' Ibid.: 242.

Hindu thought. Although many academics (especially the German Indologists) saw parallels between Hinduism and Christianity and put forward their belief in the equal validity of both religions, this admiration for Hinduism in works which were intellectually accessible to the common man was present by and large only in French works. Explaining that the Indian pantheon consisted of the Trinity at the top (Brahma, Vishnu and Siva) and that the concept of hell and heaven (*naraka-svarga*), of rebirth and transmigration governed the morals of Indians, Duruy traced the process by which Hinduism had tried over the centuries to regenerate and reform itself.[14] He cited Buddhism as the great revolt against Brahminical supremacy which advocated the equality of men.[15] The Buddha, or *Çâkyamouni*, was portrayed as a sage who preached the attainment of nirvana or deliverance by individual purity and morality.[16]

This aspect of Indian history was a mid-century phenomenon which followed the work of anthropologists (see Chapter Five) and the resulting changes in Indology (Chapter Six). Duruy was certainly not alone in his beliefs. Lamairesse, *ancien ingénieur* in chief for the French establishments in India in 1890, and author of two histories dealing with India before the birth of the Buddha and India after the Buddha[17] believed that the knowledge of Indian history and culture was necessary to know the Aryan antecedents of Europe. His argument centred on the Aryan origins of the Vedic culture of India. According to Lamairesse the Christian virtues of morality and compassion were contained in the Aryan religions of India: Brahminical Hinduism and Buddhism.[18] These religions therefore provided a

---

[14] Ibid.
[15] Ibid.: 243.
[16] Ibid.
[17] E. Lamairesse, *L'Inde avant le Bouddha*. (Paris: Georges Carré, 1891) and *L'Inde après le Bouddha*. (Paris: Georges Carré, 1892). Lamairesse, born in 1817 was inducted into the *Legion d'Honneur*.
[18] Lamairesse, *L'Inde avant le Bouddha*: 10–11.

valuable window to study the development of religion in the West. According to him, 'The conclusion of the Eastern religions of Aryan origin of the East seems a prelude or a reflection of the great religion of Aryans of the Occident.'[19] Demarcating the development of religion into the capabilities of each race to transcend the primitive religions of animism and fetishism, Lamairesse concluded that the superiority of the Aryan race, both in the East and the West was clearly visible through its religious expression. It was this link between the Eastern and Western Aryans that made it relevant to study the origins of Aryan religion in India.

The link between Christianity and Hinduism as representing a common genius of the Aryan race was certainly a mid-century phenomenon, but its inclusion in Lamairesse's works indicate the long-lasting effects of race theory, since Lamairesse was writing towards the end of the century. However, the link between Christianity and Hinduism itself was an older tradition of French writings on India dating back to Jourdain de Séverac in the thirteenth century (see Chapter One). From Séverac to Voltaire, French writers had compared the Christian and Hindu religious traditions, in a sense justifying the superiority of the latter by pointing out its similarity with the former, another example of 'Christianizing Hinduism' (see Chapter One, footnote 43). As late as 1814, Collin de Bar, the Magistrate of the Pondichéry High Court, and author of the two-volume *Histoire de l'Inde ancienne et moderne de l'Indoustan*,[20] recounted the Puranic mythology of the Great Flood and compared it with the story of Noah and the Ark, further drawing a parallel between the Hindu god Brahma and the

---

[19] 'La conclusion des religions d'origine Aryenne de l'Orient semble un prelude ou un reflet de la grande religion des Aryens de l'Occident.'Ibid.: 16.

[20] de Bar, *Histoire de l'Inde ancienne et moderne de l'Indoustan*.

Hebrew Adam. 'Brahma was the first man for the Hindus, like Adam was the first man of the Hebrews.'[21]

Recent scholarship on racism in France[22] has demonstrated that, the republican ideal of being colour-blind aside,[23] France long struggled with issues of racism, directed particularly against Jews, and in the more modern period, towards colonial minorities. In the nineteenth century, the trend of race theory being directed against Jews and culminating with the notorious *Affaire Dreyfus* cannot be glossed over. As Leon Poliakov points out, even the famous nineteenth-century philosopher at the *Collège de France*, Ernest Renan supported Gobineau's notion of the pre-eminence of the Aryan race.[24] Directly in the Indian context, while the prominent theosophist Louis Jacolliot's thesis that there was a close link between Christianity and Hinduism[25] was scoffed at by German Indologists like Max Müller,[26] interest in this theory in France was strong enough to commission at least eight editions of Jacolliot's *Bible dans l'Inde* within a few years.[27]

---

[21] 'Brahma fut le premier homme des Indous, comme Adam fut le premier homme des Hébreux.' Ibid.: 47.

[22] For example, *Race in France: Interdisciplinary Perspectives on the Politics of Difference*. Edited by Herrick Chapman and Laura L. Frader (New York: Berghahn, 2004).

[23] See Sue Peabody, *'There are no Slaves in France': The Political Culture of Race and Slavery in the Ancien Régime* (Oxford: OUP, 1996).

[24] Leon Poliakov, *The Aryan Myth: A History of Racist and Nationalist Ideas in Europe*. Translated by E. Howard. (New York: Basic Books, 1971): 206–8. Ironically, Renan was professor of Semitic Studies.

[25] Louis Jacolliot, *Christna et le Christ* (Paris: A. Lacroix et cie, 1874) and *The Bible in India: Hindoo Origin of Hebrew and Christian Revelation* (New York: Carleton, 1870). Jacolliot was a prolific writer, and, having spent some years in India as a colonial administrator, considered himself eminently qualified to write about the parallels between Hinduism and Christianity.

[26] See Friedrich Max Müller, 'On False Analogies in Comparative Theology (1870)' in *The Essential Max Müller: On Language, Mythology, and Religion*. Edited by Jon R. Stone (Palgrave Macmillan, 2002).

[27] Poliakov, *The Aryan Myth*: 209.

For Duruy India was a land which deserved more study, if not for her material accomplishments, at least for her spiritual and philosophical advances. According to him,

> We insist on this moral history of India, first because of its political history, then because this country was the large reserve of the philosophical and religious ideas [from] which, took their courses in various unknown directions.... Let us add that it is covered with imposing monuments of a rare elegance, of which we know yet very little; it had the [kind of] three glories of Greece: thought, poetry and art.[28]

The belief that India had provided, if not many material contributions to the world, many advanced systems of thought, was another longstanding French tradition. For Duruy, the difference between the Eastern and Western religion was that Western religion placed the individual and his actions first. In the East man was insignificant before God and ultimately strove to unite with the God-soul. For this reason the Hindu had less ambition than the Jew, Musulman, or Christian since he aimed only to unite with God in death rather than to improve his material existence in his present life.[29] Duruy's summary of the nature of the Hindu was very much influenced by Gobineau's description of the Hindu as striving for other-worldly aims rather than a focus on the present life.[30] As Duruy put it, 'One sees,

---

[28] 'Nous insistons sur cette histoire morale de l'Inde, d'abord parce qu'on ne connaît point son histoire politique, ensuite parce que ce pays a été le grand réservoir des idées philosophiques et religieuses qui, de là, ont pris leurs cours en différentes directions... Ajoutons qu'elle est couverte de monuments grandioses et d'une rare élégance, dont nous ne connaissons encore que la plus faible partie; de sorte qu'elle a eu trois des gloires de la Grèce: la pensée, la poésie et l'art.' Duruy, *Histoire de l'Orient*: 246–47.

[29] Ibid.: 246.

[30] Ibid. For Gobineau, see Chapter 4: 11–12.

by this short history, that if India has done little [achieved little], she has thought much.'[31]

The antecedents for Duruy's belief can be seen in Collin de Bar's early-century work, which described India as 'mysterious and sacred!... the cradle of mankind, the traditional ground religion and morals... the most beautiful area of Asia, the noblest place of the sphere [globe]...'[32] By the end of the century, Alfred Le Dain, a member of the *Société Asiatique* and recipient of an award from the *Société Ethnographique de la gironde* for his work on ancient India[33] was insisting that the exploration of India's past was a fitting beginning to the study of history since India was the 'alma mater of all nations';[34] a great fount of classical religion, philosophy and literature.

In most histories, the importance of India as an ancient society lay in her Aryan antecedents. According to Duruy, 'It was the Aryans, however, who gave India its place in history.'[35] Chapter Seventeen of Duruy's text on the Orient was exclusively devoted to India. Titled '*Les Aryas*', the chapter briefly ran through Indian history and culture since the advent of the Aryans in India. Duruy described the beginning of Aryan culture in India with the Epics, the Ramayana and the Mahabharata, which he compared to the Iliad and other works of Homer and Virgil.[36] The Vedas

---

[31] 'On voit, par cette brève histoire, que si l'Inde a peu agi, elle a beaucoup pensé.' Ibid.: 247.

[32] 'mystérieuse et sacré!...le berceau du genre humain, la terre classiques de la religion et de la morales...la plus belle région del'Asie, le plus noble séjour du globe...' de Bar, *Histoire de l'Inde ancienne et moderne de l'Indoustan*: xii, introduction.

[33] Alfred le Dain, *L'Inde Antique*. (Paris: Société cooperative des letters et des arts, 1896). Even though le Dain's thesis, a Theosophist one, was radically different from most histories of the day in insisting that the 'Rutas' or the Dravidians were the true originators of Indic culture rather than the Aryans, he still believed that India was the source of most ancient religions, including Christianity.

[34] '<*alma mater*> de toutes les nations'Ibid.: I, introduction.

[35] Duruy, *Ancient History of the East*: 16.

[36] Ibid.: 17.

according to him demonstrated the common origins of many of the ancient beliefs of Greece, Italy, and Europe in their Aryan heritage. He accepted the Epics as historical proof of the Aryans in India and of the history of ancient India. Yet he noted that in terms of documenting Indian history there was no real history of India written until the Greeks invaded, once again echoing the commonly held notion that India's past had been documented due to the organization and method of the Western mind.[37] As Duruy put it, 'This poetic and religious race unfortunately does not have other history than that of its gods.'[38] In a single page he summed up the rest of the history of ancient India with a catalogue of invasions:Darius, Alexander, the Bactrians, the Ghaznavids and finally the advent of the European settlements in India with the arrival of Vasco da Gama in India in 1498. The political history of India was described as a string of invasions rather than in terms of the evolving political institutions and forms of government, since monarchy in India was accepted to be a stagnant form of government based upon a vague notion of oriental despotism. This was a common enough feature of French histories of India; the lumping together of centuries of history, the complete lack of a sense of evolving political institutions, and the focus rather, on the Marxist creation of Oriental Despotism. Noting that India had attracted many conquerors for her riches, pearls, spices, perfumes, ivory and precious metals, Duruy continued, 'Thus here [we have] this intelligent and soft race [which] for [the] nearly ten centuries that [it] existed [has] lost its independence, but kept its social organization, religion and its literature.'[39]

---

[37] Ibid.: 18.

[38] 'Cette race poétique et religieuse n'a pas malheureusement d'autre histoire que celle de ses dieux.' Duruy, *Histoire de l'Orient*: 240.

[39] 'Ainsi voilà près de dix siècles que cette race, intelligente et douce, a perdue son indépendance, mais elle a gardé son organisation sociale, sa religion et sa littérature.' Ibid.: 241.

In this manner Duruy dispensed with historical event and chronology.

This aspect of Duruy's history of ancient India was another longstanding tradition. Located in the efforts of early colonial officials to make sense of the myriad mythological and genealogical stories abounding in India, the conclusion that Indians had no sense of historical chronology in the context of accurate and unbiased reporting meant that Western historians prided themselves on 'retrieving Indian history' from the morass of myths and half-fantastic stories.[40] According to de Bar, 'For the rest the Hindus do not have history itself, and there still does not exist a complete body of history of the peoples of India. All their chronicles are very imperfect, especially those concerning times before the Moslem invasions.'[41] Not surprisingly, de Bar's narrative was drawn from external sources—Greek, Roman, Arab, Persian and European. The only mention of Indian individuals was made in reference to their interaction with foreigners. The situation in India itself was presented as an unchanging milieu into which the march of history, in the form of successive invasions, formed a minor interruption. The Indians themselves resisted any change in their religion and custom. According to de Bar, 'This

---

[40] The most widely read work which publicized this view of India was J.S. Mill's *History of British India*. 6 vols (London: Baldwin, Cradock, and Joy, 1817). In addition, H.M. Elliot and J. Dowson's monumental *History of India as Told by her Own Historians*, 8 vols (London, Truübner and co., 1867–77) perpetuated this myth by beginning Indian 'history' from the period of Islamic invasions in the 10th century. Several excellent monographs have examined this aspect of constructing India's past, including Ronald Inden's *Imagining India* (Oxford, UK; Cambridge, Mass., USA: Basil Blackwell, 1990).

[41] 'Du reste les Indous n'ont pas d'histoire, proprement dit, et il n'existe point encore un corps d'histoire complet des peoples de l'Inde. Toutes leurs chroniques sont très-imparfaites, celles surtout qui concernant les temps antérieurs aux invasions musulmanes.'de Bar, *Histoire de l'Inde ancienne et moderne de l'Indoustan*: 48–49.

theology [of the Indians] was maintained without change, through a succession of centuries [to] which one could not assign the origin; it preserved its system intact during foreign invasions....'[42]

Following this the 'Hindu' religion was presented as a uniform set of beliefs.[43] According to de Bar,

...the attentive observer will notice that these vicissitudes, these various changes never affected the Hindu race in a significant manner, [they were] always constant in their manners, their opinions, belief and control. For twenty-two centuries, history has represented them such as we see them today. All changed around them, and in the middle of so much physical and moral change, the original character the Hindu hardly altered.[44]

The major themes of this textual Hindu culture and religion revolved around the caste system and the supremacy of the Brahmins.

In the light of these views it is only natural that the remaining description of Duruy's history was centred on social institutions, particularly the caste system. The caste

---

[42] 'Cette théologie (of the Indians) s'est maintenue sans alteration, à travers une succession de siècles dont on ne put assigner l'origine; elle a conservé son système intact pendant les invasions étrangères...' Ibid.: 67.

[43] This element was not a uniquely 'French' aspect of writing about India, nor was it a unique quality of De Bar's work; most European work on India presented Indian religion in much the same manner, describing Hinduism as being textually derived, without noting the enormous diversity of practice, belief and philosophy.

[44] '...l'observateur attentive remarquera que ces vicissitudes, ces divers changemens n'affectèrent jamais d'une manière sensible la véritable race des Indous, toujours constante dans ces moeurs, dans ces opinions, dans sa croyance et dans sa conduite. Depuis vingt-deux siècles, l'histoire les représente tels que nous les voyons aujourd'hui. Tout a changé autour d'eux, et au milieu de tant de révolutions physiques et morales, le caractère originel de l'Indous n'a presque éprouvé aucune altération.'Ibid.: 93.

system was ordained, according to the 'Books of the Saints', by the God Brahma, who divided the people into priests (*Brahmins*), warriors (*Xatryas*) (*sic*), laborers/merchants (*Vaïçyas*) and artisans/cultivators (*Soudras*). The first three castes represented the Aryans and were the dominant castes. Intermarriage between castes was forbidden and the offspring of such unions were low castes, with the offspring of the result of a union of a higher caste with a *Soudra* being the lowest of the low, a *Paria*. The Brahmins alone had the right to read and explain the sacred books and became the doctors, priests, judges, and poets of India owing to their education and wisdom.[45]

These histories were propagating a view of the caste system as a stagnant system which, once ordained, did not change for the centuries that it had existed. In fact, the caste system was an evolving, living organism where the interaction of different castes was always changing.[46] In different regions of India the caste system had different hierarchies[47] and significance in governing day-to-day

---

[45] Duruy, *Histoire de l'Orient*: 241.

[46] See Karen Leonard, *Social History of an Indian Caste: the Kayasths of Hyderabad* (California: UC Press, 1978); Adrian Mayer, *Caste and Kinship in Central India: A Village and its Region* (Berkeley: UC Press, 1960); Milton Singer, *When a Great Tradition Modernizes* (New York: Praeger, 1972); Frank Conlon, *A Caste in a Changing World. The Chitrapur Saraswat Brahmans, 1700–1935* (Berkeley: UC Press, 1977); Mattison Mines, *The Warrior Merchants: Textiles, Trade and Territory in South India* (Cambridge: CUP, 1984); Robert Hardgrave, *The Nadars of Tamilnad. The Political Culture of a Community in Change* (Berkeley: UC Press, 1969); Pauline Kolenda, *Caste in Contemporary India: Beyond Organic and Solidarity* (California: UC Press, 1978).

[47] See Gloria Goodwin Raheja, *The Poison in the Gift: Ritual, Prestation and the Dominant Caste in a North Indian Village* (Chicago: University of Chicago Press, 1988); McKim Marriot, *Caste Ranking and Community Structure in Five Regions of India and Pakistan* (Poona, 1960); Brenda Beck, *Peasant Society in Konku. A Study of Right and Left Sub-castes in South India* (Vancouver: University of British Columbia Press, 1972); Niels Brimnes, *Constructing the Colonial Encounter. Right*

life.[48] Colonial histories thus portrayed a never-changing continuum where institutions ordained centuries earlier, existed without any alteration or addition in the present. According to Duruy, the Indian government was marked by a 'regular, changeless machine'.[49] In this manner the complexities of individual choice, historical process, and changing situations in the diverse subcontinent were ignored in favour of a monolithic construct of India which was imagined and propagated by colonialists.

Another manner in which India was 'constructed' was her physical extent. In his first chapter, titled *'Monde connu des anciens'*, Duruy sketched the physiological environment of India. Touching briefly upon the trade routes of the ancient world (among which India figured prominently due to her easy accessibility via water bodies like the Arabian Sea and the Bay of Bengal), he noted that the Indian mountains, the Hindukush range or the Indian Caucuses, and the Himalayas were prominent among ancient geographers as were the rivers Brahmaputra, Ganga and Indus. In addition, Duruy included India as one among the six major physical and political regions of the ancient world, alongside the Mediterranean, Red Sea, the land between the Euphrates and Tigris, between the Tigris and Indus and North Asia.

Most historians believed that an extensive topographical description of India was necessary to understand the development of her culture. For instance, according to Lacroix de Marles, author of an extensive six-volume history of India,

---

and *Left Hand Castes in Early Colonial South India* (Richmond, Surrey: Rutledge and Curzon, 1999); M. N. Srinivas, *Religion and Society among the Coorgs of South India* (London: OUP, 1952).

[48] See Gerald Berreman, *Caste and other Inequities: Essays on Inequality* (Chicago: University of Chicago Press, 1978); Irawati Karve, *Hindu Society: An Interpretation* (Poona: Sangam Press, 1968).

[49] Victor Duruy, *Ancient History of the East*. Translated by Edwin Augustus Grosvenor and Thomas Spencer Jerome (T. Y. Crowell & company, 1899): 16.

I thought that a geographical note, to which statistical details and interesting descriptions would be linked, would not only arouse curiosity, but that it would facilitate the intelligence of history... the geographical note will form approximately half of the first volume. One will find there a general description of the ground, mountains, rivers, climate, and positive concepts of knowledge that the ancients had of India....[50]

Despite this attention to topographical detail, most French authors used several different terms to describe the land, in particular, the terms 'l'Inde' and 'Hindoustan' were used interchangeably, even though these areas indicated different parts of the subcontinent. Marles discussed the origin of the term 'India' and the various theories which variously attributed the word 'India' to the river Indus, a derivation of 'Hindu', and other theories. Nowhere did Marles express the realization that 'India' meant different geographical limits in the ancient and modern times and that even the boundaries of the entity of 'India' were constantly shifting.[51] In a seamless move from ancient to modern times, Marles described the geography of ancient India in the time of Alexander and Ptolemy to the modern

---

[50] "J'ai pensé qu'une notice géographique, à laquelle s'uniraient des détails statistiques et des descriptions intéressantes, ne piquerait pas seulement la curiosité, mais qu'elle faciliterait l'intelligence de l'histoire...La notice géographique formera environ la moitié du premier volume. On y trouvera une description générale du sol, des montagnes, des fleuves, du climat, et des notions positives sur la connaissance que les anciens ont eue de l'Inde..." Jean Lacroix de Marles, *Histoire Générale de l'Inde Ancienne et moderne depuis l'an 2000 avant J. C. jusqu'a nos jours* (Paris, 1828): 21–22.

[51] See, for example, Susan Gole, *Early Maps of India* (New York: Humanities Press, 1976); Matthew H. Edney, *Mapping an Empire. The Geographical Construction of British India, 1765–1843.* (Chicago: University of Chicago Press, 1997); and Ian Barrow, *Making History, Drawing Territory. British Mapping in India, c.1756–1905* (New Delhi: OUP, 2003).

colonial government and administrative organization. Acknowledging that India was composed of diverse peoples like the Sikhs, Rohillas, Jats and Marathas who each had their own cultural and religious belief systems, and that furthermore the divisions within India were made even more complicated by the diversity of origin and religion,[52] he nevertheless continues to describe these mini-nations as existing within a recognizable 'India', underlining the process by which colonial powers literally created a geographical space where India was defined.[53] In a basic sense, French cartographers and writers were part of the European creation of 'India'.[54] They were as persuasive as British cartographers and writers that a natural geographical region unified by cultural, religious, linguistic, and political bonds existed as 'India' even though this was simply not the case. As Ian Barrow and Mathew Edney both suggest, maps were a powerful tool for claiming and even creating colonial spaces.[55] By the time Duruy wrote a history text on the modern world,[56] he too referred to India as 'l'Inde' and 'Hindoustan' interchangeably as a

---

[52] Lacroix de Marles,*Histoire Générale de l'Inde Ancienne et moderne depuis l'an 2000 avant J. C jusqu'a nos jours* (Paris, 1828), introduction.

[53] Prior to British colonization the term 'India' could not be applied to the geographical limits of what is now India. There were independent kingdoms, tribal areas, the massive limits of the Mughal Empire popularly referred to as Hindustan, and the stark division between the Northern and Southern halves of the subcontinent. As Susan Gole has demonstrated in her work on *Early Maps of India*(New York: Humanities Press, 1976), 'India' or the 'Indies' could signify a range of areas from Madagascar to the Spice Islands.

[54] See Nigel Leask, 'Francis Wilford and the colonial construction of Hindu geography, 1799–1822', *Romantic Geographies: Discourses of Travel, 1775–1844*, edited by Amanda Gilroy (Manchester and New York: Manchester University Press, 2000).

[55] Ian Barrow, *Making History, Drawing Territory*; Matthew H. Edney, *Mapping an Empire*.

[56] V. Duruy, *Histoire des Temps Modernes depuis 1453 jusqu'a 1789* (Paris: Librairie Hachette, 1870), 5th edition.

recognizable geographical entity which corresponded to the modern extent of India. For example, he described the Portuguese empire in India as, 'By Diu, on the Gujarat coast, Goa on the Malabar coast, the island of Ceylon, and Nagapatam on the Coromandel coast, they encompassed all of Hindustan.'[57]

Duruy's seems to have been the rare school textbook which described ancient India. Most other textbooks concentrated only on the modern, colonial period of Indian history. Histories written by Isaac and Malet, which were used by schoolchildren well into the twentieth century, contained little or no reference to pre-colonial India. For instance, in Isaac and Malet's *L'Orient et La Grèce*,[58] there was no reference at all to the Far East, the Orient in this case being defined as Egypt, Persia and other areas of the Near East. The reference to India was entirely incidental and occurred in the context of Alexander the Great's invasion of India.[59] The textbook is comparable to Duruy's sixth-grade textbook in content, covering many of the ancient societies of the world. Yet the focus had shifted from the nineteenth to the twentieth century and to a more Eurocentric approach to ancient civilizations, where the empires of Greece and Rome were the sole reason for the spread of civilization overseas. This was arguably an indication of the development of colonial doctrine. Whereas sixth-grade students had earlier learned about ancient India and some of her history and customs they were now presented with one sentence about ancient India in the context of her conquest by Greece.

---

[57] 'Par Diu, sur la côte du Guzzerat, Goa, sur celle du Malabar, l'île de Ceylan, et Negapatam sur la côte de Coromandel, ils enveloppaient tout l'Hindoustan.' Ibid.: 134.

[58] Isaac Malet, *L'Orient et la Grèce* (Paris: Hachette, 1932). The text was composed after the official history curriculum prescribed in 1931. Meant for the sixth grade, the programme specified that students needed to receive an hour and a half of historical instruction per day.

[59] Ibid.: 303.

In the light of this gap Duruy's work was important for how it portrayed India in terms of her Aryan heritage, spirituality and other worldliness, caste system and philosophy. This was presumably the first time that children were encountering India academically making it an influential guide as to how they continued to perceive India. Since Duruy was not a specialist in Indian history, all of his narratives were drawn from other, influential French histories of India. His sources included historical, philological, and anthropological sources which are clearly recognizable in his narrative. His work therefore was a hybrid coming together of diverse academic images of India and as such provided a space within which a single, recognizable entity of 'India', however artificial, was presented to French schoolchildren. Thus, the academic construction of pre-colonial India by Indologists and anthropologists made its way into the school textbooks of the Francophone world. In these pages, one can see the resonances of pedagogical influences which were to stay with many of these French students (including the students in the French Indian *Comptoirs!*) to adulthood and beyond.

ANGLO-FRENCH COLONIAL RIVALRY

In contrast to Duruy, Isaac and Malet's textbooks, which dominated the twentieth century, focused on the colonial period. Jules Isaac, born in 1877 was greatly influenced by the Dreyfus affair (he was 20 when *J'Accuse* was published) and by World War I (he was wounded at Verdun) Albert Malet was *Professeur agrégé d'histoire au Lycée Louis-le-Grand*. Isaac held the same position at the Lycée Saint-Louis. Together they wrote the history textbooks which were used in schools in the first part of the twentieth century. Between 1923 and 1930 seven volumes of history textbooks written by Isaac and Malet were released by Hachette. In 1936 Isaac was made Inspector General of Education, a post which was revoked in 1940 by the Vichy

Regime. In the history manuals he was considered a radical teacher by his peers because of his inclusion of primary documents, the profusion of illustrations with prominent figures given pride of place, as well as images of inventions and great art.

While Duruy emphasized the ancient greatness of India in the nineteenth century, Isaac and Malet minimized the importance of the ancient period of Indian history. They chose instead to relate the history of the colonial enterprise in India, especially highlighting the growing Indian movement for independence from British rule. While Duruy did include the colonial period in his textbooks, his remarks were for the most part innocuous in opposition to Isaac and Malet's criticism of British rule. This was a new aspect of French interests in India. Since 1815, French hostility to Britain over colonies overseas had been veiled, flaring up in the colonial lobby and pro-colonial press only when France was actively pursuing colonies in Africa and Asia during the mid-nineteenth century. By the end of the century and into the twentieth century however, this simmering hostility had developed into an open criticism of British colonial policy and enterprise as selfish and oppressive.

In textbooks such as Isaac and Malet and even Duruy's later work, the chief sentiment by the early twentieth century was a comparison of French and British colonial methods, a reflection of the primacy of Anglo-French rivalries and the need to prove that French colonization was superior to the British. For example, following the empire of the Portuguese, Duruy recounted the formation of the East India Companies of England and France in the seventeenth century and their subsequent rivalry over India. Focusing on the efforts of individual French generals, Duruy noted that, 'The French Company extended then [expanded its territories] with speed... profited, like the English, of these competitions to consolidate its establishments, and it charged the care of its interests in these remote areas to two remarkable men: Bourdonnais... and Dupleix....'[60] The focus on individual efforts was very typical of histories which described the French colonial period in India. Duruy continued the military exploits of Dupleix with the career of Bussy in the Deccan, and of Lally-Tolendal following which he recounted the heroic defence by Hyder Ali and his son, Tipu Sultan of Mysore (in alliance with the French), against the British, even describing the latter as 'Frederic II of the East: he was at least an energetic representative of Indian nationality, and one of the most remarkable men of modern Asia.'[61] Unfortunately, Tipu died defending his capital, Seringapatam in 1799. 'Since this moment the English were the true Masters of India; they still have this vast and rich country where they have 150 million subjects which their first governors exploited with a pitiless cruelty.'[62] The description of British colonization in India as an exploitative and oppressive regime was not a new aspect of French writing although it was infrequently expressed.

The element of Anglo-French rivalry was a long-standing tradition in French histories of India. In the *Avertissement* to De Bar's early history, the editors described his personal interests in advancing the cause of his country and of the métropole.[63] In fact, as the editors

[60] 'La Compagnie française s'éntendit alors avec rapidité...profita, comme l'anglaise, de ces rivalités pour consolider ses établissements, et elle chargea du soin de ses intérêts dans ces régions lointaines deux hommes remarquables: la Bourdonnais... et Dupleix...' V. Duruy, *Histoire des Temps Modernes depuis 1453 jusqu'a 1789* (Paris: Librairie Hatchette, 1870). 5th edition: 486–87.

[61] 'Frédéric II de l'Orient: il fut du moins le représentant énergique de la nationalité indienne, et un des hommes les plus remarquables de l'Asie moderne.' Ibid.: 490.

[62] 'Depuis ce moment les Anglais furent les véritables maîtres de l'Inde; ils possèdent encore ce vaste et riche pays où ils ont 150 millions de sujets que leurs premiers gouverneurs exploitèrent avec une impitoyable cruauté.' Ibid.: 490.

[63] de Bar, *Histoire de l'Inde ancienne et moderne de l'Indoustan*: *Avertissement*: iii.

pointed out, De Bar wrote his History during eight years of captivity, presumably at the hands of the British. His further advantage in possessing the original *Mémoires* of Dupleix and Bussy allowed him to retrace France's glorious moments in India with passion.[64] However, according to the editors, this partiality did not preclude him from producing an excellent history of India. According to them, 'For the rest, his work is not limited only to the history of the competitions of France and of England in the peninsula of India, he embraces a wider framework, and as a whole forms a complete body of history.'[65] And again,

> But the part of this work which... deserves more [of] the attention of the historians, the publicity agents, the statesmen, it is indisputably that which treats, with as much interest as of impartiality, of progress and the development of the exclusive domination of Great Britain on almost the totality of the peninsula of India. One especially sees there by which means this imposing power today managed to found one of the richest empires of the world in this end of the world, worsens it is perhaps indebted [i.e., Britain maintains the empire in India] only with the systematic and permanent oppression that it exerts there.[66]

---

[64] Ibid., *Avertissement:* iv.

[65] 'Du reste, son ouvrage ne se borne pas seulement à l'histoire des rivalités de la France et de l'Angleterre dans la presqu'île de l'Inde, il embrasse un cadre plus étendu, et forme un corps d'histoire suivi et complet dans son ensemble.' Ibid.

[66] 'Mais la partie de cet ouvrage qui...mérite le plus l'attention des historiens, des publicistes, des hommes d'Etat, c'est sans contredit celle qui traite, avec autant d'intérêt que d'impartialité, des progrès et du développement de la domination exclusive de la Grande-Bretagne sur la presque totalité de la péninsule de l'Inde. On y voit surtout par quels moyens cette puissance aujourd'hui si imposante est parvenu à fonder un des plus riches empires du monde dans cette extrémité de la terre, empire dont elle n'est peut-être redevable qu'à l'oppression systématique et permanente qu'elle y exerce.' Ibid.,*Avertissement:* vii.

Anglo-French colonial rivalry over India tended to flare up periodically during the nineteenth and twentieth centuries, based on the larger colonial currents of the day. Initially centred on India herself and Anglo-French rivalry over the subcontinent, the early loss of the French in the latter half of the eighteenth century and the definitive defeat of French national aims by 1815 was only exacerbated by mid- and late century colonial rivalries in Africa and the Far East where France and Britain were squabbling over territories.

Focusing as they did on the modern period of colonialism, Isaac and Malet's later textbooks, were written with this colonial agenda of expansion and Anglo-French rivalry. A textbook titled *Cours abrégé d'histoire*[67] followed the programme of instruction for '*primaire supérieur*' of 1920 and was meant for the schools of *primaries supérieures, Cours complémentaires, and Préparation au Brevet élémentaire*. The work provided a brief account of French colonial efforts to build an empire in India under Dupleix and Dumas. In the laudatory strain common among French historians recounting colonial efforts in India, Isaac and Malet noted the role of Dupleix in 'founding in India a grand French Empire'.[68] Glorifying the exploits of this adventurer, at once 'extremely active and audacious'[69] they described Dupleix' efforts bearing fruit. 'In 1752 French possessions with vassal states formed an empire of thirty million people, twice as large as France.'[70] In another text, Isaac and Malet elaborated on this feat: 'It was thus a question not only of making trade, but of establishing French domination in India....These extraordinary results had been

---

[67] Albert Malet and Jules Isaac. *Cours abrégé d'histoire* Second edition (Paris: Librairie Hatchette, 1922).

[68] 'fonder dans l'Inde un grand empire français', Ibid.: 96.

[69] 'extrêmement actif et audacieux', Ibid.: 97.

[70] 'En 1752, les possessions françaises avec les pays vassaux formaient un empire de trente millions d'habitants, deux fois grande comme la France.' Ibid.

obtained with limited resources, less than 2,000 Europeans and approximately 4,000 cipayes, natives commanded by Europeans.'[71] However, the English were not pleased. 'But the policy of Dupleix ran up against the resistance of the English; he was obliged to ask for reinforcements. However in France, the government and the Company preferred peace: Dupleix, ignored and considered a dangerous adventurer, was treated brutally....'[72] With the Treaty of Godeheu, the French East India Company renounced all her ambitions in India: 'thus, without... doubt, France lost the empire of India.'[73] Isaac and Malet were unequivocal about the decision. Calling it 'this terrible sacrifice'[74] they concluded that '...the Franco-English competition over the colonies ended in the total ruin of France and the triumph... of England.'[75] In fact, the primary source at the end of the chapter detailing the colonial rivalry between France and England was 'La programme de Dupleix exposé par lui-même', taken from P. Cultru (ed.), *Dupleix, ses*

---

[71] 'Il s'agissait donc non plus seulement de faire du commerce, mais d'établir la domination française dans l'Inde...Ces résultats extraordinaires avaient été obtenus avec de faibles moyens, moins de 2000 Européens et environ 4000 *cipayes*, indigènes exercés à l'européen.' Malet and Isaac. *XVII & XVIII siècles* (Paris: Librairie Hatchette, nd): 572–73.

[72] 'Mais la politique de Dupleix se heurta à la resistance des Anglais; il fut obligé de demander des renforts. Or en France, le gouvernement et la Compagnie préféraient la paix: Dupleix, méconnu et considéré comme un dangereux aventurier, fut rappelé brutalement...' Malet and Isaac. *Cours abrégé d'histoire*: 97. This sentiment demonstrates the influence of colonial desire in the late nineteenth century in France and the return to an older school of historiography which glorified men who had helped to further these temporal ambitions.

[73] *ainsi, sans...doute, la France perdit l'empire de l'Inde* (original italics—says much about their views about losing the Indian empire),Ibid.

[74] 'ce terrible sacrifice', Ibid.

[75] '...la rivalité franco- anglaise aux colonies se terminait par la ruine totale de la France et le triomphe...de l'Angleterre.' Ibid.: 98.

plans politiques, sa disgrace. Paris: Hatchette, nd)[76] high-lighting the feeling that the loss of India was far greater than any other colonial loss.

The notion of the loss of the French India Empire was exacerbated by the inclusion of the incorrect map showing the extent of French territories in India in 1752 (see Image 7.1).[77] The same map was also included as late as *Atlas Général Larousse* (Paris: Librairie Larousse, 1959). Even though the French *Comptoirs* in India were negligible both in size and economic contribution to the French empire, there was a sense of the past grandeur of 'French-India'. The maps indicating that France had once possessed an empire spanning almost the entire peninsula were classic of this desire to aggrandize their claims of an empire that never was;[78] a phenomenon that Magadera and Marsh term 'France's imaginary empire';[79] India thus constituted a space which could have and indeed *should* have been

---

[76] Malet and Isaac,*XIX siècle. Histoire contemporaine, 1815–1920*: 590–92.

[77] Malet and Isaac, *Cours abrégé d'histoire*: 97. Similar map in Malet and Isaac. *XIX siècle. Histoire contemporaine, 1815–1920*: 568.

[78] Matthew H. Edney, *Mapping an Empire*. According to Mathew Edney, cartography and imperialism was fundamentally linked in that imperial cartographers created a 'spatial recognition of territory and empire' (p. 1), a sense of the extent of territorial possession in order to boost national pride as well as challenge other colonial powers. Edney traces the process by which British cartographers created the territory of 'India'. Thus, maps were fundamental to the process of national pride in colonial possessions.

[79] See Kate Marsh, *Fictions of 1947: Representations of Indian Decolonization in French-language texts* (New York: Peter Lang, 2007). Also see Kate Marsh, 'Les cinq noms sonores: The French Voice in the Story of British India 1763–1954', in *Journal of Romance Studies*, 5 (2005): 65–77 (co-authored with Ian H. Magadera), and 'Representing Indian Decolonization in the Parisian Press 1923–54', *International Journal of Francophone Studies*, 5 (2002): 74–84. Marsh argues that French notions of India were shaped by a triad of India, France, and Britain, interacting with each other.

French territorially speaking, failing which she could be 'an empire in mind'. At the height of her colonial expansion in India, France had merely extended diplomatic and military aid to the rulers of peninsular India, who had employed many French mercenaries as their military advisors. Yet the inclusion of these areas as part of her 'empire' indicates the extent of French *desire* for India temporally.[80] Kate Marsh notes the persistence of this theme of a 'lost empire' in a school textbook on geography under the Third Republic—L.-H Ferrand's *Géographie de la France et de ses colonies: Cours moyen certificate d'études* (Paris: Cornély, 1904).[81] This agenda extended to the press as well. *La Politique Coloniale*, which published bi-weekly issues of the news in French colonies as well as serving as the organ of the *Parti Coloniale* even referred to the French *Établissements* in India as '*notre colonie dans l'Inde*', a true enough but misleading description of the actual extent of French ownership of India.[82] As Camille Guy insisted in his handbook to the 1900 Exposition, 'our posts in French India are all that remains of our immense Indian empire.'[83]

The information about British India contained in the Isaac and Malet textbooks were to be found in the texts prescribed for the advanced classes of philosophy and mathematics. Focused on the nineteenth century, the book

---

[80] As Ian Barrow points out, all colonial cartography was a site for power contestations. Ian Barrow, *Making History, Drawing Territory*: 333.

[81] Kate Marsh, *Fictions of 1947*: 30.

[82] *La Politique Coloniale*, 1892.

[83] 'nos établissements de l'Inde française sont tous ce qui nous reste de l'immense empire indien.' Camille Guy, *Exposition Universelle de 1900, Les colonies françaises: Les établissements français de l'Inde.* (Paris: Levé, 1900): 1. Quoted in Kathryn Gibbs, 'The Exposition Coloniale of 1900: Representing and Forgetting l'Inde française'. Paper presented at 1st AHRC Study Day: French Subaltern Colonizers and the Grand Narrative of British India. University of Liverpool, 10 September 2007.

sketched the colonial conquest briefly, and recounted the British conquest of India in a few pages. In two editions of the book,[84] modified according to new programmes of curricula, the French belief that Britain was unfairly interfering with Indian customs clearly came through. The earlier edition, conforming to the educational curriculum of 1902, consisted of almost 1,200 pages of information about the nineteenth century. In a chapter titled *'Les Puissances européenes en Asie'*, the English conquest of India was traced from the origins of the East India Company until the Rebellion of 1857. The earlier work portrayed the Rebellion as caused primarily by the annexation of native states under Dalhousie's policy of Lapse and accorded the incident of the greased cartridge importance only as the proverbial match which lit the fire. In a text meant for the third grade, the Revolt was described as 'a military insurrection... the fundamental cause of the insurrection was the hatred of the Hindus for their winners... the pretext was the distribution of cartridges coated with cow grease, a sacred animal for the Hindus, to the cipayes.'[85] The later

---

[84] Earlier edition was Malet and Isaac. *XIX siècle. Histoire contemporaine, 1815–1920* (Paris: Librairie Hatchette, nd). There were 10 pages devoted to India. The map was on p. 910, and images provided included a picture of a Sikh man on p. 911, and a picture of Benares Brahmins with long, matted locks and covered in sacred ash on p. 915. No sources were provided. The later edition titled *'Histoire contemporaine, depuis le milieu du XIX siècle'*, of which I examined two copies, were published by Colin in 1918 (2nd edition) and Librairie Hachette, Paris in 1930 respectively. Of a total of 849 pages, only six pages were devoted to India, the emphasis now being clearly on France's larger and more prominent colonies. The source for this edition was primarily Métin's *L'Inde Contemporaine* and included extended quotations from Piriou, *L'Inde contemporaine et le movement national* (Paris: Alcan éd., 1905); and from E. de Valbezen, *Les Anglais et l'Inde*, tome 1 (Paris, 1875).

[85] 'une insurrection militaire...La cause profonde de l'insurrection fut la haine des Hindous pour leurs vainqueurs...Le prétexte fut la distribution aux cipayes de cartouches enduites de graisse de vache, animal

edition of *Histoire contemporaine* (1930) however, gave equal importance to the religious feelings of the Hindus and their belief that the English were interfering too much with their culture and religion. In this text, 'The revolt had military and religious causes.'[86] In this case, the incident of the greased cartridges was the last straw. Nikki Frith's study demonstrates a similar trend in contemporary newspapers and journals, like the *Journal des Débats, La Presse, La Patrie, Le Constitutionnel,* and *Le Siècle,* which referred to the event as a 'people's revolt', 'national revolt' and 'revolution'.[87] According to Louis Jourdan of *Le Siècle,* 'The revolt of English India is a supreme warning... if, after the victory, they [English] were shown also inhuman, as unknowing of their mission as they were to it... the last hour of their domination would have sounded.... More slavery! More constraint! More supreme oppression.'[88]

Both editions of Isaac and Malet also recounted the infamous massacre at Kanpur of British women and children by Nana Sahib but while the earlier edition concluded with a brief sentence describing the British reprisals for the massacre and their eventual suppression of the

---

sacré pour les Hindous.' Isaac and Malet, *L'Epoque contemporaine* (Paris: Hatchette, 1907): 552–53.

[86] 'La révolte eut des causes militaires et religieuses.' Isaac and Malet, *Histoire contemporaine, depuis le milieu du XIX siècle.* (Paris: Librairie Hachette, 1930): 484.

[87] Nikki Frith,' "Natural and Necessary Enemies": French-Language Representations of the Indian "Mutinies" and Britain's Colonial "Failure"', Paper presented at 1st AHRC Study Day: French Subaltern Colonizers and the Grand Narrative of British India. University of Liverpool, 10 September 2007: 4. Also see attached table of Journal nomenclatures.

[88] 'La révolte de l'Inde anglaise est un Avertissement suprême...si, après la victoire, ils (les Anglais) se montraient aussi inhumains, aussi inintelligens de leur mission qu'ils l'ont été...la dernière heure de leur domination aurait bientôt sonné...Plus d'esclavage! Plus de servitude! Plus d'oppression supreme.' Louis Jourdan, 'Esclavage', *Le Siècle,* 16 and 17 August 1857: 1. Quoted in Nikki Frith, ' "Natural and Necessary Enemies": 4.

Rebellion,[89] the later edition included an extended quotation from Valbezen which recounted, in detail, the manner of British reprisal and the violence wreaked on Indians who were seen as responsible for the massacre.[90] According to Ernest Dréolle, 'it is what one does not like in France, it is to hear about the sheets [newspapers] of London, [who] after having expressed horror [about] the wild excesses which inspired the companions of Nana Sahib, excite the troops of S M Britannique to the same crimes and to the same vengeances.'[91] Jules Verne's 'The Steam House' which was published in 1880 was a condemnatory novel of 1857 which portrayed the British as killing thousands of innocent non-combatant Indians.[92] Jean Richepin's play 'Nana Sahib' first performed in 1883 cast Nana Sahib as the first Indian leader to inspire a revolution against British oppression.[93] According to Frederick Quinn, it almost seems that Verne lifted his plots from the popular press. His finger was always on the pulse of French readers and he both reflected and helped shape their perceptions of the world beyond their borders, as fanciful and contradictory as it

---

[89] The text, *L'Epoque contemporaine* (Paris: Hachette, 1907): 553 described 'De là de terribles représailles de la part des Anglais. Il leur fallut plus d'une année et demie pour écraser l'insurrection.'

[90] Isaac and Malet, *Histoire contemporaine, depuis le milieu du XIX siècle'*: 486.

[91] 'ce qu'on n'aime pas en France, c'est d'entendre les feuilles de Londres, après avoir exprimé l'horreur que leur inspire la conduite sauvage des compagnons de Nena-Saïb, exciter les troupes de S.M. Britannique aux mêmes crimes et aux mêmes vengeances.' Ernest Dréolle, Le Constitutionnel, 7 September 1857: 1. Quoted in Nikki Frith, '"Natural and Necessary Enemies"': 2.

[92] Verne's most famous character, Captain Nemo, of *Twenty Thousand Leagues Underthe Sea* and *The Mysterious Island* was also revealed to be a prince of Indian ancestry and a fervent opponent of imperialism, having lost his family and kingdom to the British in the Revolt of 1857.

[93] Cited in *ibid.*: 3.

had been in centuries past.[94] Rousselet's novel about the mutiny also demonstrated the French sympathy with the Indians. Noting that,

> ...After many centuries, Europeans, attracted by the renown of our riches, came to our country; first of all as humble men full of good words. Instead of driving them away as our neighbours the Chinese did, we Hindoos received the white men courteously, we opened our towns to them, and gave them part of our treasures. Little by little they insinuated themselves amongst us, taking advantage of our quarrels and dissensions. At last, becoming the stronger, under the pretext that our skin was dark, and that we worshipped idols, they robbed us of our cities and lands, and shared our wealth among them, as though it belonged to them by right. Now the oppressed Hindoos are rising up against their masters. Who can say they have not right on their side?[95]

Isaac and Malet continued to follow the course of British colonization of India with the declaration of Queen Victoria as the Empress of India and the transfer of authority from the East India Company to the Crown in the wake of the Rebellion. They described the works which the British undertook in India in the name of development, including reforms in education and society, the building of roads and rails, improving agricultural systems and introducing industries to India, the establishment of a regular administration, civil service, and police to govern India and the

---

[94] Frederick Quinn, *The French Overseas Empire.* (Westport, CT and London: Praeger, 2000): 170. Also see Nikki Frith, 'Competing Colonial Discourses in India: Representing the 1857 Kanpur Massacres in French- and English-Language Texts and Images', Unpublished doctoral thesis, University of Liverpool, 2008. Frith studies the mostly negative French representations of the British during the Mutiny and explains it in terms of their national and colonial rivalry with Britain.

[95] Louis Rousselet, *The Serpent Charmer* (New York: Charles Scribner's Sons, 1889): 265–66.

other 'civilizing' projects of the British. Having concluded this account of the 'civilizing' mission of the British they then questioned the validity of these works by pointing out that the greatest difference of opinion between the British and the 'Hindus' was over these very projects.

'Such is the English thesis. But the few million Hindus who are able to be interested in public affairs bitterly dispute these alleged benefits' (original italics).[96] Accepting that people who questioned British presence in India were in a small majority in the earlier edition of the history, and that the very geographical entity of India was a result of the British conquest, this edition pointed out that the continuation of the British presence in India was a result of the internal disunity among Indians. The later edition however expended more space on the agenda of the Indian nationalists and especially on their critique of colonial rule as being beneficial only to Britain, while draining India of her resources.[97] It detailed the Indian nationalists'

---

[96] *'Telle est la thèse anglaise. Mais les quelques millions d'Hindous qui sont capables de s'intéresser aux affaires publiques contestent âprement ces prétendus bienfaits.'* Isaac and Malet, *Histoire contemporaine, depuis le milieu du XIX siècle'* (Paris: Colin, 1918) 2nd edition: 488.

[97] Most histories which included a discussion of European colonization and of contemporary India also focused on the British drain of Indian wealth and the rapid impoverishment and exploitation of the country. See for example Baron Auguste Barchou de Penhoën, *L'Inde sous la domination anglaise* (Paris, 1827) and Paul Boell, *L'Inde et le problem Indien* (Paris, s.d.). What is very interesting is the close intellectual ties which existed between French Indologists and Indian Nationalists who were working for a greater Indian participation in governance and for eventual independence. As Kate Marsh points out, the French press continually compared the Nationalist movement in India to the French Revolution in terms of the desire to overthrow oppression and tyranny. See Kate Marsh, "Representing Indian Decolonization in the Parisian Press, 1923–54", *International Journal of Francophone Studies* 2002, 5.2. The mutual admiration of Indian intellectuals for French support and political ideals is reflected in countless writings and speeches which lauded the Revolutionary ideals of 1789, exhorted Indians to overthrow

economic and political critique of colonial rule and pointed out that the British exploited the differences between Hindus and Muslims for their own gains.[98] Quoting Piriou, the text pointed out that under other foreign conquerors India had not suffered the material and moral drain that English rule had effected.[99] 'Lastly, India succumbs under the triple burden of the treatments of the civil servants [salaries], the national debt and all the diplomatic and military expenditures that England makes in Asia, under the pretext that they [the revenue] are used to maintain the safety of India.'[100] The fact that by 1932 Indians were fairly visible (in public spaces) in Europe and that the movement for independence in India had gathered considerable

---

British tyranny like the peasant of the French Revolution and incorporated French notions of Aryanism which argued that India being the original home of the Aryans was well capable of self-rule. This aspect of French images of India is particularly strong in the speeches of Subhas Chandra Bose. Nationalist writings adopted the tone of Aryan greatness to push the concept that India may have declined over the centuries but that she was essentially home to a superior race which could regain that position of greatness. For example Swami Dayanand Saraswati's main argument was of a return to Aryan greatness. The writings of most Arya Samaj followers continue to echo this idea. These writings also fixed India in a timeless continuum which amplified the philosophical and spiritual achievements of the ancient Indians. When nationalists acknowledged the present social inequalities of caste they did so in an accusatory vein which blamed either racial intermixing or the Islamic influence for the ills of Indian society, two scapegoats which had been the creation of French Indologists. This is an intriguing aspect of the nationalist movement which has not been researched.

[98] Isaac and Malet, *Histoire contemporaine, depuis le milieu du XIX siècle'* (Paris: Colin, 1918) 2nd edition: 490.

[99] *Ibid.*, 1930 edn: 489 from E. Piriou, *L'Inde contemporaine et le mouvement national* (Paris: Alcan, 1905).

[100] 'Enfin, l'Inde succombe sous le triple fardeau des traitements des fonctionnaires, de la dette publique et de toutes les dépenses, militaires et diplomatiques que l'Angleterre fait en Asie, sous prétexte qu'elles servent à maintenir la sécurité de l'Inde.' Ibid. The same sentiment is in Malet and Isaac. *XIX siècle. Histoire contemporaine, 1815–1920*: 914.

momentum undoubtedly had a lot to do with this expanded account of Indian nationalist activities. But it was also in keeping with the French focus on the many dissatisfactions of colonial peoples of the British and their suggestion that British *mise en valeur* was only in the nature of lip service to what was actually an exploitation of colonies, while France genuinely had her colonies' interests in mind as Saussure's work had foretold decades before.[101]

In his early work on *Psychologie de la colonization Française*, Saussure had made a distinction between colony and possession categorizing India as a possession of Great Britain.[102] Furthermore, according to him character was paramount to determining the quality of civilization and life. It was the specific British character that allowed 60,000 English to rule over 250 million Hindus, who were no less than them in intelligence and by far surpassed them in artistic sense and philosophical views.[103] It was not religion that constituted civilization but the hereditary mental characteristics of a race. In India, for example, Islam had not freed Muslims from practising caste, or even a form of Islam closer to Brahmanism than Islam. Mohammad was worshipped in idol form, the mosque was akin to a temple, etc.[104] In France, the doctrine of assimilation took into account the racial characteristics of each colony and allowed the colony to preserve its culture and way of life. Domination alone could not achieve colonization as was seen from the example of 1857. The policy of assimilation ensured the civilizing effects of colonization without destroying colonial culture. Assimilation was primarily achieved through education, institutions (such as

---

[101] Léopold de Saussure. *Psychologie de la colonization Française. Dans ses rapports avec les sociétés indigenes* (Paris, 1899).

[102] Ibid: 19.

[103] Ibid: 48.

[104] Ibid: 59.

political institutions for democracy, administration, and justice) and language. This last point was hammered home in the volume by Isaac and Malet in many ways. Noting that the colonial policy of England varied in each country, the authors pointed out that while colonies with a dominant European population like Canada and Australia were governed benevolently, other colonies were much oppressed and the natives were subjected to a rigorous tutelage. In countries with a long history like India and Egypt, this had led to a violent nationalist agitation which had forced the English to grant some concessions. According to them,

> Generally, England was liberal with regard to the colonies where the European element dominated.... With regard to the other colonies, the English policy was more oppressive; the natives were subjected to a rigorous supervision. From there, in the countries of ancient civilizations like India and Egypt, a violent nationalist agitation obliged England to make concessions....[105]

Indeed, these textbooks provided official confirmation to the views prevalent in the popular press about the vicious colonial policies of the British. After recounting the efforts of the British to improve the social and economic conditions of the Indians by combating famines and floods, they noted nevertheless that, 'but these measures were impotent to make the plague disappear which, periodically, decimated the population. The famine of 1899–1900 had four million

---

[105] 'D'une façon générale, l'Angleterre s'est montrée libérale à l'égard des colonies où dominé l'élément européen....A l'égard des autres colonies, la politique anglaise a été plus oppressive; les indigènes ont été soumis à une tutelle rigoureuse. De là, dans les pays de civilisations ancienne comme l'Inde et l'Égypte, une violent *agitation nationaliste* qui a obligé l'Angleterre à des concessions....',Isaac and Malet, *Cours abrégé d'histoire*: 247.

victims.'[106] Moreover, while education was encouraged and developed, 'it is neither free nor obligatory and, consequently, hardly gave results.'[107] On the other hand, education was free in French India until the secondary level with the *écoles primaries, écoles centrales,* and *collèges* teaching in the French medium.[108]

The French colonial policy on the other hand was characterized by 'la *mise en valeur*' whereby France actively worked for the economic development of her colonies.

In addition, it is necessary [for France] to practise, with respect to the indigenous populations, *a policy of education, of collaboration and of friendship* which creates insoluble bonds between the colonies and the metropolis: thus will constitute [themselves in] the world of 'new France' which will be the best representation of old France (original italics).[109]

As the protagonist of Rousselet's *Le Charmeur des Serpents,* André, declared to his faithful servant,

...it must be confessed that we Europeans are the cause of all these frightful calamities. One thing, however, consoles me, which is, that the French, my ancestors, when they

---

[106] 'mais ces mesures ont été impuissantes à faire disparaître le fléau qui, périodiquement, décimé la population. La famine de 1899–1900 a fait *quatre millions de victimes.*' Malet and Isaac. *XIX siècle. Histoire contemporaine, 1815–1920*: 915.

[107] 'il n'est ni gratuit ni obligatoire et, par suite, n'a guère donné de résultats.' Ibid.

[108] Preeti Chopra, 'Pondicherry: A French Enclave in India', in *Forms of Dominance. On the Architecture and Urbanism of the Colonial Enterprise,* edited by Nezar AlSayyad (Aldershot and Brookfield: Avebury, 1992): 117.

[109] 'D'autre part, il lui faut pratiquer, vis-à-vis des populations indigènes, une *politique d'éducation, de collaboration et d'amitié* qui crée entre les colonies et la métropole des liens indissolubles: ainsi se constitueront dans le monde des <<Frances nouvelles>> qui seront le meilleur soutien de l'ancienne France.' Albert Malet and Jules Isaac. *Cours abrégé d'histoire* Second edition: 309.

were masters of India for a time, knew how to rule with a light hand and make themselves beloved of their subjects.

To which his servant Mali replied, 'Quite true the French were not masters, but brothers, and their memory has always been held dear. All India still deplores their departure.'[110] While French newspapers reported the progress of the Independence movement, and particularly the role of Gandhi with sympathy and commiseration,[111] the Parisian press noted with complacence that, the inhabitants of the Comptoirs, referred to as 'citoyens français' did not desire Independence from 'la mère patrie'.[112] According to the newspaper *Le Monde*,'they fear, perhaps not without reason, of not enjoying the same freedoms [in Independent India] which they benefit from in French India.'[113]

By the mid-nineteenth century, the second wave of French colonialism in the Far East and in Africa was contextualized within the Indian experience. On the one hand, India, and the French loss of an Indian empire, was cited repeatedly as an important lesson to French colonialists: 'Africa must not become for us a trading post like India.'[114] On the other hand, these advances would be 'a

---

[110] Louis Rousselet, *The Serpent Charmer* (New York: Charles Scribner's Sons, 1889): 266.

[111] See Kate Marsh, 'Representing Indian Decolonization in the Parisian Press 1923–54': 74–84.

[112] From *Le Monde*, 5 August 1947: 1–2. Quoted in ibid.: 82.

[113] 'ils craignent, non sans raison peut- être, de ne pas y en (en Inde independant) jouir des mêmes libertés dont ils bénéficients dans l'Inde française.'Ibid.

[114] '*l'Afrique ne doit pas être pour nous un comptoir comme l'Inde.*' Lucien-Anatole Prévost-Paradol, *La France Nouvelle*, Livre III: Quelques notions d'histoire nationale et quelques conseils à la generation présenté (Paris: Lévy, 1868): 417. Cited in Gibbs, 'The Exposition Coloniale of 1900: Representing and Forgetting l'Inde française'.

compensation for the loss of India'.[115] The French colonial enterprise could even demonstrate the true spirit of the *mission civilisatrice* to the British in India. In the coverage of the Revolt of 1857, Louis Jourdan wrote, 'England missed with [in] its duty.... This formidable teaching [lesson] should be lost neither for our allies, nor for we who fulfil in Algeria a role similar [analogous] to that of Great Britain in India.'[116] As Frith concludes,

> In short, the Indian mutinies are exploited as a narrative space in which French writing can not only imagine France as a preferable colonial power, but can offer as early as 1857 the [burgeoning] reality of 'French Algeria' as its rhetorical proof. Simultaneously, the apposition of *l'Afrique française* and *l'Inde anglaise* erases the memory of France's disappointed desires for India to which the presence of its marginalized Indian *comptoirs* continued to attest.[117]

Similarly, Indo-China was to fulfil France's thwarted destiny in India. As Camille Guy wrote, 'Our [Indochinese] empire has compensated for the losses of the last century.'[118] In fact, he went so far as to describe Dupleix, Lally and Mahé de la Bourdonnais as 'the direct ancestors

---

[115] *'une compensation de la perte de l'Inde.'* in reference to Indo-China. Publication de la Commission, *Exposition Universelle de 1900, Les Colonies françaises: un siècle de l'expansion coloniale* (Paris: Challamel, 1902): 16. Cited in Gibbs, 'The Exposition Coloniale of 1900: Representing and Forgetting l'Inde française'.

[116] *'L'Angleterre a manqué à son devoir...Ce formidable enseignement ne doit être perdu ni pour notre alliée, ni pour nous qui remplissons en Algérie un rôle analogue à celui de la Grande-Bretagne dans l'Inde.'* Louis Jourdan, 'Esclavage', *Le Siècle*, 16 and 17 August, 1857. Cited in Frith, ' "Natural and Necessary Enemies"': 4.

[117] Ibid.: 5.

[118] *'notre empire (Indo-Chinois) a compensé pour les pertes du dernier siècle.'* Camille Guy, *Exposition Universelle de 1900, Les colonies françaises: Les établissements français de l'Inde* (Paris: Levé, 1900): 1. Quoted in Gibbs, 'The Exposition Coloniale of 1900: Representing and Forgetting l'Inde française'.

and educators of Francis Garnier, Doudart de Lagrée and Coubert in Indochina.'[119] Guy, an enthusiastic proponent of colonial expansion and the *mise en valeur*, was the head of the geographical service of the Ministry of Colonies.[120] He was also the author of the handbook on the Indian *Comptoirs* for the 1900 *Exposition coloniale*, demonstrating the close link between the production and the dissemination of information about India.[121] Further, according to him, '...the Indo-Chinese Empire will console France for the Indian Empire, conquered by Dupleix and Lally-Tollendal and lost by the Government of Louis XV.'[122] In *'L'Affaire Myngoon Min ou les tribulations d'un prince birman entre rivalités imperialists et entente cordiale* (1884–1921)', Karine Delaye notes the tension between Anglo-French colonial lobbies in the latter half of the nineteenth century, particularly with the increasing French presence in South East Asia.[123] The idea of revenge, of avenging French loss in India, by conquering the Indo-Chinese peninsula, was the central aim of French colonialists. Labelling this 'the Dupleix syndrome', the notion that France had unfinished business in India was a persistent element in French colonial writings. Pointing to several references to 'l'Inde perdue', the sentiment that England had snatched India

---

[119] '*les ancêstres directs et les éducateurs de Francis Garnier, Doudart de Lagrée et Coubert en Indo-Chine.*' *Ibid.*: 13.

[120] Camille Guy, *Les colonies françaises: la mise en valeur de notre domaine coloniale*. This was volume III of *Les Colonies françaises*, Exposition Universelle de 1900, Publications de la Commission.ᶜhargée de préparer la participation de la Ministère des Colonies (Paris: Augustin Challamel, 1900). He later became the Lieutenant-Governor of Senegal (1903–5) French Guinea (1910–12).

[121] Guy, *Exposition Universelle de 1900, Les colonies françaises*.

[122] Camille Guy, 'French Colonial Expansion in the Nineteenth Century', *The International Monthly* (July–December 1901) Vol IV: 527.

[123] Karine Delaye, 'L'Affaire Myngoon Min ou les tribulations d'un prince birman entre rivalités imperialists et entente cordiale (1884–1921)' in *Les Relations entre la France et l'Inde de 1673 à nos jours*. Edited by Jacques Weber (Paris: Les indes savantes, 2002): 181.

away from the French, and the feeling of avenging Dupleix ('jusqu'à ce que nous ayons vengé Dupleix et affirmé notre savoir faire en matière coloniale'), the French empire in Indo-China was spurred by the need, after 1870, to redress her defeat in India.[124]

Penny Edwards has studied the results of the intense sense of loss which the French felt over India and manifested itself in French constructions of Indo-China, particularly the temple of Angkor Vat, which became a site for the exercise of fantasies of what *Inde* could have become under French rule.[125] According to Edwards,

> Through on-site renovation and global representations, the construction of Angkor both as site of memory and a site for the exercise of fantasies of what Inde could have become under French rule...saw the celebration and elaboration of a Hindu heritage for Angkor, within the schema of past glory [which the French Protectorate would restore], and the construction of a Buddhist religion for Cambodge, construed through the prism of contemporary degeneracy [from which French scholarship would rescue it].[126]

She points out that the very impetus for protecting and preserving monuments in Indochina was begun by Indologists, who initially constructed Angkor as the French preservation of Hinduism in stark contrast to the British desecration of Indian monuments. As a monument to *l'Inde Perdue*,[127] Angkor was frequently compared to the Taj Mahal in India, the constant emphasis remaining on the role of the French in preserving the culture of Indo-China.

---

[124] Ibid.: 182.

[125] Penny Edwards, 'Taj Angkor: Enshrining *l'Inde* in le *Cambodge*, Paper presented at 'Indochina', India and France: Cultural Representations, University of Newcastle upon Tyne, Newcastle, England, 5–7 September 2003): 3.

[126] Ibid.

[127] Marcel Dubois, Preface in *Empire Colonial de la France: L'Indochine* (Paris: Librairie Coloniale Augustin Challamel, s.d): ix.

Colonial officials, newspapers and administrators openly expressed their belief that Britain was only exploiting India and that France would have made a far more sympathetic and enlightened ruler. The French resentment over India was especially clear once she had colonized Indo-China. While the anxiety of British officials that the French conquest of Indo-China would constitute a challenge to their own Indian Empire had been well-documented[128] it also sharpened the colonial rivalry with Britain. Beginning with philologist and explorer Henri Mouhot's plea to France in 1860 to add Angkor to her imperial glories before the British could snatch it away as they had done in India,[129] to the report of the *Saigon Courier* gleefully reporting the discomfiture of the British in 1864 at having to watch their precious Indian empire being threatened by the Tricoleur in Indo-China,[130] the contestation for colonial pasts and the French humiliation in India was played out in the construction of Indo-Chine as a Buddhist land.

In the twentieth century, the Anglo-French rivalry was echoed in the British resentment at the French insistence on 'harbouring Indian nationalists who were exiled from British India'. The *Morning Post* of 14 January 1909, wrote

---

[128] S. P. Sen describes some of these attempts by individual French to launch military campaigns to regain French territory and empire in India. He also documents the correspondence between British officials in India and the Directors of the East India Company in London, particularly the British unease with French colonial gains in Indo-China which would constitute a challenge to their Indian empire. See S. P. Sen, *The French in India, 1763–1816* (Delhi: Munshiram Manoharlal, 1971). For French attempts to regain India see Jean Marie Lafont, *La présence française dans le royaume sikh du Penjab: 1822–49* (Paris : École française d'Extrême-Orient, 1992), and *Indika. Essays in Indo-French Relations 1630–1976* (New Delhi: Manohar, 2000).

[129] Penny Edwards, 'Taj Angkor: Enshrining *l'Inde* in le *Cambodge*, Paper presented at 'Indochina', India and France: Cultural Representations, University of Newcastle upon Tyne, Newcastle, England, 5–7 September 2003): 2.

[130] Ibid. : 4. Cited from 'Comment Angkor fut révélé au grand public', *Courrier de Saïgon*, 10 February 1864.

that 'the anarchist agitation in India which causes intense concern to the British government, is probably directed from Paris' and the *Madras Times* of 12 November 1910 marked Pondichéry as a refuge for the most dangerous malcontents of British India.[131] Pondichéry also became the headquarters of Sri Aurobindo, who, exiled from British India as a result of his seditious activities, first fled to Chandernagore after his acquittal in the Alipur Bomb case of 1908 and then sought refuge in Pondichéry. It was from here that he directed various operations in British India and eventually, decided to renounce his worldly life and retreat into spiritualism. He founded an ashram or retreat for like-minded people and his first 'foreign' disciple, was Sylvain Lévi. Eventually the working of the Ashram was taken over by a Frenchwoman, who preferred to be called 'Mother', and who remained the head of the Ashram until her death in 1973. Indo-French relations continued to be based on mutual admiration especially with the founding of the Friends of France Society in India and the Franco-Indian Committee of 8 April 1914 which implicitly recognized India as a free nation. Subramania Bharathi also went to Pondichéry after his press was raided in 1908 and continued to publish the Tamil weekly *India* which had news of radical nationalists, for the next 18 months from Pondichéry. Pondichéry was also the port of entry for nationalist literature from nationalists abroad which was then smuggled into British India.

CONCLUSION

The histories of India which were written in France at the end of the nineteenth century provided a convenient

---

[131] Cited in Emmanuelle Ortoli, 'The Time of Friendship', *L'Aventure des Français en Inde. XVII–XX siècles*. Edited by In Rose Vincent (Kailash Editions: 1995). Translated in English as *The French in India: from Diamond Traders to Sanskrit Scholars* (Bombay: Popular Prakashan, 1990): 146.

space to articulate French desires in India as well as colonial rivalries with England. The fact that these sentiments were incorporated into school textbooks demonstrates the strength of such desires and the manner in which they were inculcated in the minds of ordinary French boys and girls, as well as the subjects of France's vast colonial empire.

Duruy's themes revolved around the issue of the Aryan origins. He believed that the Aryans had created all that was great in Indian civilization: language, customs, and institutions. The degenerated condition that contemporary India found herself in was due to centuries of racial dilution, a theory easily traced to the influence of anthropologists like Le Bon.

Isaac and Malet addressed themselves directly to the colonial enterprise and denounced Britain's role in impoverishing and ravishing India. Stressing that France would have made a fitter ruler, they underscored both the heightened colonial aims of France under Jules Ferry as well as the continued resentment at losing India to the British. Although France had no plans to actually recoup India, the sense of loss translated into a particularly rancorous commentary against the British Raj.

In contrast to these French histories of India, the image of India in British history textbooks from 1890–1914 was that of an unruly, impoverished and motley collection of small kingdoms and principalities, which had been developed and rescued from their deplorable plight by the effort of the British. Like the French, British school texts were written according to a centrally created syllabus.[132] Kathryn Castle, who has studied the representation of India in British history textbooks notes that the primary goal of these school texts was to impress young children with their duty towards maintaining the Britain's imperial presence

---

[132] See Richard Aldrich, 'Imperialism in the Study and Teaching of History', in *'Benefits bestowed?': Education and British Imperialism*, edited by J.A. Mangan (Manchester: Manchester University Press, 1988).

in India.[133] To that end the history of India prior to British rule was described only in passing, and as a period of time when the chaos and decay in India was arrested only with British intervention. The British in taking over from the oppressive and debauched native princes, provided India with peace and stable government. Any challenge to British authority (particularly the Rebellion of 1857) was represented as the natural unruliness and resistance of native Indian nature to civilized government. The achievement of British administration in providing a stable, prosperous, and modern life to Indians was emphasized.

Indians like Dayanand Saraswati, Tilak, Gandhi and even Ram Mohun Roy, writing accounts of India in the nineteenth and early twentieth centuries accepted French paradigms of a degenerate caste system, glorious Aryan past, decline of Sanskrit as expressed in the contemporary vernaculars of India, all of which could be rectified by a 'return' to the older Aryan civilization. I oppose the suggestion by scholars like Chetan Bhatt,[134] and Peter van der Veer[135] that Indians were influenced by British studies on Aryanism to conceptualize a revisionist notion of India as returning to a mythic Aryan past in order to recapture the glory of a previous age. Rather, this notion was developed *in opposition* to British works on the degeneration of India, and found support in German and French works on Aryanism. German works were by and large romantic in their paeans to the Vedic origins of the Aryan race. French works actu-

---

[133] Kathryn Castle, *Britannia's Children* (Manchester: Manchester University Press, 1996); and Kathryn Castle, 'The Imperial Indian: India in British History Textbooks for Schools, 1890–1914' in *The Imperial Curriculum: Racial Images and Education in the British Colonial Experience*, edited by J. A. Mangan (London and New York: Routledge, 1993).

[134] Chetan Bhatt, *Hindu Nationalism: Origins, Ideologies and Modern Myths* (Oxford: Berg Publishers, 2001).

[135] Peter van der Veer, *Imperial Encounters: Religion and Modernity in India and Britain* (Princeton: Princeton University Press, 2001).

ally described the process by which the Aryans in India had apparently become degenerate owing variously to racial intermarriage, climate and inferior cultural traditions of indigenous (defined as Dravidian) peoples. In terms of providing a call to action, the French works allowed Indians who dreamed of a return to the Vedic greatness of India a tangible method, a method that has become associated with the radical Hindu movement of *'Hindutva'*.[136] The French connection to Hindutva has become stronger with the adoption of Sri Aurobindo as a champion of the Vedic heritage movement.

Simultaneously, British-educated Indians like the early leaders of the Indian National Congress (moderates like Dadabhai Naoroji, W. C. Bonnerji and Baddruddin Tyabji) internalized and propagated clichés of corrupt, inept local rulers, the need for India to modernize according to British-defined standards of industrialization and Western education, as well as the notion that inbuilt divisions of caste, race and religion among Indians was only overcome with the central government and administration of the British. Among many modern Indian historians, the fear of appearing revisionist or sectarian leads them to adopt a hyper-critical stance towards the Indian past and particularly caste, as stagnant and backwards. For these scholars, development can only be made by adopting a Western standard of progress, measured in technological terms as well as India's ability to conform to international linguistic and cultural norms. The perpetuation of English as the language of rule and of a westernized mode of behaviour is implicit in the process of conforming.

History textbooks provide a good view of the image of India. French images were drawn from more than a

---

[136] See for example, Antony Copley, *Hinduism in Public and Private Reform, Hindutva, Gender, and Sampraday* (Oxford: OUP, 2009) and Jyotirmaya Sharma, *Hindutva: Exploring the Idea of Hindu Nationalism* (New Delhi: Penguin, 2003).

century of Indic traditions in France. The depiction of India in these textbooks clung obstinately to certain images such as the romantic view of India as a great civilization while simultaneously presenting contemporary India in a state of degeneration. The contradictions in these images do not seem to have bothered Duruy or Isaac and Malet. India in nineteenth-century France had served so many purposes that it was impossible to reconcile all of them to a logical image of India. Moreover, the understanding of India as a mass of contradictions could be admirably harnessed to support different theories. India was thus presented as a great culture *in theory*. In ancient times, she had achieved much great thought and philosophy. India in the contemporary period suffered from many ailments; some such as the tyranny of caste were social evils brought about by racial dilution. The other major evil was the oppressive and exploitative rule of the British.

In contrast, British textbooks sought to highlight the civilizing mission in India. Both traditions of writing have had their impact not just on how the West views India, but on how India views herself.

The conclusion moves the debate on the construction of India into the public sphere. A comparison of India at the Imperial Exhibition of Wembley in 1924–25 and at the Exposition coloniale of Paris in 1931 provides not just a summary of the themes of the previous chapters, but also a vicarious jaunt into the heart of the public conceptions of India in Britain and France.

IMAGE 7.1: L'Inde coloniale

Source: Atlas Général Larousse. Paris: Librairie Larousse, 1959. The same map
is incorporated in Isaac and Malet's history textbooks: Isaac and Malet, *Histoire
contemporaine, depuis le milieu du XIX siècle'*. Paris: Colin, 1918. 2nd edition,
and Albert Malet and Jules Isaac. *Cours abrégé d'histoire* Second edition. Paris:
Librairie Hachette, 1922.

Chapter 8

Imperial Showcase: The Visual Presentation of 'India'

Few countries in the world, without doubt, hold the spirit of 'mysterious India'. Few countries possess such attraction and magnetism.[1]

India was significant for the French notion of colony and Empire. Despite possessing a mere handful of outposts in India surrounded by the might of the British Raj, the French India Establishments retained an identity of 'Frenchness', defiant in the face of Anglican *sahibdom*. This book has examined the presence of India in the French academic sphere during the nineteenth century. This chapter explores the problematic representation of India in the International Colonial Exhibition, held in Paris in 1931, specifically in the context of the clear construction of India as devoid of British rule.

The grand Colonial Exhibition, held in Paris from 6 May to 15 November 1931 celebrated France's accomplishments in civilizing the 'noble savage'. Portugal, the Netherlands, Belgium, Denmark, Italy and the United States joined France in this unashamed showcase of empire. The only colonial power missing was Britain, financially unable to participate after her own aggrandizing Colonial Exhibition at Wembley in 1924–25 and reluctant moreover, to play second fiddle to France's demonstration of colonial might.

---

[1] 'Les Établissements français de l'Inde', *L'Illustration* (19 September 1931).

Germany had been stripped of its colonies after World War I, and Japan was only starting out on her colonial venture. The 1931 Exhibition was the last great demonstration of colonial power, attracting more than 33 million entries from France and abroad.

The mastermind behind the brave showing at Vincennes was Maréchal Lyautey who envisaged two larger goals for the Exhibition: the promotion of French industrial and business investment in the colonies and the raising of French public awareness of their nation's colonial grandeur. National pride was at stake and the exhibition was meant to counter the image of the lethargic French who cared nothing for their colonial holdings.[2] It was an effort to galvanize the French public to participate in the colonial effort.

The representation of India at the International Colonial Exhibition of 1931 was really a microcosm of France's attitudes and policy towards the French settlements in India and of greater India as a cultural entity. Despite having lost her principal Indian empire to Britain in the late eighteenth century, France continued to retain certain outposts for the prestige of possessing parts of India within her colonial empire. While the French comptoirs were certainly prosperous, they were by no means comparable to French colonies like Algeria or Indo-China in terms of the geographical extent of rule. It seems probable therefore, that the primary aim of France in showcasing her India posts to a far greater degree than their actual importance to French colonial interest warranted, was due to the ideological need to define 'Frenchness' in the colonial context, as an enlightened colonial power that truly cared about her colonies and made genuine efforts to develop them philanthropically and raise their people to a 'civilized' level.[3]

---

[2] Patricia Morton, 'National and Colonial: the Musée des colonies at the Colonial Exposition Paris 1931', *Art Bulletin*, 80 (June 1998): 357.

[3] This was the crucial ideological component of French colonial policy and the key to Anglo-French colonial rivalry.

The *Exposition coloniale internationale de Paris* elaborated a world view of 'Greater France'. Indigenous buildings were reconstructed along French avenues of order, marking the unity of French progress and colonial exoticism in an exhibition that constructed a particular understanding of the French colonial empire.[4] Hailed as the *apothéose de la plus grande France*, the Exposition featured pavilions from all its various colonies and depots. The highpoints of the colonial exhibit were the reproductions of Angkor Vat, Sudanese earth buildings and the North African Casbah. Watching benevolently over these was the *palais d'exposition*, the headquarters of the French exhibition of colonies. The colonial pavilions showcased French colonial achievements as *la plus grande France*—an attempt to rival 'Greater Britain'. Yet the central puppeteer was the *palais*. The colonial pavilions were placed along French avenues just as the French had attempted to re-construct the French *quartiers* in their colonies by blending indigenous architectural styles with the broad principles of French town planning, broad avenues and open spaces.[5]

India was represented in many ways at the 1931 Exhibition, structurally, culturally, politically and economically. Structurally, India was represented through two pavilions: the Establishments of French India as part of the French global colonial presence, and the pavilion of Hindustan. Culturally, events such as the Hindu dance night, operas reflecting Indian influence, films, paintings, and frescoes depicting India, the arts and crafts of India and even Indian cuisine formed a solid corpus of a typically Indian experience.

---

[4] Panivong Norindr, 'La Plus Grande France', *Identity Papers. Contested Nationhood in Twentieth-century France*, edited by Steven Ungar and Tom Conley (Minneapolis and London: University of Minneapolis Press, 1996): 324.

[5] Ibid.: 235–36.

The Commissariat of French India was constituted by a decree in 1927 by the planning committee for the *Exposition Coloniale Internationale* and headed by M. Ginestou, Commissaire. M. Gaudart, the adjoint engineer to the public works of Colonies, was Adjoint Commissaire.[6] In October 1931, M. Gaudart left for India and was replaced by M. Raoux.

Although the pavilion did not have any other official or administrative support, a local Indian committee composed of volunteers helped during the duration of the Exposition.[7] It is not recorded whether the committee was composed of French residents in India or of Indians, or even a mix of both. In any case the representation of French India was a significant insight into the opinion of the inhabitants of French India of their colonial masters. Despite being a considerably exoticized version of India, there seems to have been complete collaboration on the part of the committee, and that there was no criticism by Indian visitors to the pavilion like the disgust expressed by Egyptian visitors for the similarly exoticized representation of their land speaks of the high regard for the French in India.

The site for the India pavilion was chosen bordering on the greater French colonies and in the vicinity of the ancient colonies.[8] Even though the significance of the French India Posts in terms of France's colonial empire was modest, the size and location of the pavilion

---

[6] *Rapport Général de Exposition Coloniale Internationale de 1931,* présenté par Gouverner Général Olivier (Paris: Imprimérie Nationale, 1933), Vol.V, part II: 613.

[7] Ibid.: 614.

[8] Ibid.: 615. This statement leads me to view with suspicion Patricia Morton's statement that the colonial pavilions were scattered with no apparent regard to geography or manner or period of acquisition. In fact, this superficial disregard of logical systems of planning may have been a deliberate attempt of the planners of the Exposition to impress the viewer with the diversity and the vastness of the French colonial presence.

representing India implied otherwise. Entering from the *Cité des Informations*, the visitor to the Exposition would have been whisked off to the *Grande Avenue des Colonies Français*, upon which the pavilion of *Indes Français* was the second on the left. While it was only a modest 20 m by 6 m, the pavilion was placed in clear view and would have been among the first that the visitor would have seen. It was larger than many older colonies like the pavilions of Martinique and Guadeloupe and had an enormous number of visitors. The average was calculated based on estimates made 10 times each month for the duration of the Exposition and totalled 40,000 people during the week and between 60,000–75,000 on Sunday.[9] The official record of the Exposition notes that the pavilion was allocated two guards and no untoward incident occurred during the six months of the Exposition.[10]

The pavilion was allocated a very modest budget, which precluded the hosting of fêtes, or other celebrations other than those organized by the central committee for the Exposition. However, India was a prominent cultural presence during the Exposition. Represented in the fine arts display as well as the displays of songs and dances, India was also a theme of the films shown at the Exposition. Among the various conferences held during the Exposition under the aegis of the Commissariat, India was the sole subject of one held under the presidency of Gouverneur Général Olivier.[11] The conference appears to have been well attended and was distinguished by the presence of Senator M. le Moignac.[12] The pavilion was also

[9] Ibid.: 624.

[10] Ibid.

[11] This conference was in addition to the numerous conferences discussing the resources, cultural, religious and moral progress of French colonies where French India was also studied.

[12] Moignac was India's representative in the French Senate. *Le Livre d'Or de l'Exposition Coloniale Internationale de Paris, 1931* (Paris: Librarie ancienne Honoré Champion, 1931): 175.

highly visible in the awards that the Exhibition officials made to various categories of products and artefacts displayed by the colonies.

Inaugurated on 22 May 1931, the rose-coloured pavilion consisted of three rooms, devoted in turn to India's arts, economy and history. One entered the pavilion by way of a grand entrance, which was flanked by sculptures of two huge white elephants (Image 8.1) These sculptures were unprecedented in Indian architecture and evocative more of a temple entrance than the entrance to a Hindu house, which was the aim of the Commissaire. Represented with huge tusks, these male elephants were yet calm and submissive, domesticated and docile creatures much in the manner of actual temple elephants used even today in temples in South India. They were adorned with tassels and brocades. The first impression of the pavilion of French India was of these huge, benign creatures flanking the entrance to a flat-roofed one-storey house topped by a small tower.

The temple-like appearance of the pavilion was further heightened by the construction of a flat roof and a small tower over the entrance, very much like the *gopuram* entrances to temples, and by the ornate pillars supporting the roof (Images 8.2 and 8.3). The most striking aspect of the interior of the pavilion was the central sculpture of the interior courtyard—Shiva as Nataraja, the Prince of Dancers (Image 8.4). Presumably, Lyautey's directives to interpret loosely the architecture of a typical Hindu house were taken rather literally to present an exoticised version of the Hindu house as a cross between the interior of a well-to-do Hindu house with rooms constructed around a central courtyard, and the exterior, which was almost entirely the façade of a local temple except for the scale and grandeur on which it was built, which was less ornate than a normal temple. The rose-coloured pavilion, constructed by the firm of M. M. Girves was also constructed to serve the needs of a museum (Image 8.5).

It is significant that the reproduction of palaces, buildings and villages at the Exposition were almost always designed by European or American architects, not by the inhabitants of the colonies, even if native materials and craftsmen were used. All sorts of liberties were taken with indigenous styles to fit the demands of the exhibitions.[13] In the case of the French India pavilion this was certainly true. The pavilion represented neither a temple nor a domestic residence. The architectural elements which were chosen to be incorporated into this 'authentic' representation of India were strictly from the point of view of maximizing the exotic quality of the pavilion while providing a logical pattern for examining its interior.

A verandah, enveloped in green palms greeted visitors. The verandah contained a 'poyal', a largish swing which was meant for high-caste Hindus to greet lower caste visitors to their home so that the interior would not be defiled. Ritual lamps provided light to the verandah during the evening and night. The European visitor to the pavilion was free from all cultural restrictions which may have been imposed upon them in India. The visitor to the pavilion was permitted a view into the life of high-caste Indians that even lower caste Indians presumably did not have. They could bypass the disagreeable restrictions of caste to experience the full beauty and skill of India.

As Demaison instructed the visitor to the India Pavilion,

All is ritual and caste in India. You are not a stranger or of an inferior caste—walk right in to the centre of the house, to the historical room of high interest, to the commercial room where you will find the artistic products of India— jewellery, brocades, furniture, ivory, precious gems and other artefacts of this civilization older than ours, a splendid civilization where gold, gems, ivory and precious wood

---

[13] Burton Benedict 'International Exhibitions and National Identity', *Anthropology Today*, Vol. 7.3 (June 1991): 7.

are fashioned into delicate and magnificent fantasies by the Hindu artisans.[14]

Each of the three rooms in the interior of the pavilion was painted with frescoes to heighten the effect of the themes of the room. The first, the artistic room, was painted by M. Montassier, who represented scenes from Hindu mythology to form a harmonious ensemble with the figures of Gods and divinities. He depicted, among others, Brahma with four hands and heads holding the four Vedas, four-headed Vishnu with his conch, lotus and discus, Shiva in all his forms (including the *Ardhanari*: half-man, half-woman), *Trimurti* (associated with the forms of Shiva, Vishnu, Brahma), Kali, Goddess of Destruction and Death as an old woman riding on a tiger with a garland of skulls, and Ganesha, son of Shiva and Parvati with an elephant-head and accompanied by his *vahana* (chariot), the rat.[15] Thousands of Gods and Goddesses in wood, in bronze and marble and mostly produced by the school of arts and industries of Pondichéry added to the richness of the room. The final touch to the room was the display of Indian jewellery; intricate patterns designed in emeralds, gold, silver, diamonds, for which Indian artisans were world-famous, complementing the granite structures of the pavilion perfectly.

On the left was the commercial room. The room was painted by M. Portevin, and was less classical and freer, representing scenes of agriculture and industry. The room displayed the agricultural and industrial products of French India: cotton, jute, copper objects of domestic and religious use, choir mats, precious and exquisite textiles which affirmed the centuries of progress in Indian weaving,

---

[14] André Demaison, *A Paris en 1931. Exposition Coloniale Internationale 'Votre Guide'* (Paris: Editions Mayeux, 1931): 47.

[15] *Rapport Général*, Vol. 5, part II: 619. Quoted from *Le Monde illustré*, numéro de septembre 1931.

reptile skins, shells, essences, cereals, oils, conserves, and examples of the exotic foods of India and of industrial production. Among the new activities of women was an important contribution of beautiful lace and needlework items, for domestic and decorative use, done under the teaching of the Sisters of Saint-Joseph of Cluny in Pondichéry.[16]

One entered on the right by the historical room—rich and precious souvenirs, parchments and maps, engravings and local archival curiosities. Among the treasures of the room were the plans of Pondichéry, dated between 1700 and 1720, loaned by the bureau of the Archives of the Ministry of Colonies.[17] M. Poisson, painter of the room, had represented scenes from the history of the French conquest of India. He was also the installer of the precious objects from the colonies and the invaluable art treasures from the collection of M. Loo.[18]

The blue ceiling of the whole pavilion was decorated by M. Lafitte, the decoration and interior by Claude Salvy, the magnificent floral decoration by M. Nonin and exotic trees of the horticulturist Dupoux.[19] The most striking aspect of the interior of the pavilion was the central sculpture of the interior courtyard—Shiva as Nataraja, the Prince of Dancers. This sculpture was loaned to the Commissaire from the collection of M. Loo and left an indelible impression on the visitor of the colourful nature of Indian culture and religion.

Interestingly, most of the artefacts represented in the French India pavilion were not truly 'Indian' in any sense of the word. They certainly did not represent the work of Indian craftsmen. Many of the contributions that comprised the life of the pavilion were by Frenchmen. The exhibit on Indian jewellery was by M. Charpentier, paintings by

---

[16] Ibid.: 620.
[17] Ibid.: 620.
[18] Ibid.: 617.
[19] Ibid.: 619.

Montassier, Portevin and Poisson, elephants by Magrou, ceiling decoration by Lafitte, interior decoration by Salvy, and the floral decoration by Nonin, all of these purporting to represent the true Indian style.[20] Charpentier was even awarded a medal for his production of 'Indian' jewellery. Except for a few examples of crafts produced by the artisanal workshops at Pondichéry and by the women of Pondichéry under the tutelage of the Sisters of Saint-Joseph of Cluny, most of the arts and crafts in the pavilion were by French contributors. Significantly enough, even the two workshops representing the work of the Indians were institutions that had been established by the colonial government for the education and development of Indians. Even the division of the pavilion into three rooms was a French categorization. According to Breckenridge, a collection ordered India's unruly and disorderly *past*, and at the same time it pointed to India's present by ordering her unruly and disorderly *practices*. A collection also created an illusion of control for the colonial masters, in their orderly categorization and compartmentalization.[21] A 'traditional' Indian home would not have been divided up into these compartments.

The pavilion was highly visible in the awards that the Exposition officials made to various categories of products and artefacts displayed by the colonies. The people exhibiting their wares in the pavilion won a total of 16 medals: four grand prizes, two gold medals, six silver and five bronze. Collaborators and those who had contributed to decorating the pavilion also won 10: two *diplômes d'honneur*, two gold, four silver and two bronze medals. Among the winners was the School of Arts and Industries in Pondichéry, Edmond Gaudart and others.[22]

---

[20] Ibid.: 625.

[21] Carol Breckenridge 'The Aesthetics and Politics of Colonial Collecting: India at World Fairs', *Comparative Study of Society and History*, 31.2 (April 1989): 209.

[22] *Rapport Général*, Vol. 5, part II: 625.

The pavilion of French India was the main representation of Indian life. However, there were other exhibits, and cultural performances that provided the visitor with a range of 'India images' (Image 8.6). The *Section Retrospective* at the *Musée des Colonies* was a great aide to discovering the life and history of the French India establishments and especially that of Pondichéry. Prof. Jouveau-Dubreuil, an eminent Indologist was the brain behind the exhibit which included a remarkable collection of objects, engravings, tableaux and other artefacts of the history of French colonialism in India. These objects were original artefacts transported to the *Musée* from India under the supervision of the professor to represent the artistic and historical accomplishments of French India.[23] The display included a reproduction of a room in French India from the time of Dupleix. The Commissariat of the *Séction Retrospective* also sponsored a programme on 28 October 1931 in the *salles des fêtes* of the *Musée permanent des Colonies* that included fragments of the musical *Les Indes galantes* from the time of Dupleix, composed by Rameau and conducted by Poulet as well as performances of music and dance by Indians.[24]

Other expressions of Indian culture were provided by the Hindu night, which formed one of the many *nuits coloniales* that were among the highlights of the Exposition. The performance by the dancer Mme. Nyoka Inyota of Bengali dances was the highlight of the *nuit hindoue*. Ironically Mme Inyota was not herself Indian. However, she was a prominent expression of the performing arts during the Exposition and made several appearances on 8 July 1931 in the presence of the President of the Republic and other members of Government as part of a grand soirée,[25] and other receptions for foreign dignitaries visiting the Exposition.[26] Other expressions of Indian performing arts

---

[23] Ibid.: 134.
[24] Ibid.: 145.
[25] *Rapport Général*, Vol. 4: 359.
[26] *Rapport Général*, Vol. 5, part I.

included a number of musical performances by Uday Shankar and his company.

Uday Shankar, older brother of the famous sitarist Ravi Shankar, placed Indian dance on the world map. While in London at the Royal College of Art, he choreographed two Indian ballets; 'Krishna and Radha' and 'A Hindu Wedding'. The first performance was held at Covent Garden in September 1923. He formed a troupe of 'Hindu dancers' from among his family and friends and on 31 March 1931 at the Theatre Champs-Elysées in Paris, he presented *Tandava Nritya* or the fearsome Dance of Death attributed to Shiva.

What Isadora Duncan and Martha Graham were to western dance, Shankar was to Indian dance forms. A breath of fresh air in the traditional, guru-disciple-dominated field of Indian dance, and performing both traditional and interpretive dances with finesse, Uday Shankar was the first Indian dancer and musician to open these fields to modern methods. He began a school of music, art and dance where students could learn the arts without being bound by the *gurukul* tradition of Indian education,[27] freeing the students from nepotism and opening up the fields of art to talent rather than family tradition. Shankar performed in the Exposition a number of times, including a programme sponsored by the Commissariat of the Section Retrospective

---

[27] The *gurukul* was the system of ancient learning. The pupil actually lived with the teacher for a period of some years, performing household tasks and learning simultaneously until the teacher decided that the former's education was complete. Although this system had become obsolete in India by the nineteenth century in formal education and Western forms of schooling were in vogue, the field of performing and applied arts still followed the old system of *gurukul* education. There are still some schools which operate on this basis, most notably, Tagore's University, Shanti Niketan. While the *gurukul* system had many advantages, there was a lack of exposure and multi-culturalism, the student being bound to learn the techniques of only one teacher which was what Shankar attempted to resolve by establishing an Academy of Dance in 1939.

on 28 October 1931 in the *salles des fêtes* of the *Musée permanent des Colonies*. Shankar's choices were an array of cultural interpretations that encompassed classical dances such as the *Tandava* dance and a musical rendering of *Raga Pahari*, a peasant dance, and even a sword dance performed by Uday Shankar and Simkie, a member of his troupe.[28]

Among colonial influences on French music, a number of Indian-inspired airs were performed at the Exposition. *Lakmé* by Léo Delibes, and the duet from the opera *Roi de Lahore* by Massenet, were among the musicals of Indian origin which were composed in the nineteenth century while fragments of Padmavati by Albert Roussel and the Hindu chant of Sadko conducted by Rimsky-Korsakov represented the influence of India on French music in the twentieth century. Two of the nine performances that represented colonial influences on French music in the nineteenth century were Indian, the majority of the remaining being Middle Eastern; while for the twentieth century, two from among 13 performances were Indian, while four were Middle Eastern, one Japanese, one Chinese, and two Indo-Chinese.[29]

India figured prominently among the expressions of the fine arts. The importance of the exhibition of colonial art was expressed in a letter by Lyautey to Emile Bayard, in the preface to the latter's book, *L'Art de Reconnaître les Styles Coloniaux de la France*.[30] The letter, dated 26 September 1930, praised Bayard for his efforts to educate the West about the thoughts, institutions, works and lives of the peoples of the Mediterranean, Africa and Asia through a study of their art. Lyautey pointed out that the civilization of a people could be defined by their art style and the knowledge of this was '*la condition de toute politique*

---

[28] *Rapport Général*, Vol. 5, part I: 145–46.

[29] Ibid.: 98.

[30] Emile Bayard, *L'Art de Reconnaître les Styles Coloniaux de la France* (Paris: Librarie Garnier Frères, 1931).

coloniale' [the main goal of colonial policy].[31] In addition to the frescoes decorating the interior of the Pavilion of French India and the sculptures of elephants flanking the entrance of the pavilion, art inspired by India was an attraction at the Palace of Fine Arts. The most prominent among these were paintings by Fouqueray—*le bain sacré, Côte de Malabar,* and *Le Port de Malabar*—who was renowned for his exotic paintings.[32] Among more eclectic selections were a series of paintings by Mlle Louise Hervieu who represented exotic themes of distant travel and longing for Oriental imagery in her images of India, *Mirage indien,* and *Bouddha.*[33] The *Salon du Maréchal,* also called the *Salon Lyautey* or *Salon de l'Asie* was decorated with panels representing Oriental religions and myths. Bayard emphasized the influence of religion on the art of the Orient and this was clear in the works included in the Salon.[34] The frescoes represented panels from the lives and teachings of Krishna, Buddha and Confucius. Other panels depicted scenes of Oriental music and drama. Painted by the Lemaître brothers, André-Hubert and Ivanna, the paintings were a relatively accurate depiction of the 'inscrutable Orient' of mysterious religions and complicated mythologies given the Lemaître's interest and understanding of Oriental religion.[35] The Exposition also screened a number of films at the *Cité des Informations.* Among 10 films on Asia, three were about India—*L'Ami hindoue, Mungo, Chasseur de serpents,* and *Les Indes mystérieuses*—while at least half were inspired by the culture of the subcontinent.[36]

---

[31] Ibid., preface: VIII.
[32] Ibid.: 433.
[33] Ibid.: 430.
[34] Ibid.: 4–5.
[35] Patricia Morton, 'National and Colonial: the Musée des colonies at the Colonial Exposition Paris 1931', *Art Bulletin,* 80 (June 1998): 372–73.
[36] *Rapport Général,* Vol. 6, part I: 323–24.

The element of exoticism, however, continued to dominate these representations of Indian culture as much as the pavilion. Mme Nyoka Inyota was not Indian and her dances represented a stylistic rendition of her interpretation of India. The paintings of India were produced by French artists, none of whom had even visited India. Films and music with Indian themes were created by directors and composers to whom India was by and large a mysterious, exotic construct. While I am not suggesting that the performance of a culture by one who is removed from it is necessarily Orientalist, the same becomes true when the performer uses a repertoire of secondary images and descriptions to depict that culture. Thus, the exposition of the French-Indian colonies in the *Palais des beaux-arts* was faithful to its original, having been supervised by Jouveau-Dubreil, who had spent several years in India learning about the culture of the land that he exhibited.

The representation of French India in the Exposition was a summation of the paradoxes in French colonial policy. French India was the epitome of the French policy of association. France had extended citizenship rights to her thereby confirming that she was truly interested in democratic associationism with her colonies rather than outright autocratic rule. While on the one hand, colonialism proceeded along the lines of the imperial conquest of the nineteenth century in that France sought to impose political and cultural hegemony over her colonies, France also claimed that her colonialism was actually different from the simple economic exploitation and Drain of Wealth[37]

---

[37] The Drain of Wealth Theory was first propounded by Dadabhai Nauroji, an early Indian nationalist, who pointed out that colonial exploitation was not merely composed of the visible economic drain through unequal trade, high tariffs and taxes. The Drain also took the form of payment by the colony for the administrative structure, payment of the salaries of British officials in India, remittances to Britain by these personnel and the creation and extension of India government bonds to these personnel.

since the political heritage of France was radically different from other colonial nations in Europe. French colonial ideology was developed along with and to accommodate the needs of French national identity in the nineteenth century. To this end, the former was different from the 'normal' process of colonial expansion since France had a republican, democratic foundation to national identity, which had to be extended, at least in theory, to her colonies in order to justify the *mission civilisatrice*. Albert Sarraut's *Mise en valeur des colonies françaises* published in 1923 claimed that 'What characterized its [France's] colonial policy and gives it its particular definition, is its sense of humanity; it proceeds essentially from the great idea of human solidarity.'[38]

The Pondichérians in French India, for example, were declared citizens of France and some of them continue to be citizens of France even though they are born and live their whole lives in India. The French policy of assimilation was extremely potent in shaping the loyalties of the Pondichérians to France and in creating a social group of 'foreigners' as Kristeva puts it, who owed their loyalties to France and yet remained beyond the pale of true 'Frenchness'. In terms of nationalism therefore, French India was an ideal example not only of the way in which it perceived itself as part of France but also how the French perceived French India.

The pavilion of *Indes Français* at the *Exposition Coloniale* of 1931 was meant to stand for the enlightened rule that France had provided to the French-Indian posts. Unlike the British, the French had not only disseminated the superior advantages of French language and culture in the posts, they had also successfully maintained and supported the indigenous cultures and achievements of the

---

[38] Albert Sarraut's *Mise en valeur des colonies françaises* (1923) Preface. Quoted in Raymond Betts, *Tricouleur: The French Overseas Empire* (Gordon and Cremonesi, 1978): 40.

Indians. French India could truly be cited as an example of *la mission civilisatrice*. The relative importance of the pavilion of *Indes Français* must be seen in the context of the fact that the 1931 Exposition stood as France's answer to Britain's Colonial Exhibition at Wembley in 1924–25. *Indes Français* was the perfect antithesis to the British Indian Empire, which by the 1930s was increasingly coming under attack not least so from the rising tide of Indian nationalism and demand for independence.

The Hindustan Pavilion was a late and intriguing addition to the Exhibition (Image 8.7). Apparently completely overlooked in the *Rapport Général* which was published in 1933, two years after the Exhibition and which therefore had no excuse to exclude even late additions, the pavilion does not seem to have had any official opening ceremony or any receptions, though these were a standard feature of all other pavilions, and faithfully catalogued in the daily calendar of events presented in the *Rapport*. The pavilion was situated next to the pavilion of the United States, right on the railway line which transported visitors around the Exhibition, another reason why it could not have been overlooked, since it was not hidden away from sight.

Commissioned by M. Bhumgara and constructed under the supervision of M. Heyman, the committee overlooking the activities of the pavilion consisted of an assemblage of high-ranking Indians—both Muslims and Hindus—including the Maharajas of Kapurthala, Baroda, Patiala, Burdwan, the Aga Khan, the Begum Shah Nawaz, Sir Mirza Muhammed Ismail and other grand persons who came to attend the Round Table Conference in England.[39] The Magazine *L'Illustration* carried a prominent article on the visit of Mahatma Gandhi to Paris, before the start of the Round Table Conference.[40] The article detailed his rail journey from Marseille to Paris and his immense popularity among

---

[39] Demaison, *A Paris en 1931*: 176–77.
[40] *L'Illustration*, 19 September 1931.

the crowds of French people who had gathered to see him at each stop. It also described Gandhi's simple lifestyle, his piety, and his philosophy of non-violence, underlining the peaceful nature of his mission to seek freedom for India. The news coverage of India's mission for independence from the British was reinforced by the presence of the Hindustan pavilion.

The monument represented was the tomb of Itmad-ud Daulah, commissioned by his daughter, the Mughal Empress Nur Jahan, wife of Jahangir in 1623. The architectural style was classic Mughal, with arches. The original monument was built in white marble and inlaid with precious and semi-precious stones in the *pietra dura* style that became popular in the late Mughal period. The pavilion was surrounded by gardens and fountains in true Mughal style. At one side was a reproduction of the Badshahi mosque of Lahore and the Khas Mahal of Agra, which also held an Indian restaurant and a theatre.[41] The pavilion contained treasures from the private collection of members of the committee as well as examples of the arts and industries of India.

The description of the Hindustan pavilion being absent from official accounts of the Exhibition, I have relied primarily on sketchy descriptions in two guide books. While one could suggest that this exclusion was due to an oversight, it is far more likely that the political repercussions of the inclusion of the Hindustan pavilion were far too great from the point of view of Anglo-French relations, even though the pavilion itself existed as an ironic testament to civil disobedience to British rule. It is no coincidence that the committee for the Hindustan pavilion was composed entirely of royalty or high-ranking Indians who had come to England to attend the first Round Table Conference to

---

41 Ibid. Also see *Le Guide. Exposition Coloniale Internationale. Paris 1931* (Paris: Édition de l'Imprimerie Union, 1931): 54.

discuss the issue of Home Rule for India.[42] It was a statement of the capability of indigenous rulers to rule India successfully while not being a direct challenge to British authority.

In 1921 the Minister of Colonies had invited Great Britain and her colonies and dependencies to participate.[43] Britain declined due to financial reasons and in October 1929, Sir Edward Crowe, Controller of the Department of Commerce had communicated to M. Condurier de Chassaigne, on mission to London, his government's acceptance of participating in the foreign section in the *Cité des Informations*, which was formally reiterated in November 1929.[44] Great Britain's Dominions and Colonies also declined the offer to participate in the Exhibition due to the prevailing atmosphere of economic depression, except for the Union of South Africa and Canada who also participated in the *Cité*.[45] Clearly the Hindustan pavilion was not part of the British stand.

The monument represented a subtle exercise in political tact. The representation of a Mughal monument was a testimony to the unity of Indians, Mughal culture being one of the few issues that bound the diverse cultures of India together and a key issue debated at the Round Table conference. Moreover, the representation of the glory of Indian architectural and cultural achievement prior to British conquest simultaneously made it impossible for England to take offence and sent out a subtle message of the glories of India that had been destroyed by the advent of British

---

[42] The members of the committee were by and large supporters of British rule in order to rule their kingdoms at least nominally, and most had British residents at their courts. However, they played important roles in the organization of the nationalist movement underground, while remaining outwardly loyal supporters of the Crown.

[43] *Rapport Général*, Vol. I, p. 347.

[44] Ibid.: 350–51.

[45] Ibid.: 351.

rule.[46] The pavilion was guarded by troops of Indians thus heightening the sense of exoticism for the visitor as well as reinforcing the message that the rulers of India were well capable of self-rule.

This was a constant theme in the guidebooks. As Demaison wrote: 'Contemplate and reflect once again upon India, before the tap of manufacture and the truck of the automobile brutally transformed the people and dried up the human sources of their beauty.'[47] The curious use of the word 'Hindu' and 'Hindustan' to denote India, which was essentially a British creation, is significant too. The French described their settlements in India as the 'Establishments of French India', yet chose to use an indigenous term *Hindu* to erroneously describe a country when it really connoted a religious or cultural community. The Indian committee naturally chose to represent their contribution as 'Hindustan' since this was a hybrid term that was inclusive of the diverse peoples of India and yet not an English import. While their choice of words was an obvious part of passive non-cooperation with the British government, the insistence on the word Hindu to describe Indians, and Hindustan to describe India in all French accounts of the pavilion is significant. It is indicative of a whole imagery of exoticism and romance, indeed of another country which

---

[46] This image of an unsullied India before the British ravaged the fabulously wealthy land was glorified in colonial paintings depicting the French conquest in India under Dupleix, Lally and Bussy in the eighteenth century. The French campaigns in India were reproduced and prominently displayed in fantastic paintings and frescoes in the Retrospective Section of the *Musée Permanent des Colonies*. See *Rapport*, p. 622. Ironically it was acceptable for France to wage a war of colonial conquest on India but the British were described implicitly as marauders and looters.

[47] Demaison, *A Paris en 1931*: 176–77. The reference to manufacture is obviously to the introduction of modern industry, transport and communication by the British in order to better exploit the resources of India.

was not overrun by Britain. Demaison extolled the pristine culture of India as,

> ... the land of the Vedas—immortal books of the wisdom of the sages; of the epics the Ramayana and Mahabharata, where divine animals play an important role in a single lifetime, as the heroes and demi-Gods. It is the land of many languages, spoken by numerous castes and which has given us many literary masterpieces.
>
> It is the land of famous monuments, of unimaginable joys, of thousands of trades, which are world-renowned for their work, the country of grand human movements and of sacred temples which have the inspired fantasies of magnificent artists, yet perfected by their extreme attention to detail.[48]

While the French had always been far more impressed by the theology and culture of India they had tempered their admiration of India by a reference to the lack of reason, the pervasiveness of superstition and prejudice, and the strange, sometimes barbaric acts of Indians. While the description of a once-great country that had fallen prey to disorder and moral corruption fits perfectly into the Imperial episteme, Demaison's whole-hearted paean to Hindu culture was strangely unlike his tempered descriptions of the French-Indian establishments.

In his description of the monument, Demaison described the construction of the tomb by the Empress Nur Jahan,

> whose filial piety was as renowned as her beauty. Nur Jahan, or as she was known, 'Light of the Day', was the wife of the Mongol Emperor Shah Jahan. When she died, Shah Jahan was inconsolable and in her memory, he ordered that a splendid mausoleum be constructed in her

---

[48] Ibid.: 177.

memory in Agra. He built the Taj Mahal—one of the world's architectural wonders. This souvenir of the nobility and beauty of Nur Jahan are a timeless testimony.[49]

The passage had several errors. Nur Jahan, literally 'Light of the World', was the wife of the Mughal Emperor Jahangir who was actually the father of Shah Jahan. The Taj Mahal was in fact constructed by Shah Jahan in memory of his wife Mumtaz Mahal. This erroneous description of the glories of India and the great and ancient culture, which had been trampled upon ruthlessly by British conquest, was a theme of the guidebooks describing the Hindustan pavilion. As Patricia Morton notes, the description of pavilions was important to Western visitors, whose gaze and understanding of events was mediated by the often-erroneous explanation contained in the guidebooks.[50] The French-Indian pavilion, on the other hand, was represented as the classic colonial French effort to preserve indigenous cultures and yet introduce them to the material advantages of Western civilization. Thus, the arts and crafts of French India were presented as original and authentic manufactures produced under the tutelage of French colonial rule.

This aspect of veiled rivalry between France and Britain was apparent even in scholarly writings on India at the Exhibition. Sir Aurel Stein, distinguished British Indologist, visited Paris during the Colonial Exhibition of 1931. His description of the importance of the exhibition for showcasing Indian culture formed a scholarly, informed view which eluded most visitors to the Exhibition but was influential among other Indologists and their propagation of Indology as a discipline.[51] Stein emphasised the impact

---

[49] Ibid.: 176.

[50] Patricia Morton, *Hybrid Modernities: Architecture and Representation at the 1931 Colonial Exposition, Paris* (Cambridge Mass. and London, England: The MIT Press, 2000).

[51] See Aurel Stein, 'The International Colonial Exhibition in Paris and the Indian Visitor', *The Asiatic Review*, 27 (October 1931).

of Indian culture on Indo-China, on cultural exchanges with China and with the Middle Eastern and African parts of the French empire, as an indication of the influences that India both had and felt during several centuries of civilization in Asia before Imperialism. His description of the Sanskrit inscriptions in Indo-China and the powerful Hindu architectural traditions of Angkor Vat and Borobodur spoke of the long cultural and religious impact that India had on Southeast Asia. Moreover, Stein's suggestion that Indo-China had been colonized by a South Indian dynasty propelled the studies which eventually established that the Chola Empire of South India had in fact extended their empire to Sri Lanka and Indo-China. Stein thus extended the importance of India to include Indo-China and beyond.

> The Indian section, it is true, occupies but a modest pavilion among the array of great structures, including a permanent colonial museum, exhibition galleries, halls, etc., which, interspersed with ornamental gardens, places of entertainment and the like, spreads itself over an area of more than 250 acres. Yet there is probably at the present day no other place to be found where the powerful influence exercised by the old civilization and art of India over great regions of Asia outside its own limits is presented to the eye in more impressive a fashion.[52]

Presenting the greatness of Indian civilization as a Western discovery, and therefore part of the showcasing of Western Empires, Stein's descriptions of Indian culture credited the Archaeological Survey of India with the 'unearthing' of India's past. Similarly, he credited the French *École française d'Extrême Orient* with the discovery and careful preservation of the cultural heritage of Indo-China, and Marshall Lyautey's efforts to preserve the 'authenticity' of traditional crafts in Morocco. Stein advised the Indian visitor to the Exhibition to learn about the greatness of India's

---

[52] Ibid.: 599.

past through a tour of the Exhibition and by correlating the Indian elements in the Exhibition architecture with India's cultural impact in Asia.

The vast extension of Indian cultural influences, from Central Asia in the north to tropical Indonesia in the south, and from the border lands of Persia to China and Japan, has fully revealed to the world at large only during the last seventy years or so and almost entirely through the researches of Western scholars. They have shown that ancient India was the radiating centre of a civilization which by its religious thought, its art and literature was destined since two thousand years to leave its deep mark on races wholly diverse and scattered over the greatest part of Asia. Yet India herself may be considered to have remained until quite recently unconscious of this its great rôle in the past. This curious fact can largely be attributed to the peculiar features of traditional Indian mentality. These *inter alia* account for the fact that amidst the vast stores of Indian classical literature there are to be found but very scanty relics of what may be properly classed as written historical records.

However, the fertilizing contact with Western thought through modern education has made its effect felt in this direction also. Some knowledge of a 'Greater India' is gradually being brought home now to a wider circle of the Indian public. It is bound to be justly pleasing to patriotic pride and may be expected to command increasing attention.[53]

In this spirit of veiled rivalries, one can clearly discern a competing discourse for claiming credit for 'discovering' pasts of colonial countries. While Stein praised the efforts of French scholars in this aspect, he unequivocally established the greater antiquity and influence of the Indian civilization upon the civilization of Indo-China.

---

[53] Ibid.: 599–600.

If we leave aside the great region to the north-west and north, including Afghanistan, Central Asia, and Tibet, the main share in the work of elucidating the facts concerning that expansion of early Indian culture must be attributed chiefly to French scholars....It is an achievement of which France, that home of sound critical methods in the fields of historical and antiquarian researches, may be proud, and a worthy accompaniment of its great past as a colonizing power. The work was begun by French scientific missions from the very time when French protectorates were first established on the coasts of Indochina in the third quarter of the last century....[54]

Among French writers however, there was no reference to the cultural exchange, far less the cultural colonization of Indo-China by South India. Only one writer, Claude Farrère, acknowledged the heavy Hindu and Indian influence in the pavilion of Indochina. Describing the immense kilometre-long bas-relief on the walls of Angkor from the Ramayana, he marvelled at the depiction of *apsaras* (nymphs) and serpents, the representation of a civilization of Sikandar (Alexander the Great), and the conquest of the Ganges valley by Alexander in these panels.[55] However, Farrère did not fail to mention the movement for independence against the British at the time, led primarily by the Bengalis. French descriptions of Indo-China by and large limited themselves to descriptions of the indigenous history and culture of the area, with marginal reference to the impact of colonization by South India in the late middle ages—the introduction of Hinduism and of Sanskrit, Tamil and regional Indian languages, Indian literary epics, dance, music, and architectural forms in particular. The re-enactment of the Ramayana as an Indo-Chinese classic comprising over 200 actors was a spectacular performance

---

[54] Ibid.: 601.
[55] Claude Farrère, 'Angkor et l'Indochine', *L'Illustration*, 23 Mai, 1931.

during the Exhibition and had no reference at all to the importation of the epic and its dance form from India, underscoring the French gloss over the colonial influence of India in Indo-China.[56] Instead the political unrest and the growing movement for independence in British India was a constant theme of French writings on India. Here was a case of French superiority. Clearly the peaceful India posts and the faithfulness of their population were testimony to the superior nature of French colonization. The *Livre d'Or* sums up this attitude succinctly. Mentioning that the French-Indian posts had experienced some political troubles, which the Governor-General, M. Juvanon termed regrettable, isolated incidents which were under control, a distinction was created between the political upheavals in British India and those in French India.

> In British India there is a national uprising, an organized rebellion against the British system of exploiting the earth and the people, against the whip of Britain. In French India the conception of colonization has always been different and the methods diametrically opposite.[57]

Thus, pre-colonial pasts became grounds of rival claims of superiority between Britain and France in the imperial enterprise.

The political significance of the pavilion, indeed of the French-Indian Posts, was summed up by Maurice Larrouy who hailed the pavilion as 'a testimonial to the vibrant culture of the French India posts, which faithfully

---

[56] *Rapport Général*, Vol. 6, part I: 320.

[57] *Le Livre d'Or de l'Exposition Coloniale Internationale de Paris 1931* (Paris: Librarie ancienne Honoré Champion, 1931): 177. 'Dans l'Inde anglaise, il s'agit d'un soulèvement national, d'une rebellion organisée contre- disons le mot- le système britannique d'exploitation de la terre et des gens, contre le cravache anglaise. Dans l'Inde fançaise, la conception de colonisation a toujours été différente et les méthodes diamétralement opposées.'

persist in their allegiance to France'.[58] French India was a showcase of France to the British, who at this time were struggling with the nationalist movement in India.

Burton Benedict points out that the Exhibitions were key to the definition of national identity in the inter-war years when many colonial empires were threatened by rising movements for independence. Contemporary observers too noted this fact: 'The fact that the French Republic has gathered and held together a rich, varied and colourful world empire was impressed upon us over and over again.'[59] The Exhibitions served to reinforce power both for the Imperial powers as well as for the colonies that they were striving so desperately to control. According to Benedict, 'the imperial powers were displaying their colonies as the era of empires was drawing to a close.'[60]

The importance of India and, in fact the representation of what was a minor colony of the French, lay in many strands of colonialist propaganda and claims. First, as Carol Breckenridge has pointed out, India was represented at all the major world exhibitions, a process which continues today. At some fairs, illustrative collections of India's objects were framed and shaped in the India court or the India pavilion by traders, and at other fairs by professionals and/or officials in government service.[61] India served to remind spectators that France too possessed part of what had come to be known as a huge treasure of wealth and exoticism.

---

[58] Maurice Larrouy, 'Les possessions océaniques', *L'Illustration*, 23 Mai 1931.

[59] Frances Parkinson Keyes, 'Tricolor and Stars and Stripes Float Together Over the Greatest Show on Earth', *Good Housekeeping Magazine*, November 1931: 196.

[60] Burton Benedict, 'International Exhibitions and National Identity', *Anthropology Today*, 7.3 (June 1991): 8.

[61] Carol Breckenridge, 'The Aesthetics and Politics of Colonial Collecting: India at World Fairs', in *Comparative Study of Society and History*, 31.2 (April 1989): 201.

French India was, after all, the remains of a glorious period in French colonial history. It was all that remained of the wise administration of great colonists like Dupleix, Mahé de la Bourdonnais, Bussy, Lally-Tollendal and Dumas. These figures had achieved great feats of development and colonization in India in keeping with the grand enterprise of the French civilizing mission. The India Posts represented all that remained of the moral patrimony of France in the glorious epoch of colonialism.[62]

> This tiny colony was the object of much attention on the part of the mother country [France] in the past. Unfortunately, the position of French India today is that of a poor parent to the flashy French empire.[63]

Another factor in the display of artefacts and cultural expressions of Indian culture beyond its actual political presence in France was Anglo-French imperial rivalry, which, though veiled, was nevertheless pervasive in the definition of France's colonial mission and in fact in the very expression of twentieth-century French nationhood. French India was also a foil to other colonies of France who at this time were fighting for independence. Indo-China had begun demanding a freer hand, as had Algeria and France's African colonies. French India served to remind spectators of the peaceful nature of French colonies that

---

[62] *Le Livre d'Or de l'Exposition Coloniale Internationale de Paris 1931* (Paris: Librairie ancienne Honoré Champion, 1931): 176. This tiny colony was the object of much attention on the part of the mother country (France) in the past. Unfortunately, by the nineteenth century when France claimed her vast colonial Empire in Asia and Africa, the position of French India had been reduced to a mere mention in histories of past colonial enterprises.

[63] Ibid.: 176. 'Cette petite colonie qui nous est si chère par tant de souvenirs devrait être l'objet d'une plus grande sollicitude de la part de la mère- patrie. Aujourd'hui l'Inde Française apparaît malheureusement trop comme le parent pauvre dans notre fastueux empire colonial.'

were content to learn under French tutelage. Indeed, French India was treated very well compared to France's high-handed treatment of the Algerians and Indo-Chinese. The use of coercion was minimal, the inhabitants of French India were allowed to rise higher in the colonial administration than in these other colonies, and Indians had a greater say in the administration and the system of justice. Part of the reason for this was the value and size of the India Posts. Being maintained primarily for prestige there was really no need to crush the inhabitants with the might of western military and police force. Instead the Posts, being highly urbanized settlements, were models of French education policies, cultural development and peaceful co-existence. Demaison's statistics—'a tiny territory of 510 km, yet a huge population of 265,000 people...'[64]—served once again to drive home to the colonial powers and especially Britain, that France had truly succeeded in colonizing and winning the allegiance of her peoples. The peace in the French India posts was attributed to the administration, its high moral qualities and cordial relations and a sympathetic attitude to the land, which allowed order to be rapidly restored with benign justice in a land where 'imponderables' played a major role.[65] The disturbances were set at the door of those marginal social elements, who, like the nationalists in Indo-China, were infected by Socialistic and Communist sentiments. However, they could only manage to create minor ripples in the peaceful India Posts which remained loyal to France and the *patrie*.[66]

The role of India in French colonial thought in the twentieth century was complicated. While a large part of the educated public would have known that India formed part of the British Empire, the dissemination of India in

---

[64] Demaison, *A Paris en 1931.*: 176.

[65] *Le Livre d'Or de l'Exposition Coloniale Internationale de Paris 1931* (Paris: Librairie ancienne Honoré Champion, 1931): 176.

[66] Ibid.

French popular culture belied this fact. French India stood as a subtle challenge to the British model of colonialism. The impact that these images of India made upon the French public can be captured in the opening words of a memoir by Taya Zinkin, 'I thought India was French.'[67] The pavilions of French India at the various *expositions coloniale* which were held during the late nineteenth and early twentieth centuries were powerful visual statements about the conception of India in France. The single most obvious fact about all these pavilions were that they were always reproductions of temples (Images 8.1, 8.8, 8.9), reinforcing the religious and spiritual aspect of India over any other. The Indian natives who worked at the pavilions were dressed modestly with an absence of ostentatious jewellery or towering headdresses or even a lack of clothing (like the popularity of naked fakirs at the Philadelphia and New York World Fairs in the early twentieth centuries).

In contrast to the French pavilions, the Empire Exhibition of Britain at Wembley presented India as a land of palaces,[68] oriental despots, a land of immense wealth, and simultaneously a land which had been immeasurably improved by British colonization (Image 8.10).[69] One of the many guides to the Exhibition titled, 'British Empire Exhibition: The Businessman's Opportunity' (Wembley, 1925) described the India pavilion.

The steel and plaster pavilion of India, covering three acres of ground, will again enshrine the wonders of many

---

[67] Taya Zinkin, *French Memsahib*, (Dorset, United Kingdom: Thomas Harmsworth Publishing Co, 1989): 1. Zinkin was French-born and -educated, and later married an Englishman, Maurice Zinkin, who was part of the Indian Civil Service.

[68] According to Beinart and Hughes, at least 24 palaces were built to represent India at the various British imperial exhibitions between 1886 and 1939. William Beinart and Lotte Hughes, *Environment and Empire* (Oxford, OUP, 2007): 225.

[69] See Denis Judd, *Empire: The British Imperial Experience from 1765 to the Present* (Basic Books, 1998).

a native state. How far have the arts and crafts of India reached the world beyond? That they have travelled a great way cannot be gainsaid; that they have received full justice must be denied. India's carpets and curtains, her carved work in wood and metals and ivory, her great and growing timber trade—all these things will be seen at Wembley this year on a scale worthy of them. The result should be satisfactory to exhibitor and merchant alike.[70]

The huge size of the pavilion was meant to impress visitors with the place of India in Britain's empire (Image 8.11). Yet the above passage conveyed the idea that native crafts, which had been neglected by Indian rulers, would finally get their due acclaim as a result of being displayed at the British Exhibition.[71] The India Palace at Wembley occupied the same place of prominence as the temple of Angkor Vat did at the *Exposition Coloniale* of 1931 in Paris. Purported to loosely resemble the Taj Mahal, the palace was placed behind a lake, where visitors could rent boats and enjoy a luxury cruise. The pavilion, illuminated at night, reinforced the notion of an 'oriental fairyland' (Image 8.12), albeit one which was constructed by the London architectural firm of Messrs. White, Allom and Co.[72]

The interior of the palace contained images of princely India, of strapping guards with ornate uniforms and elaborate moustaches and beards, paintings, reproductions of

[70] *British Empire Exhibition: The Businessman's Opportunity* (London, Wembley: Waterlow and Sons ltd, 1925): 12.

[71] See Tapati Guha Thakurta, 'Careers of the Copy: Travelling Replicas in Colonial and Postcolonial India', *Firth Lecture, Annual Conference of the Association of Social Anthropologists of the UK and Commonwealth*, 'Archaeological and Anthropological Imaginations' (Bristol University, 8 April 2009). Website: http://www.theasa.org/publications/firth/firth09.pdf. Accessed on 16 October 2009. Thakurta has discussed this aspect of 'displaying India' in more detail.

[72] Ibid.: 20–21. Cited from *Official Guide, British Empire Exhibition, Wembley, 1925*, edited by G. C. Lawrence (London: Fleetway Press, 1925): 74–75.

the Peacock Throne and of other riches of India. A bazaar street which resembled Chandni Chowk or the Street of Silver, which was traditionally the street where the Mughal Emperors shopped in Delhi allowed visitors to shop like the Mughal Emperors from among the choicest arts and crafts of India. The bazaar street led visitors to a restaurant where patrons had a choice between native foods and typical English tea services. They were served by native bearers or waiters, to allow visitors to experience the grandeur of being in the Raj.[73] Finally visitors could visit a theatre where jugglers, acrobats, and snake charmers rounded off this experience of being in Imperial India. The impact of the Wembley Exhibition on the British public was immense and included newspaper and journal articles, references in juvenile and adult fiction, dramas, TV, radio, and even popular songs of the day.[74]

The pavilions of India displayed at the French and British colonial exhibitions of the late nineteenth and early twentieth centuries provided a three dimensional, visual image of their different conceptions of India. The French-Indian pavilions of temples, decorated with religious paintings and local crafts clearly contradicted the British Indian palaces of ostentatious wealth, oriental royalty, and power. The conceptualization of India in the intellectual spheres of France and Britain had successfully parlayed their creations into their public imagination and understanding of 'India'.

---

[73] Elizabeth M. Collingham, *Curry: A Tale of Cooks and Conquerors* (Oxford: OUP, 2006): 153.

[74] John Mackenzie, 'The Popular Culture of Empire in Britain', *The Oxford History of the British Empire* edited by Judith Brown and William Louis (Oxford: OUP, 2001).

IMAGE 8.1: Postcard representing the Pavilion of Inde Française at the Exposition Coloniale internationale, Paris, 1931

IMAGE 8.2: The exterior of the pavilion. Exposition Coloniale: pavillon de l' Inde Française: [photographie de presse] / Agence Meurisse

Source: Bibliothèque nationale de France, département Estampes et photographie, EI-13 (2880)

IMAGE 8.3: THE PILLARS OF THE PAVILION

IMAGE 8.4: POSTCARD DEPICTING THE INNER COURTYARD

IMAGE 8.5: [Exposition coloniale de Paris, 1931: projet pour le] pavillon d'honneur, section belge : [Photographie] / Sartony Laffitte

Source: Ville de Paris / BHdV / Roger-Viollet.

IMAGE 8.6: Panel depicting India

Source: Exposition coloniale internationale de 1931 : rapport général

IMAGE 8.7: The Hindustan Pavilion

Source: Andre de Maison.

IMAGE 8.8: Postcard of the French India pavilion at the Exposition Universelle of 1889

IMAGE 8.9: Postcard of the French India Pavilion at the Exposition Universelle, Paris 1900

IMAGE 8.10: Postcard of the India palace at the Wembley Exhibition, 1924–25

IMAGE 8.11: POSTCARD OF THE INDIAN COURTYARD AT WEMBLEY

IMAGE 8.12: POSTCARD OF THE INDIA PAVILION AT NIGHT

Conclusion: Was India Really 'French'?

In this book, I have examined the French intellectual elite's efforts in the eighteenth and nineteenth centuries to understand India, and the relationship of this endeavour to the creation of colonial knowledge. From the early formulation of India as a great Brahminical civilization, then as the home of Buddhism to the home of the Aryans and finally the creation of a complex Hindu identity full of contradictions, simultaneously advanced and oppressive, the study of India in France during the nineteenth century proceeded side by side with French colonial expansion. Sometimes coincidentally, but more often not, India was used as an example to support the prevailing colonial ideologies of race, assimilation and association. She was also an intrinsic part of the continuing national rivalry with England, at once an example of British self-centeredness and of the superior French colonizing mission.

In the preceding chapters, I have examined the construction of an academic image of 'India' which was distinctly French and marked by its reliance on the spiritual and religious aspects of India, its antiquity, and Aryan heritage. The work was inspired, in part, by the need for such an intellectual focus. While scholars have long paid attention to the literary and artistic impact which India has made upon France,[1] and more recently examined how the French popular press represented India,[2] the roots of this

---

[1] For example, Lisa Lowe, *Critical Terrains. French and British Orientalisms* (Ithaca: Cornell University Press, 1991) and Binita Mehta, Widows, *Pariahs and Bayadères. India as Spectacle* (Lewisburg: Bucknell University Press and London: Associated University Presses, 2002).

[2] For example, Kate Marsh, *Fictions of1947: Representations of Indian Decolonization in French-language texts* (New York: Peter

familiarity with India, which lay with the Parisian school of Indology during the nineteenth century, have not been examined. In this book, I begin the task of recovering the image of India that French universities and research institutions created.

According to S. P. Sen, French historical writing on European activities in India really started in the last quarter of the nineteenth century.[3] After the success of their second colonial venture in the latter part of the nineteenth century, the French were enthused with writing about their colonies. However, I think Sen is mistaken in his analysis. Undoubtedly, a great burst of writing about colonies took place with the colonial expansion of Napoleon III and Jules Ferry, but a steady stream of writing from the eighteenth century characterized French images of India. What distinguished nineteenth-century writing was its compartmentalization into institutional forms;writing on colonies came to be demarcated into literary, historical, and Indological (linguistic, philosophic, religious and cultural studies on India) genres.

The missionaries' accounts offered a perspective on Indian religion which was corrupted by its association with Islam. Described as a religion which imbued its followers with a warlike, greedy quality, their narrative believed that Islam eventually destroyed ancient civilizations such as India.

The French observers also saw India as a great example of the results of different races intermarrying and causing a degeneration of 'superior' racial qualities. Mid-nineteenth century French anthropologists, particularly

---

Lang, 2007); and Nicki Frith, 'Competing Colonial Discourses in India: Representing the 1857 Kanpur Massacres in French- and English-Language Texts and Images', Unpublished doctoral thesis, University of Liverpool, 2008.

[3] S. P. Sen, 'French historical writing on European activities in India', in *Historians of India, Pakistan and Ceylon,* edited by C. H. Philips (London, 1961).

those who were anti-Semitic, used the 'unfortunate racial history' which India presented. This history was one in which a presumably superior Aryan race, inter-married with inferior races and thereby lost its superior qualities and indeed, lost its superior civilization. Thus, in their view, India had become a sad example of a fallen race, indeed a mongrel race unable to reclaim its once-glorious Aryan heritage due to the dilution in superior 'blood'. While these writings focused entirely on India as an 'other' exotic entity, far from the comfortable civilizing presence of France, the warning that French civilization could just as easily be corrupted by allowing lesser races to imprint themselves on French culture was a powerful argument in certain French circles.

Another important way in which India helped to develop notions of 'Frenchness' among apologists for colonial expansion was in her situation as a British colony during the nineteenth century. As colonies became an accepted part of 'national wealth' French nationalism within the colonial lobby also became a fierce rhetorical and cultural expression of everything that was *not* British.[4] As Brunschwig points out, France aimed at building a colonial Empire in order to boost national pride rather than a quest for financial enrichment.[5] Colonial policies like assimilation were geared to showcase the superior culture and colonial achievements of France and this aim was underscored by the proponents of Empire in France. Unlike England, where Empire was pursued by merchants, industrialists and financiers, the French colonial enterprise was

---

[4] See Linda Colley, *Britons: Forging the Nation, 1707–1837* (New Haven and London: Yale University Press, 1992). Colley describes the definition of British national identity in opposition to 'the other' which was France. Similarly, French national identity too was shaped by Anglo-French rivalry and hence French identity came to be defined in terms of things 'not British'.

[5] Henri Brunschwig, *French Colonialism 1871–1914: Myths and Realities* (London: Pall Mall Press, 1966). Revised edn.

taken up by geographers, journalists and intellectuals who saw Empire as a means to restore national pride after humiliating defeats to England and Germany during the course of the nineteenth century.

The colonial progress of France in the nineteenth century was very much reflected in the writings on India. The romanticism and military vainglory of the eighteenth century was present in most works of the period on India, which praised France for her efforts to understand and associate with such an ancient civilization. The Revolution was a huge break when France was too busy with her internal conflicts and the crushing colonial losses to England to pay much attention to her empire. Colonial dreams, which were resurrected with Napoleon, soon died a quiet death. The Restoration government under Louis Philippe was as timid as the King himself. Having concluded several peace treaties with England which stripped France of her most lucrative colonial possessions, France was in no position to challenge England. Colonization proceeded sedately and unremarkably. The proclamation of the Second Republic in 1848 and the rise of Louis Napoleon once again fired France's colonial dreams. New expansion into Africa with the conquest of Algeria and Senegal, and East Asia into Indo-China put France back on the list of colonial contenders. The period saw the introduction of colonial policies of assimilation, followed in the 1870s with the Third Republic and the stewardship of Jules Ferry in the 1890s, with the policy of association, which proclaimed France's greatness and uniqueness as a colonial power and also her real desire to civilize her colonies.[6]

The French colonial lobby pushed their spiritual and religious image of India in an attempt to challenge British dominance in India by pointing to the superior achievements of India in philosophy and intellect. German

---

[6] See Thomas Power, *Jules Ferry and the Renaissance of French Imperialism* (New York: Octagon Books, 1966).

Indological work, deeply influenced by France[7] presented India through a lens of Romanticism and spirituality, furthering this image. In addition, one has to remember that nineteenth-century Europe was still a land where French was spoken and understood more than English. Therefore, the consumption and imagination of India on French terms was far stronger than the British representations of India even though Britain was well on her way to establishing her empire in India. In stark contrast to the image of British India suffering under constant famines, and back-breaking poverty, the French comptoirs were consistently represented as peaceful, content towns,sleepy little outposts of *la plus grande France*.[8] Indians were extended French citizenship and taught the glorious language and culture of France, all proof of France's superior mission civilisatrice. Simultaneously colonial leaders lost no opportunity to criticize British rule. As Albert Sarrault declared as late as 1931, 'India is not governed, she is exploited.'[9] In contrast, inhabitants of the French comptoirs seemed content with French rule, possibly because of their belief in the French character which was inclined to emphasize the attributes of equality and legality and to a greater extent than in British India, those of fraternity and liberty as

---

[7] Although Germany and France were bitter rivals during the nineteenth century in Europe, France was the first country to actively embrace Indology as an academic discipline with established Chairs in Sanskrit and Indic studies. German Indologists were among the first foreign students of these French Indologists in the early nineteenth century and took back the ideological framework of Romantic thought in viewing India with them. Thereafter they continued to work with a strong Romantic current, which is reflected even today.

[8] Pierre Loti, for instance, described Pondichéry as 'this tiny corner of old France, lost on the edge of the Bay of Bengal'. Pierre Loti, *L'Inde (sansles Anglais)* (Paris: Calman-Levy, 1903): 227.

[9] Cited in Jacques Weber, 'Cent ans de colonies', in *L'Aventure des Français en Inde. XVII–XX siècles*. Edited by Rose Vincent (Kailash Editions: 1995): 203.

well.[10] Not only were the French treating their Indian citizens like equals[11] but in their eagerness to preserve their civilization, French scholars were the leaders in Indology. The relationship between France and India was therefore not a simple imposition; if French was *imported* into the Comptoirs, Sanskrit was *exported*, underlining the French desire to preserve the civilization of India. The notion that this civilization was as artificial and imposed, a construct of those in power, as the selfsame British, was not important to address. This aspect of French intellectualism, more than any other single achievement, served to challenge British claims of 'rehabilitating' India.

Despite British territorial dominance in India, the conception of India as a land of spiritual and intellectual greatness was still strongly French and it continues to endure in Europe even today. This fact alone necessitates the study of how and why the French chose to involve themselves so closely with the study of India. This book begins that fascinating journey into the politics of academic portrayals and their accuracy.

---

[10] Joseph Minattur, *Justice in Pondicherry* (New Delhi: The Indian Law Institute, 1973): 1–2.

[11] The granting of citizenship and the so-called advancement of the Comptoirs under the French was also questionable. However, these issues have only recently begun coming to light in the work of scholars such as Narayani Gupta, 'The Citizens of French India: the issue of cultural identity in Pondicherry in the XIX century', in *Les relations historiques et culturelles entre la France et l'Inde XVII–XX siècles.* 2 volumes (Sainte-Clotilde, 1987), Jacques Weber, 'Chanemougam, the King of French India', *EPW*, 9 February 1991; Jacques Weber, Pondichéry *les comptoirs de l'Inde après Dupleix* (Paris: Denoël, 1996); L. S. Vishwanath, 'Social Stratification in Colonial India', in K. S. Mathew (ed.) *French in India and Indian nationalism 1700–1963.* 2 vols (Delhi, 1999), Vol. 1.

Appendix

TABLE A1: List of articles about India, *Magazin Encyclopédique ou Journal des sciences, des lettres et des arts*, 1795–96. Paris, Imprimérie du Magazin Encyclopédique

Year	No	Title	Author	Content
1795	2	Notice sur les travaux typographiques et littéraires des Anglais dans l'Inde	Louis Langlès	Bibliographic catalogue
1795	3	Suite de la Notice sur les travaux typographiques et littéraires des Anglais dans l'Inde	Louis Langlès	Bibliographic catalogue
1795	4	–	–	–
1795	5	–	–	–
1795	6	Notice sur l'Indoustan, tirée des manuscripts de la Bibliothèque Nationale	Louis Langlès	Bibliographic catalogue
1795	6	The history of Hindostan, c'est-à-dire, Histoire de l'Indoustan, de ces arts, de ses sciences, envisages dans leur connexion, avec l'histoire des autres grands empires de l'Asie, aux époques les plus reculées, avec un grand nombre de planches explicatives, par l'auteur des Antiquités de l'Inde.	Louis Langlès	Book review
1795	6	Le mort de Raynal		Death notice of Abbé Raynal
1796	1	Notice sur la vie et des ouvrages de Gauillaume- Thomas Raynal, member de l'Institut national, lui à la séance publique de 15 germinal	Joachim Le Breton, secrétaire de la classe des sciences morales et politiques	Biography of Raynal
1796	1	A Journey overland to India, etc; c'est-à-dire, Voyage dans l'inde par terre, et en partie par une route qui n'a été pratiquée jusqu'ici par aucun Européen, par Donald Campbell		Book review

TABLE A2: List of articles about India, 1803–5, *Journal des Débats et des Décrets*

Number	Date	Title	Author	Content
	30 October 1803	Spectacles: review of Aline ou la Reine de Golconde, playing at the Théâtre de l'Opéra-Comique		Theatre review
	20 February 1804	Translation of Robert Percival's work on Ceylon: Voyage à l'île de Ceylan	P. F. Henry	Travels
	1 March 1804	Mémoire sur les laines et les moutons du Cachemire et du Boutan, le à la Société d'agriculture de Paris, dans la séance du 7 frimair, an IX	Le Goux de Flaix	Travels
		Voyage à l'île de Ceylan, part II	P. F. Henry	Travels
	11 March 1804	Histoire naturelle des deux Eléphans... de l'Inde		Travel/ accounts of curiosities
		Mémoire sur les laines et les moutons du Cachemire et du Boutan, le à la Société d'agriculture de Paris, dans la séance du 7 Frimaire, an IX. Part II	Le Goux de Flaix	Travels
	10 April 1804	Notice des travaux de la Classe de littérature et histoire anciennes de l'Institut Nationale. The article included a 3 page discussion of Anquetil Duperron's opinion of India	C. Ameilhon	Comparative literature
	10 May 1804	Anecdotes Anglaises		Colonial rivalry between England and France

(Continued)

TABLE A2: (Continued)

Number	Date	Title	Author	Content
	9 June 1804	Notice historique et critique sur cette question: Est-il vrai que les veuves de l'Indoustan soient dans l'usage de se brûler sur le bûcher de leurs époux?	Le Goux de Flaix	Travels/ Ethnologies
	22 October 1804	Notice regarding a new edition of the Lettres Édifiantes		Book announcement
	10 November 1804	Histoire d'Hérodote, including extracts from his accounts of Persia and India		Book review
	21 November 1804	" " Part II		" "
	20 December 1804	Lettre à M. le Senateur Lanjuinais, à l'occasion de ses extraits du livre sacré des Hindous, traduit du persan en latin, sous le titre d'Oupnek'hat, par M. Anquetil du Perron		Scholarly critique/review
	Jan. 10, 1805	Deuxième lettre sur l'Oupnek'hat de M. A D P		" "
	Feb. 19, 1805	Review of Langlès' Recherches sur la découverte de l'essence de rose		Book review
		Notice of the death of Anquetil Duperron		

TABLE A3: Articles on India by topic, *Journal des Savants*, 1817–99

Year	Total Number of Articles on India	Hinduism	Buddhism	Literature	Colonialism/ Ethnology
1817–29	52	25	5	33	14
1830–39	47	13	6	32	5
1840–49	23	6	5	17	5
1850–59	54	19	23	46	8
1860–69	53	36	5	38	7
1870–79	36	12	9	28	7
1880–89	49	26	3	27	15
1890–99	48	17	17	31	4

TABLE A4: Articles on India by topic, *Journal Asiatique*, 1822–1902

Year	Total Articles on India	Buddhism	Hinduism	Islam	Philology	Indo-European Ethnology
1822–27	48	5	20	12	6	0
1828–35	38	6	12	5	9	1
1836–42	32	6	11	5	9	2
1843–52	27	4	14	6	4	0
1853–62	37	1	10	2	22	0
1863–72	16	7	3	0	0	0
1873–82	23	19	0	1	0	0
1883–92	43	26	11	2	6	0
1893–1902	8	4	0	1	0	0

TABLE A5: Articles on India by topic, *Revue des Deux Mondes*, 1829–1900

Period	Total	Academic	Hinduism	Buddhism	Islam	Sanskrit
1829–39	25	6	3	1	2	3 (12%)
1840–49	29	8	4	–	4	2 (6%)
1850–59	37	12	12	–	1	9 (24%)
1860–69	18	2	1	1	–	1 (5%)
1870–79	10	–	–	–	–	–
1880–89	15	4	3	1	–	3 (20%)
1890–1900	23	9	7	5	–	3 (13%)

TABLE A6: Comparison of article content among articles on India, *Journal Asiatique*, 1822–1902

Year	Total Articles on India	Buddhism	Hinduism	Islam	Philology	Indo-European Ethnology
1822–27	48	5	20	12	6	0
1828–35	38	6	12	5	9	1
1836–42	32	6	11	5	9	2
1843–52	27	4	14	6	4	0
1853–62	37	1	10	2	22	0
1863–72	16	7	3	0	0	0
1873–82	23	19	0	1	0	0
1883–92	43	26	11	2	6	0
1893–1902	8	4	0	1	0	0

TABLE A7: Comparison of Article Content among Articles on India in the *Bulletins de la Société d'anthropologie de Paris*, 1822–1902

Year	Ethnography	Anthropometry	Aryan/Dravidian	Total
1860–70	18	7	26	50
1871–80	15	14	5	32
1881–90	56	14	5	72
1891–1900	4	6	1	10

Missing: Vol. 9, series 2 (1874), Vol. 1, series 4 (1890), Vol. 6, series 4 (1895), Vol. 9, series 5 (1898).

TABLE A8: Comparison of Article Content among Articles on India in the *Journal Asiatique*, *Revue d'Ethnographie*, *Revue d'Anthropologie* and *Bulletins de la Société d'anthropologie de Paris*, 1860–1900

Year	Philology	Religion	Anthropology	Aryan/Race
1860–70	0	9	49	26
1871–80	8	11	31	6
1881–90	27	20	71	8
1891–1900	5	4	10	3

Bibliography

BIBLIOGRAPHIC AIDS

Gaebele, Yvonne Robert. Catalogue général des livres de la Bibliothèque publique de Pondichéry. Pondichery: Imprimerie du gouvernement, 1960.

Gaudart, Edmond. Catalogue des manuscrits des anciennes archives de l'Inde française. 8 vols. Paris: Leroux; Pondichéry: Bibliothèque coloniale, 1922–36.

Martineau, Alfred (ed). Bibiographie d'histoire coloniale: 1900–1930. Paris: E.Leroux, 1932.

Société Française d'histoire d'outre-mer: 90 ans de publications. Tables bibliographiques. 1913–2003. Paris and Saint-Denis: Publications de la Société Française d'histoire d'outre-mer, 2003.

Sources de l'Histoire de l'Asie et de l'Oceanie dans les Archives et K. G. Saur, 1981.

Table des publications de la Société de l'histoire des colonies française (1913–1922) suive de la Table des publications de la Société de l'histoire de l'Inde française (1911–22). Paris.

Tranchell, Henry George. Catalogue des cartes, plans et projets d'études du Dépôt des annciennes archives de Pondichéry. Paris: E. Leroux, 1930.

Quatre Siècles de Colonisation Française. Paris: Bibliothèques Nationales de France, 1931.

JOURNALS AND NEWSPAPERS

Annales de géographie.

Annales du Musée Guimet, Paris, 1918–27.

Asiatick Researches, vols 1–22.

Bulletin de l'Ecole Française d'Extrême Orient.

Bulletin de la Société Anthropologique de Paris.

Bulletin de la Société Ethnologique de Paris.

Bulletin de la Société Géographique de Paris.

Dépèche Coloniale.

Histoire de l'académie royale des inscriptions et belles lettres, Paris: Imprimérie Royale.

Journal Asiatique.
Journal de l'Empire.
Journal des Savants.
Journal of the Asiatic Society, 1832–1905. Vols 1–75.
Journal of the Royal Asiatic Society of Great Britain and Ireland.
La Politique Coloniale, 1892.
Mémoires de l'Acadêmie des inscriptions et belles-lettres.
Mémoires de la Société de l'Anthropologie.
Mémoires de la Société de l'ethnologie.
Revue Brittannique.
Revue d'Anthropologie.
Revue de l'histoire des religions.
Revue de linguistique et de philologie comparée.
Revue des Deux Mondes.
Revue d'ethnographie.
Revue historique de l'Inde française.
*Revue d'Histoire des Colonies françaises,*1913–30.
Revue d'Histoire des Colonies, 1931–58.
Revue française d'histoire d'outre-mer.

PRIMARY SOURCES

E. Amann, 'Malabares (Rites)' *Dictionnaire de théologie catholique,* edited by Vacant, A., Mangenot,. E., and Amann, E. Paris, 1927. Volume 9: 1704–46.

Ampère, Jean-Jacques. 'Histoire du Bouddhisme. Relations des Royaumes bouddhiques. Traduit du chinois et accompagnée d'un commentaire, par Abel Rémusat', *Revue des Deux-Mondes,* no. 9, (15 June 1837): 731–51.

———. et Charles Daremberg. *La science et les lettres en Orient.* Paris: Didier, 1832

Anquetil-Duperron, Abraham Hyacinthe. *Législation orientale, ouvrage dans lequel, en montrant quells sont en Turquie, en Perse et dans l'Indoustan, les principes fondamentaux du government.* Amsterdam: M. M. Rey, 1778.

———. *Oupenek'hat.* Strasbourg, 1801.

———. *Recherches historiques et géographiques sur l'Inde.* 2 vols. Berlin: P. Bourdeaux, 1786–87.

———. *L'Inde en rapport avec l'Europe,* 2 vols. Paris: Lesguilliez frères,1798.

———. *Zend-Avesta, discours préliminaire, commentaires et notes J. Deloche, M. et P.-S. Filiozat.* Paris: Maisonneuve et Larose, 1997.

Atlas colonial illustré. Paris: Larousse, 1902–03.

Atlas pittoresque des colonies françaises: recueil de vues géographiques et pittoreques de toutes les colonies françaises, accompagnées de notices géographiques et de légendes explicatives. Paris: Éditions pittoresques, 1929.

Bader, *La femme dans l'Inde Antique.* Paris, nd.

Bailly, Sylvain. *Lettres sur l'origine des sciences et sur celle des peoples de l'Asie, adressées à M. Voltaire.* Paris, 1777.

Barchou de Penhoën, Baron Auguste. *L'Inde sous la domination anglaise.* Paris, 1827.

———. *Histoire de la conquête et de la fondation de l'empire anglais dans l'Inde.* 6 vols. Paris, 1840–41.

Barth, Auguste. *Quarante ans d'indianisme: Ouevres, recueillés à l'occasion son quatre-vingtième anniversaire.* 5 vols. Paris: E. Leroux, 1914–27.

———. *Les religions de l'Inde.* Paris: G. Fischbacher, 1879. Reprinted from Encyclopédie des sciences religieuses.

Barthelémy Saint-Hilaire, J. *Eugene Burnouf. Ses Travaux et sa Correspondance.* Paris, 1891.

———. *M Victor Cousin. Sa vie et sa correspendance.* Paris: Hatchette and Félix Alcan, 1895. 3 vols.

———. *Etat actuel de l'Inde.* Paris, 1885.

Bédier, Achille and Joseph-Marie-Emmanuel Cordier. *Statistiques de Pondichéry, 1822–1824.* Pondichéry: Institut français de Pondichéry, 1988.

Bergaigne, Abel. *Les dieux souverains de la religion védique.* Paris: F. Viewig, 1877.

Bernier, François. *Voyage dans les États du Grand Mogol.* Paris: Fayard,1670.

Bernoulli, Jean. *Description historique et géographique de l'Inde.* 3 vols. Berlin, 1786–89. *Voltaire's Correspondence.* Edited by Theodore Besterman.Paris: Gallimard, 1964.

J. Bertrand, *Mémoires historiques sur les missions des ordres religieux et spécialement sur les questions du clergé indigène et des rites malabares d'après des documents inédits.* 2nd edn (Paris: P. Brunet,1862).

Billot, Fréréric. *L'Inde, l'Angleterre et la France.* Paris, 1857.

Bochinger, Georges. *La vie contemplative, ascétique et monastique chez les Indous et chez les peuples bouddhistes.* Strasbourg: F. G. Levrault, 1831.

Boell, Paul. *L'Inde et le problem Indien.* Paris, s.d.

Bosc, Ernest. *Yoghisme et Fakirisme Hindous.* Paris: G. A. Mann, 1913.

Bouglé, Celestin. *Essai sur le régime des castes.* Paris: F. Alcan, 1908.

Brehat, Alfred de. *Souvenirs de l'Inde Anglaise.* Paris, 1876.

Colonies Françaises. Edited by Ch de Brossard. Paris: E. Flammarion, 1906.

Burnouf, Eugène. *Choix de lettres d'Eugène Burnouf, 1825–1852, suivi d'une bibliographie*. Edited by Laure Burnouf Delisle. Paris: H. Champion, 1891.

———. *L'Inde française*. Collection of lithographs. 2 vols. Paris: Chabrelle, 1827–35.

———. 'Seconde lettre à M. le Rédacteur du Journal Asiatique, sur quelques denominations géographiques du Drâvida ou pays des Tamouls', *Nouveau Journal Asiatique*, vol. 2, (Oct 1828): 241–77.

———. 'Discours sur la langue et la littérature sanscrite, prononcé au collége de France', *Journal Asiatique*, Series 2, vol. 11, (Jan–Jun 1833): 251–72.

Burnouf, Eugène and Christian Lassen. *Essai sur le pali*. Paris: Dondey-Dupré père et fils,1826.

Campbell, George. 'The Ethnology of India', *Journal of the Asiatic Society of Bengal*, 35.2 (special number on Indian Ethnology, 1866.

———. 'On the Races of India as Traced in Existing Tribes and Castes', *Journal of the Ethnological Society of London*, ns, 1.

Carré, Barthélemy. *Nouvelle Relation d'un Voyage aux Indes Orientales*. Paris, 1699.

Chardin, Jean. *Journal du voyage du Chévalier Chardin en Perse et aux Indes orientales par la mer Noire et par la Colchide*. London, 1686.

Chauvelot, Robert. *L'Inde Mystérieuse, ses rajahs, ses Brahmes, ses fakirs*. Paris: Librairie Chapelot, 1920.

Chevrillon, André. *In India*. Translated by William Marchand. London: William Heinemann, 1897.

Chézy, Antoine Léonard de. *La mort d'Yadjnadatta, épisode extrait du Ramâyana*. Paris: F. Didot, 1826.

———. *La reconnaissance de Sacountala, drame sanscrit et pracrit de Calidasa*. Paris: Dondey-Dupré père et fils, 1830.

———. *Discours prononcé au Collège royal de France, à l'ouverture du cours de langue et de littérature sanskrite*. Paris: J.-M. Eberhart, 1815.

Closets d'Errey, Henri de. *Histoire de l'Inde française, 1664–1814. institutions religieuses et artisanales de l'Inde; son folklore*. Pondichéry, 1940.

———.*Précis chronologique de l'histoire de l'Inde française*. Pondichéry: Bibliothèque publique, Paris: Librairie E. Leroux, 1934.

———. *Étude sur les fetes religieuses brahmaniques et musulmanes au sud de l'Inde*. Pondichéry, 1935.

Closets d'Errey, Henri de. and Alfred Martineau. *Resumé des actes de l'État civil de Pondichéry.* Pondichéry: Bibliothèque publique and Paris: Librarie Ernest Leroux, 1917.

Colebrooke, H. T. 'Enumeration of Indian Classes', *Asiatick Researches*, vol. 5, (1788): 53–67.

Collin de Bar, Alexis Guillaume Henri. *Histoire de l'Inde ancienne et moderne ou Indoustan considéré relativement à ses antiquités.* Paris: Le Normant, Imprimeur-Librairie, 1814. 2 vols.

Congrès national d'Action et de Propagande colonials sous le haut patronage de M. le Ministre de Colonies et de M. le Maréchal Lyautey: Paris, Exposition coloniale internationale (11, 12 mai 1931): Compte-rendu des séances. Paris: Editions de l'Institut colonial français, 1931.

Courtillier, Gaston. *Les anciennes civilizations de l'Inde.* Paris: A. Colin, 1930.

Cousin, Victor. *Premiers essays de philosophie.* Paris: Librairie Nouvelles, 1855.

———. *Histoire générale de la philosophie depuis les temps le plus anciens jusqu'à XIXe siècle.* Paris, 1884.

Crawfurd, John. 'On the Physical and Mental Characteristics of the European and Asiatic Races of Man', *Journal of the Ethnological Society of London*, 5, (1867): 58–81.

———. 'On the Supposed Aborigines of India as Distinguished from its Civilised Inhabitants', *Journal of the Ethnological Society of London*, 6 (1868).

Le Dain, Alfred. *L'Inde Antique.* Paris: Société cooperative des letters et des arts, 1896.

Darmesteter, James. *Essays Orientaux.* Paris: A. Levy, 1883.

———. *Lettres sur l'Inde.* Paris: A. Lemerre, 1888.

Diderot's Encyclopédie vol. 8. Paris, 1765.

Dubois, Jean Antoine, Abbé. *A Description of the Character, Manners and Customs of the People of India.* London, 1816.

———. *Expose de quelques des principaux articles de la théogonie des brahmes.* Paris, 1825.

Dubois de Jancigny, A. Philibert. *Inde.* Paris, 1845.

Dufrenoy, L. 'Étude statistique des tendencies en littérature', *Journal de la Société statistique de Paris*, (Nov–Dec 1945): 260–70.

Du Jarric, Fr. *Akbar and the Jesuits: An Account of the Jesuit Missions to the Court of Akbar.* Oxon: Routledge Curzon, 2005 reprint.

Duruy, Victor. *Histoire de France.* 2 vols. Paris, 1866.

———. *Histoire de l'Orient.* Paris, 1890.

———. *Histoire des Temps Modernes depuis 1453 jusqu'a 1789.* Paris: Librairie Hatchette, 1870. 5th edition.

Eichoff, F. G. *Parallèls des langues de l'Europe et de l'Inde.* Paris, 1836.

Elliot, *The History of India, as Told by Its Own Historians. The Muhammadan Period.* Edited by John Dowson. London: Trubner Company, 1867–77.

Esquer. A. *Essai sur les castes dans l'Inde.* Pondicherry, 1871.

Farrère, Claude. *L'Inde perdue.* Paris: E. Flammarion, 1935.

———. *Forces spirituelles de l'Orient.* Paris, 1937.

De La Flotte. *Esais historiques sur l'Inde (precedes d'un journal de voyages et d'une description géographique de la côte de Coromandel.* Paris: Hérissant, 1769. 8 vols.

Fontaine, Maurices. *Inde Védique. De 1800 à 800 avant J. C.* Paris, 1881.

Forgues. *La Révolte des Cipayes.* Paris, 1860.

Foucaux, Philippe Edouard. *Doctrine des bouddhistes sur le nirvana.* Paris: Benjamin Duprat, 1864.

Foucher, Alfred. *L'art Greco-bouddhique du Gandhara: Etude sur les origins de l'influence classique dans l'art bouddhique de l'Inde et de l'Extrême-Orient.* 2 vols. Paris: E. Leroux, 1905–22.

———. *La vie du Bouddha, d'après les textes et les monuments de l'Inde.* Paris: Payot, 1949.

Gaebelé, Yvonne, Mme Robert. *Histoire de Pondichéry, de l'an 1000 à nos jours.* Pondichéry: Imprimérie du gouvernement, 1960.

———. *Créole et grande dame, Johanna Bégum, marquise Dupleix, 1706–1756.* Pondichéry: Bibliothèque coloniale; Paris: E. Leroux, 1934.

———. *Une Parisienne aux Indes au XVII siècle.* Pondichéry: Bibliothèque coloniale, Paris: Éditions Leroux, 1937.

Garcin de Tassy. *Histoire de la littérature Hindoui et hindoustani.* Paris : Printed under the auspices of the Oriental Translation Committee of Great Britain and Ireland, 1839–47. 2 vols.

———. *Mémoire sur les particularités de la religion musulmane dans l'Inde d'après les ouvrages hindoustanis.* Paris: A. Labitte, 1869 2. éd.

Gnanadicom, F. *L'Inde Française-sa régéneration.* Toulon, 1894.

Gobineau, Comte de. *Essai sur l'inégalité des races humaines.* Paris: Librairie Firmin-Didot, second edition, 1884.

Gopaljee, Samboo. *Les comptoirs français dans l'Inde nouvelle de la Compagnie des Indes à nos jours.* Paris, 1950.

Grousset, René. *Les civilizations de l'Orient.* Paris: les editions G Cres, 1929. Translated as Civilizations of the East by Catherine Alison Phillips. 4 vols. New York: Alfred Knopf, 1931.

———. *Histoire de la philosophie orientale: Inde, Chine, Japon.* Paris: Nouvelle librairie nationale, 1923.

———. *L'Inde.* Paris: Plon, 1949.

Guenon, René. *Introduction générale à l'étude des doctrines hindoues.* Paris: M. Rivière, 1921.

Guimet, Emile. *Huit Jours aux Indes*. Paris, 1876.

Guy, Camille. *Notices coloniales. Exposition universelle de Paris*. Paris, 1900.

———. *Les colonies françaises: la mise en valeur de notre domaine coloniale*. Volume III of Les Colonies françaises, Exposition Universelle de 1900, Publications de la Commission chargée de préparer la participation de la Ministère des Colonies. Paris: Augustin Challamel, 1900.

———. *Exposition Universelle de 1900, Les colonies françaises: Les établissements français de l'Inde*. Paris: Levé, 1900.

———. 'French Colonial Expansion in the Nineteenth Century', *The International Monthly* (July–December 1901) Vol. IV.

De Guignes, Joseph. *Recherches historiques sur la religion indienne*. 1776.

Havell, Ernest Binfield. *The History of Aryan Rule in India, from the Earliest Times to the Death of Akbar*. Np: Frederick A. Stokes, 1918.

Herman, Louis. *Histoire de la rivalitité des Français et des Anglais dans l'Inde*. Paris, 1852.

Hovelacque, Abel and Julien Vinson. *Études de linguistiqe et d'ethnographie*. Paris, Reinwald and Co, 1878.

Hough, Rev. James. *A Reply to the Letters of the Abbé Dubois on the State of Christianity in India*. London, 1824.

Huillet, Dr. N. *Hygiène des blancs, des mixtes, et des Indiens à Pondichéry*. Pondichéry: Géruzet, 1867.

Inauguration du monument éléve à la Mémoire d'Abel Bergaigne. Discours prononcés a Vimy. Souvenir du Oct 9, 1898.

Jacolliot, Louis. *La femme dans l'Inde: La femme aux temps védiques, aux temps brahmaniques, et dans l'Inde de la décadence*. Paris: Lacroix, 1877.

———. *La Bible dans l'Inde. Vie de Iezeus Christna*. Paris: Lacroix, Ver-Boeckhoven & Cie., 1869.

———. *Les traditions indo-européennes et africaines*. Paris: A. Lacroix, 1876.

———. *Le pariah dans l'humanité*. Paris: A. Lacroix et Cie, 1876.

———. *Rois, prêtres et castes*. Paris: Lacroix et Cie, 1877.

Jacquemont, Victor. *Correspondance de Victor Jacquemont avec sa famille et plusieurs de ses amis, pendant son voyage dans l'Inde (1828–1832)*. Paris: H. Fournier, 1833. Translated as Letters from India: Describing a Journey in the British Dominions of India, Tibet, Lahore and Cashmere. London: E. Churton, 1834.

Jordanus. Mirabilia Descripta. *The Wonders of the East*. Translated by Col. Sir Henry Yule. Hakluyt Society Publication no. 31, first series,

1863. Also published as Receuil des Voyages et de Mémoires publié par la Société de Géographie, vol. 4.

Jouveaux-Dubreuil. 'Indes françaises', *Revue des Deux-Mondes*, no. 4, (1937).

——.*Vedic Antiquities*. Pondichéry, 1922.

Julien, Stanislas. *Histoire de la vie de Hiouen-Thsang et de ses voyages dans l'Inde, depuis l'an 629 jusqu'en 645*. Paris: Imprimérie impériale, 1853.

Kermorgant, Alexandre. *Hygiène coloniale*. Paris: Masson, 1911.

Labaume, A. *Recherches Asiatiques. Mémoires de la sociéte établis au Bengale. Paris, 1805* (translation of Asiatick Researches).

Labernadie, Marguerite. *Le vieux Pondichéry, 1674–1815. histoire d'un ville coloniale française*. Pondichéry, 1936.

Lacroix de Marlès, M de., *Histoire générale de l'Inde ancienne et moderne (depuis l'an 200 avant J.C jusqu'a nos jours)*. 6 volumes. Paris: Emler Frères, Libraires-Éditeurs, 1828.

Lacroze, V. *Histoire du christianisme des Indes*. La Haye, 1758.

Lamairesse, E. *L'Inde avant le Bouddha*. Paris: Georges Carré, 1891.

——. *L'Inde apres le Bouddha*. Paris: Georges Carré, 1892.

La Mazelière. Mis de. *Essai sur l'évolution de la Civilisation Indienne*. Paris, 1903. 2 vols.

Lanessan, J. M. A. de. *L'expansion coloniale de la France*. Paris, 1886.

Langlès, Louis Mathieu. *Recherches asiatiques, ou Mémoires de la Société*. Paris: Impremerie imperiale, 1805.

——. *Monuments anciens et modernes de l'Indoustan*. Paris, 1821.

Langlois, Alexandre. *Monuments littéraires de l'Inde ou Mélanges de littérature sanscrit*. Paris: Lefevre, 1827.

Lanoye, F. de. *L'Inde contemporaine*. Paris, 1858.

Laude, F. N. *De la femme dans la société Indoue*. 1805.

Laude, Procureur Général. *De la souveraineté chez les peuples Indous dans l'Antiquité*. Pondichéry, 1870.

Launay, Adrien. *Histoire des Missions de l'Inde*. Paris, 1898.

La Vallée-Poussin, Louis de. *Indo-Européens et Indo-Iraniens: L'Inde jusque vers 300 ans avant Jésus-Christ*. Part of Histoire du monde, edited by M. E. Cavaignac. 3 vols. Paris: E de Boccard, 1924.

Le Bon, Gustave. *Les civilisations de l'Inde*. Paris: Ernest Flammarion, 1900.

——. *Les lois psychologiques de l'évolution des peuples*. Paris, 1894.

Leconte, Casimir. *Des colonies françaises aux Indes orientales*. Lettre adressée à la Chambre des députés. Paris, 1834.

Legoux de Flaix. *Essai historique, géographique et politique sur l'Indoustan*. Paris, 1807.

L'empire français et ses resources: conférences d'information organisées en février-mars, 1942. Paris: Presses universitaires de France, 1942.

Leroux, Pierre. 'De l'influence philosophique des etudes orientales', *Revue Encyclopédique*, (April 1832): 69–82.

Lescure, N. *Précis historique sur les établissements français dans l'Inde.* Pondichéry, 1864.

Lettres édificantes et curieuses écrits des missions étrangères. 8 vols. Paris, 1703–8.

Lettres Inédites d'Henri IV et de pleusiers personages célèbres. Paris: Henri Tardieu, An X (1802).

Lévi, Sylvain. *L'Inde et le monde.* Paris: H. Champion, 1928.

———. *L'Indianisme.* Paris: Larousse, 1915.

———. *La Science des religions et les religions de l'Inde.* Paris,1892.

———. *L'Inde Civilisatrice.* Paris, 3rd edition,1928.

———. 'La formation religieuse de l'Inde contemporaine', *Conferences faites au Musée Guimet.* Paris, 1907.

Lhande, Père. *L'Inde sacrée: grandeur et pitié d'un monde.* Paris: Plon, 1934.

Loti, Pierre. *L'Inde (sans les Anglais).* Paris: Calman-Levy, 1903.

Lyall, Alfred. *The Rise and Expansion of the British Dominion in India.* New York: H. Fertig, 1910.

Maël, Pierre. *The Land of Tawny Beasts.* Translated by Elizabeth Luther Cary New York: Frederick Stokes Co., 1895.

Malet, Albert and Jules Isaac. *Cours abrégé d'histoire* Second edition. Paris: Librairie. Hachette, 1922.

———. *L'Orient et la Grèce.* Paris: Hatchette, 1932.

———. *XVII & XVIII siècles.* Paris: Librairie Hatchette, nd.

———. *XIX siècle. Histoire contemporaine, 1815–1920.* Paris: Librairie Hatchette, nd.

———. *Histoire contemporaine, depuis le milieu du XIX siècle.* 2nd edn. Paris: Colin, 1918. Also a later edition by Librairie Hatchette, 1930.

———. *L'Epoque contemporaine.* Paris: Hatchette, 1907.

Malleson, G. B. *History of the French in India from the Founding of Pondicherry in 1674 to the Capture of that Place in 1761.* London, 1868.

———. *Final French Struggles in India and on the Indian Seas.* London, 1878.

Martineau, Alfred. *Discours prononcé par M. Martineau à l'inauguration du cours d'histoire coloniale au Collège de France, le 4 mai 1921.* Abbeville: Imprimérie de F. Paillart, 1921.

Martineau, Alfred. *L'histoire et les études historiques dans le sud de l'Inde*. Pondichéry: Société de l'Histoire de l'Inde française, 1917.

———. et Hanoteaux, G. *Histoire des colonies françaises et de l'expansion française dans le monde*. Vol. 5. Paris, 1932.

Masson-Oursel, Paul. *La spécificité de la psychologie Indienne*. Melun, 1928.

———. 'Bibliographie sommaire de l'indianisme', *Isis*, no. 3(1920): 171–218.

———. *Esquisse d'une histoire de la philosophie indienne*. Paris: P. Geuthner, 1923.

———. *La philosophie en Orient*. Paris: F. Alcan, 1938.

———. Helena Grabowska and Philippe Stern. *L'Inde antique et la civilisation indienne*. Paris: La Renaissance du Livre, 1933.

Métin, Albert. *L'Inde d' aujourd'hui*. Paris, 1918.

Mélanges d'histoire et de géographie orientales. 4 vols. Paris: J. Maisonneuve et fils, 1914–23.

Michaud, P. R. I. *Histoire des progrès et de la chute de l'empire de Mysore sous les règnes d'Hyder-Ali et Tippoo-Saïb*. 2 volumes. Paris, 1801.

Michelet, Jules. *Bible de l'Humanité*. Paris, 1864.

Mill, James. *The History of British India*. 6 vols. London, 1818.

Mohl, Jules. *Vingt-sept ans d'histoire des etudes orientales: Rapport faits à la Société Asiatique de Paris de 1840 à 1867*. 2 vols. Paris: Reinwald, 1879–80. 2 vols.

Montesquieu, Charles. *De l'esprit des lois*. Paris: Garnier frères 1922 new edn. 2 vols.

———. *Persian Letters*. 1721.

Muir, John. *Original Sanskrit texts on the origin and history of the people of India : their religion and institutions*. 5 vols. London: Trübner & Co., 1873–90, 3rd edn.

Max Müller, Friedrich. *India: what can it Teach Us? A Course of Lectures Delivered Before the University of Cambridge*. Cambridge: Longmans Green, 1883: Lecture I.

———. 'On False Analogies in Comparative Theology (1870)', *The Essential Max Müller: On Language, Mythology, and Religion*. Edited by Jon R. Stone. Palgrave Macmillan, 2002.

M. Naudet, 'Notice historique sur MM. Burnouf, Père et fils', *Mémoires de l'Académie des inscriptions et belles-lettres* 20. Paris, 1854.

Nawrath, Alfred. *Eternal India: The Land, the People, the Masterpieces of Architecture and Sculpture of India, Pakistan, Burma and Ceylon*. New York: Crown Publishers, 1956.

Nilsson, Sten Ake. *European Architecture in India, 1750–1850*. London: Faber and Faber, 1968 edn. *Notes on Pondicherry or The French in*

India. By an Officer of the Madras Artillery. Calcutta: W.Thacker and Co., 1845.

Oltramare, Paul Jean. *L'histoire des idées théosophiques dans l'Inde.* 2 vols. Paris: E Leroux, 1906–23.

Pascal, Blaise. *Pensées,* nos 817 and 818. Translated by W. F. Trotter. 1660.

Pellenc, Baron Jean. *Diamonds and Dust. India through French Eyes.* London, 1936.

Pernot, Maurice. *L'inquietitude de l'Orient sur la route de l'Inde.* np, 1927.

Phear, Sir John. *The Aryan Village in India and Ceylon.* London, 1880.

Piriou, Ernest. *L'Inde contemporaine et le Mouvement nationale.* Paris, 1905.

Pope, G U. *Textbook of Indian History.* London, 1880.

Poulain, Claude. *Notes sur l'Inde française.* Chalon-sur-Saône: Imprimérie de L. Marceau, 1894.

Rajkumar, Nagoji. *The Problem of French India.* New Delhi: All-India Congress Committee 1951.

Ranga Pillai, Ananda. *Journal.* 12 volumes. Trans. from Tamil to English. Madras, 1874.

Rapport Général de Exposition Coloniale Internationale de 1931, présenté par Gouverner Général Olivier. Paris: Impremerie Nationale, 1933.

Raymond, Xavier. *Inde.* Paris, 1845.

Raynal, Abbe. *Histoire philosophique et politique des établissemens et du commerce des Européens dans les deux Indes.* Geneve: Chez J.L. Pellet, 1780.

Regnaud, Paul. *Matériaux pour server à l'histoire de la philosophie de l'Inde.* Paris: F. Vieweg, 1876–78. 2 vols.

———. *Le Rig-véda et les origines de la mythologie indo-europé-enne.* Paris: E. Leroux, 1892.

———. *Les premières formes de la religion et de la tradition dans l'Inde et la Grèce.* Paris: E. Leroux, 1894.

———. *Études védiques et post-védiques.* Paris: E. Leroux, 1898.

Reinaud, Joseph. 'Mémoire géographique, historique et scientifique sur l'Inde antérieurement au milieu du XI siècle, d'après les écrivains arabes, persans, et chinois. 1845–49', *Mémoires de l'Académie des inscriptions et belles-lettres.* Paris: Imprimerie nationale, vol. 18. 2, 1849).

———. *Question scientifique et personnelle soulevée au sein de l'Institut au sujet des dernières découvertes sur la géographie et l'histoire de l'Inde.* Paris: Imprimérie de Cosse et J. Dumaine, 1859.

Renou, Louis. *Anthologie sanskrite: Textes de l'Inde ancienne*. Paris: Payot, 1947.

———. *Littérature sanskrite avec en appendice une table de concordance du Rigveda*. Paris: Maisonneuve, 1946.

———. *Les maîtres de la philology védique*. Paris: P. Geuthner, 1928.

———. *The Influence of Indian Thought on French Literature*. Madras: Adyar Library, 1948.

Reynaud, Gustave A. *Hygiène coloniale*. Paris: Baillière, 1903. 2 vols.

Rousseau, Jean-Jacques. *The Social Contract*, 1762.

———. *Confessions*, Vol. 2. New York: Blanchard, 1857.

Rousselet, Louis. *L'Inde des rajahs: Voyage dans l'Inde centrale et dans les présidences de Bombay et du Bengale*. Paris: Hatchette, 1875. (First published as a series of articles in Le Tour du Monde, vols. 22–1871, 23–1872, 24–1872, 25–1873, 26–1873 and 27–1874).

———. *Tableau des races de l'Inde septentrionale*. Paris: E. Leroux, 1875.

———. *The Serpent Charmer*. New York: Scribner and Sons, 1889.

Silvestre de Sacy, Antoine Isaac. *Mélanges de littérature orientale*. Paris: E Docrocq, 1861.

———. *Mémoires d'histoire et de littérature orientale*. Paris: Academie des Inscriptions et Belles-Lettres, 1823–32.

———. *Notice sur la vie et les ouvrages de m. de Chézy, lue à la séance publique de l'Académie des inscriptions et belles-lettres, du 14 aout 1835*. Paris: Imprimérie de C. Eberhart, 1835.

De Saussure, Leopold. *La psychologie de la colonisation française dans ses rapports avec les sociéties indigènes*. Paris, 1899.

Schoebel, Charles. *Inde française. L'histoire des origines et du developpement des castes de l'Inde*. Paris, 1884.

Sénart, Émile. 'Origines Bouddhiques', *Conferences faites au Musée Guimet*. Paris, 1907.

———. 'Le théâtre indien', *Revue des Deux Mondes* (1 Mai, 1891): 84–123.

———. 'Les castes dans l'Inde', *Revue des Deux Mondes* (1 Mai, 1894).

———. Rajas et la théorie indienne des trois gunas, *Journal Asiatiques*. (July–Aug 1915): 151–88.

———. 'Essai sur la légende du Buddha, son caractère et ses origins', *Journal Asiatiques*, (Aug–Sept 1873: 113–302, Jan–Jun 1874: 249–256, Jul–Dec 1874: Jul–Dec 1875: 97–234.

———. 'Les castes dans l'Inde: Le Présent', *Revue des Deux Mondes*, (1st Feb 1894): 596–636.

———. 'Les Castes dans l'Inde: Les Origines', *Revue des Deux Mondes*, (15 September 1894): 313–47.

———. 'Les Castes dans l'Inde: Le Passé', *Revue des Deux Mondes* (1 March, 1894): 94–120.

Sivaswamy, Kodaganallur. *The Political Struggle in French Establishments in India. Madras, 1947.*

Subbaiah, V. *Saga of Freedom of French India: Testament of my Life.* Madras: New Century Book House, 1990.

Topinard, Paul. *Science and Faith.* Translated by Thomas McCormack. Chicago: Open Court, 1899.

———. *L'Anthropologie.* Paris, 1876.

Travels of the Jesuits into Various Parts of the World, particularly China and the East Indies. Translated by Lockman, John. 2 vols. London, 2nd edition, 1762.

De Valbezen, Eugen. *Les Anglais et l'Inde.* Paris, 1875.

Vinson, Julien. *L'Inde Française et les études indiennes de 1882 à 1884.* Paris: Maisonneuve frères et Ch. Leclerc, 1885.

———. 'Les populations de l'Inde française', *Les Colonies françaises.* Paris, sd. Vol. 2.

———. *L'Inde et le mahométisme.* Np, 1906.

———. *Ethnographie dravidienne. Les castes du sud de l'Inde.* Paris, 1864–69.

———. and Abel Hovelacque. *Études de linguistiqe et d'ethnographie.* Paris: Reinwald and Co, 1878.

Viollis, Andrée. *L'Inde Contre les Anglais.* Paris, sd.

Vivien de Saint-Martin. 'Compte rendu de l'Essai sur les castes de l'Inde par M. Esquer, président du tribunal de Pondichéry', *Bulletin de la Société de géographie,* (November 1872): 534–42.

Voltaire, *Oeuvres Completes de Voltaire: Annales de l'Empire: Fragments sur quelques révolutions dans l'Inde and sur le mort du Comte de Lalli,* vol. 24. Paris: Imprimérie de la Société Littéraire,1785–89.

Voltaire, *Mélanges.* Paris, 1961.

Warren, Comte Edouard de. *L'Inde anglaise avant et après l'insurrention de 1857.* Paris, vol. I 1857, vol. II 1858.

SECONDARY SOURCES

Ageron, Charles-Robert. *L'anticolonialisme en France de 1871 à 1914.* Paris: Presses Universitaires de France, 1973.

Alsayyad, Nezar (ed.). *Forms of Dominance: On the Architecture and Urbanism of the Colonial Enterprise.* Brookfield: Aldershot, 1992.

Ames, Glenn J. and Ronald Love (eds). *Distant Lands and Diverse Cultures: The French Experience in Asia 1600–1700.* Westport Ct and London: Praeger, 2003.

Amin, Shahid. *Event, Metaphor, Memory: Chauri Chaura, 1922–1992.* Berkeley: University of California Press, 1995.

Anderson, Benedict. *Imagined Communities*. London and New York: Verso, 1991.

Anderson, Richard. *India in Romantic and Parnassian French Poetry*. New Haven, 1950.

Annasse, Arthur. *Les comptoirs français de l'Inde : 1664–1954, trois siècles de présence française*. Paris: la Pensée universelle, 1975.

Ansari, S. M. Razaullah 'Introduction of Modern Western Astronomy in India during 18–19 Centuries', *History of Indian Astronomy*, edited by Sen, S. N. and K. S. Shukla. New Delhi: INSA, 1985.

Appadurai, Arjun. 'Right and Left Hand Castes in South India', *Indian Economic and Social History Review* 11 (2–3): 216–60.

Aronson, Alex. *Europe Looks at India*. Bombay: Hind Kitabs, 1946.

Ashcroft, Bill, Gareth Griffiths and Helen Tiffin. *The Empire Writes Back: Theory and Practice in Post-Colonial Literatures*. London: Routledge, 1989.

Assayag, Jackie. 'L'Inde dans le théâtre des Lumières une tragédie théologico-politique inédite de Jean-François de la Harpe : Les Brames (1783)', *Purusartha* (1998), vol. 20: 301–25.

———. *L'Inde fabuleuse: le charme discret de l'exotisme français : XVII-XXe siècles*. Paris: Kimé, 1999.

August, Thomas. *The Selling of the Empire: British and French Imperialist Propaganda 1890–1940*. Westport, Connecticut: Greenwood Press 1985.

———. 'The Colonial Exhibition in France: Education or Reinforcement?', *Proceedings of the Sixth and Seventh Annual Meetings of the French Colonial Historical Society*. 1980/82.

Bailey, F. G. *Caste and the Economic Frontier*. Manchester: Manchester University Press 1957.

Balibar, Etienne and Immannuel Wallerstein, *Race, Nation, Classe: Les identités ambigués*. London and New York: Verso, 1991.

Ballantyne, Tony. *Orientalism and Race. Aryanism in the British Empire*. New York: Palgrave, 2002.

Ballhatchet, Kenneth. *Race, Sex and Class under the Raj*. New York: St. Martin's Press, 1980.

Bamboat, Zenobia. *Voyageurs français dans l'Inde aux XVII et XVIII siècles*. Introduction by A. Martineau. Paris: Société de l'histoire des colonies françaises, 1933.

Bancel, Nicholas (ed.). *Images et Colonies: iconographie et propagande coloniale sur l'Afrique française de 1880 à 1962*. Pascal Blanchard et Laurent Gervereau. Nanterre: Bibliothèque de documentation internationale contemporaine and Paris: Association Connaissance de l'histoire de l'Afrique contemporaine, 1993.

Barrier, Gerald (ed.). *Census in India*. New Delhi: Manohar, 1981.

Colonialism and the Object: Empire, Material Culture and the Museum. Edited by Barringer, Tim and Tom Flynn. London and NY: Routledge, 1998.

Barrow, Ian. *Making History, Drawing Territory. British Mapping in India, c.1756–1905.* New Delhi: OUP, 2003.

Bartlett, Robert. 'On the Politics of Faith and Reason: The Project of Enlightenment in Pierre Bayle and Montesquieu', *The Journal of Politics,* 63.1 (Feb. 2001): 1–28.

Barua, Pradeep. 'Inventing Race. The British and India's Martial Races', *The Historian* 58.1, (1995): 107–16.

Basquel, Victor. *Castes. L'Inde tragique.* Paris: Éditions Jean Cres, 1935.

Baumgart, Winfried. *Imperialism. The Idea and Reality of British and French Colonial Expansion, 1880–1914.* Oxford: OUP, 1982.

Bayly, C. A. *Imperial Meridian: The British Empire and the World, 1780–1831.* London and NY: Longman, 1989.

———. *Indian Society and the Making of the British Empire.* Cambridge: CUP, 1988.

Bayly, Susan. *Caste, Society and Politics in India from the 18th Century to the Modern Age.* Cambridge: CUP, 1999.

Bearce, George D. *British Attitudes towards India, 1784–1858.* Oxford: OUP, 1961.

Beck, Brenda. *Peasant Society in Kongu. A Study of Right and Left Subcastes in South India.* Vancouver, 1972.

Behdad, Ali. *Belated Travelers: Orientalism in the Age of Colonial Dissolution.* Durham: Duke University Press, 1994.

Benedict, Burton. 'International Exhibitions and National Identity', *Anthropology Today*, vol. 7.3. June 1991: 5–9.

Beteille, Andre. *Caste, Class and Power. Changing Patterns of Social Stratification in a Tanjore Village.* Berkeley: University of California Press, 1965.

———. 'The reproduction of inequality. Occupation, caste and family', *Contributions to Indian Sociology* 25.1 (1991): 3–28.

Betts, Raymond. *Tricouleur: The French Overseas Empire.* London and NY: Gordon & Cremonesi, 1978.

———. *France and Decolonization 1900–1960.* New York: St. Martin's Press 1991.

———. *Assimilation and Association in French Colonial Theory, 1890–1914.* New York: Columbia University Press, 1961.

Bhabha, Homi K. *The Location of Culture.* London and New York: Routledge, 1994.

———. *Nation and Narration.* London and New York: Routledge, 1990.

Bhatt, Chetan. *Hindu Nationalism: Origins, Ideologies and Modern Myths.* Oxford: Berg Publishers, 2001.

Biardeau, Madeline. *Hinduism. The Anthropology of a Civilization.* Delhi and New York: Oxford University Press, 1989.

Biès, Jean. *Littérature française et pensée hindoue des origines à 1950.* Paris: C. Klincksieck, 1974.

Bigot, A. 'The Advantages of Anthropological Researches at Pondicherry', *Man in India,* vol. 28.24 (1948).

Bissoondoyal, B. *India in French Literature.* London: Buzac,1967.

Blanchard, Pascal and Nicholas Bancel (eds). *Culture post-coloniale 1961–2006.* Paris: Éditions Autrement, 2005.

Blanks, David R. and Frassetto, Michael (eds). *Western Views of Islam in Medieval and Early Modern Europe: Perception of Other.* New York: St. Martin's Press, 1999.

Blavatsky, Madame. *Isis Unveiled.* 1877.

Blet, Henri. *La Colonisation Française: Les étapes d'une renaissance coloniale, 1789–1870.* Grenoble: B. Arthaud, 1946–50.

Blom, Philip *Enlightening the World: Encyclopédie, The Book That Changed the Course of History.* New York: Palgrave Macmillan, 2005.

Bolt, Christine. *Victorian Attitudes to Race.* London: Routledge and K. Paul, 1971.

Booker, M. Keith. *Colonial Power, Colonial Texts: India in the Modern British Novel.* Ann Arbor: The University of Michigan Press, 1997.

Bouger, Louis. *François Bernier, sa vie, ses voyages, sa classification des races.* Paris: L. Arnette, 1937.

Boulle, Pierre. 'La Construction du Concept de Race dans la France d'Ancien Régime', *Outre-Mers: Revue d'Histoire* (France) 89.2. (2002): 155–75.

Boyé, Jérôme. *Pondichéry, Chandernagore, Karikal, Mahé, Yanaon: les anciens comptoirs français de l'Inde.* Np: Editions C & D, 1992.

Brantlinger, Patrick. *Rule of Darkness: British Literature and Imperialism 1830–1914.* Ithaca, NY: Cornell UP, 1988.

Breckenridge, Carol. 'The Aesthetics and Politics of Colonial Collecting: India at World Fairs', *Comparative Study of Society and History,* 31.2 (April 1989): 195–216.

Breckenridge, Carol and Van der Veer, Peter (eds). *Postcolonialism and the Orientalist Predicament: perspectives on South Asia.* Philadelphia: University of Pennsylvania Press, 1993.

Brimnes, Niels. *Constructing the Colonial Encounter. Right and Left Hand Castes in Early Colonial South India.* Richmond, Surrey: Curzon, 1999.

Bristow, Joseph. *Empire Boys: Adventures in a Man's World.* London and New York: Unwin Hyman, 1991.

Brunschwig, Henri. *French Colonialism 1871–1914: Myths and Realities.* London: Pall Mall Press, 1966. Revised edn.

Burton, Antoinette. *Burdens of History: British Feminists, Indian Women, and Imperial Culture, 1865–1915*. Chapel Hill and London: University of North Carolina Press, 1994.

Butel, Paul. 'French Traders and India at the End of the Eighteenth century', *Merchants, Companies and Trade. Europe and Asia in the early Modern Era*, edited by Chaudhury, Sushil and Morineau, Michel. Cambridge, UK: CUP, 1999.

Camiscioli, Eliza. 'Producing Citizens, Reproducing the "French Race": Immigration, Demography and Pronatalism in Early Twentieth-Century France', *Gender and History*, 13.3 (Nov. 2001): 593–621.

Carr, Philip. *The French at Home in the Country and in Town*. London: Methuen & Co., 1930.

Castle, Kathryn. *Britannia's Children*. Manchester: Manchester University Press, 1996.

Celestine, Fr. Peter. *Early Capuchin Missions in India: Pondicherry, Surat, Madras. 1632–1834*. Sahibabad, 1982.

Çelik, Zeynep. *Urban Forms and Colonial Confrontations: Algiers Under French Rule*. Berkeley, Los Angeles, London: University of California Press, 1997.

Chafer, Tony and Sackur, Amanda (eds). *French Colonial Empire and the Popular Front: Hope and Disillusion*. New York: St. Martin's Press, 1999.

———. *Promoting the Colonial Idea. Propaganda and Visions of Empire in France*. New York: Palgrave, 2002.

Chakrabarty, Dipesh. *Provincialising Europe*. Princeton: Princeton University Press, 2000.

Chakravarty, Suhash. *The Raj Syndrome: A Study in Imperial Perceptions*. Delhi: Chanakya Publications, 1989.

Chapman, Herrick and Frader, Laura L. (eds). *Race in France: Interdisciplinary Perspectives on the Politics of Difference*. New York: Berghahn, 2004.

Chatterjee, Amal. *Representations of India, 1740–1840: The Creation of India in the Colonial Imagination*. New York: St. Martin's Press, 1998.

Chatterjee, Partha. *The Nation and its Fragments. Colonial and Postcolonial Histories*. Princeton, NJ: Princeton University Press, 1993.

———. *Nationalist Thought and the Colonial World. A Derivative Discourse?* London, UK: Zed Books for the United Nations University, 1986.

Chaudhury, Sushil and Michel Morineau (eds). *Merchants, Companies and Trade. Europe and Asia in the Early Modern Era*. Cambridge and NY: Cambridge University Press, 1999.

Chester, Lucy. 'The Mapping of Empire: French and British Cartographies of India in the Late Eighteenth Century,' *Portuguese Studies* 16 (October 2000): 256–65.

Chézaud, Patrick. *Louis Rousselet et l'image de la culture de l'autre.* Saint Pierre de Salerne, G. Monfort, 2005.

Chopra, Preeti. French Colonial Urbanism: A Case Study of Pondicherry. MA Thesis. University of California, Berkeley, May 1993.

Clancy-Smith, Julia and Gouda, Frances (eds). *Domesticating the Empire: Race, Gender and Family Life in French and Dutch Colonialism.* Charlottesville and London: University Press of Virginia, 1998.

Clines, David 'In Search of the Indian Job', *Vetus Testamentum*, Vol. 33. 4 (Oct., 1983): 398–418.

Clooney, Francis. *Fr. Bouchet's India: An 18th Century Jesuits' Encounter with Hinduism.* Chennai: Satyam Nilyam Publications, 2005.

Cohn, Bernard. *An Anthropologist and other Essays.* Delhi, New York: Oxford University Press, 1987.

———. *Colonialism and its Forms of Knowledge.* Princeton: Princeton University Press, 1996.

Colley, Linda. Britons: *Forging the Nation, 1707–1837.* New Haven and London: Yale University Press, 1992.

Comaroff, John L. and Comaroff, Jean. *Of Revelation and Revolution* 2 vols. Chicago and London: University of Chicago Press,1991.

Conklin, Alice L. *A Mission to Civilize: The Republican Idea of Empire in France and West Africa, 1895–1930.* Stanford, California: Stanford University Press, 1997.

Conlon, Frank. *Caste in a Changing World.* Berkeley: University of California Press, 1977.

Cooper, Frederick and Stoler, Laura Ann (eds). *Tensions of Empire: Colonial Cultures in a Bourgeois World.* Berkeley, Los Angeles, London: University of California Press, 1997.

Creer, Lelaud. *Napoleonic Interests in India, 1797–1807.* Washington DC, 1929.

Cronin, Richard. *Imagining India.* London; Macmillan Press Limited, 1989.

Daniel, Valentine. *Fluid Signs. Being a Person the Tamil way.* Berkeley: University of California Press, 1984.

Das, Sudipta. *Myths and Realities of French Imperialism in India, 1763–1783.* New York: P. Lang, 1992.

Das, Veena. *Structure and Cognition.* Delhi: OUP, 1977.

Defrance, Jacques 'Les Gymnastiques et l'Idéologie Eugeniste en France pendant la Prémière Moitié du 20eme siècle', *Stadion,* 26.2 (2000): 155–77.

Delavignette, Robert Louis. *Christianity and Colonialism.* New York: Hawthorn Books, 1964.

Delaye, Karine. 'L'Affaire Myngoon Min ou les tribulations d'un prince birman entre rivalités imperialists et entente cordiale (1884–1921)', *Les Relations entre la France et l'Inde de 1673 à nos jours*. Edited by Jacques Weber. Paris: Les indes savantes, 2002).

Deleury, Guy. *Les Indes florissantes: Anthologie des voyageurs français en Inde (1750–1820)*. Paris: R. Laffont, 1991.

Deliège, Robert. *The Untouchables of India*. New York and Oxford: OUP, 1999.

———. 'Replication and Consensus', *Man* ns 27 (1992): 155–73.

Diagou, Jaganou. *Résumé d'histoire de l'Inde française, 1742–1814*. Pondichéry: J. Diagou, 1990.

Dirks, Nicholas. *The Hollow Crown. The Ethnohistory of a Small Kingdom*. Cambridge: CUP, 1987.

Dirks, Nicholas (ed.). *Colonialism and Culture*. Ann Arbor: The University of Michigan Press, 1992.

———. *Castes of Mind*. Princeton: PUP, 2001.

Divien, Emmanuel. The Development of Tamil Society in Pondicherry, 1706–1898. PhD Thesis, University of Madras, 1975.

Duchet, Michèle. *Diderot et l'Histoire des deux Indes: ou, L'écriture fragmentaire*. Paris: A.G. Nizet, 1978.

Dumézil, Georges. *Les dieux des Indo-Européens*. Paris: Presses universitaires de France, 1952.

Dumont, Louis. *Homo Hierarchicus: The Caste System and its Implications*. London: Weidenfeld and Nicolson, 1970.

Eastern Encounters: Orientalist Painters of the Nineteenth Century. London: The Fine Art Society, 1978.

Edney, Matthew H. *Mapping an Empire. The Geographical Construction of British India, 1765–1843*. Chicago: University of Chicago Press, 1997.

Edwardes, Michael. *British India 1772–1947*. New York: Taplinger Pub. Co., 1967.

Edwards, Elizabeth. *Anthropology and Photography, 1860–1920*. New Hampshire: YUP, 1994.

Edwards, Penny. 'Taj Angkor: Enshrining l'Inde in le Cambodge' Paper presented at 'Indochina', India and France: Cultural Representations, University of Newcastle upon Tyne, Newcastle, England, 5–7 September 2003.

Elias, Norbert. *The Civilising Process*. Oxford, 1978–1982, vol.1.

Engels, Dagmar and Shula Marks (eds). *Contesting colonial hegemony. State and Society in India and Africa*. London: British Academic Press, 1994.

Ezra, Elizabeth, *The Colonial Unconscious: Race and Culture in Interwar France*. Ithaca and London: Cornell University Press, 2000.

Ezra, Elizabeth. 'The Colonial Look: Exhibiting Empire in the 1930's', *Contemporary French Civilization* 19.1 (1995).

Fanon, Frantz. *Black Skin, White Masks*. Translated by Charles Lam Markmann. New York: Grove Press, 1967.

Figuiera, Dorothy. *Translating the Orient: The Reception of Sakuntala in Nineteenth-century Europe*. Albany: State University of New York Press, 1991.

———. *Aryans, Jews, Brahmins: Theorizing Authority through Myths of Identity*. Albany: State University of New York Press, 2002.

Filliozat, Jean. 'La Naissance et l'essor de l'indianisme', *Bulletin de la Société des* études indochinoises de Saigon, 29.4 (1954): 1–32.

———. 'Une grammaire sanskrit du XVII siècle et les debuts du l'indianisme en France', *Bulletin de la Société des Études Indochinoises*, 29.4 (1954): 275–84.

———. 'Les échanges de l'Inde et l'empire romaine', *Revue historique*, no. 201 (1949).

———. 'La france et l'Inde dans la creation de l'Indianisme', *France-Orient* (January 1947).

Fletcher, Yaël Simpson. 'City, Nation and Empire in Marseilles, 1919–1939', PhD Diss. Thesis, Emory University, 1999.

Foucault, Michael. *Discipline and Punish: The Birth of the Prison*. New York: Vintage, 1995.

Frith, Nicki. 'Competing Colonial Discourses in India: Representing the 1857 Kanpur Massacres in French- and English-Language Texts and Images' Unpublished doctoral thesis, University of Liverpool, forthcoming 2008.

———. 'Natural and Necessary Enemies': French-Language Representations of the Indian 'Mutinies' and Britain's Colonial 'Failure', Paper presented at 1st AHRC Study Day: French Subaltern Colonizers and the Grand Narrative of British India. University of Liverpool, 10 September 2007.

Gibbs, Kathryn. 'The Exposition Coloniale of 1900: Representing and Forgetting l'Inde française'. Paper presented at 1st AHRC Study Day: French Subaltern Colonizers and the Grand Narrative of British India. University of Liverpool, 10 September 2007.

Gole, Susan. *Early Maps of India*. New York: Humanities Press, 1976.

Gopaljee, Samboo. *Les Comptoirs Français dans l'Inde Nouvelle*. Paris: Fasquelle Editeurs, 1950.

Gouda, Frances. 'Mimicry and Projection in the Colonial Encounter', *Journal of Colonialism and Colonial History*, 1.2 (2000).

Greenberger, Allan. *The British Image of India: A Study in the Literature of Imperialism, 1880–1960*. London: OUP, 1969.

Greene, John 'Some Early Speculations on the Origin of the Human Species', *American Anthropologist*, 56 (1954): 31–41.

Gros, François (ed.). *Passeurs d'Orient. Encounters between India and France*. Paris: Ministry of External Affairs, 1991.

Guha, Ranajit. *Dominance without Hegemony: History and Power in Colonial India*. Cambridge: CUP, 1997.

———. 'Not at Home in Empire', *Critical Inquiry* 23 (Spring 1997): 482–93.

Guha, Sumit. 'Lower Strata, Older Races, and Aboriginal Peoples: Racial Anthropology and Mythical History Past and Present', *JAS* 57.2 (May 1998): 423–41.

Halbfass, Wilhelm. *India and Europe*. Albany, NY: State University of New York Press, 1988.

Hall, Catherine. *Civilizing Subjects*. Chicago: University of Chicago Press, 2002.

Haller, John 'The Species Problem: Nineteenth-century Concepts of Racial Inferiority in the Origin of Man Controversy', *American Anthropologist*, 72 (1970): 1319–29.

Hankins, Frank H. *The Racial Basis of Civilization*. New York and London: A. A. Knopf, 1926.

Hawley, D. S. 'L'Inde de Voltaire', *Studies on Voltaire and the 18th Century*, vol. CXX (1974): 139–78.

Haynes, Douglas and Gyan Prakash (eds). *Contesting Power: Resistance and Everyday Social Relations in South Asia*. Berkeley: University of California Press, 1992.

Hengen, Orville. Comparative Colonialism: An Analysis of the British and French Colonial Practices and Procedures in India and Vietnam. M A Thesis, University of Kansas, 1973.

Horvath, Sandra. Victor Duruy and French Education, 1863–1869. PhD Thesis, Catholic University of America, 1971.

Hulin, Michel, Christine Maillard, and Gérard Fussman (eds). *L'Inde inspiratrice*. Strasbourg, 1996.

Hyam, Ronald. *Britain's Imperial Century*. New York: Barnes & Noble Books, 1976.

———. *Empire and Sexuality: The British Experience*. Manchester and New York: Manchester University Press, 1990.

Inden, Ronald. *Imagining India*. Oxford: UK; Cambridge, Mass., USA: Basil Blackwell, 1990.

Irschick, Eugene. *Dialogue and History*. Berkeley: University of California Press, 1994.

Irwin, Lee 'Western Esotericism, Eastern Spirituality, and the Global Future', *Esoterica* III (2001): 1–47.

Jasanoff, Maya. *Edge of Empire, Lives, Culture, and Conquest in the East, 1750–1850*. NY: Knopf, 2005.

Johnson, G. Wesley (ed.). *Double Impact: France and Africa on the Age of Imperialism*. Westport, Connecticut and London, England: Greenwood Press, 1985.

Jullian, Philippe. *The Orientalists: European Painters of Eastern Scenes*. Oxford: OUP, 1977.

Kabbani, Rana. *Europe's Myths of the Orient*. London: Macmillan, 1986.

Kasturi, Malavika. 'Law and Crime in India. British Policy and the Female Infanticide Act of 1870', *Indian Journal of Gender Studies* 1.2 1994: 169–93.

Kaviraj, Sudipta. 'The Imaginary Institution of India', *Subaltern Studies 7*.

Keller, Richard 'Madness and Colonization: Psychiatry in the British and French Empires, 1800–1962', *Journal of Social History*, 35.2 (2001): 295–326.

Khilnani, Sunil. *The Idea of India*. Delhi: Penguin, 1997.

Kochhar, R. K. 'Secondary Tools of Empire: Jesuit Men of Science in India', *Discoveries, Missionary Expansion and Asian Cultures*. Edited by Teotonio R de. Souza. New Delhi: Concept Publishing Company, 1994.

Lacote, Felix. 'L'Indianisme', *Société Asiatique: Livre du centenaire*. Paris: La Société Asiatique, 1922.

Lacroix, Paul. Manners, *Custom and Dress During the Middle Ages and During the Renaissance Period*. Project Gutenberg EBook.

Lafont, Jean Marie. *Indika. Essays in Indo-French relations 1630–1976*. New Delhi: Manohar, 2000.

———. *Chitra: Cities and Monuments of 18th–century India from French Archives*. Oxford: OUP, 2001.

———. *La présence française dans le royaume sikh du Penjab : 1822–1849*. Paris : École française d'Extrême-Orient, 1992.

———. *Seminar: Indo-French Relations: History & Perspectives*. New Delhi: Office of the Counsellor for Cultural, Scientific & Technical Cooperation, Embassy of France, 1990.

Lahor, Jean. *L'Influence de la pensée religieuse indienne dans le romantisme et le Parnasse*. Paris: A. G. Nizet, 1962.

Leask, Nigel. 'Francis Wilford and the Colonial Construction of Hindu Geography 1799–1822', *Romantic Geographies. Discourses of Travel 1775–1844*. Edited by Amanda Gilroy. Manchester and New York: Manchester University Press, 2000.

Lebovics, Herman. *True France: The Wars over Cultural Identity 1900–1945*. Ithaca and London: Cornell University Press, 1992.

———. 'Donner à voir l'Empire colonial: l'exposition coloniale internationale de Paris en 1931', *Gradhiva*, no. 7, hiver 1989–90: 18–28.

Le Collège de France (1530–1930). Livre Jubiliare composée a l'occasion de son quatrième centenaire. Paris, 1932.

Leopold, Joan. 'The Aryan Theory of Race', *Indian Economic and Social History Review*, 7 (1970): 271–91.

———. 'British Application of the Aryan Theory of Race to India', *English Historical Review* 89.3 (1974): 578–603.

Les relations historiques et culturelles entre la France et l'Inde XVII–XX siècles. 2 volumes. Sainte-Clotilde: Le Chaudron, 1987.

Lewis, Martin Deming. 'One Hundred Million Frenchmen: The "Assimilation" Theory in French Colonial Policy', *Comparative Studies in Society and History*, vol. 4.2 (Jan. 1962): 129–53.

L'Inde, études et images. Paris: l'Harmattan and Saint-Denis: Université de la Réunion, 1993.

L'Inde française dans la guerre: vers 1942 Pondichéry: Imprimérie de la Mission, s.d.

Lokke, Carl Ludwig. *France and the Colonial Question: A Study of Contemporary French Opinion 1763–1801*. New York: Octagon Books, 1976, reprint of 1932 ed. *Curators of the Buddha: the Study of Buddhism under Colonialism*.

Lopez, Donald. Chicago: University of Chicago Press, 1995.

Lorcin, Patricia 'Imperialism, Colonial Identity and Race in Algeria, 1830–1870: the Role of the French Medical Corps', *Isis*, Vol. 90, No. 4 (Dec. 1999): 653–79.

———. *Imperial Identities: Stereotyping, Prejudice and Race in Colonial Algeria*. St. Martin's Press: New York, 1999.

Lorenzen, David. 'Who invented Hinduism?', *Society for Comparative Study of Society and History*, (1999): 630–59.

Lowe, Lisa. *Critical Terrains. French and British Orientalisms*. Ithaca: Cornell University Press, 1991.

Mainardi, Patricia. 'The Double Exhibition in Nineteenth Century France', *Art Journal* 48.1, Spring 1989: 23–28.

Maingueneau, Dominique. *Les Livres d'école de la république 1870–1914. Discours et idéologie*. Le Sycomore. Paris, 1979.

Mangan, J. A. (ed.). *The Imperial Curriculum: Racial Images and Education in the British Colonial Experience*. London and New York: Routledge, 1993.

Marseille, Jacques. *Empire colonial et capitalisme français: histoire d'un divorce*. Paris: Éditions Albin Michel, 1984.

———. *L'Age d'Or de la France Coloniale*. Paris: Éditions Albin Michel, 1986.

Marsh, Kate. *Fictions of 1947: Representations of Indian Decolonization in French-language texts*. New York: Peter Lang, 2007.

———. 'Les cinq noms sonores: The French Voice in the Story of British India 1763–1954', *Journal of Romance Studies*, 5 (2005), 65–77 (co-authored with Ian H. Magedera).

Marsh, Kate. 'Representing Indian Decolonization in the Parisian Press 1923–1954', *International Journal of Francophone Studies*, 5 (2002), 74–84.

Marshall, Bruce D. *The French Colonial Myth and Constitution-Making in the Fourth Republic*. New Haven and London: Yale University Press, 1973.

Marshall, Peter (ed.). *The British Discovery of Hinduism in the Eighteenth Century*. Cambridge: Cambridge University Press, 1970.

Masui, Jacques (ed.). Approches de l'Inde. Texts et études. *Les Cahiers du Sud*, 1949.

Masuzawa, Tomoko. *The Invention of World Religions, Or, How European Universalism was Preserved in the Language of Pluralism*. Chicago: University of Chicago Press, 2005.

Mathew, K. S. (ed.). *French in India and Indian nationalism 1700–1963*. 2 vols. Delhi, 1999.

Mathew, K. S. and Stephen, S. Jeyaseela (eds). *Indo-French relations*. Delhi: Published by Pragati Publications in association with Indian Council of Historical Research, 1999.

Maxwell, Anne. *Colonial Photography and Exhibitions. Representations of the 'Native' and the Making of European Identities*. London and New York: Leicester University Press, 1999.

———. *Picture Imperfect. Photography and Eugenics, 1870–1940*. Brighton and Portland: Sussex Academic Press, 2008.

McClellan III, James E. 'The Academie Royale des Sciences, 1699–1793: A Statistical Portrait', *Isis*, Vol. 72, No. 4 (Dec. 1981): 541–67.

McCully, Bruce T. 'The Origins of Indian Nationalism according to Native Writers", *Journal of Modern History*, 7.3 (September 1935): 295–314.

———. *English Education and the Origins of Indian Nationalism*. Gloucester, Mass.: P. Smith, 1966.

McGetchin, Douglas T. 'Wilting Florists: The Turbulent Early Decades of the Societe Asiatique, 1822–1860', *Journal of the History of Ideas*, Vol. 64, No. 4 (2003): 565–80.

Mehta, Binita. *Widows, Pariahs and Bayadères. India as Spectacle*. Lewisburg: Bucknell University Press and London: Associated University Presses, 2002.

———. The Image of India in the Works of Voltaire, Lemierre, and Bernardin de Saint-Pierre. MA Thesis, University of Georgia, 1985.

Metcalf, Thomas. *Message Actuel de l'Inde*. Cahiers du Sud, 1941. *Ideologies of the Raj*. Cambridge: CUP, 1994.

Michaud, Roland and Sabrina. *Mirror of India*. London, 1990.

Miles, William F. S. *Imperial Burdens: Countercolonialism in Former French India*. Boulder, London: L. Rienner Publishers, 1995.

Miles, William F S. and Clive Schofield. *Absorbing International Boundaries within a National Framework. Pondicherry and the French Indian Experience.* Durham: Duke University Press, 1993.

———. 'Comparative Decolonization: French West Africa, French Caribbean, French India,' *Contemporary French Civilization*, 14.2 (Summer/Fall 1990): 212–26.

Miller, Christopher 'Hallucinations of France and Africa in the Colonial Exhibition of 1931 and Ousmane Socé's Mirages de Paris', *Paragraph* 8.1: 39–63.

Minattur, Joseph. Administration of Justice in French Indian settlements. Punjab, 1978.

———. *Justice in Pondicherry.* New Delhi: The Indian Law Institute, 1973.

Misra, Udayon. *The Raj in Fiction: A Study of Nineteenth Century British Attitudes Towards India.* Delhi: B.R. Pub. Corp, 1987.

Mitchell, Timothy. *Colonising Egypt.* Cambridge, New York: Cambridge University Press, 1988.

———. 'The World as Exhibition', *Comparative Study of Society and History*, 31.2, April 1989: 217–36.

Mitter, Partha. *Much Maligned Monsters. History of European Reactions to Indian art.* Oxford: Clarendon Press, 1977.

Mohan, Jyoti 'British and French Ethnographies of India: Dubois and his English Commentators', *French Colonial History*, Vol. 5 (2004): 229–46.

———. 'La civilisation la plus antique: Voltaire's Images of India', *Journal of World History*, Vol 16.2 (June 2005): 173–86.

———. '"I thought India was French": The Images of India at the Exposition Universelle, Paris 1931', *Francophone Postcolonial Studies*, 3.1 (Spring/Summer 2005).

Morrison, Charles. 'Three Styles of Imperial Ethnography. British officials as Anthropologists in India', *Knowledge and Society* (1984).

Morton, Patricia. 'National and Colonial: the Musée des colonies at the Colonial Exposition Paris 1931', *Art Bulletin,* LXXX number 2 (June 1998).

———. *Hybrid Modernities: Architecture and Representation at the 1931 Colonial Exposition, Paris.* Cambridge Mass. and London, England: The MIT Press, 2000.

Moule, Arthur C. 'Brother Jordan of Sévérac', *Journal of the Royal Asiatic Society of Great Britain and Ireland* (1928): 349–76.

Ch. Mouzon, 'Pondichéry: Études de géographie humaine' *Acta geographica*, (19, Paris, 1954).

Murr, Sylvia. *L'Inde philosophique entre Bossuet et Voltaire.* Two volumes. Paris, 1987.

Murr, Sylvia 'Les conditions d'émergence du discours sur l'Inde au siècle des Lumières, Inde et Littératures', *Purusartha*, 7 (1983): 233–84.
——. 'N. J. Desvaulx (1745–1825), véritable auteur des Moeurs, institutions et cérémonies des peuples de l'Inde' de l'Abbé Dubois,' *Collection Purusartha*, 3 (1977).
Murti, Kamakshi P. *India: The Seductive and Seduced 'Other' of German Orientalism.* Westport, CT: Greenwood Publishing Group, 2001.
Nandy, Ashis. *The Intimate Enemy: Loss and Recovery of Self under Colonialism.* New Delhi: OUP, 1983.
Neogy, Ajit. *Decolonisation in French India: Liberation Movement and Indo-French relations, 1947–1954.* Pondichéry: Institut français de Pondichéry, 1997.
Norindr, Panivong. *Phantasmatic Indo-China: French Colonial Ideology in Architecture, Film and Literature.* Durham and London: Duke University Press, 1996.
Robert Nye. An Intellectual Portrait of Gustave Lebon. PhD thesis, University of Wisconsin, 1969.
Oaten, Edward Farley. *European Travellers in India during the Fifteenth, Sixteenth and Seventeenth Centuries.* 1909. New York: AMS Press, 1971 reprint
O'Hanlon, Rosalind. 'Recovering the Subject: Subaltern Studies and Histories of Resistance in Colonial South Asia', *Modern Asian Studies* 22.1 (1988): 189–224.
Okada, Amina and Enrico Isacco (eds). *L'Inde au XIXe siècle: voyage aux sources de l'imaginaire.* Marseille: AGEP, 1991.
Osbourne, Michael A. *Nature, the Exotic, and the Science of French Colonialism.* Indianapolis: Indiana University Press, 1994.
Pandey, Gyanendra. *The Construction of Communalism in Colonial North India.* Delhi: OUP, 1990.
Parry, Benita. *Delusions and Discoveries. Studies on India in the British Imagination, 1880–1930.* Berkeley: University of California Press, 1972.
Paxton, Nancy. *Writing under the Raj: Gender, Race and Rape in the British Colonial Imagination, 1830–1947.* New Brunswick, New Jersey: Rutgers University Press, 1999.
Peabody, Sue. *There are no Slaves in France: The Political Culture of Race and Slavery in the Ancien Régime.* New York: Oxford University Press, 1996.
Pels, Peter and Salemik, Oscar (eds). *Colonial Subjects. Essays on the Practical History of Anthropology.* Ann Arbor: University of Michigan Press, 1999.
Petr, Christian. *L'Inde des romans.* Paris: Ed Kailash, 1995.
Pinney, Christopher. 'Representation of India. Normalism and the "other"', *Pacific Viewpoint*, 29.2 (1988): 144–62.

Pinney, Christopher 'Classification and Fantasy in the Photographic Construction of Caste and Tribe', *Visual Anthropology* (2–3): 259–88.

————. *Photography's Other Histories*. Co-edited with Nicolas Petersen. Durham, NC: Duke University Press, 2003.

Pol-Droit, Roger. *L'Oubli de l'Inde*. Paris: Presses Universitaires de France, 1989.

Poliakov, Leon. *The Aryan Myth: A History of Racist and Nationalist Ideas in Europe*. Translated by E. Howard. New York: Basic Books, 1971.

Ponnou-Delaffon, Bernard. *Les paysans du territoire de Pondichéry*. Montpellier: Imprimérie de L'Abeille, 1945.

Pouchepadass, Jacques and Maurice Aymard (eds). *Indo-French relations. History and Perspectives: History & Perspectives*, Seminar 17, 18, 19 April 1990. New Delhi: India International Centre, 1990.

Power, Thomas F. *Jules Ferry and the Renaissance of French Imperialism*. New York: Octagon Books, 1966.

Pratt, Mary Louise. *Imperial Eyes: Travel Writing and Transculturation*. London and New York: Routledge, 1992.

Priestley, H.I. *France Overseas: A Study of Modern Imperialism*. New York, London: D. Appleton-Century, 1938.

Priolkar, A.K. (ed.). *The Goa Inquisition, Being a Quarter-centenary Commemoration Study of the Inquisition in India*. Bombay: Bombay University, 1961.

Pyenson, Lewis. *Civilising Mission. Exact Sciences and French Overseas Expansion 1830–1940*. Baltimore: Johns Hopkins University Press, 1993.

Quinn, Frederick. *The French Overseas Empire*. Westport, Connecticut and London: Praeger, 2000.

Raheja, Gloria Goodwin. 'Power and dialogue in the production of colonial ethnographies in 19th century India', *South Asia Research*, 19.1 (Spring 1999): 1–4.

Raina, Dhruv. *Nationalism, Institutional Science and the Politics of Knowledge: Ancient Indian Astronomy and Mathematics in the Landscape of French Enlightenment Historiography*, (Institutionen för vetenskapsteori, Göteborgs Universitet, 1999) Rapport Nr. 201.

————. 'Jean-Baptiste Biot on the History of Indian Astronomy (1830–1860): The Nation in the Post-Enlightenment Historiography of Science', *Indian Journal of History of Science* 35.4 (2000): 319–46.

————. 'Betwixt Jesuit and Enlightenment Historiography: The Context of Jean-Sylvain Bailly's History of Indian Astronomy', *Revue d'Histoire de Mathématiques* 9 (2003): 101–53.

Raina, Dhruv 'The Mystery of French Jesuit Manuscripts on Indian Astronomy: The Narratology and Impact of a Late Seventeenth Early Eighteenth Century Project' (paper presented at a workshop on 'Looking at it from Asia: The Processes that Shaped the Sources of History of Science.' Recherches Epistémologiques et Historiques sur les Sciences, Paris, Sept. 2006).

Raj, S. D. Pondicherry: A Planning Study. MA thesis. New Delhi: SPCA, 1961.

Ramaswamy, Sumathi. *Passions of the Tongue.* Berkeley: University of California Press, 1997.

Ravi, Srilata. *L'Inde romancée: l'Inde dans le genre romanesque français depuis 1947.* New York: P. Lang, 1997.

Raychoudhuri, Tapan. *Europe Reconsidered. Perceptions of the West in 19th-century Bengal.* Delhi: OUP, 1988.

Relations historiques et culturelles entre la France et l'Inde : XVIIe-XIXe siècles. Actes de la Conférence internationale France-Inde de l'AHIOI (Association historique internationale de l'Océan indien), Saint-Denis de la Réunion, 21–28 juillet 1986. Sainte-Clotilde (la Réunion): AHIOI, 1987.

Reminiscences. The French in India. Delhi: INTACH, 1997.

Renou, Louis. *The Influence of Indian Thought on French Literature.* Adyar, 1948.

———. and Jean Filliozat. *L'Inde Classique. Manuel des Etudes Indiennes.* Vol 1 Paris, 1947. Vol. 2 Hanoi, 1953.

Rich, Jeremy. '"Une Babylone Noire": Interracial Unions in Colonial Libreville, c. 1860–1914', *French Colonial History*, 4 (2003): 145–69.

Richards, Thomas. *The Imperial Archive: Knowledge and the Fantasy of Empire.* New York and London: Verso, 1993.

———. 'Archive and Utopia', *Representations*, vol. 0.37, winter 1992.

Ridley, Hugh. *Images of Imperial Rule.* London: Croom Helm and New York: St. Martin's Press, 1983.

The Concept of Race in South Asia. Edited by Robb, Peter. Delhi: Oxford University Press, 1995.

Rocher, Ludo. *Ezourvedam. A French Veda of the Eighteenth Century.* Philadelphia: University of Pennsylvania Press, 1984.

Rosenblum, Mort. *Mission to Civilize: The French Way.* San Diego, 1986.

Ryan, James 'European Travelers before Columbus: The Fourteenth Century's Discovery of India', Catholic Historical Review, vol. 79, Issue 4 (October 1993): 648–90.

———. *Picturing Empire: Photography and the Visualization of the British* Empire. Chicago: University of Chicago Press, 1998.

Said, Edward W. *Orientalism* New York: Vintage Books, 1978.

Recasting Women. Essays in Colonial History edited by Sangari, Kumkum and Sudesh Vaid, Delhi: Kali for Women, 1989.

Sareen, Tilak. *India and the French Revolution: A Collection of Documents and Writings.* New Delhi, 1989.

Sarkar, Indira. *Social Contacts of French Women in Calcutta.* Calcutta, 1947.

Sarkar, Sumit. *Modern India.* Delhi: Macmillan, 1983.

———. *Writing Social History.* Delhi: OUP, 1997.

Sarton, George 'Anquetil-Duperron (1731–1805)', *Osiris,* vol. 3 1937: 193–223.

Schneider, William H. *An Empire for the Masses: The French Popular Image of Africa, 1870–1900.* Westport, Connecticut and London, England: Greenwood Press, 1982.

———. 'Race and Empire: The Rise of Popular Ethnography in the late Nineteenth Century', *Journal of Popular Culture,* 11.1 (1978): 98–109.

Schiller, Francis. *Paul Broca: Founder of French Anthropology, Explorer of the Brain.* Berkeley: University of California Press, 1979.

Schwab, Raymond. *La Renaissance orientale.* Paris: Payot, 1950.

Schwarz, Henry. 'Laissez-faire linguistics. Grammar and the codes of empire', *Critical Inquiry* 23 (Spring 1997): 509–35.

Seillière, Ernest. *Le Comte de Gobineau et l'Aryanisme Historique.* 1903.

Sen, Amartya. 'Indian Traditions and the Western Imagination', *Daedalus,* vol. 126, no. 2, Human Diversity. Spring, 1997: 1–26.

Sen, S. P. *The French in India: First Establishments and Struggle.* Calcutta, 1947.

———. *The French in India, 1763–1816.* Delhi: Munshiram Manoharlal, 1971.

Shapiro, Ann-Louise, 'Fixing History: Narratives of World War I in France', *History and Theory* 36.4 (1997): 111–30.

Sharma, Radha. 'India Mirrored in Contemporary French Writings', *Encountering the Indian. Contemporary European Images of India* edited by Vibha Maurya. New Delhi: Aryan, 1999.

Sharma, Virendra Nath. 'The Impact of Eighteenth Century Jesuit Astronomers on the Astronomy of India and China', *Indian Journal of History of Science* 17.2 (1982): 345–52.

Sharpe, Jenny. *Allegories of Empire. The Figure of Woman in the Colonial Text.* Minneapolis: University of Minnesota Press, 1993.

Shaw, Wendy. 'Stylizing the French Sudan', *Jusûr,* 9, 1993.

Singaravélou, Pierre. *L'École française d'Extrême-Orient ou L'institution des marges, 1898–1956.* Paris and Montréal: L'Harmattan, 1999.

Sinha, Mrinalini. *Colonial Masculinity : The 'Manly Englishman' and the 'Effeminate Bengali' in the late nineteenth century.* Manchester: Manchester University Press, 1995.

Société Asiatique. *Le livre du centenaire (1822–1922): cent ans d'orientalisme en France.* Paris: Geuthner, 1922.

Société Asiatique. *Les Fêtes du Centenaire.* Paris, 1922.

Spurr, David. *The Rhetoric of Empire: Colonial Discourse in Journalism, Travel Writing and Imperial Administration.* Baltimore: JHU Press, 1993.

Sreenivasan, C.V. French Colonial Planning in Pondicherry. MA thesis. New Delhi: SPCA, 1970.

Srinivas, M. N. *The Cohesive Role of Sanskritisation and other Essays.* Delhi: OUP, 1989.

Staum, Martin. *Labeling People: French Scholars on Society, Race and Empire, 1815–1848.* Montreal: McGill-Queen's University Press, 2003.

Stocking, George W. *Race, Culture and Evolution. Essays in the History of Anthropology.* New York: Free Press, 1968.

Strain, Ellen. 'Exotic Bodies, Distant Landscapes: Touristic Viewing and Popularized Anthropology in the Nineteenth Century', *Wide Angle* 18.2 (1996): 70–100.

Streets, Heather. *Martial Races: The Military, Race and Masculinity in British Imperial Culture, 1857–1914.* Manchester: Manchester University Press, 2004.

Stuurman, Siep. 'François Bernier and the Invention of Racial Classification', *History Workshop Journal* 50 (2000): 1–21.

———. 'Cosmopolitan Egalitarianism in the Enlightenment: Anquetil-Duperron on India and America', *Journal of the History of Ideas,* 68.2 (April 2007): 255–78.

Suleri, Sara. *The Rhetoric of English India.* Chicago: University of Chicago Press, 1992.

Sundararajan, Saroja. *Pondicherry,* Lalitha Publications. 1997.

Surface, Esther. *The Rivalry of the British and the French in India, 1670–1754.* MA Thesis, University of California, 1929.

Teltscher, Kate. 'Maidenly and Well-nigh Effeminate: Constructions of Hindu Masculinity and Religion in 17th-century English Texts', *Postcolonial Studies* 3.2 (2000): 159–70.

———. *India Inscribed: European and British Writing on India, 1600–1800.* Delhi: OUP, 1995.

Thompson, Edward and G.T. Garratt. *Rise and Fulfilment of British Rule.* Allahabad: Central Book Depot, 1969.

Thornton, A. P. *The Imperial Idea and its Enemies; A Study in British Power.* London: Macmillan and New York: St. Martin's Press, 1959.

Trautmann, Thomas. *Aryans and British India*. Berkeley and LA: University of California Press, 1997.

———. *Languages and Nations. The Dravidian Proof in Colonial Madras*. CA: University of California Press, 2006.

Trivedi, Harish. *Colonial Transactions. English Literature and India*. Manchester: Manchester University Press, 1995.

Trois siècles de présence française en Inde. Paris, 1994.

Ungar, Steven and Conley, Tom (eds). *Identity Papers. Contested Nationhood in Twentieth-Century France*. Minneapolis and London: University of Minneapolis Press, 1996.

vander Veer, Peter. *Imperial Encounters: Religion and Modernity in India and Britain*. Princeton: Princeton University Press, 2001.

Venturi, Franco. 'Oriental Despotism', *Journal of the History of Ideas*, vol. 24. 1 (Jan–March 1963): 133–42.

Vergès, Françoise. *Monsters and Revolutionaries. Colonial Family Romance and Métissage*. Durham: Duke University Press, 1999.

Vigato, Jean-Claude 'The Architecture of Colonial Exhibitions in France,' *Daidalos* 15, March 1986: 24–37.

Vincent, Rose (ed.). *L'Aventure des Français en Inde. XVII–XX siècles*. Delhi: Kailash Editions: 1995.

Viswanathan, Gauri. *Masks of Conquest: Literary Study and British Rule in India*. New York: Columbia University Press, 1989.

Wagner, Kim A. *Thuggee: Banditry and the British in Early Nineteenth-century India*. Basingstoke: Palgrave Macmillan, 2007.

Weber, Jacques. *Les etablissements français en Inde au XIX siècle*. Five volumes. Paris: Librairie de l'Inde, 1988.

———. *Pondichéry et les comptoirs de l'Inde après Dupleix*. Paris: Denoël, 1996.

———. (ed) *Compagnie et comptoirs de l'Inde des Français, XVII–XX siècles*. Paris, 1991. Special edition of Revue française d'histoire d'outre-mer. 1er trimestre 1991.

———. (ed) *Les relations entre la france et l'Inde de 1673 à nos jours*. Paris, 2002.

———. Acculturation et assimilation dans les Établissements français de l'Inde, *Comtes Rendus trimestriels des séances de l'Académie des Sciences d'Outre-Mer*, vol. 38.2 (1978): 187–215, 219–24.

———. "Les Français en Inde sous le Second Empire", *Revue d'histoire Diplomatique*, nos 3–4 (1989): 221–42.

———. 'Chanemougam, the King of French India', *Economic and Political Weekly* (9 February 1991).

———. Les institutions representatives en Inde au XIXe siècle, *Les Cahiers du Sahib*, no. 3 (1995):135–67.

———. 'La politiques républicaine d'assimilation dans les comptoirs de l'inde', *Révolution française et ocean Indien. Prémices, paroxysms, heritages et deviances* edited by Claude Wanquet and Benoît Julien. Réunion: Université de la Réunion and Paris: L'Harmattan, 1996: 499–510.

Weinberger, Catherine (ed). *India in Western Fiction*. Paris, 1988.

Elizabeth Williams, 'Anthropological Institutions in Nineteenth-Century France', *Isis*, 76.3 (Sept. 1985): 331–48.

Wood, Roy. *The Sociology of the Meal*. Edinburgh, 1995.

Wright, Gwendolyn. 'Tradition in the Service of Modernity: Architecture and Urbanism in French Colonial Policy, 1900–1930', *Journal of Modern History*, Vol. 59.2 (1987): 291–316.

———. *The Politics of Design in French Colonial Urbanism*. Chicago: University of Chicago Press, 1991.

Young, Robert. *Colonial Desire: Hybridity in Theory, Race and Culture*. London and New York: Routledge, 1995.

Zeldin, Theodore. *The Political System of Napoleon III*. London: Macmillan and New York: St. Martin's Press, 1958.

Zinkin, Taya. *French Memsahib*. London, 1989.

Zubaida, Sami. 'Exhibitions of Power', *Economy and Society* 19.3, August 1990: 357–75.

Županov, Ines G. *Disputed Mission: Jesuit Experiments and Brahmanical Knowledge in Seventeenth Century India*. Delhi: Oxford University Press, 1999.

———. *Missionary Tropics: The Catholic Frontier in India (16th–17th Centuries)*. Ann Arbor: University of Michigan Press, 2005.

Index

About the Author

Jyoti **Mohan** has taught numerous courses on South Asian, South Asian American, Asian American, and World History at the University of Maryland College Park, University of Maryland, Baltimore County, and Morgan State University. Most recently, she was a Lecturer at Morgan State University for 11 years.

She currently serves on the Board of Editors for *H-French-Colonial*, after having served several years as Reviews Editor and List Editor. She is also a List Editor for an Academci Listserv on French–India academics.

Mohan has published articles in *French Colonial History*, *Journal of World History*, and *Francophone Postcolonial Studies*, as well as in edited anthologies of academic essays like *Beyond National Frames*.